WARRIORS
OF THE
QUEEN

WARRIORS
OF THE
QUEEN

FIGHTING
GENERALS
OF THE
VICTORIAN
AGE

WILLIAM WRIGHT

First published 2014
by Spellmount, an imprint of The History Press

The Mill, Brimscombe Port
Stroud, Gloucestershire, GL5 2QG
www.thehistorypress.co.uk

British Library Cataloguing in Publication Data.
A catalogue record for this book is available from the British Library.

ISBN 978 0 7524 9317 6

Typesetting and origination by The History Press
Printed in Great Britain

CONTENTS

INTRODUCTION

*T*his book is the first to bring together in one volume the lives of 170 Victorian army generals. Not wanting to write pure hagiography of the kind offered in nineteenth-century works (and often in the *Dictionary of National Biography*), I have, where possible, tried to analyse these men and include contemporary criticisms alongside modern historical opinion.

Critics will rise up en masse, I have no doubt, to complain that a favourite soldier is omitted – there is no Raglan here, nor famous heroes like Bromhead and Chard – so a word or two in explanation: the book deals with soldiers who reached the rank of major-general or higher before the death of the Queen-Empress on 22 January 1901. Inclusion has had to be a personal choice since the list is long, so brigadier-generals or those who reached major-general rank after Victoria's death have been excluded, along with men like Bromhead and Chard, who reached the ranks of major and lieutenant-colonel, respectively.

To further help me I have restricted the book to officers who saw action in three campaigns or more. When considering early Victorian generals I have treated the continental war against Napoleon as one campaign, hence no Raglan, who followed the Iron Duke and then had four decades of peace-time soldiering until the Crimean War.

Let me be clear: this is a book of sketches in the same way that Commander Charles Robinson's *Celebrities of the Army* (1900) sketches seventy-two commanders (not all of them generals) at the time of the South African War. It is impossible within the space I can permit myself to do more than shine a small torch on an individual officer's career but, if the book encourages you to delve further or research more, then the exercise will have been worthwhile. The book includes familiar names (**Baden-Powell**, **Gordon** of Khartoum) and important warriors (**Frederick Roberts**, **Garnet Wolseley**), along with the men of their Rings (**Adye**, **Hamilton**, **Maurice**,

McCalmont, Pole-Carew), Indian Army generals (Brownlow, Fraser-Tytler, Palmer, Stewart), and old Africa hands (Carrington, Grenfell, Molyneux, Woodgate). A large number of the men who I think worth remembering and re-assessing will be unknown to all but the most specialist scholars – names like Robert Bright, Patrick Grant, Charles Palliser and Henry Stisted.

There is not a warrior in this book who did not believe in the British Empire as a force for good in the world and wanted to defend it to the best of his ability. But in war mistakes happen and they cost men's lives. Thus, besides the great all-rounders (Gasalee, Macpherson) are some who failed in battle (Pomeroy-Colley, Primrose) and others who, while generally successful, brushed against disaster (Graham, Rowlands). The book includes generals who viewed themselves as scapegoats (Buller, Methuen) and others who fell victim to the political axe (Appleyard, Blood).

Twenty-six of these generals won the coveted Victoria Cross, including names largely forgotten today, such as George Channer and Frederick Maude. A great number received battle wounds (Alison, Tytler); indeed, sometimes reading of their battle scars makes one wonder how they possibly survived (Reynell Taylor, Watson). Some never got the glorious bronze cross, but were every bit as brave (Delafosse, Hope Grant). Fifteen of them were born in India (two more in Sri Lanka, then known as Ceylon). All the India boys returned to the land of their birth and the Indian Army (the Battye and Gough brothers, for example).

Within these pages you can read of martinets and tyrants (Brown, Franks), romantic idealists (Butler), a brilliant amateur botanist (Collett), snobs (the Crealock brothers) and eccentrics (Colville, Charles Napier). Some generals saw action in only one theatre of war, such as John Bissett on the Eastern Frontier of Cape Colony, or Charles Keyes on the North-West Frontier of India. Old-school generals of the kind favoured by the reactionary Duke of Cambridge, C-in-C of the British Army 1856–95, let us not forget, were brave fighting men in their younger days (Dillon, Horsford). They contrast with the later and younger generation of Victorian scientific soldiers (Brackenbury, Nicholson). The officer-class of the Victorian Army was a relatively close-knit institution but it was possible to rise from relatively humble beginnings (Clyde, O'Connor) to great fame and riches. More typical were the aristocratic officers (Chelmsford, Somerset), the sons of wealthy churchmen (Wood) and landed county families (Drury-Lowe, Yeatman-Biggs). Thirty of the generals in this book belonged to the cavalry and 110 to the infantry, with ten gunners, sixteen sappers and two doctors.

A book of this size containing so much biographical data is bound to have accidentally incorporated some errors. I can only apologise and hope these are few while begging the reader's indulgence.

To make the book additionally useful to those interested in a particular campaign, an appendix lists the wars of all the warriors. **Bold type** indicates a soldier featured in the book for purposes of cross-reference.

Finally, my thanks to Shaun Barrington at the History Press for his support and encouragement on this project, and Kristina Elias for re-photographing the generals and helping prepare the index. Illustrations are from my own collection.

William Wright
Budapest

WARRIORS
OF THE
QUEEN

ADYE, GENERAL SIR J. – BEST OF STAFF OFFICERS

A GUNNER WITH family associations in the Royal Artillery back to 1762, John Adye saw service in several wars but always in a staff capacity. He remains an interesting personality because, as the years rolled by, he became somewhat old-fashioned in his views on artillery, yet he remained a progressive thinker on other subjects, including the defence of India and the treatment of subject peoples.

Born in 1819, Adye entered the Royal Military Academy at Woolwich in 1834 to train as a gunner. He first saw action in the Crimea on the staff of Lord Raglan (years later, in his autobiography, he strongly defended his old chief). Staff duties put Adye under fire on several occasions; on one, during the Battle of Inkerman, a shell passed amongst the group of officers near Raglan, killing two horses and mortally wounding General Strangways, whose left leg was taken off below the knee. In escorting the dying officer from the field, Adye was almost captured by the enemy.

His most severe fight was at Cawnpore in the Mutiny, where he served under General Windham. Left to hold the city by Colin Campbell as he marched on Lucknow, Windham was given purely defensive orders and a steadily growing army as driblets of troops marching up-country reached Cawnpore. Then a massive rebel army of 25,000 men arrived to challenge the British. The defenders had just ten guns and 1,700 bayonets. As AAG, Adye had his work cut out for him and was often under intense fire. On the night of 27 November 1857 he led a dangerous sortie into the rebel-held city to rescue a naval 24-pounder. He described the task as 'rather like looking for a needle in a bundle of hay'. Led by a native guide on a roundabout route, Adye thought that the man might be leading them into a trap, but eventually they found the gun in a narrow lane with its wheels sunk into a drain. As silently as possible, his fifty infantry, aided by some sailors, pulled the gun upright and marched back triumphantly to their lines, where every man got a glass of grog and the guide a bag of rupees.

General Windham was out-generalled by the wily rebel, Tatya Tope, and was barely holding his own when Campbell returned with his army. Adye wrote a book in defence of his chief, whose position had been precarious and whose courage never in doubt, aiming to set the record straight. History has largely validated his opinion that Windham 'was a brave soldier and an excellent leader, and [his] difficulties were by no means understood and appreciated'.

Six years later, Adye was sent to Umbeyla on the North-West Frontier to report on the campaign turning disastrously wrong against the tribes. Once there he was asked to stay on as a staff officer and was one of the small party that was permitted, under escort by the tribesmen, to see Malka, the fanatics' stronghold, being put to the torch. One of Adye's colleagues, Frederick **Roberts**, noted that if a shot had been fired on either side, 'the desire for blood would quickly have spread, and in all probability not one of our party would have escaped'.

In 1870 Adye was made director of artillery and stores at the War Office. Here he became a firm advocate of the reforms being made by the War Minister, Edward Cardwell. It has been argued by some that during his tenure, 'British artillery development failed to keep pace with technological advances and rival nations'. He seems to have been a little too close to the Armstrong armaments family, marrying a daughter to one of its sons, while promoting an Armstrong rifle-barrel breech loading gun that, after many trials, had to be abandoned. Other high positions followed; governor of the 'shop' at Woolwich in 1875 and surveyor-general of the ordnance in 1880.

Adye's war services were not at an end; in 1882 he was a most competent chief of staff to Garnet **Wolseley** in Egypt. One writer claims that Adye was 'chagrined' at serving under an officer fourteen years his junior but, if so, he kept it to himself. He rode with his chief to witness the capture of Mahsama and was present with the rest of the staff during the battle of Tel-el-Kebir. After the war Adye defended the medical and hospital services at a royal commission, though Wolseley noted in his diary that Adye had painted too rosy a picture.

In the last two decades of the nineteenth century, when Roberts and his friends held sway on all matters Indian, Sir John Adye was bold enough to write that 'the war of 1878-79 was bad in policy and unjust in principle from beginning to end', and 'there is no cause for war, or indeed probability of it, between Russia and England, in that part of the world'. Time was to prove Adye right. Remarkably free of colour prejudice, he was also one of the few soldiers of his age to predict that British days in India were numbered. Indian self-government, he always thought, was inevitable, and natives needed to be made part of the governmental system. 'If such principles are *not* carried out, we shall not only lose India, but shall deserve to do so. Others talk of the people of India as being composed of inferior races. I am not aware that God has created any races of men who are inferior.'

Wise and brave, a classic gentleman and fine soldier, John Adye died in his eightieth year on 26 August 1900.

AIREY, LIEUTENANT-GENERAL SIR J. – CHEERY AFGHAN CAPTIVE

DURING THE FIRST Afghan War, when a few British, such as Lady Sale and George **Lawrence**, became captives in the mountains, a handful of their countrymen had already agreed to be prisoners at Kabul. One of these was Lieutenant James Talbot Airey.

Born in 1812, James was commissioned an ensign in the 30th Foot in 1830, exchanging into the 3rd Foot in 1833. He served as an aide to the Governor of Madras 1834–37 and went to Afghanistan in the same capacity with the gout-ridden British commander General Elphinstone. Once there, Airey found himself sleeping most nights on the floor outside 'Elphy Bey's' room in case he was required to deliver orders. He was also in several skirmishes with the Afghans and acted as aide on occasions to the hot-tempered Brigadier Shelton. Assisting Robert **Sale** in the Khoord-Kabul Pass, his horse was killed beneath him. In December 1841, with the Afghans demanding hostages during negotiations, Elphinstone asked his young aide if he would volunteer. Being a bachelor, and realising that many of his fellow officers had wives or family, he agreed and went into captivity two days before the British envoy, Sir William Macnaghten, was murdered. In a letter to his brother, Lt-Colonel Richard Airey, James explained how Kabulis 'on several occasions surrounded the house … and demanded our blood in anything but a civil manner,' adding, 'I shall not be surprised to find myself, some fine morning, tending sheep as a slave in Tourkistan [sic], but … having grown grey from confinement, I shall fetch a very small price.' He concluded a letter on 19 June with the cheery words: 'I am as healthy a ghost as you generally see … I am a little tired … of sitting cross-legged and eating Pillau with my fingers.'

After his release by Pollock's army on 21 September 1842, James heard the good news that he had been promoted and also that Elphinstone had kindly left him £300 in his will. He then joined Brigadier McCaskill's force in Kohistan, fought in 'the thick' of the bloody storming of Istalif and was twice mentioned in despatches. A year later he served with the 3rd Foot in the Gwalior War.

Peacetime soldiering, with an exchange into the Coldstream Guards, kept Airey busy until the Crimean War broke out in 1854; he was present at all the main battles as AQMG of the Light Division (his elder brother, Richard, was Lord Raglan's confidante as QMG). James was mentioned three times in despatches. He stayed with the Coldstreams until 1868, when he was promoted to major-general; lieutenant-general rank followed nine years later. A bachelor all his life, Sir James died in London on 1 January 1898.

ALISON, GENERAL SIR A. – SCOTLAND'S ONE-ARMED HERO

WHEN, IN 1882, Madame Tussauds waxworks displayed a model of the new peer and victor of Tel-el-Kebir, General Lord **Wolseley**, the only other hero of the Egyptian War afforded a similar honour was Sir Archibald Alison. His courage at the head of the Highland Brigade made his name a household word, especially north of the border.

The eldest son of an eminent historian of the same name, Alison was born on 21 January 1826. He was commissioned an ensign in the 72nd Foot (later the Seaforth Highlanders) and served in various parts of the globe before first seeing action in the Crimean War. It was his coolness under fire at Sebastopol and during one of the assaults on the Redan that brought him to the attention of Scotland's great hero, Major-General Sir Colin **Campbell**.

In July 1857 Campbell set sail for India to quell the uprising which threatened to engulf the sub-continent. With him went Alison as his military secretary while his younger brother, Frederick, was ADC. During the final assault at Lucknow, a cannon ball took one of Archibald's arms and knocked him off his horse. It took him four years to recover, but during the following decade he artfully rose up the ladder of promotion in a series of staff positions.

Much to the chagrin of Wolseley, the rising star in the military firmament, Alison was chosen in 1873 to command the European Brigade, with the local rank of brigadier-general, in an expedition against the warlike Ashanti of West Africa. 'I don't care much for him and I don't think he is the man I want', wrote Wolseley, who had been forced to accept Alison by the Duke of Cambridge, the British Army's C-in-C. Despite Alison's bravery and cool handling of his men at Amoaful, on 31 January 1874, he never became a real member of Wolseley's inner circle. Alison was critical of Wolseley's transport arrangements for the campaign and told his wife that the staff officers were too young and inexperienced. They responded by spreading the rumour that a sick Alison would have retreated after Amoaful if he had been in charge. Wolseley was most annoyed that Alison always had the ear of the Duke of Cambridge. Knighted shortly after his return from the Gold Coast, Sir Archibald also complained to Cambridge about errors he saw in the unofficial history of the Ashanti War, written by Wolseley's assistant military secretary.

Stints in Aldershot, Ireland, and as commandant at the new Staff College at Camberley led, in 1878, to Alison's appointment as DQMG for intelligence at the War Office, a position he held until the outbreak of the

Egyptian War in 1882. Clever, discreet and shrewd, Alison probably knew more about the military situation in Egypt than anyone, including Wolseley. This was to lead to another clash of egos.

Sent to Egypt as head of an advance force, with instructions to safeguard the Suez Canal, Alison found himself at the centre of a confused situation; while he had been on the high seas a British fleet had gone into action and bombarded Alexandria. He landed at Port Said with instructions to head back to Cyprus. Sensibly, Alison told his staff that if they had to turn back it was appropriate to do this via Alexandria. Here he took charge as British regiments started to arrive. Wolseley's idea was that nothing should disturb things until he landed, but, ten days before his chief's arrival, Alison led a reconnaissance that turned into a small battle at Kafr Dawar. This action, hailed as a British victory in London was, in reality, pretty inconclusive. But it encouraged Alison to plan a bigger feint towards the Egyptians at Abourkir Bay. This impertinent plan to fight his own little war on the Egyptian coast was quashed on Wolseley's arrival, but his greatest moment of glory was at hand; just after 5 a.m. on 13 September 1882, riding at the head of his Highland Brigade, he led the attack on the Egyptian fortified trenches at Tel-el-Kebir. The fighting was intense and in the close-quarter scrum Sir Archibald had his horse shot from under him. Unperturbed, he strode about, using a pistol when necessary and urging on his troops. It was a tough fight and even Alison praised the Egyptians, saying 'I never saw men fight more steadily.'

Back in Scotland after the campaign, the press lauded Alison's exploits. He made himself more popular by wearing a sprig of heather in public and stating how proud his old chief, Colin Campbell, would have been of his highland boys. Eleven years later, in 1893, Alison retired. Among his last important duties were those of adjutant-general during Wolseley's absence in the Sudan 1884–85 and his membership of the Indian Council. He died as one of Scotland's best loved warriors in 1907.

APPLEYARD, MAJOR-GENERAL F. – THE MAN WHO UPSET A VICEROY

IT WAS A dangerous move to antagonise a Viceroy of India. One career that illustrates this rather well is that of Frederick Appleyard, a gallant soldier who offended the highly strung Lord Lytton and was removed from his command during the Second Afghan War.

He enlisted in 1850 as an ensign in the 80th Foot and within a few weeks set sail with his regiment for India. Two years later the 80th sailed again to take part in the Second Burmese War. Appleyard was present at the taking of Prome and the first officer to force his way through the huge pagoda gate at Rangoon. 'Caught sight of the tail end of the Burmese troops escaping on the opposite side,' he recalled, 'pursued them with about half a section down the steps, and came to some sheds in which were some ponies, one of which I bagged – a really good one – but as the enemy were still in force, firing at us, and no help near, we had to return ...'

Dysentery soon saw him sent home on sick leave. He next joined the 7th Royal Fusiliers in time for the Crimean War, was wounded in the shoulder carrying their colours at the Alma and fought in the thick of things at Inkerman and the first assault on the Redan. It was said that Appleyard did more various duties than any other officer in the 1st Brigade, Light Division; these included over ninety nights in the trenches, sometimes not being relieved for seventy-two hours in the cruel winter of 1854. Next Frederick sailed to India and the Mutiny, but arrived too late to see action. He transferred to the 85th Regiment in 1861 and remained with them for the next nineteen years. When the 85th were ordered to India in 1868 the ambitious Appleyard went as their commanding officer.

It was at a *durbar* in the spring of 1878, where Lord Lytton was meeting the rulers of Oudh, that the hapless colonel 'unfortunately, and quite unintentionally' incurred the Viceroy's displeasure. In his autobiography Appleyard does not reveal exactly what he said to upset the impulsive and neurotic Lytton – who once wrote, 'I am as variable as the wind, and I certainly don't know myself' – but when the commands for the invasion of Afghanistan were announced, his name was erased from the list. He complained to headquarters and was given command of the 3rd Brigade, Peshawar Valley Field Force. Then, despite being the senior brigadier in the 1st Division, he found this command mysteriously taken from him as he was posted to the rear. Appleyard quickly telegraphed his complaints to the War Office in London and in March 1879 got back his earlier command.

During the attack on the Afghan fortress at Ali Musjid, high above the Khyber Pass, Appleyard was as courageous as he had been in Burma and was the first officer through the breach. He was now put in charge of the Lundi Kotal-Ali Musjid section of the Khyber and, according to the war's historian, Colonel Hanna, the energetic Appleyard did sterling work keeping the supply line open despite attacks from Afridis and other tribes.

Fate now dealt Appleyard a cruel blow; the loss on 23 May 1879 of about fifty mules and some supplies (due, he thought, to transport department deficiencies beyond his control), brought him eventually to the Viceroy's desk. Lytton accused him of 'lamentable errors of judgment' and of 'unfitness to move troops in a difficult country, of inertness, incompetence, a want of zeal and enterprise …' The unfortunate Appleyard complained to anyone who would listen, up to and including the C-in-C, and his protests dragged on for the next fifteen years. It was all to no avail.

Frederick Ernest Appleyard never held another field command, though he became a major-general in 1884, after being placed on half-pay. One can guess that he went to his grave in 1911 still feeling bitter. Ten years earlier an officer had described him as 'a most pompous little old gentleman'. Some small satisfaction came with a letter the general received in his later years from his old PVFF commander, Sam **Browne**, who wrote: 'I consider Lord Lytton's treatment of you was most unjust and most harsh.'

BADEN-POWELL, LIEUTENANT-GENERAL LORD R. – ALWAYS 'B.P.'

NO VICTORIAN SOLDIER has had his career and personality examined under the microscope of historical reassessment quite like Robert Stephenson Smyth Baden-Powell. Many contemporaries called him 'brilliant', 'indefatigable', and 'a 'prince of scouts' as well as a 'prince of good fellows'. Recent historians have tended to view him as an energetic eccentric, a man with a tendency to stretch the truth when it suited him and a callous regard for native life.

He was born in 1857 and aged 19 was commissioned into the 13th Hussars. Sent to India and dull cantonment life, 'B.P.', as he was known to his friends, was a cheery subaltern with a ready wit, always happy to sketch the *memsahibs* or dress up in comic plays. His commanding officer, Baker **Russell**, liked him and he was popular in society. Sent to Afghanistan in 1880 with the 13th, 'B.P.' saw no fighting but managed to shoot himself in the leg.

Eight years later, serving as an aide to his peppery uncle, General Sir Henry Smyth, Baden-Powell took part in suppressing a Zulu rising. This was part of a civil war in Zululand and 'B.P.' had with him a large contingent of 'splendid' Zulu scouts. He saw little fighting but on 10 August allowed his irregulars to charge into some caves, stab a woman and two men to death and take several Zulus prisoners. There was a hullabaloo because the incident occurred in Boer territory. 'B.P.' claimed it was a mistake at the time, but years later confessed: 'We disregarded the border and followed them up, attacked and got them.' The matter reveals how Baden-Powell had a tendency to shift the truth if it enhanced his position.

Riding across the magnificent valleys and hills of Zululand inspired Baden-Powell to make a study of scouting techniques and irregular warfare. In 1895–96 he was given command of a native levy in the bloodless Ashanti expedition that abducted King Prempeh. On the other side of Africa 'B.P.' was propelled into another war as the Matabele and Mashona tried to resist the white men encroaching on their lands. In his role as chief staff officer to Frederick Carrington, our fast-balding hero at last saw some real action; on 5 June 1896 he took part without a sword but firing wildly with his revolver in his first and last cavalry charge. It was, in truth, an ugly massacre, with just four whites wounded and, according to Baden-Powell, 200 Matabele killed.

'B.P.' once again demonstrated his method of getting results after he captured a proud chief called Uwini. Injured in fighting (where Baden-Powell was not present), Uwini tore off his bandages after his wound was dressed. Despite a warning from Carrington not to shoot prisoners, Baden-Powell decided that if an example was made of this 'fine, truculent-looking savage' many other headmen might lay down their arms. Accordingly, after a sham trial that Uwini quite rightly deigned not to recognise, he was shot. Many headmen did surrender in the next few days, but the High Commissioner, Lord Rosmead, appalled by 'B.P.''s actions, demanded a court of inquiry which, hardly surprisingly, exonerated the cavalryman. Rosmead continued to maintain, however, that 'B.P.' had behaved in an 'illegal and immoral' manner.

Returning to India, and command of the 5th Dragoon Guards, 'B.P.' got permission to visit the North-West Frontier during the 1897 Pathan Revolt. With Bindon **Blood**'s agreement he observed actions against the Mohmands and was impressed by one brave *ghazi* who, all alone, attacked an entire battalion of infantry. In his private life, 'B.P.' was getting more eccentric; so well-known was he for dressing up and playing the women's parts in amateur theatricals that he was even asked to give recitals in a fake soprano!

This neat, dapper, eccentric exhibitionist with 'a boyish enthusiasm for hard work and new knowledge', accompanied by a rather unpleasant veneer of self-promotion, was catapulted to fame when he led the defence of Mafeking, a small tin-roofed town of 1,500 whites and 5,000 natives besieged by the Boers from 13 October 1899 to 17 May 1900. Modern studies have revealed that there is some justification in the charge that 'Baden-Powell was deliberately prolonging the siege for the sake of his reputation, while bringing upon the town unnecessary damage from Boer shelling.' Locals, like auctioneer Edward Ross, also complained that while many in Mafeking suffered privations, 'B.P.' and his staff were 'filling themselves with fiz, brandies and sodas etc.' and getting all the praise and honours that followed. It can also be argued that Baden-Powell worked hard to keep people's spirits up. His chief clerk thought him 'a wonderful man'. Others were less sure; Charles Weir, a leading citizen, thought 'he might have done more to save the lives of the natives' (354 Africans were officially recorded as dying, but the actual toll was considerably higher). Historian Brian Willan, an authority on the siege, has written: 'From a purely military point of view ... it is difficult to resist the conclusion that his reputation was built on somewhat shaky foundations. Certainly he displayed a good deal of ingenuity in securing the defence of Mafeking ... But on the few occasions that he took the offensive the results were, to say the least, unfortunate.' News of Mafeking's relief was greeted with fervour in Britain. After so many confused disasters and so much loss of life, this strange victory – more an avoidance of a defeat – seemed like a plucky game of cricket. Within days Mafeking's commandant was promoted to major-general, the youngest in the British Army. Lord **Roberts** told the Queen that 'B.P.''s 'pluck and resource are quite wonderful'. As time passed Roberts changed his mind, complaining that 'it is curious Baden-Powell should not be acting with more vigour. He certainly showed himself to have resources while defending Mafeking, but he disappointed me afterwards, & I gather those who were with him at Mafeking, do not look upon him as a great commander.' By July 1901 his lordship simply dismissed 'B.P.' as 'not a General'.

Whatever Roberts privately thought, Baden-Powell went on to become a lieutenant-general, though he saw no more campaigning. He directed his energies to developing his ideas for the character-building youth organisation that would become the Boy Scouts. He retired in 1910, aged 53, and his new life's work won him a baronetcy in 1929 as Lord Baden-Powell of Gilwell. He died in Kenya, the continent of his military triumphs, on 8 January 1941.

BAKER, LIEUTENANT-GENERAL SIR T. – BETWEEN THE RINGS

DESPITE THE RIVALRY between the rings of **Roberts** and **Wolseley**, it was possible for a good soldier to work closely with both of these generals and be mutually respected. One such was Thomas Durand Baker. Born in the year of the Queen's accession, he went to Cheltenham College before being commissioned into the 18th Foot in 1854. He served with this regiment, first as an ensign and then a lieutenant, his bravery noticed in the attack on the Redan at Sebastopol. Next he and his fellow Royal Irish were sent to India and took part in the sweaty work of pursuing some of the final rebel bands in 1858.

On 2 April 1863 the 2nd Battalion, 18th Foot, set sail for New Zealand where a fierce war with the Maoris had broken out. Captain Baker was appointed DAAG and later AAG under General Cameron, frequently getting mentions in despatches. The most notable event was at Orakau on 31 March 1864, where Baker leapt off his horse and personally led a vain third assault on the staunchly defended Maori *pah* (or fort). At the close of the campaign he was rewarded with a brevet majority.

After passing out of the Staff College he applied in 1873 to join Wolseley's intended Ashanti expedition. Baker was made AAG, then QMG and finally Chief of Staff. Wolseley was full of praise for an officer 'who does his work well, but I fear he will break down as it is too much for one man'. On 11 October in a confidential letter to the War Minister a fairminded Wolseley pointed out Baker for future honours and promotion. Finally, when George **Greaves** arrived to take up chief of staff duties, Baker went down with fever, but 'won't confess he is ill and won't go on board the Commodore's ship … He is a splendid fellow …'

In 1878, now a full colonel, Baker won the plum appointment of Military Secretary to the bellicose Viceroy, Lord Lytton. When the Afghan War broke out it was Roberts's opinion that much of the British planning had been done not by **Haines**, but by Baker and **Pomeroy-Colley**, the Viceroy's closest military advisors, commenting that he considered the colonel more clever than **East** or **Elles**. During the war's second phase he requested Baker as a brigadier; at Charasiab near Kabul the new general was told to lead the attack, which he did, according to a contemporary officer, 'cool, confident and quiet'. The Afghans, outflanked and enfiladed by Baker, lost almost 300 while the British had only eighteen fatalities. After the battle there was a furious spat between Baker and the cavalry commander, Brigadier Massy. Fellow officers took sides, but the majority disliked Massy, thinking him as 'arrant an imposter as ever drew a sword. [A] self-indulgent, timid, good-for-nothing fellow'. Baker was soon kept busy fighting around Kabul and led one of Roberts's three infantry brigades in the push to Kandahar.

After the war he got a KCB and was made AG in India 1884–88, during which period he saw his last active service in Burma. In 1886 Roberts recommended him for a division, which he got two years later. In 1890 he returned to London and the War Office as QMG, a post he held for three years until his death at a relatively early age, the result of a West African ague that had never left him. Had he lived another seven years he almost certainly would have taken a senior field command in the South African War.

BARTON, MAJOR-GENERAL G. – FUSSY LITTLE MAN OF ACTION

GEOFFREY BARTON SPENT most of his career in the Royal Fusiliers, seeing plenty of action along the way. It was his misfortune, during the South African War, to fall foul of Lord **Kitchener**.

He joined the 7th Foot (Royal Fusiliers) in 1862 at age 18 and had a quiet first decade in the army until he volunteered as a special service officer for the 1873–74 Ashanti War. This saw him mentioned in despatches. Four years later he went out to Africa again on special service and commanded the 4th battalion of the Natal Native Contingent. He soon saw fighting again at the Battle of Gingindlovo in which over 1,000 Zulus were slain. Two mentions in despatches quickly followed.

After attending the Staff College and now accepted as a junior member of **Wolseley**'s ring of bright young officers, Barton served as staff officer in the Egyptian War in 1882. Ostensibly commanding the regular police, he managed to see action at Kassassin and again at Tel-el-Kebir. Three years later he served in a similar staff role with Gerald Graham fighting the Mahdists in the Eastern Sudan. In 1890 Lt-Colonel Barton took command of the 2nd Battalion, Royal Fusiliers. A year later he exchanged into the 1st Battalion serving in India.

With his Staff College and Wolseley credentials, it was not surprising that he was given command of the 6th Brigade, South African Field Force in Natal on the outbreak of war with the Boers. Barton was one of that clutch of generals who, within a year, had failed to impress the new warlords – **Roberts** and Kitchener. According to the gossipy Ian **Hamilton**, by the end of 1901 Lord Kitchener considered him of 'very little use now ...'

Hamilton went on to say that he did not entirely agree; Barton was, he declared, a 'fussy little man, who is inclined to devote all his attention to details, and to disregard, in doing so, more weighty matters. These are serious faults, but still he has a good deal of energy and keenness and he certainly seems to have worked out the defences of Pretoria and neighbourhood in a very satisfactory style. Of course, I have always understood that he is no leader of troops in the field, but this is mere hearsay'. Harsh words perhaps but, unfortunately, valid. Barton's big moment had come at Colenso on 15 December 1899. It is true that he and his fellow commanders were saddled with instigating the plan of their C-in-C, Redvers **Buller**, for a 'frontal attack directed on three points of an insufficiently reconnoitred position held in unknown strength by an entrenched enemy', but Barton raised no objections. Towards the end of this frightful battle, in which British losses totalled 1,138 killed, wounded and missing, the cavalry commander, Lord Dundonald, saw a chance to cut off the Boer line of retreat and asked for Barton's brigade to assist him. The request was denied. Barton was in the right strictly speaking but, as one historian has noted, 'By Barton's refusal the last chance of redeeming the day was lost.'

Despite Lord Kitchener's lack of faith in him, Barton retained his command and served in the Western Transvaal until the end of the war in 1902. It was almost the end of his fighting career. He died in 1922.

BATTYE, LIEUTENANT-GENERAL SIR A. – HIGHEST RANKED OF THE 'FIGHTING TEN'

NO FAMILY SOLDIERED and died for the Empire quite like the Battyes. It came to be said that it was rare for a Battye to die in his bed, though, in truth, only four died in action (Quintin, Wigram, Richmond and Fred), but the 'fighting ten' brothers certainly carved a niche for themselves in the pantheon of imperial heroes, and especially in the Indian Army.

The career of Arthur, highest ranked and longest serving, must stand for the rest. He was born in 1839, the seventh son, and aged 17 was gazetted an ensign in the 19th Bengal Native Infantry at Berhampur. Broadly built and not exceptionally clever (according to his biographer), Arthur was a kindly, sensitive, religious youth who was mercilessly bullied by his fellow subalterns. On one occasion they even set light to him and threw him down the steps of the mess. In these first months he saw his regiment disbanded when they threatened to mutiny. He was also present at Barrackpore when the *sepoy*, Mangal Pandey, stoned on hashish, tried to incite rebellion and was hanged.

Transferring to the 1st Bengal Fusiliers, Arthur served at the Siege of Delhi where his brother Quintin was to die in action leading his Corps of Guides with the final words, 'Ah well, old fellow, *"Dulce et decorum est pro patria mori."* That's how it is …' (the words were meant as an ironic jest, says his biographer). Arthur's regiment, called 'the dirty shirts' because of the amount of fighting they took part in, often went into battle with the Guides, or the Sirmoor Gurkhas, both of which were quartered beside them. In the final assault at Delhi the 1st Bengal Fusiliers took part in the leading first column under the command of the courageous and possibly half-mad Brigadier-General John Nicholson. Young Arthur climbed the glacis near the Kashmir Gate under terrific shelling and pressed into the teeming city with a deadly hail of gunfire all around him. He was not far from Nicholson when the latter fell, mortally wounded.

Seven of the Battye brothers fought in the Mutiny and, after Quintin's death, half a dozen of them were present at the Siege of Lucknow. Getting a reputation as a superb horseman, Arthur was recruited by William Hodson, the dashing and unorthodox commander of a newly formed irregular cavalry regiment called Hodson's Horse. Rapidly proving himself an adept leader, Arthur was mentioned several times in despatches for his gallantry as he led his *sowars* in mopping-up operations in Oudh throughout 1858. He remained in the saddle hunting mutineers until March 1859.

That May saw the disbandment of Arthur's 3rd Squadron and he transferred to the 2nd (Sirmoor Rifles) Gurkha Regiment. In 1863 he marched with them to take part in the Umbeyla expedition on the North-West Frontier, but the fighting was over before the regiment arrived. Within days they were ordered to relieve the fort of Shabkadar in Mohmand country. Battye and his Gurkhas arrived just in the nick of time; on 2 January 1864 over 5,000 tribesmen attacked the fort. Sword in hand, Arthur joined the 7th Hussars and units of the 2nd and 6th Bengal Cavalry in a mounted charge that had the enemy running for the hills, but not before his horse was shot under him and he narrowly escaped with his life. Seven years later, in a north-east frontier expedition against the Lushai tribe, who had kidnapped the young daughter of a British tea planter and kept her as a hostage, Battye was almost killed again. While attacking the abductor's village he was impaled (along with two of his non-commissioned officers and nine of his men) on the sharp bamboo spikes of a palisade.

Rated a first-class regiment, the 2nd Gurkhas under Battye, now a major, were sent to Cyprus in 1878 when war seemed likely between Russia and Turkey. It was a sham manoeuvre, but within months war broke out for a second time with Afghanistan and the Battye family were once more in the thick of things. Wigram Battye died nobly leading his Guides at Futtehabad and Arthur Battye took part in General **Roberts**'s tough and duly celebrated march from Kabul to Kandahar. In the battle that followed, he was shot in the shoulder as his Gurkhas raced to secure a village that was the key to breaking the enemy line. Following the war's close and two more mentions in despatches, Arthur was raised to a full colonelcy and gained a CB.

It was his last campaign; on retirement he settled in Torquay. He died in 1909. One obituary noted that 'it has become an unusual event for a soldier Battye to die in his bed, though he gave fate every opportunity, was wounded, and in the thick of the Indian warfare for many years …'

BISSET, LIEUTENANT-GENERAL SIR J. – TELLER OF TALL TALES

IT WAS UNCOMMON for a soldier to spend his campaigning fighting just one tribe, but that was the proud boast of John Jarvis Bisset, who fought in the sixth, seventh and eighth frontier wars against the Xhosa of South Africa. His memoirs, *Sport and War*, are replete with tall tales and economies of truth. What is not in dispute is that he packed an awful lot of action into his first fifteen years in the army.

The son of an officer who had fought in the Napoleonic Wars, Jack Bisset was just 15 when in 1834–35 the Sixth Xhosa War broke out and he joined a civilian militia known as the Bathurst Volunteers. On his first patrol this tender youth saw fighting and found two Boers who had been attacked – one with nineteen assegai wounds, the other with twenty-three – 'a portion of his entrails were protruding … three men actually fainted from the sight …'

In the same year young Bisset gallantly saved a chief's daughter from being mistakenly shot, but his greatest feat was taking part in the pursuit and death of the supreme Xhosa chief, Hintsa. On 9 May 1835, while leading British troops into his territory (it has never been clarified if he was a guide, a hostage or a prisoner), Hintsa suddenly galloped off in the direction of his hills. Fast in pursuit was the British commander, Sir Harry **Smith**, who, in a bit of close-quarters action, managed to unseat his opponent. Bisset and a small body of men now took up the chase and Hintsa was shot and killed as he rested in a stream. In his memoirs Bisset claimed, 'I was the first to reach the dead chief' and 'took his assegais and the charm from around his neck ...', while tactfully omitting the fact that Hintsa had begged for his life and that his ears were hacked off as grisly souvenirs.

Bisset won his commission that same day and soon joined the Cape Mounted Rifles, a corps he was associated with for the remainder of his life. For a decade an uneasy peace reigned along the Cape frontier, but a number of warriors, especially the clever Sandile, chief of the amaRharhabe Xhosa, and his brother, Maqoma, were soon to give the British authorities several years of severe fighting.

During the invasion of the Amatola hills, heartland of the Xhosa, in the 1846–47 'War of the Axe', all three advancing columns ran into difficulties and over fifty wagons were abandoned (HM 7th Dragoon Guards lost all their regimental silver). Bisset's horse was shot from under him in the fighting and 'my gun was shattered to pieces in my hands ...' Sent to recover an ammunition wagon, he found a soldier who had been lashed to the limber and burnt alive. During the relief of Fort Peddie, while leading his troopers, Bisset ran into an ambush, one bullet grazing his forehead and another denting a barrel of his shotgun. A few days later, on 8 June 1846, he charged with his regiment at the Battle of the Gwanga, but was unable to draw his sabre as he needed to hold tightly to the reins of his headstrong horse. During the mopping-up operations in which 300 Xhosa were killed he shot seven men, though all were, he later claimed, 'in the act of firing at me ...' To be fair, Bisset was also the only British officer to take prisoners, one of whom was an important chief. It was on 19 October 1847 that he won his greatest fame; riding out with just one interpreter, he convinced Sandile to meet with senior officers and discuss a closure of the war. Bisset afterwards said that he guaranteed the chief only his personal safety, but on arrival at the British camp Sandile was made a prisoner. It seems likely that Bisset used subterfuge to convince Sandile and this act, though of no matter to contemporaries, has rankled with historians ever since. Sandile was later released. Sir Harry Smith's intentions to have him deposed as chief were, Bisset felt, 'a great mistake'.

Events proved him correct when an eighth frontier war broke out in 1850. Appointed AG and later QMG, Bisset was ambushed with a 700-strong column in the narrow Boomah Pass on Christmas Eve 1850 – his birthday. In the hand-to-hand fighting he was shot through the thigh by a warrior who shouted out gleefully, 'I have shot him!' Bisset could not resist yelling back in Xhosa, 'I have got it!' He was one of twenty-three wounded;

the same number again were killed. The Xhosa harried the British all the way to Fort White, where Bisset was left in the care of doctors as the army moved on. Two days later Sandile led a major attack on the fort, which was repulsed by Bisset, a small detachment of Cape Mounted Rifles and several civilians. It was six weeks before Fort White was relieved.

This was the last fighting of Bisset's career, though many might say he had seen enough for ten men. He quickly rose to the rank of general and was a worthy temporary acting governor of Natal in the 1860s. A hardy old fighter with a 'ferocious squint', long-time foe of the Xhosa and teller of tall tales, John Jarvis Bisset died in 1895.

BLACK, MAJOR-GENERAL SIR R. – ZULU WAR FACTOTUM

ONE OF THE men omitted from Greaves and Knight's excellent *The Who's Who in the Zulu War* is Robert Wilstone Black. The historian Sonia Clarke describes him as 'the Central Column's general factotum', and in *Zulu Rising* Ian Knight calls Black 'indefatigable'. Black was with **Chelmsford** at Isandlwana on the morning before and night after the battle, and led the first search back there in March, when a strong stench of death still hung over the place. Zulus tried to cut off his party. He returned on 15 May, but once again the Zulus fired on his patrol. Black's most celebrated moment came when he led a party of volunteers to Fugitives Drift. The bodies of his comrades Melvill and Coghill were found and buried temporarily under a pile of rocks. Then, with Zulus watching from the opposite riverbank, Black bravely instigated a search for the Queen's colour of the 24th that had been taken from the battlefield by the dead officers. It was miraculously found in its case and handed to Black, the only officer of the 24th who was present. Later, in a moving ceremony, he returned it to his regiment.

Robert Black was born in in Glasgow in 1833 and commissioned in to the 42nd Highlanders in 1854, serving almost immediately in the Crimean War. He later transferred into the 24th Foot and sailed with them for South Africa. During the Ninth Frontier War, 1877–78, he learned some of the Xhosa languages and acted as regimental interpreter.

Despite seeming to be everywhere, Black fought in none of the major Zulu War battles. Yet on 11 January, when Sihayo's *kraal* was attacked in the first fighting of the war, he temporarily commanded the 3rd Regiment, Natal Native Contingent. When his men wavered, Black urged them on at the point of his sword (and some 24th bayonets). Then he got off his horse and led the fight on foot. In the close-quarter action a bullet tore his hat from his hand. Calmly, he bent down and picked it up. A few minutes later an observer recalled Black standing 'with his back turned to the rock and … waving his sword when the Zulus hearing him rolled over some stones; one struck the gallant Major on the – well, not the head – and he fell on his knees and poured forth a volume of Gaelic that filled my non-coms with delight'. At Isandlwana one fateful morning Black led some of his regiment as an escort for the guns accompanying Chelmsford's column. Later, when firing was heard in the camp's direction, he urged a return to investigate. That night, as troops shakily returned in the inky darkness, he was a tower of strength. One officer wrote: 'Every now and then Black's voice would ring out, "Steady the 24th – be ready to fire a volley – and charge."' John North **Crealock**, usually acidic towards everyone, was generous in his praise of a man he called 'energetic and plucky and liked by the men …' Later in the war, as the columns converged on Ulundi, the Zulu capital, Crealock once again praised Black for his 'initiative' while 'keeping our right flank open'. Hamilton-Browne, one of the tough NNC officers, described him as 'brave as his own sword … but with a temper, well may I say it, just a little peppery'.

His reputation enhanced by the Zulu campaign, Black held various peacetime military commands across the Empire until his retirement in 1899. He died ten years later.

BLOOD, GENERAL SIR B. – LONG-SERVING SOLDIER OF MANY WARS

A VERY CAPABLE commander, the splendidly named Bindon Blood was a fighting soldier on the Indian frontier, famously shepherding the career of the young Winston Churchill. Less well known is the rebuttal he got from Lord Curzon, probably the harshest censure ever made of a general by a civilian in authority.

Born in Jedburgh of an old Anglo-Irish family, Blood was commissioned in the Royal Engineers on 19 December 1860. Eleven years later he was sent to India and he continued, apart from home leave and African campaigning, to be associated with the Raj until 1907. He was seventeen years in the service before he saw action in the Jowaki Afridi expedition 1877–78 but, to Blood's annoyance, in this campaign, as with the Zulu War 1879 and second Afghan War, he always seemed to arrive too late for the main show or was sidelined. He also made some enemies; the acerbic Charles Metcalfe **Macgregor** called him 'an ass and a sycophant' in Afghanistan.

Blood was luckier in 1882, when he arrived in Egypt in time to take part in the final big battle at Tel-el-Kebir where he had a hot seat for most of the firefight, guarding some ammunition wagons. A few days later he acted courageously, with shell splinters and bullets whizzing around, when several trains laden with ammunition and supplies caught fire at the Cairo railway station.

The next ten years saw Blood in a number of staff positions, gradually rising in rank as his abilities as a senior engineer were noticed by the top brass. In 1895, as a brigadier-general, he became chief of staff on the Chitral relief expedition sent to the assistance of an isolated fort on the North-West Frontier. This six-week campaign in which Blood, as a staff officer, witnessed most of the major actions, enabled him to use the full scope of his outstanding planning abilities to assist the army to force the steep Malakand Pass and cross the swirling Swat River at Chakdara. At the war's close Blood was knighted.

He suspected a second frontier war might soon be in the offing. Sure enough, when tribes along almost the entire length of the North-West Frontier region rose in 1897, he was appointed to command the Malakand Field Force to punish the Swat Valley insurgents. A friend of the Churchill family, Sir Bindon allowed the young Winston to take part in the campaign as a war correspondent. Churchill thought Blood 'kind' and 'charming'. He dedicated his first book, *The Story of the Malakand Field Force*, to him.

The frontier revolt of 1897–98 was the biggest campaign fought by the Indian Army since the Mutiny and Blood was one of the few officers to emerge with an enhanced reputation. The fact that he had covered much of the same ground in 1895 proved invaluable. 'I knew exactly what I intended to do,' he later wrote; 'I assumed command at once, cleared everybody out of the office and had orders out in less than an hour.' The Swat tribes punished, Blood was given command of the Buner Field Force in January 1898 and in a fortnight his troops successfully coerced the Bunerwals and other tribes of the region into submission. Blood was now, as Churchill told his mother, 'a made man'.

For the next two years Sir Bindon commanded the Meerut Division before being sent to South Africa at the express wish of Lord **Kitchener** in January 1900. His handling of operations in the Eastern Transvaal were considered good, though he was outsmarted on a number of occasions by the wily Boer general, Ben Viljoen.

Nine months later Blood returned to India and the important command of the Punjab. It was his bad luck that on 9 April 1902 a cook named Atu was beaten to death in the lines of the newly arrived 9th Queen's Royal Lancers at Sialkot. Before he died, Atu blamed men of the regiment. Several of his claims were later disputed. It is clear, however, that Sir Bindon took the side of this 'fine regiment' and believed the victim's statement to be 'unjustifiable'. Punjab military command did not rush to investigate the matter or do a very thorough job when it did so. Finally, Blood sent a report to the Viceroy that was a whitewash. The matter was made worse by a second outrage; a private of the same regiment kicked a punkah-wallah to death, though Blood reported that there was 'only one kick, and that "a slight one with the bare foot"', wrote Curzon in disgust.

The report from the Punjab landed on the desk of the Adjutant-General, Sir Horace Smith-Dorrien, who remarked wittily to an assistant that Sir Bindon had 'fallen into the jaws of the lion'. Lord Curzon, full of reforming zeal, was determined to stamp out, as he termed it, 'the theory that a white man may kick or batter a black man to death with impunity because he is only a "damned nigger."' The Viceroy castigated Blood in a withering document of many pages. 'Really,' he wrote, 'can ineptitude further go?' The report he described as 'a purely *ex-parte* statement, couched in the style of an advocate and animated by the spirit of a partisan'.

Sir Bindon found the whole matter distressing and described Curzon's reply as 'rude'. He was a defender of the institution he loved and its men, but Blood was not an overt racist (his memoirs contain a portrait of his favourite native orderly and I have a book he presented to an Indian gentleman he called 'my good friend'). The army closed ranks and supported him, though it must be said that Kitchener agreed with the Viceroy's censure of the 9th Lancers and the regiment's punishment. Blood retired five years later, but remained active on ceremonial occasions. He was 90 when he wrote his memoirs and died seven years later on 16 May 1940. It was said his name had appeared in the army lists for eighty years.

BOURCHIER, MAJOR-GENERAL SIR G. – INDIAN ARMY GUNNER

ROUND-FACED WITH LONG white mutton-chop whiskers, George Bourchier was a most gallant gunner during the Indian Mutiny. Later he saw more action in Bhutan and commanded a column in the 1871–72 Lushai expedition.

Bourchier was born in 1821, the son of a parson, was educated at Addiscombe and entered the Bengal Artillery in 1838. Five years later he took part in his first battle at Punniar in the Gwalior campaign. Promoted to captain in 1853, George was commanding No. 17 field battery when the Sepoy Rebellion broke out. He was soon in the thick of things during the siege and capture of Delhi, the march towards Cawnpore and Lucknow and Campbell's battles for the relief and capture of the latter. Perhaps Bourchier's biggest success was his pursuit of the Gwalior Contingent at Cawnpore, where he led his gunners as they poured volley after volley into the retreating rebels. With the events fresh in his mind, Bourchier swiftly wrote *Eight Months Campaign against the Bengal Sepoy Army*, a work that covered events up to December 1857 – and was on sale in the bookshops by May 1858. This remains one of the best accounts of the Delhi siege and especially of the work of Greathed's column marching up-country.

During the Bhutan War in 1865, now a colonel, Bourchier commanded the Royal Artillery. Promoted brigadier in 1871, he was given command of the Cachar column in the Lushai expedition with young Fred **Roberts** as his quartermaster. One of two columns sent to invade this hill country on the borders of Assam and Burma, Bourchier led half a mountain battery, one company of sappers and miners, 1,500 infantry composed of three Indian Army regiments, along with 100 police and 1,200 coolies. It was an arduous little war that sapped the strength of all who took part. The other column, entering Lushai territory from Chittagong, was led by Charles **Brownlow** and rescued Mary Winchester, the 6-year-old daughter of a tea planter whose abduction had sparked the campaign. But it was Bourchier's troops who had the stiffest fight, on 25 January 1872 at Kangnung. The Lushais had stockaded a village at the top of a steep ascent, the narrow path having a 300ft drop on one side. A participant wrote how 'the gloom of the forest was lighted up by a myriad of flashes, and bullets and slugs fell around us' as Bourchier and his staff approached with an advanced guard of fifty men. The general's orderly was shot dead and Bourchier received multiple wounds. The Lushais were beaten with a loss of over 100 dead (the British lost four dead and six wounded). Bourchier had taken a slug through his hand, but when he removed his coat it was found that 'a hole was discovered under and behind his left elbow; and a wound which was under his left fore-arm at once accounted for the pain he felt there'.

Ninety-one days of continuous marching, some of it at altitudes of over 6,600ft, often in pestilential jungle, took its toll on Bourchier and all who served in the expedition. Worn out at its close (some of his staff thought he might die), Bourchier praised his troops in a final despatch and wrote: 'The history of the expedition from first to last has been sheer hard work.' Barely 50 years old but looking older, Bourchier retired in 1872 after being knighted and promoted to major-general. He died on 15 March 1898.

BRACKENBURY, GENERAL SIR H. – ALMOST TOO CLEVER

'THE CLEVEREST MAN in the British Army' was how Lord **Wolseley** described Henry Brackenbury. This famously 'ugly' soldier, labelled 'a very dangerous man' by the ultra-conservative Duke of Cambridge was, as his biographer admits, 'the most radical of Britain's military reformers in the Victorian era'. Then and now Brackenbury had critics. He was variously described by contemporaries as 'arrogant' and 'sarcastic'. The gossipy Ian **Hamilton**, who had a penchant for cruel remarks, called him 'the most competent administrator in our Army', but added that he hated 'live soldiers. On paper he appreciated them well ... but Brackenbury, the real Brackenbury, hated them in practice. He had never worked with soldiers; never kept in touch with them; always tried to keep out of cannon-shot range of them'. To be fair, this 'scientific soldier' belonged to that wealthy class who rarely came into contact with the ordinary rankers on a social level (unless the matter touched on army reform), and had no interest in them whatsoever on a personal one.

An extremely loud 'haw-haw' silly-ass kind of voice, an affected lisp (pronouncing his own name as 'Bwackenbaywe') and a fondness for cosying up to European royalty marked him out as a snob. Perhaps he was. But no one ever denied his genius. One of his Intelligence Department juniors later remembered his 'pasty-yellow, black moustache face and almost uncanny power of getting at the root of a complicated matter in a word or a question or two'. To some extent, 'Brack', as his assistants called him (though only behind his back), was a mass of contradictions. He had the manner of seeming superior, with an effortless knowledge, yet he declined the plum job of C-in-C India in third-person self-deprecating terms: 'He is unknown to the Indian Army. He has not the gift of attaching soldiers to him, which is possessed by Lord Roberts and Sir George White. He has no practical knowledge of the Indian Army. He is an indifferent horseman. He has been for the last seven years dissociated from the command of troops.' Hardly the words of an egotist.

Brackenbury was also more than a desk soldier. He was on active service frequently between 1858 and 1885 and took part in his fair share of fighting. As a 20-year-old artilleryman he served with the Saugor Field Force under **Whitlock**, who, in April 1858, defeated the Indian mutineers at Banda. British losses in the battle were trifling, but the 'gruesome' sight of good men killed by sun stroke on that campaign, as a result of inadequate equipment, haunted Brackenbury for the rest of his career and helped explain his zeal as a reforming organiser.

In 1868 he was appointed professor of military history at Woolwich. During this five-year spell he also visited the Franco-Prussian battlefields, getting to the front line, and wrote a book of his observations. Brackenbury's lucky break came in 1873 when his advocacy of reform brought him to the attention of Garnet Wolseley, who selected him to be his military secretary in the Ashanti campaign. On the way to Kumasi he was one of two officers who led the frontal assault on the enemy held village of Essaman, and he was also with Wolseley in the hard-fought battle at Amoaful which saw the Ashantis defeated. Brackenbury then penned a 795-page history of the war in six weeks. The book was a bestseller and helped cement Wolseley's fame, though Brackenbury was left exhausted.

Wolseley now found 'Brack' to be 'indispensable' and used him again as his military secretary in Cyprus 1878–79, Zululand 1879 and in the short campaign against the BaPedi chief Sekhukhune. Once again, Brackenbury proved he was no mere intellectual soldier by joining in the final charge against the enemy's mountain redoubt.

For a few months in 1880 he served as private secretary to Lord Lytton as Viceroy, then acted as military attaché in Paris, before reluctantly becoming intelligence chief in Ireland. An attempt to join Wolseley in Egypt in 1882 saw his dismissal from Ireland by a furious home secretary.

His career was then helped by his old mentor, Wolseley, who in 1884 took him to the Sudan as his DAG. Here he was sent to be second-in-command of the river column under General **Earle**. The death of Earle, shot at Kirbekan, followed by the news that **Gordon** had perished at the hands of dervishes who had captured Khartoum, led to Brackenbury commanding the whole of the army's withdrawal down the Nile.

Returning to England a major-general, Brackenbury was next given a free hand to overhaul the army's intelligence department. This he did for six years until 1891, when he went to India for four years as military member of the Viceroy's Council. He worked tirelessly to develop Indian defence policy, curbing the worst excesses of the Forward school, while trying to strengthen India's military resources and enable the army to fight its border wars.

In the summer of 1895 a battle royal developed over who would succeed the Duke of Cambridge as C-in-C of the British Army. 'The two men with the most brains to do it are Wolseley and Brackenbury,' noted the intelligence expert John Ardagh, but he went on to say that Brackenbury's talents were 'marred to some extent by an under-lying self-seeking and selfishness, which has made him distrusted in the past ...' Brackenbury was Director-General of Ordnance throughout the South African War. A colleague in the 1890s described him as 'keen, energetic, ambitious and extraordinarily quick on the uptake ... he possessed in unusual measure the gift of expressing himself appositely, clearly and concisely'.

After a life spent promoting efficiency and recruitment within the army, author of numerous articles on reform and ever the expert, Sir Henry retired to France in 1904 and died on the eve of the greatest war in history on 20 April 1914. Ironically, many of the changes he had championed or predicted would come to pass during the First World War.

BRIGHT, LIEUTENANT-GENERAL SIR R. – HOLDING THE KHYBER LINE

THE SPLENDIDLY NAMED Robert Onesiphorus Bright was one of the senior generals, though one of the less well-known names, who served in the Second Afghan War. Tasked with holding the Khyber line into Afghanistan, he was constantly bedevilled by the volatile, swerving allegiances of the frontier tribes.

Born in 1823, Robert joined the 19th Regiment as an ensign in 1843 and served with them for twenty-eight years. In the Crimea he saw action in all the major battles commanding the sharpshooters of the Light Division. During this campaign he demonstrated a remarkable constitution, never being sick or absent from duty throughout the awful winter of 1854–55. In 1871 Bright assumed a brigade command in India and left his regiment. One of the most noted Victorian Army cricketers, he was also keen on other sports and even retained his own pack of foxhounds called, hardly surprisingly, 'The Green Howards'.

Bright demonstrated singular skills at handling troops in action when he took command of the 1st Brigade of the Hazara Field Force in 1868, sent to punish once again the fierce tribesmen of the Black Mountain.

This 9,500-strong expedition was led by veteran campaigner Alfred **Wilde**, commanding the Punjab Frontier Force. At Kungali and Chilabat, where fir-clad peaks had to be stormed, Bright led his soldiers with flair. The 20th PNI and 5th Gurkhas were frequently under fire. Finally, the Machai Peak, defended by thousands of tribesmen, had to be taken. Major-General Wilde later declared it to be the strongest mountain position he had ever seen. Bright's troops captured it with a loss of just one man killed and seven wounded.

A decade later Bright, now a major-general, was given the 2nd (Khyber) Division of the Kabul Field Force. He essentially commanded all troops in the Second Afghan War west of the Indus, divided initially into four brigades by 1880, some 16,000 men with twenty-eight heavy guns. Under constant threat of attack, it was wearisome work for all involved, hot in summer and freezing in winter. Just as one tribe was subdued another seemed to rise hydra-like to menace the supply columns. Despite the difficulties, Sir Robert proved himself to be an able commander. The often cruel C.M. **Macgregor** called him 'a good enough fellow, but weak as water', yet genuinely seemed to like the man whom he frequently alluded to in his diary as 'old Bright'.

In 1894 this fine old regimental soldier, frontier warrior and sportsman was made a lieutenant-general. He died two years later, on 15 November 1896.

BROWN, GENERAL SIR G. – IRRITABLE MARTINET

OFFICERS OBSESSED WITH discipline, order and punishment have always existed in the services; one of the most infamous was Sir George Brown, described by one historian as 'the most unpopular officer' to serve in the Crimean War. Contemporaries thought the same: the 'old wretch is more hated than any man ever was … He blusters and bullies everybody, he dares and damns and swears at everything an inch high', reported one subaltern, while another officer thought him an 'old imbecile bully'. Regulation-bound men like Brown can be sadistic and stupid, but in the Victorian army they were also often brave; high on his horse he led his men into battle and was wounded in action at Inkerman. He also had a strong sense of loyalty – to the memory of the Iron Duke and to his friend, Lord **Raglan**, commanding the British troops in the Crimea.

In 1806, aged 16, Brown was commissioned an ensign in the 43rd Foot. A year later action came in the Copenhagen expedition, followed by years fighting in Spain and Portugal, including service under Moore at

Corunna. Sent to the Americas, he was wounded fighting against the young republicans at Bladensburg in 1814. For the next forty years, rising from lieutenant-colonel to lieutenant-general, he stagnated and grew old and increasingly irritable in a series of staff appointments at home and abroad, including many years at the Horse Guards. Sir George resigned in 1853 after an argument with the C-in-C, Viscount Hardinge, over some minor reforms. I 'never knew a man who so cordially hated all change', said the War Minister, Lord Panmure. Floggings, pipe-clayed equipment and stiff uniforms were the essence of an army in Brown's opinion.

A long-time confidante of Raglan, having served with him for decades at the Horse Guards, Brown was given command of the 5th (Light) Division in the Crimea. The two men conferred rather too much and Brown gave his advice freely. Those who served under him continued to grumble. This discontent grew in 1855 after he led an abortive raid on Kertch and the unsuccessful assault on the Redan on 18 June. One participant wrote that Brown, 'inflated by the bloodless conquest of Kertch directed the operations as if the garrison of Sebastopol were a body of serfs'. Most officers agreed with Captain Arthur Earle that 'We are prepared to try it again provided Sir G. Brown has nothing to do with it ...'

While his officers and men continued to die, Sir George was invalided home just ten days after the Redan attack, and promoted full general. He was then appointed to command the troops in Ireland and had retired from that post due to ill health just four months before his death, aged 75, on 27 August 1865. Writing nearly forty years later, Field-Marshal Lord **Wolseley**, who had been a captain in the Crimea and seen his fair share of foolish generals, wrote the best commendation Sir George ever received, calling him 'a fine soldier of the old school ... [who] was under fire an object lesson to all who saw him ... No matter how hot the day he was never seen without his leather stock; indeed, it was generally believed that he slept in it. A braver man of the Peninsula school never wore the Queen's uniform'.

BROWNE, GENERAL SIR J. – 'BUSTER' OF BALUCHISTAN

GENIAL, HEARTY, INTELLIGENT, brave, with a thick, full beard, Browne, known throughout the Indian Army as 'Buster', was a huge bear of a man who became one of the Raj's great engineers. Born in Le Havre, France, in 1839, the son of a doctor with a Calcutta practice, the young James soon learned to speak French and German fluently. This gift for languages would be a boon in his career; later he would learn to be fully conversant in Afghan and several Indian dialects, along with Persian and Russian.

In December 1857 he left the East India Company's college at Addiscombe second in the list of engineers and set sail for India and the Bengal Army. Within three years he was lucky to see his first fighting in an expedition against the Waziris led by Neville **Chamberlain**. At dawn on 23 April 1860 a large force of tribesmen attacked the British camp. Unable to find his sword and still dressed in his nightshirt, Browne seized a tent pole and flattened several intruders.

The burly officer soon carved a name for himself as a hands-on engineer. Whether destroying tribal fortifications, constructing roads or building bridges, he was always to be seen shirt sleeves rolled up, or even in his underpants in a river, getting the job done. A legendary story told about him concerned a *memsahib* who was being shown a bridge under construction and asked, 'Who is that native in the water there? He looks almost white.' A wit replied (in the punning way beloved by the Victorians), 'Oh, he may look white, but actually he is Browne!'

In 1863 he was sent under Chamberlain again to serve in the Umbeyla expedition. Every day for almost eight weeks the British were under attack and Browne took part in many vicious hand-to-hand struggles besides his engineering and interpreting duties. Just one example will suffice: trying to help strengthen an outlying picquet of the 20th Punjabis one dark night, he had to fight off two attacks by tribesmen; the first man he cut down, but the second assailant was armed with a fine *tulwar* and at one stroke shattered Browne's sword to the hilt. Unfazed, the furious engineer, bleeding from a slashed arm, smashed the hilt into the *ghazi*'s face and despatched him with the *tulwar*.

Engineering works, such as a road across the Kangra Valley, and the design of a great iron bridge at Sukkur occupied him for the next decade. Sukkur, on the borders of Sind and Baluchistan, led inexorably to Browne's association with that area in the 1870s after he was assigned to undertake a reconnaissance, in view of roads and railways, throughout the region. The Viceroy, Lord Lytton, was so impressed with Browne's report that he invited him to stay at the Viceregal Lodge at Simla, where the two found they held similar views on the Russian threat to India. Seconded to the political department, Browne was soon back in Baluchistan with a wide brief to conduct secret intelligence work along the Afghan frontier. So effective was he at this task that a legend grew among the tribes that he was not a British officer at all but an Afghan *mullah* in disguise.

When the Second Afghan War broke out in 1878, Colonel Browne accompanied the Quetta column heading towards Kandahar. His *mullah* legend now proved a boon when the army reached the hulking mountain fortress of Khelat-i-Ghilzie. Here 'Buster' was able to meet its Afghan commander in front of the fort, detain him with threats, then ride into the fortress with just sixteen *sowars* and so overawe the garrison that they gave him the keys. It was a stunningly audacious act that probably saved many lives.

Back in England on leave when the second phase of the war broke out, he defended Lytton and lectured on the Russian menace in Central Asia. Active service came as a welcome relief in 1882, when he was sent to Egypt as Commanding Royal Engineer of the Indian Contingent. With the troops under Herbert **Macpherson**, he charged along the banks of the canal at Tel-el-Kebir as Egyptian soldiers ran for their lives. At the war's end he found himself twice mentioned in despatches and made a CB.

It was to be Browne's last campaign. Before him lay the immense task of constructing the Hurnai railway across Baluchistan. Blasting through rocky chasms, building bridges and laying tracks on a line that rose from 500ft above sea level to 6,800ft, took him and his labour force five years, battling tunnel falls, floods and mud slides. In 1889 he was rewarded with promotion to QMG at army headquarters, and three years later had the honour to succeed the famous Sir Robert Sandeman as Governor-General's agent in Baluchistan. It was while working there that he died, a relatively young general, on 13 June 1896.

BROWNE, GENERAL SIR S. – ONE-ARMED VICTORIA CROSS HERO

BEARDED, KINDLY, COURAGEOUS Sam Browne was perhaps the classic beau *sabreur* of the Indian Army. He is still remembered by the belt he designed which bears his name and has been in use ever since.

His father was an HEIC doctor and Samuel was born in India on 3 October 1824. After an English education, he returned to the land of his birth in 1840 and was commissioned in the 46th Bengal Native Infantry. The period was one of great expansion of British power and though he missed some wars, the young Browne was active throughout the Second Anglo-Sikh War 1848–49, including the bloody battle of Chillianwallah and the decisive victory at Gujerat.

With the Sikhs conquered, the British set their sights on bringing order to the mountainous Punjab-Afghan frontier north of Peshawar. A new kind of irregular cavalry and infantry were needed to police these badlands and Browne began to carve out a name for himself and his new regiment – the 2nd Punjab Cavalry. He took part in frequent skirmishes against the wily tribesmen and in major campaigns against the Waziris, Bozdars and Black Mountain fanatics in 1851–52 and 1857.

The year 1857 saw the Great Uprising break out across northern India and Sam, now commanding his regiment, led them in countless actions before winning his coveted Victoria Cross in an amazing display of courage at Seerporah on 31 August 1858. In a fierce engagement that saw 300 mutineers slain, Browne galloped with just one orderly *sowar* against a 9-pounder gun and its crew who were about to fire on the advancing British infantry. Surrounded by increasing numbers of the enemy, he managed to kill one gunner before receiving a severe sword wound on the left knee. With blood spurting, he fought on until a mutineer sliced his left arm off at the shoulder. The blow was struck so hard that Brown's horse toppled over on top of him. Luckily *sowar*s of the 2nd PC then arrived and saved their commandant.

The famous belt that Browne designed is usually ascribed to the loss of his arm, but recent research suggests otherwise; as early as 1852 he told a visiting English politician that he was 'designing a new belt for his regiment and was finding out the best way of carrying his arms'. It seems Sam experimented with bits of harness and in 1856 he paid a London saddler to make a belt based on his Indian design. The old-style cavalry belt caused the sword to trail on the ground when a trooper was dismounted and it had no easy attachment for pistols. His new design allowed a man to easily reach his sword, pistol and ammunition. The waist belt also gave greater support to the back and the whole thing frankly looked smarter. The old belt stayed in use for some years, but by 1859 several officers in the 2nd PC had adopted the 'Sam Browne belt' and it gradually became universal in the British Army.

Another VC hero, Sir Dighton **Probyn**, commented that soon after the 1857–59 uprising, officers of the 2nd PC had lengths of bridle chain sewn across the shoulders of their jackets. Clearly, the loss of Sam's arm had an effect and shoulder chains became an increasingly common dress feature of Indian cavalry regiments.

Sam Browne served nineteen years with the 2nd PC and in 1865 was given the prestigious command of the Corps of Guides. The rank of major-general came five years later and in 1875 he was chosen to escort HRH the

Prince of Wales on his Indian tour. This resulted in a knighthood and further promotion. In 1878 he was made Military Member of the Viceroy's Council. Here Browne and the C-in-C India, Sir Frederick **Haines**, both tried, without success, to curb the rash fantasies of Lord Lytton, warning that Afghanistan would not be an easy nut to crack if war broke out, but the Viceroy was determined on a show of force.

When invasion came, Browne was given command of the northern column. His Peshawar Valley Field Force immediately ran into transport difficulties (largely not his fault as the other two invading armies had grabbed the best animals and supplies). Then, in attacking the fort of Ali Musjid that dominated the Khyber Pass, his frontal assault failed because the three brigades involved were not well co-ordinated. One critic who took part, the religious Colonel Ball-Acton, wrote that 'the whole thing was a mistake … We were much too weak to attack so strong a position … We ought to have waited a day or two …' Luckily, the Afghans evacuated the fort under cover of darkness (Browne had warned the Viceroy of the dangers that would be faced attacking Ali Musjid before the war even started). He was now able to advance on Jellalabad and by 2 April occupy Gandamak, where a treaty brought a short-lived peace in May 1879.

Lytton now had a petty revenge on the man who had cautioned him a year earlier. He told British government that Browne should have been court-martialled instead of being honoured with a GCB, that he 'was utterly unfit for any responsible command, had neglected every duty of a commander and displayed almost every disqualification; at the end of the campaign, his troops were demoralized and nearly mutinous through lack of confidence in their commander and his neglect of their simplest requirements'. The Viceroy's wrath was harsh indeed and Browne was relegated to command the Lahore Division and not sent to the front when war resumed. Lytton's censure was vindictive, but it was not wholly unfair; one Gurkha officer wrote at the time that Browne had 'a well-earned reputation of being a regular old woman and quite unfit to command an army'.

Sam Browne retired soon after the war but lived for two more decades, until 14 March 1901. A monument 'to his perpetual memory', showing a Punjab cavalryman, was unveiled in St Paul's Cathedral (with a copy in Lahore Cathedral), where it can be seen today. At the time, Lord **Roberts** said there never was 'a truer man, a firmer friend, a braver soldier'.

BROWNLOW, FIELD-MARSHAL SIR C. – INDIAN EXPERT

AS A YOUNG man, Charles Brownlow was a brave and intelligent officer who was allowed to raise his own regiment during the Indian Revolt. Skinny, with fishy eyes accentuated in later life by a droopy walrus moustache, he became one of those acerbic old officers who regularly write letters to *The Times* on all matters military.

He was born on 12 December 1831 and arrived in India just before the outbreak of the Second Anglo-Sikh War. He got a medal for the campaign, but saw little real action. That came soon enough in the 1852–53 Hazara expedition, when he was adjutant of the newly formed 1st Sikh Infantry, a regiment composed of men from the disbanded Sikh Army. Brownlow was noted in despatches as 'a gallant and efficient officer'. A year later, he was on campaign against the Michni Mohmands. On 31 August 1854, while trying to secure the heights above a village being destroyed by the troops, Brownlow was shot through both lungs. He was again mentioned in despatches and got a personal letter from the Governor-General, Lord Dalhousie, praising his 'conspicuous spirit and gallantry'. Three years later, fully recovered from his wounds, he was in action on the frontier again in the Bozdar expedition.

Clearly a brave officer, he was chosen by Sir John Lawrence, Chief Commissioner of the Punjab, to form a new regiment to be called the 8th Punjab Native Infantry. It was composed of new recruits and detachments from the 4th and 5th PNI (many of whom were not happy at first to leave their old corps). Drilled by Brownlow, the new regiment went on campaign on 21 August 1858 – just eight months after being raised. Having impressed with their toughness fighting the Kudu Khel and Hindustani fanatics, the regiment was honoured by being sent to fight in China in 1860. Here Captain Brownlow commanded them at the taking of the Taku Forts and at Peking, where the Chinese opened the An-tung gate to the city minutes before a bombardment had been ordered. This allowed the 8th PNI to be the first regiment of the British-French Expeditionary Force to march into the capital and plant its colours on the city walls.

Brownlow's greatest days of glory came three years later in the tough Umbeyla campaign. His regiment, now designated the 20th [Brownlow's] Punjabis (following a re-organisation of the Bengal Army), lost 167 out of all ranks killed and wounded from a total of 350 officers and men. After one of the stiffest fights at the Crag Picquet, their commander was overjoyed to hear men in camp say, 'Brownlow's men hold the Crag tonight –

we may sleep in peace.' Later he wrote: 'I cannot recall a compliment to the Regiment that pleased me more.' Many officers felt that Brownlow deserved a Victoria Cross for his bravery at Umbeyla, but he was at least promoted. Five years later he led the 20th PNI in his third campaign against the fanatical *Wahhabi* Muslims of the Black Mountain.

Though he would remain an honoured colonel of the 20th Punjabis until his death, Charles Brownlow's fighting days as a regimental commander now came to a close. He was promoted again, made an aide to the Queen and given command, in 1871, of the Chittagong column of the Lushai Expeditionary Force. It must have been a distinct change after two decades serving on the North-West Frontier to conduct a campaign in the steamy jungles of north-eastern India. His army, one of two columns, fought several small actions as well as two minor battles at heavily stockaded villages on 3 and 21 January 1872 before its objectives were finally achieved. The political officer with the column noted the general had 'a genial smile and a kindly blue eye'. Despite suffering from the climate, Brownlow still insisted on walking much of the way and sharing the meagre diet of his officers – chapatis, tinned mutton and rum.

High honours continued to fall; a KCB and command of the Rawal Pindi Brigade led to the coveted appointment in 1879 of Assistant Military Secretary for Indian Affairs at the Horse Guards. This plum post allowed Brownlow to have the ear of the C-in-C, George, Duke of Cambridge. In Whitehall he managed to influence Indian Army policy for ten years. Surprisingly, perhaps, he got on well with **Wolseley**, but as an old India man he campaigned quietly, and successfully, for **Roberts** to be made C-in-C of India in 1885.

In retirement Sir Charles was a frequent contributor to the newspapers. He was a stern critic of the Forward Policy and scorned any British interference in tribal territory. Afghanistan and the fighting tribes would always be a bulwark against any Russian advance on India, he argued, and the tribes would never be completely conquered, though periodic campaigns were a necessary way of punishing them and of training the Indian Army in hill warfare. The Russian invasion of India was 'a bogey', wrote Brownlow. 'The tribes will settle down if we withdraw from their country,' he wrote in 1897, 'and the Cossack will patrol the Pamirs in vain'. Sir Charles lived on, occasionally fulminating in the press, until his death in 1916. The town of 'Brownlow' in South Australia was named in his honour by an admiring governor, though he never visited the continent.

BULLER, GENERAL SIR R. – VICTORIA CROSS HERO AND SCAPEGOAT

TO WIN A Victoria Cross is the ultimate symbol of courage that can be shown by a British soldier. To fail in battle or lead troops through a series of ignominious defeats is the mark of a poor general. It was Redvers Buller's fate to achieve both, and it is hardly surprising that his career and personal character are still the subject of historical debate and revision.

The son of an MP, he purchased his commission into the elite 60th Rifles in 1858, was quickly en route to India and saw fighting against the Chinese in 1860. Much of that decade he spent in Canada, but returned home in 1869; a year later, at the invitation of Garnet **Wolseley**, he agreed to serve in the Red River expedition.

Three years later, following a spell at the Staff College, 34-year-old Buller served as Wolseley's chief intelligence officer on the 1873–74 Ashanti expedition. His reward after this arduous little war was a CB and the brevet rank of major. The 1870s were the high point of Buller's prowess; he saw action in the Ninth Xhosa War and led the Frontier Light Horse against the Zulus in 1879. The natives called him 'the Steam Engine' because 'he was always rushing out of unexpected places'. Impulsiveness can be dangerous. On 28 March he won the Victoria Cross during the retreat from Hlobane Mountain, a disastrous battle in which he showed great courage under fire and rescued a fellow officer, but it was only the British success next day at Kambula that saved his reputation since, as even his most sympathetic biographer has written, 'Undoubtedly Buller was to blame.' Plain-speaking and hot-tempered, Buller was starting to make enemies. After Hlobane it was whispered that Buller and Evelyn **Wood** (the latter in overall command) had shifted much of the censure onto another officer. A gossipy staff officer described Buller as 'a man of the most perverse turn of mind I think I ever met', with an inclination 'to crab everybody', and 'not always to be trusted'.

In 1882 Buller broke off his honeymoon when Wolseley asked him to head his intelligence department during the war against the Egyptian nationalists. About the last officer to arrive on service, he was nonetheless instrumental in helping to plan the victory at Tel-el-Kebir. Awarded a knighthood and further promotion, he served in the Sudan in 1884, commanding a brigade in the Red Sea area battles of El Teb and Tamai. His commander, Gerald **Graham**, praised Buller's 'coolness in action, his knowledge of soldiers and experience in the field'. Rewarded with the rank of major-general, Buller was to act as Wolseley's chief of staff in the unsuccessful attempt to save **Gordon** at Khartoum in 1885. By now many of the older Ring members were jealous of one another. Wolseley thought Buller complained too much and was egotistical, summing up that he 'works hard and he is, all round, one of our best men, but he is better as an executive than as a Staff or Administrative Officer. He is too fond of argument'. The 'dashing' young officer of the 1850s was aging rapidly. The most savage description of Buller in 1885 comes from the pen of the historian, Michael Asher, who describes him as 'a beefy man', with a 'berserk appetite for killing savages'; 'an alcoholic' who was 'essentially a loud-mouthed but inarticulate tough who might have made a competent sergeant, but should never have been promoted to high command'. Harsh words indeed. A far cry from Wolseley, who praised him as 'always cheery, always prepared to take on any job no matter how unpleasant it may be', and gave him the task of supervising the withdrawal of the expedition down the Nile.

In London between 1887–97, first as QMG and latterly as AG, Buller helped re-organise the army and its support branches. A problem occurred in 1895 when the Earl of Roseberry planned to promote Buller to C-in-C over the heads of Wolseley and **Roberts**, but the government fell, and the Unionists who took power gave the job to his old chief. Wolseley ceased to trust his old friend (naming an unreliable horse in his stable 'Sir Redvers'), but recent evidence suggests that Buller had not asked for the promotion. He did have friends in high places; the Queen thought him 'most honest and straightforward; I believe him to be a thorough gentleman', in contrast to Wolseley, whom she always found to be 'very imprudent, full of new fancies'.

When war broke out with the Boers in 1899, Buller was bullied into taking command of the South African Field Force. Once at Cape Town he soon found all his actions criticised and failures amplified. Under intense pressure to relieve the besieged garrisons in Kimberley, Ladysmith and Mafeking, he divided his forces into three, but was soon personally repulsed at Colenso on 15 December 1899 (after British failures at Stormberg and Magersfontein all in the same week). Even worse was his failure to crush the Boers in a major battle at Spion Kop on 23–24 January 1900. There were now huge cries for his dismissal from politicians and the press, though ordinary Tommies remained loyal. Still popular in some circles, he was replaced by Lord Roberts and finally departed the Cape in October 1900.

He returned to his command at Aldershot, but was clearly a broken man – disappointed and drinking heavily. To be fair to Buller, it must be said in mitigation that he had begged not to be sent to South Africa unless in a subordinate command to Wolseley or Wood. His former chief was now 'thoroughly disgusted in him'; Wolseley was saddened that 'he has not shown any of the characteristics I had attributed to him; no military genius, no firmness, not even the obstinacy which I thought he possessed when I discovered him. He seems dazed and dumbfounded.'

In October 1901 Buller's chief critic, Leopold Amery of *The Times*, provoked him into defending his actions in public. Most prominent of these was a notorious telegram he had written shortly after arriving at Cape Town that said, 'My view is that I ought to let Ladysmith go ... I now feel that I cannot say I can relieve Ladysmith with my available force.' A furious Buller now felt that he had been 'goaded past endurance' by a gang 'basely, and I know, falsely, attacking me', but it was too late; a displeased Roberts insisted he be put on half-pay for indiscipline. Buller requested a court-martial, but was refused. It was a sad end to his military career.

Amery continued to snipe, editing a monumental history of the South African War and criticising Buller more than 100 times in the text. His adversary, truly a scapegoat, grew weaker and died in his beloved Devon in 1908. Three years earlier the citizens of Exeter had unveiled an equestrian statue of their local hero that bore the simple words, 'He Saved Natal'. Shortly before his death Buller had appeared before a Royal Commission on the war and one member noted he was 'unpleasing in appearance, with no command of temper', but was 'a brave and capable soldier, admirably adapted to hold a high secondary command, but unfitted, by his temperament, to be placed in supreme command of an Army in the field'. Ironically, poor Buller had said very much the same thing in 1899 and his career might have ended on a better note if others had listened to his own self-criticisms. Not all the failures of the British Army in South Africa can be laid at his door; there was much he could not control and mistakes for which he deserved no blame. A century later most historians are charitable to him and one of his defenders, Thomas Pakenham, suggests that he was an 'innovator in countering Boer tactics'. In essence, the problem with Buller was summed up by Amery when he wrote: 'In every great war there have been unexpected failures, and always must be, Buller was one of these.'

BUTLER, LIEUTENANT-GENERAL SIR W. – ROMANTIC IDEALIST

EVERY AGE OF soldiering deserves a general who is its conscience. Just such a man was William Butler, the romantically inclined Irish Catholic from an old pro-British landowning family who served all over the globe in defence of the Empire, yet always had a passionate, idealistic affinity for the underdog. A lover of wild, open spaces, Butler recounted his adventures in a series of travel books that, despite some florid prose, also contain superb descriptive passages. Works such as *The Great Lone Land* (about a journey across the Canadian north-west) or *'Akim-Foo'* (recounting his hellish adventures in the Ashanti jungle) mark him out as one of the great Victorian travel writers. He also wrote biographies (George **Colley**, Charles **Gordon** and Charles **Napier** among their subjects) and an amazing fantasy, *The Invasion of England,* in which he predicted that a badly prepared British Army might be defeated by a German one sometime in the future, a work published, remarkably, thirty-two years before the outbreak of the First World War.

Joining the 69th Regiment as an ensign in 1858, Butler travelled extensively and was in Canada when he heard of **Wolseley**'s planned Red River expedition. He made a perilous trip alone to take part and eventually reached his goal in a canoe propelled by eight Iroquois, to the delight of Wolseley, who exclaimed, 'Where on earth have *you* dropped from?' It was typical of Butler that twelve days earlier he had made an unaccompanied and dangerous visit to see Louis Riel, the idealistic leader of the Metis half-breeds whom Wolseley had pledged to bring to justice.

Alongside Redvers Buller and Evelyn Wood, he was soon one of that remarkable circle of officers brought together by Wolseley. When his chief was assembling staff for the Ashanti War, the energetic Irishman cabled: 'Remember Butler'. Wolseley had need of him to head his intelligence department, just as he had done in Canada. He was also sent to form a second front against the Ashanti leading 1,400 Akim tribesmen, but after many setbacks and weeks spent trudging through the steamy West African jungle, Butler considered his efforts a 'failure'. Where Wolseley went Butler was sure to follow; this path took him to South Africa (in 1875 and 1879), Cyprus (1878), Egypt (1882) and the Sudan (1884–85). Along the way he wooed and wed 28-year-old Elizabeth Thompson, Britain's leading painter of battle scenes (including 'Quatre Bras', 'The Defence of Rorke's Drift' and many others). It was a very happy marriage of artistic minds.

Butler was at his chief's side at Mahsama and Tel-el-Kebir, and when the **Gordon** Relief Expedition was mounted he was put in charge of the River column – the boat flotilla utilising the Nile to get to Khartoum. It was his task in this audacious enterprise to organise a fleet of whalers crewed by West African *kroomen* and 400 hardy Canadian *voyageurs*, a scheme he and Wolseley believed in, though critics called it 'sheer quackery' and 'madness'.

Gordon's death at Khartoum put an end to Butler's efforts and those of his team, who had hauled and sailed boats around cataracts and up the Nile. During this period Wolseley summed up Butler as 'erratic', an officer whose usefulness was reduced by half because he was not a team player, simply 'an impulsive, talented Irishman, wanting in method'. The two men had a falling-out when Wolseley failed to agree with Butler's criticisms of Redvers **Buller** as chief of staff and his precious boats were made to carry extra weight. Wolseley prevented Butler from personally proceeding beyond the Nile cataracts and Sir William replied with an intemperate letter. Despite these altercations, Wolseley was still able to write at campaign's end that Butler 'makes me very angry at times, but I always like him'. Butler fought at Kirbekan and during the British withdrawal from the Sudan he led a brigade at Giniss in what was the last battle of the 1885 Sudan War. The dervishes were forced off the field with severe loss. Butler was then furious that his soldiers were left at Assouan during the hot season and bluntly said so to the authorities in Cairo. His old comrade, Evelyn **Wood**, was moved to comment that because Butler 'was generally right in his conclusions does not indicate that he always went the right way to attain them'.

Now with the rank of brigadier-general, he returned to England and a series of peacetime commands. He was also a co-respondent in the most costly and notorious of all Victorian adultery trials, that of Lady Colin Campbell (his failure to appear in court imperilling his status as a gentleman, though it has been suggested that an innocent Butler might, under oath, have simply caused the lady more grief).

This sordid drama did not affect Butler's career and in 1898 he was appointed to command the troops in South Africa. Here he was soon on a collision course with Alfred Milner, the British High Commissioner, and financier Cecil Rhodes, both architects of war with the Boers. Shortly after his arrival at the Cape, Butler made a speech in which he bluntly said: 'South Africa ... does not need a surgical operation. She needs peace, progress, and the development which is only possible through the union of many hearts and the labour of many hands.' Milner thought him 'awful' and 'of no use'. With his usual lack of tact, Butler told the High Commissioner after one interview, 'I envy you only the books in your library', and told the War Office, with one of his famous what-to-expect predictions, that 'war between the white races ... would be the greatest calamity that has ever occurred in South Africa.' By the summer of 1899 Milner was writing in his diary: 'Butler or I will have to go.' But it was the general who offered his resignation on 4 July.

He returned to London amid much criticism and a hostile press as public appetite for war against the Boer Republics was whipped to a frenzy. 'He alone, I think, among military or South African authorities, had predicted a long and severe campaign', wrote John Adye, the son of one of Butler's old comrades (see **Adye**). Subsequent events proved him right. Promoted to lieutenant-general, Sir William retired in 1905, returned to his beloved Tipperary and devoted himself to civic duties and writing his autobiography (easily the most literary one by a Victorian general). Five years later he succumbed to a bad attack of influenza and died suddenly on 7 June 1910. The old soldier's memoirs were published posthumously a year later. One reviewer noted that Butler's sympathy 'was always given to the weak, the injured, the oppressed', while another commented that he 'had an inexhaustible fund of pity, and indignation quick as a flame'.

CARRINGTON, MAJOR-GENERAL SIR F. – IMPERIAL FRONTIERSMAN

WHEN THE RATHER sleazy series of small wars and uprisings unfolded along the South African frontier during the last quarter of the nineteenth century, one man seemed to take part in almost all of them – Frederick Carrington. One of the innovators of irregular mounted warfare, 'Old Freddy', as he became known, with his long, fleshy, beagle face and heavily drooping walrus moustache, was hardly a classic hero, yet he displayed expert horsemanship and bravery under fire, and was only finally beaten when he met similarly mounted opponents more skilful than himself.

At school he was considered a dunce whose only success was on the sports field. In 1864, shortly before his twentieth birthday, Freddy was bought a commission in the 1/24th Foot and, still only a lieutenant, was one of their officers who sailed for the Cape ten years later. By luck his skills as a horseman won him the job of forming a troop of mounted infantrymen to quell a bloodless rising of diamond miners in Griqualand West. These troops soon expanded into a squadron, called 'Carrington's Horse', and when the Ninth Xhosa War broke out in 1877 Freddy got the job of forming a volunteer cavalry regiment to be called the Frontier Light Horse. At Centane he led his men gallantly, though they were almost unhorsed in the long grass by warriors led by the astute Chief Sandile. But it was a fine blooding of the new corps and Carrington passed command of it to Major Redvers **Buller**.

Now a captain, Carrington missed action in the Zulu War as he was left to guard the Transvaal border country with a new volunteer unit he formed called the Transvaal Mounted Horse. Here he also kept one eye on the troublesome BaPedi of Chief Sekhukhune. After the Zulus had been defeated Sir Garnet **Wolseley** gave Carrington command of eight squadrons of colonial troops in the assault on these mountain warriors' stronghold, called 'the Fighting Kopje', on 28 November 1879. He was commended for his 'coolness' under fire, promoted to lieutenant-colonel and made a CMG.

Next Carrington was absorbed by what became known as the Basuto Gun War of 1880–81. Besieged for a time at Mafeteng, he broke out with a body of colonial troops and led an attack (under the overall command of General Mansfield **Clarke**) on Chief Lerothodi's village, burning it to the ground. Problems on other parts of the frontier caused Clarke to leave Carrington behind with 2,000 men and a new title of 'Colonel-Commandant' until the war drifted to a sad and ignominious end.

After leave taken in England, Freddy returned to South Africa in time to command the 2nd Mounted Rifles (one of two corps) in an expedition to Bechuanaland. At the close Carrington was made commandant of a mounted force to police the territory. He demanded the best recruits, land was cheap to buy, and soon the Bechuanaland Border Police were known as 'the Blue-Blooded Police' and 'the Top Hat Brigade'.

In 1888 Carrington resigned his command and sailed for England. Bechuanaland was on the border of Matabele territory and within a year he was back, at the request of the Colonial Office, with an enlarged BBP. 'Old Freddy' became a pal of Cecil Rhodes in his plans to expand the British Empire, joined a 'get-rich' gold syndicate and helped to train the men who invaded Matabeleland in one of history's least attractive land grabs. Home again, Carrington was sent to command troops on Gibraltar, but in 1896 he was needed in southern Africa again to command all imperial and colonial troops when the Matabele rose for a second time, now aided by the formerly peaceful Mashona. For much of this war 'Old Freddy' had chronic bronchitis, but observers criticised his 'lacklustre' generalship in directing a campaign in the boulder-strewn Matopos Hills. At dinner Rhodes used to annoy his military guests by sarcastically calculating 'how long it would take at this rate of loss for Carrington's force to be entirely exterminated'.

By 1898 Freddy was so famous that he was included in a book, *Our Living Generals*, which ranked him alongside Roberts as one of the best dozen soldiers in the army. Praise indeed! In 1900, during the South African War, Carrington was given command of over 5,000 men, mainly culled from Australia, Tasmania and New Zealand, designated the Rhodesian Field Force. Sir Alfred Milner, the British High Commissioner, thought Carrington was not 'a clever or quick-witted strategist', adding, 'He is a disciplinarian, yet despises red tape.' Another officer went further and said that 'his mental development is very small'. It was not a happy command. After dithering about, Carrington made a mess of trying to relieve the supply base at Brakfontein (suffering a short siege some said was worse than Mafeking), an incident that was described as 'one of the most mortifying episodes' of the war. A disgusted Lord **Roberts** broke up the RFF and made 'Old Freddy' return home, but not before he had the humiliation of reading a defamatory editorial about his actions in the *Rhodesian Times*.

An expert horseman and brave warrior, Carrington had, up to 1896, a very good career. He was, however, a weak general. When placed against men like De la Rey, a true master of strategy and tactics, he was out of his depth. He died in 1913, after a quiet decade spent in Gloucestershire, and it seems apposite that his passing came shortly before a new and terrible war arrived to make his own mounted forays look puny indeed.

CATHCART, LIEUTENANT-GENERAL SIR G. – METHOD AND MADNESS

THE CRIMEAN WAR historian Christopher Hibbert wrote that, after Waterloo, the career of this officer was not distinguished, while Harold Raugh, correctly in my opinion, sums up his handling of the Eighth Xhosa War as 'competent' and 'conscientious'. It is time for a reassessment of George Cathcart.

The son of an earl, he was commissioned a cornet in the 2nd Life Guards, served as private secretary to his father, the ambassador to Russia, and witnessed there many of the Napoleonic battles in 1813. At Waterloo he served as an aide to Wellington. Over the next two decades he leap-frogged through various regiments until, in 1851, he was a major-general.

In April 1852 Cathcart arrived in South Africa as successor to the energetic but often foolish Sir Harry **Smith** as governor and C-in-C. One historian, writing of his arrival at the Cape, describes Cathcart as 'tall, slim, and able … all calmness and efficiency'. Immediately and wisely he suspended military operations against the Xhosa tribes, so that the troops could have a rest, while he assessed the situation. Step by step he wore down his enemy: first he cleared them from the highway between King William's

Town and Grahamstown, then built small blockhouses, which he called 'castles', to restrict enemy movements as he pushed deeper into their country; mounted armed police forces were raised in all five frontier districts to aid the regular troops. It was a cruel guerrilla-style war; every male native captured in Xhosa territory was hanged, their heads removed and often boiled to make grisly trophies.

In December the general travelled north to extort 10,000 cattle to feed his troops from Moshoeshoe of the Basutos. The wily chief refused to comply and defeated an imperial force sent against him at the Battle of the Berea. He then cunningly complimented Cathcart on his 'victory' and sent him a token herd of cattle. A wiser man than many of his kind, Cathcart sensibly accepted this ruse and returned south to end the Xhosa War 'as quietly and inexpensively as possible'. When, in March 1853, broken by this war of attrition, Sandile and other Xhosa chiefs sued for peace, Cathcart met with them amicably but banished the Xhosa forever from their ancestral lands in the Amatolas. At the same time he intended to reward loyal native tribes by making them a homeland of the district of British Kaffraria. Land-hungry colonists were appalled. Cathcart labelled the whites 'mean [and] dishonest' and wrote that 'the Kafir is much the finer race of the two'. When war broke out again and the Xhosa tried to recover their beloved Amatola Mountains, Sir George – for he was knighted after the war – was Adjutant-General at the Horse Guards. Yet his frontier policy has been described by one modern South African historian as 'cautious and moderate'. In a book in which he allowed most of his correspondence to be printed, Cathcart called it 'military control, not colonization'.

It can be seen that Sir George did most things, as Noel Mostert has written, 'calmly, deliberately and methodically'. Crimean War historians see him in a different light. He was sent to the Crimea in 1854, aged 60, one of the two youngest generals on the campaign, holding in his pocket a 'dormant commission' to succeed Lord Raglan, the C-in-C, in the event of the latter's death or incapacitation. This document seems to have been the source of a tension that developed between the pair; Sir George acted much of the time as if he was in a quasi-independent command and it chafed him that Raglan ignored what he thought to be sound advice (such as capturing Sebastopol at the outset). At Balaklava, before the famous charge, Cathcart refused to move his troops until he had eaten breakfast and his men, who had been out all night in the trenches, had taken some rest. This was typical of him.

Less typical was his fatal behaviour at Inkerman. In the middle of this foggy battle on 5 November 1854, Sir George was bluntly told, 'Support the Brigade of Guards. Do not descend or leave the plateau ... Those are Lord Raglan's orders.' Immediately Cathcart admitted to an aide that he 'did not want to be cautioned' and set off with 400 men to charge the Russians out of a valley. In the mist, melee and excitement he failed to recognise it was a trap and that there were Russian marksmen on high ground. His troops were soon being shot in the back and Cathcart admitted to a staff officer, 'I fear we are in a mess.' Seconds later, a bullet pierced his heart and he fell dead from his horse.

He was no great general but, in the pre-Crimean, post-Waterloo age littered with military incompetents in high command, George Cathcart was more conscientious than most, less foolish than many, moderate in subjugation of his native opponents and brave in battle. It was unfortunate that he allowed his low opinion of Raglan to cloud his normally calm and sensible judgement at Inkerman.

CHAMBERLAIN, FIELD-MARSHAL SIR N. & GENERAL SIR C. – BROTHERS IN ARMS

TALL, DISTINGUISHED-LOOKING NEVILLE Bowles Chamberlain was a courageous officer, labelled 'the bravest of the brave' by Lord **Gough**, while Charles **Napier** called him 'the very soul of chivalry'. A major figure in the mid-Victorian Indian Army, he was wounded in action several times, including his last and most hard-fought campaign, one in which his style of generalship added to a notable disaster. Neville's brother Crawford, a year his junior, became one of the Indian Army's most dashing irregular cavalry commanders. Both brothers were devoted to one another.

The boys were born in 1820 and 1821, sons of a diplomat. At the tender age of 15, Neville was sent to the Royal Military Academy, Woolwich, but two years later opted for a commission in the 16th NI of the Bengal Army. He served with the 'Army of Retribution' that chastised Kabul in 1842. The young officer was shocked at the savagery meted out by British troops to the citizenry on whom they blamed the deaths of so many comrades during the awful retreat nine months earlier. He wrote that he was 'disgusted with myself, the world, and above all, my chosen profession. In fact, we are nothing but licensed assassins'. During the fighting Chamberlain was wounded six times, but went on to fight at Maharajpore in the short Gwalior War of 1843, and won praise for his conduct at Gujerat in the Second Sikh War, winning a brevet majority.

After leave, Neville returned to India and asked to be transferred to the political department within the Punjab as an assistant to Sir Henry Lawrence. Soon he was in command of a fledgling military police force; when Sir Henry's brother, John Lawrence, took over the chief commissionership he asked Chamberlain to become commandant. He took the local rank of brigadier-general, and control of the 11,000 troops of the new Punjab Irregular Frontier Force tasked with guarding the 700 miles of the North-West Frontier. Early in 1855 Neville led his men in an expedition into the Miranzai border country to punish the tribes, and in August of the same year was fighting the Afridis.

On the outbreak of the Mutiny, he headed that decisive band of officers who heeded the call to send a moveable column down to Delhi. Shortly afterwards he joined the army on the ridge before Delhi as its adjutant-general. During the stiff fighting he was wounded in the shoulder by a musket-ball as his horse leapt over a wall lined with mutineers. Weak and confined to bed, Chamberlain was unable to be with the final assault columns, but when the rear and right side of the British camp were threatened he had himself borne on a litter to supervise and restore order. A firm soldier, quite ready to blow rebels from the mouth of cannon, he was also a fair man. When cries for vengeance against Delhi were loudest and there were calls for the city to be razed to the ground, Chamberlain said: 'I am ready to pass sentence of death against all rebels and mutineers against whom any single murder or participation in an act of gross cruelty can be proved, but I would sooner resign my commission than stand a passive spectator of indiscriminate slaughter.' A fellow officer, Henry **Daly**, wrote at this time that 'Chamberlain *looks* what he truly is, a high and noble soldier.'

Back on the frontier in August 1858, Chamberlain prevented a conspiracy among Sikh troops at Dera Ismail Khan before leading an expedition against the Waziris. In 1860 he was in action again in a short campaign against the Mahsud tribe. Though only 40 years old he was, in fact, worn out by constant active service, bouts of malaria and the effects of his many injuries – it was said at the time that he bore more wounds than any other British officer.

Yet in 1863 one more campaign beckoned. It was to be his toughest and test severely his courage, strength and abilities as a soldier. Its aim was to expel the *Wahhabi* fanatics from their village of Malka, at the end of the Umbeyla Pass, less than 40 miles from the Corps of Guides headquarters at Mardan in British territory. From the outset, Chamberlain was not keen to command. He wrote to his brother: 'If duty requires the sacrifice I cannot repine, but ... I have no wish for active service.' The nest of fierce funda-mentalist tribesmen at Malka had irritated the Raj for several years and only five years earlier a force under Sydney **Cotton** had tried to snuff them out.

The Umbeyla Pass was a narrow rocky gorge on the edge of territory belonging to the Buner and Chamlawal tribes. The political officer, Reynell **Taylor**, made the mistake of thinking the tribes would let a British army pass through their lands. Against the advice of the C-in-C, Sir Hugh **Rose**, the Punjab Chief Commissioner, Sir Robert Montgomery doubled the size of the force from a flying column to an unwieldy army and demanded it set off hurriedly in October instead of the next spring. Thus, Chamberlain's army of 6,000 men entered the Umbeyla Pass on 20 October 1863.

Things had not gone well from the start, especially with the strag-gling supply train, and the pass itself was just the width of a mule track. Chamberlain now made the mistake of halting his troops at this juncture for two days while his engineers tried to improve the track. It was, in the words of one historian, a delay that 'was to prove fatal'. The tribes, suspi-cious of British intentions, turned warlike, the Akhund of Swat, mystical leader of the tribes along that part of the frontier, threw the weight of his prestige against the invaders and soon thousands of warriors joined the *jihad*. By mid-November, with losses mounting and his troops pinned down in the pass, Chamberlain was begging Montgomery for fresh troops – 'This is urgent.' Brave as ever, he led a sortie and was wounded again, a bullet smashing his elbow.

Montgomery finally decided on a withdrawal, but from his sick-bed Chamberlain cautioned against a retirement; he felt, rightly as it proved, that the Swatis and Bunerwals were starting to lose heart and the tide was turning. The seriously injured Chamberlain returned to India at this point. He was aware that the high losses of the campaign would be laid at his door, but wrote, 'I had no other course than that I adopted. An onward move would have hazarded the safety of the force. Our advance was merely the flame to set up the spark of fanaticism.'

Knighted, Sir Neville continued to rise in the service and by 1877 was a full general. One year later he headed a mission to Afghanistan. Its rebuff, encamped near the entrance to the Khyber Pass, became a *casus belli* for the start of the Second Afghan War. Chamberlain retired in 1881. He received his Field-Marshal's baton in 1900, shortly before his death on 18 February 1902.

Crawford Chamberlain's career was almost as grand; he joined his elder brother's regiment in 1837 and marched with it as part of the Army of the Indus into Afghanistan in 1838, and was present at the capture of the fortress of Ghazni. In October 1841 he was appointed adjutant of Shah Shooja's 1st Irregular Cavalry commanded by Captain John Christie. The regiment saw much fighting around Kandahar and on one occasion Crawford had a narrow escape when an opponent slashed open the seat of his trousers and injured his horse. In 1843 he formed two squadrons of irregular cavalry in Sind called Chamberlain's Horse. Three years later his unit was merged with Christie's Horse and Crawford was made second-in-command. He fought alongside Neville in the bloody battle of Chillianwallah against the Sikhs. In the same war he led a spectacular charge in which sixteen of the enemy were killed and he was wounded. An impressed Lord Gough made him the subject of a special despatch. At Gujerat, on 21 February 1849, the injured Crawford had to be lifted into the saddle, yet remained on horseback all day.

Made commandant of the 1st Irregular Cavalry, better known as Skinner's Horse, Major Chamberlain led his troopers in the 1854 Mohmand expedition. During the early stages of the 1857 Mutiny he kept order at Multan, disarming suspect regiments, while his own men stayed loyal. In September he and his regiment were besieged for three days at Cheechawtnee, but held out until relieved.

Crawford continued to rise in the service and finally reached full general in 1880. He retired four years later. In 1896, after two years of widowhood, he married Augusta Christie, daughter of his old commandant. He was knighted and made a GCIE in the 1897 Diamond Jubilee honours. Of 'splendid physique' in his prime, Crawford died in December 1902, not long after Neville's passing. The brothers in arms lie buried in the quiet churchyard of Rownhams in Hampshire.

CHANNER, GENERAL SIR G. – VC HERO OF PERAK

HANDSOME GEORGE CHANNER was the son of a soldier born at Allahabad, on 7 January 1843. After a typical education back in England he returned to India as an ensign in the Bengal infantry. Promoted lieutenant in 1861, he served in the Umbeyla expedition of 1863 and then the Lushai expedition of 1871–72. His Victoria Cross was the only one given for the little-known Perak expedition on the Malay Peninsula in 1875–76.

Stealthily, Captain Channer led a small party of the 1st Gurkha Light Infantry into an enemy stockade surrounded by a stout bamboo palisade on 20 December 1875. The rebels were quartered in a 7-yard-long loghouse of great strength. It was deemed that this position had to be taken at the point of the bayonet. Waving his sword, Channer led from the front. This small but savage little fight brought the war to a close.

Within two years Channer, now a major, was fighting the Afridis in 1877–78 and then, almost immediately, the Afghans. After the battle at Peiwar Kotal, under **Roberts**, he found himself mentioned in despatches for his superb handling of the 29th Punjab Native Infantry, a Sikh regiment. In 1888 he commanded the 1st Brigade of the Hazara Field Force. It was his last taste of fighting, but in a celebrated march in which kit was kept to a minimum and the men allowed only one day's rations, he led 980 soldiers in a descent of 1,500ft in less than six hours to surprise an enemy village, while at Pokal his troops marched 7 miles in an amazing descent of 4,500 feet, killing almost 100 of the enemy with a loss of one soldier killed and four wounded. In 1895 Channer commanded the Reserve Brigade of the Chitral Relief Force.

Considered one of the best revolver shots in the British Army, Channer's star continued to rise but ill health dogged him. He died at his home in north Devon aged 62 years on 13 December 1905.

CHEAPE, GENERAL SIR J. – FIGHTING BURMESE AND SIKHS

JOHN CHEAPE WAS a Bengal Engineer who figured prominently in the First and Second Burmese wars as well as being chief engineer at the Siege of Multan during the Second Sikh War. He was born in 1792 and set sail for India with an engineer's commission at the age of 17. Six years later he saw his first action in the 1815–16 Pindari War and later the attack on the fortress of Aseeghur in March 1819.

When the First Burmese War broke out in 1824, Captain Cheape found himself constantly employed until its close two years later; he was chief engineer at the attack and seizure of Rangoon on 7 December 1824 and received 'the greatest credit' for this British success by the C-in-C. Fourteen years later, with the rank of brigadier, Cheape joined the besieging army before Multan. In the words of historians Gough and Innes:

> On December 6th, 13th and 16th he made special reconnaissances. Major Napier had previously drawn up a project of attack, which was directed against the north-east angle of the fort … On December 12th … Cheape recorded objections to it, and proposed instead that the attack should be similar to that in the first siege – against and through the city, beginning at its southern bastion …

The city was stoutly defended by the Sikhs, but stormed and taken by the British along the lines of Cheape's proposals on 2 January 1849. Following this success he was also at the last battle against the Sikhs, Gujerat, as senior engineer.

When a second war with the Burmese broke out in 1852, and officers and *sepoy*s from the Bengal and Madras East India Company armies were being sent to fight there, Cheape commanded the Bengal Division of about 9,000 men. While based at Prome he took the surrender of the leading enemy general, Maha Bandula and co-ordinated the repulse of a whole series of attacks on the town made by the Burmese on the night of 8 December. Early in February 1853 it was decided to send a force of almost 600 men to destroy the base of a chief called Nya-Myatt-Toon (to the Burmese he was a nationalist hero, to the British a pirate who was causing havoc for their shipping on the Irrawaddy). The column, a mix of soldiers and marines, set off up river led by a naval officer, Captain Loch, who was also allowed to command on land when the force found the river blocked. Stumbling through dense and booby-trapped jungle, the column was ambushed and three officers were killed, one of them Loch, and over seventy men wounded.

It was necessary to expunge this humiliation and Cheape was sent with 1,500 to destroy Toon's camp and capture or kill him if at all possible. On 18 March 1853 Cheape's little army reached the place, which was a series of three large, heavily defended stockades filled with over 4,000 heavily armed Burmese who also turned the two guns they had captured from Loch's column on the advancing British. The final and third stockade was the most difficult. In the words of historian Edward Thackeray:

> Its length was 1200 yards, its left flank was protected by a morass, and along the whole front there was a nullah with a good deal of water and soft mud at the bottom. The ground near the right flank was nearly dry, and was covered by an abattis which was penetrable with extreme difficulty ... altogether impracticable to troops under fire. The only entrance to the stockade was a narrow path, across which at intervals pits had been dug, and this path was commanded by the two guns captured from the previous expedition and by several jingals.

Indeed, the fire was so intense on this path that the troops had to wait until a 24-pounder howitzer could blast an entrance. Cheape's army eventually silenced all the stockades, but Nya-Myatt-Toon escaped; the butcher's bill was several hundred Burmese and 130 officers and men killed and wounded. One of those who suffered a life-threatening jingal ball in the thigh was

Ensign Wolseley of the 80th Foot. This young officer, who had led one of the charges, would recover and rise to become C-in-C of the British Army.

Cheape was praised for his 'coolness, energy and prudence, with compassion for his wounded and suffering soldiers'. On his return from the expedition, a contemporary newspaper remarked that he looked 'a good deal knocked up, he says the month's campaign has been the hardest work he ever undertook in his life'. Cheape had almost been burned to death one night when his hut caught fire and he lost his favourite sword. When General Godwin departed the war, supreme command in the field devolved on Cheape until peace was declared in 1854. For his services he was made a KCB and raised in 1865 to a GCB. This fine old warrior died in 1875 in his eighty-third year.

CHELMSFORD, GENERAL LORD F. – HAUNTED BY ISANDLWANA

IT WOULD BE wrong to lay all the mistakes made in the Zulu War at Chelmsford's door, but his generalship was clearly flawed. His name will be forever linked with one of the worst defeats suffered by British arms in the nineteenth century. Modern historians have labelled him a poor general. It is sometimes forgotten that contemporary military observers were no less kind.

Frederic Augustus Thesiger, later Baron Chelmsford, was born on 31 May 1827, eldest son of a future lord chancellor. This scion of the high aristocracy was educated at Eton, entered the army in 1844 and, through dint of purchase, was a major within nine years. During the Crimean War he was an ADC to Lt-General Markham, commanding the 2nd Division. From a distance, Frederic watched the attacks on Sebastopol and wrote: 'I enjoy myself very much … The General goes out for a two hours' ride in the morning, and then we do ample justice to a very good breakfast, cheese and port wine at 2, ride again at 3, and dinner at half past 7. Not so bad for campaigners, is it?'

Wanting to see more active service Thesiger, now a lieutenant-colonel, bought his way into the 95th Foot and arrived in India just in time to take part in the last of fourteen battles fought by his regiment in the arduous Central India campaign of 1857–58 under Sir Hugh **Rose**. He then spent the next sixteen years based in India, though a third war saw him off to Abyssinia as DAG in **Napier**'s 1868 expedition. A brief period of home service followed until January 1878, when he was appointed to command the troops in South Africa.

The ninth and last Xhosa war was dragging itself to a close; with a tiny staff, doing much of the administrative work himself, Thesiger re-organised the British and colonial forces and began a series of sweeps of the bush country. These tactics were only partially successful. The fighting spirit of the Xhosa, luckily for him, was extinguished by the death in May of their great chief, Sandile. When the natives sued for peace Thesiger, an old-school soldier who liked old-school tactics, was left with a low opinion of black Africans and white colonials generally as warriors, coupled with an excessively high regard for his red-coated regulars.

When the British High Commissioner, Sir Bartle Frere, decided to goad King Cetshwayo and his Zulus into war in order to remove their perceived 'threat', Thesiger was in full support. He was well-liked, the perfect gentle-man, interested in the welfare of the ordinary soldier, a tall figure with a spade beard, hair carefully parted in the centre, soft-spoken and with cool, impeccable manners. Frederic was certain that the Zulus 'must be thor-oughly crushed to make them believe in our superiority ... I shall strive to be in a position to show them how hopelessly inferior they are to us in fighting power, altho' numerically stronger'. The disaster at Isandlwana, the victory of Rorke's Drift, the war's other battles and Chelmsford's final victory at Ulundi have been written about in hundreds of books. He was undoubtedly brave, conscientious and industrious, but these good quali-ties are out-weighed by his mistakes. He refused to delegate, relied on too small a staff, had no chief of staff and, until after Isandlwana, no intel-ligence department. Above all, his easy success in the Xhosa War clouded his judgement so that he 'wholly under-rated the enemy'. Chelmsford was clever enough to realise that terrain and distance would make an invasion of Zululand a war of logistics. His solution was to send in five (later reduced to three) columns to converge on the Zulu capital. Yet a division of forces has long been accepted as 'bad strategy'. He failed to grasp that so many columns acting alone required more, not less, staff liaison. They needed accurate maps and full cavalry support (he did little in these areas).

The historian John Laband has argued that from the start 'the command-ers of the advancing Zulu army deliberately manoeuvred Chelmsford into the fatal division of his forces'. At Isandlwana, where he had effectively taken over command of no. 3 column, he rode out on the morning of 22 January 1879 without leaving clear and specific orders for its defence. He was then 'inexcusably out of communication for much of the day' while a defeat occurred with appalling loss of life, weapons, ammunition and transport that shattered his invasion plans.

Back in Natal, a court of enquiry into Isandlwana was instituted. Chelmsford, it is generally accepted by historians, 'had no intention that it should probe too deeply into his responsibility for the disaster'. By late March he was ready to resume the offensive and again preferred to use separate columns. This time he had an early success on 2 April, when the Zulus attacked him at Gingindlovu. Buoyed by this victory (and **Wood**'s at Kambula), and increasingly supported by extra troops, equipment and commanders, Lord Chelmsford now advanced on the Zulu royal *kraal* near Ulundi 'slow and steady'. The death of the Prince Imperial of France, killed by Zulus on 1 June, was not his fault, many of the transport problems were beyond his powers to rectify, but when Sir Garnet **Wolseley**, sent from Britain to supersede him in the light of Isandlwana, ordered him not to try and force a final battle on the Zulus, Chelmsford did quite the reverse. Luck was on his side, for once, and the Zulus did not stage another fight. Sir Henry Bulwer, Governor of Natal, wrote that Chelmsford could now return to Britain 'with a certain flush of success', adding, 'He advanced prematurely. Everyone says he did it because of Sir G's coming out and I fancy they are right.' Wolseley, polite in public, wrote privately of 'poor, incapable Chelmsford'. Home in England, the Prime Minister, Lord Beaconsfield, so appalled by the mismanaged and costly small war, refused to see him. The sovereign was more compassionate; Chelmsford was made a full general in 1888, and various honorariums followed until he died playing billiards at his London club on 9 April 1905.

During those years after the war, Chelmsford was convinced he was right in all his actions and tried to make others the scapegoats for his failures. His reputation was, and remains, crippled. Shortly after his return from Zululand a full debate was held in Parliament on the war. In the House of Commons he was accused of 'military misconduct and incapacity', while in the House of Lords he was made to squirm in his seat when Field-Marshal Lord Strathnairn (who, as Hugh Rose, had commanded Chelmsford in the tough Central India campaign) said in front of fellow peers:

> I desire to call attention to mistakes which occurred in the conduct of the Zulu campaign pertaining to Isandlwana in particular ... In the first instance, I maintain that the invading columns were too far apart to allow of mutual support and communication ... Had the dangerous ground been properly reconnoitred it was quite possible the calamity would never have occurred ... the camp should have been entrenched ... the warning that the Zulus had shown themselves in force was ignored.

These and other criticisms, like so many veldt flies, continue to buzz around the reputation of this most vexed of Victorian commanders.

CLARKE, GENERAL C. – SCOURGE OF THE BASUTOS

CHARLES MANSFIELD CLARKE, known generally as Mansfield Clarke, was a competent officer who ousted Zulus and Pedi but met his match in the Basuto chief, Lerothodi.

He was born on 13 December 1839, educated at Eton and joined the 57th Foot in 1857. He was to be connected with this regiment (later the Middlesex Regiment) for much of his life. In 1862 he sailed with the 57th to New Zealand and was soon in action against the Maoris; on 6 April 1864 he was lucky to escape with his life when disciples of the cannibalistic Pai-Marire cult surprised a detachment while Clarke was out destroying Maori crops. His captain's head was cut off and subsequently smoked to shrink it! Clarke was DAQMG in the Taranaki operations 1863–66.

During the late 1870s Captain Clarke served in the rather delicate role of 'political officer' on the South African frontier trying to keep the peace between settlers and the tribes. In 1878, when the BaPedi rose up in the British-administered Transvaal, he supported Hugh **Rowlands** in the first British expedition against Chief Sekhukhune. Rowlands' biographer blames Clarke for mistakes made, but in fairness it must be said that he was, on the whole, a wise administrator and certainly impressed men like **Buller** and **Wolseley** – which Rowlands did not.

In 1879 he arrived in command of the 57th in time to take part in **Chelmsford**'s second invasion of Zululand. His seasoned old soldiers, under his able command, formed the stoutest defenders of the south, or right face, of the British square at the Battle of Gingindlovu. Every attack on them by the Zulu left horn was met with superbly controlled volley fire. Not long after this battle Clarke was one of 800 soldiers in the 1st Division crippled by fever. He recovered and commanded the advanced guard in search of Cetshwayo after the Battle of Ulundi. One of his staff officers in this hunt wrote of Clarke: 'Never was there a stricter or more exacting CO, and never was there a better soldier to serve under.' Clarke assisted Wolseley in the second Sekhukhune expedition and afterwards was offered the new post of Resident of Zululand, but wisely turned it down. Instead he was appointed commandant of all colonial forces in South Africa. Rebellions had begun in Basutoland and the Transkei. Historian Philip Gon notes that 'He was considered a capable soldier and was highly regarded by the officers who had served under him, but he still had to win the trust of the colonials.' Faced with 'defective' local forces, Clarke had to form a new frontier defence force – and quickly. Notices for volunteers were posted in all the South African colonies and the Orange Free State. Within three weeks he managed to assemble a column of 1,500 men, two-thirds of them mounted troops.

Clarke's Basutoland invasion, aimed at relieving the besieged town of Mafeteng, began badly; that same day, 19 October 1880, an advanced force of 200 men of the 1st Cape Mounted Yeomanry were ambushed at Qalabane and thirty-three of them killed. The siege of Mafeteng was lifted and Clarke was then successful in destroying Chief Lerothodi's main *kraal*. Disturbances with the Transkei tribes now kept Clarke in the saddle for the next six months, but he returned to Basutoland in March 1881 and on the 21st led 1,000 men in a major reconnaissance. Once again the Basutos lured their enemies into a trap amid a range of rocky hills and then hit them with concentrated rifle fire. Several men, including second-in-command Frederick **Carrington**, were wounded in the ensuing retreat. Clarke was now determined to crush the Basutos with an 8,000-strong army, but the Cape government, sick of a war that had raised grain prices and disturbed the diamond fields, brought this messy campaign to a close.

From 1893 to 1898 Mansfield Clarke served as C-in-C of the Madras Army, where a young subaltern named Winston Churchill thought him 'obstinate' when he was refused permission to play in a polo tournament. After holding the governorship of Malta, Clarke, now a baronet, retired in 1907. He lived on for a quarter century more as a Norfolk gentleman, dying at the ripe old age of 92 years on 22 April 1932.

CLERY, LIEUTENANT-GENERAL SIR C. – TACTICS NOT APPLIED

CORNELIUS FRANCIS CLERY has been described by the Zulu War historian Sonia Clarke as 'vain, able, critical of friend and foe, egotistical and amusing'. Ron Lock and Peter Quantrill, joint authors of other Zulu War books, are less charitable when they describe him as 'vindictive and a gossip'. A contemporary officer wrote in 1879 that Clery had a 'tendency to belittle the services of good men'. Twenty years later, in a much bigger South African war, the one-time professor of tactics was given a chance to prove his worth and failed badly.

An Irishman, born in 1838, Clery joined the 32nd Foot in 1858. Ten years later, while a captain, he entered the Staff College and passed out in 1870 but took up the post of instructor of tactics. In 1875, without campaign experience of any kind, he authored a handbook on 'minor tactics' that became a standard work. In 1878 he sailed for South Africa and briefly took part in an expedition to the diamond fields and an unsuccessful campaign against the BaPedi.

When the Zulu War broke out Clery was appointed chief staff officer to Colonel **Glyn**, commanding the centre column. Lord **Chelmsford**'s decision to ride with this column sidelined Glyn and his staff to mundane duties. Tension erupted between Clery and John North **Crealock**, Chelmsford's acerbic assistant military secretary, over their respective loyalties and duties. Clery especially disliked Crealock's attempts to transfer blame for the Isandlwana disaster away from Chelmsford and onto Glyn and his staff. Yet it was Clery who marked out the camp at Isandlwana when the army arrived there on 20 January 1879 and he later claimed to have been the officer who told Lt-Colonel Pulleine to defend the camp after Chelmsford had ridden away without leaving clear instructions. Clery later joined Evelyn Wood as a staff officer and was also present at the Battle of Ulundi. In a series of highly vindictive secret letters he informed Sir Archibald **Alison**, an old friend who headed the intelligence department at the War Office, of all that he heard and saw.

In 1882 Clery served in the Egyptian War, but was sidelined again to duties at Alexandria. Fighting and a real chance for glory came two years later when he served under General **Graham** as a brigade major in the battles at El Teb and Tamai. The troops were among the first to wear khaki on active service, but Clery conspicuously wore his red uniform. 'When at any critical period I saw his red coat,' Graham later wrote, 'I knew that matters would be going well, or, if wrong, would soon be rectified.'

Praised for his work in the Sudan, Clery finally returned home in 1887 and was made Commandant of the Staff College. When the South African War broke out he was promoted to lieutenant-general and given command of the 2nd Division. Now in his sixties, it seems as if the vigorous Clery of earlier years had lost his pep; he was supposed to get ready the Natal Field Force before **Buller**'s arrival but did surprisingly little, allowing his strategy at Colenso on 15 December 1899 'to be dictated by Buller with disastrous results', and subsequently went into 'a funk' (according to his chief). He was also becoming very eccentric, dyeing his side whiskers blue and insisting that a French chef prepare his meals. Clery remained as courageous as ever and was wounded at Vaalkrantz in February 1900. This mishap helped **Roberts** to include him in the list of generals sent home that year. As compensation he was made a KCMG, but retired from the army in 1901. He died, aged 88 years, in 1926.

CLIFFORD, MAJOR-GENERAL SIR H. – ALWAYS CONSCIENTIOUS

A BIG, TOUGH, brave man, Henry Clifford, third son of the 7th Baron Clifford of Chudleigh, won a VC in the Crimea, but later proved an invaluable administrator in the Zulu War.

Aged 20 years, he obtained his first commission in the Rifle Brigade on 7 August 1846. Noted for his fine physique, Clifford once agreed on one occasion to accompany a fellow officer who had accepted a bet to walk from Dover to Canterbury, a distance of 16 miles, in under two hours. The bet was won. The brother officer went to bed, exhausted. Clifford started back immediately and, after completing the 32-mile round trip, went and danced at a ball that same night!

In 1847 the Rifle Brigade sailed for South Africa and took part in the series of wet bivouacs and gruelling marches that concluded the Seventh Frontier War. Under Sir Harry **Smith**'s command, Clifford and his regiment saw action against rebellious Boers at the Battle of Boemplaats, followed by over 1,100 miles of marches required to bring the revolt to an end. After a brief spell of home leave he returned to the Cape frontier for the Eighth Xhosa War, taking part in General **Cathcart**'s operations to clear the Waterkloof Mountains of the enemy.

The Rifle Brigade arrived back in Portsmouth in January 1854. Six months later Lieutenant Clifford sailed for the Crimea. Here he was appointed an aide to peppery Sir George **Brown** and advanced with the rest of his staff under fire to the heights of the Alma. He was also sent riding around the battlefield, urging on various regiments. On 5 November in the dull mist at Inkerman Clifford recaptured three guns whilst leading some men of the 77th Foot. His Victoria Cross warrant noted that he displayed 'conspicuous gallantry, leading a charge, killing one of the enemy with his sword, disabling another, and saving a soldier's life'. He remained in the Crimea after Brown's departure, staying on as DAQMG of the Light Division. Subsequently, when the first VC investiture took place in Hyde Park in June 1857 Clifford's medal was pinned on by the Queen.

Sent to China in 1860, he was present at the operations resulting in the capture of Canton. More promotions followed and in 1875 he was appointed an aide to the C-in-C, HRH the Duke of Cambridge. Impressed by Clifford's organisational skills, his knowledge of South Africa and physical toughness, Prince George personally selected him to be inspector-general of forces in Natal and lines of communication after the disaster at

Isandlwana. He was, the Duke told Lord **Chelmsford**, 'a most agreeable and satisfactory man to deal with'.

At first all went well between Clifford, Chelmsford and the latter's assistant military secretary, J.N. **Crealock**, who noted that 'nothing is too small for him to look into'. Friction developed because Clifford's remit stopped at the Natal border, which he thought nonsensical, and he criticised Chelmsford for living in 'a very narrow world of his own … shut off by Crealock from many who would give him sound advice'. By June Chelmsford was complaining to Clifford that 'You have got me into terrible hot water at home.' Remarks made by Clifford in letters to Cambridge and **Wolseley** were instrumental in creating a lack of confidence in Chelmsford's abilities. These matters came to a head in a memo sent by the field commander on 2 July in which, for once, he took off his gentleman's gloves and wrote:

> General Clifford seems to imagine that when sitting at his desk in PMburg he is capable of looking after my lines of communication in the enemy's country. I am satisfied he can do nothing of the sort … [he is] strangely ignorant of the situation of the forces under my command and very foolish … to think South African warfare can be carried on according to the strict rules laid down for an European campaign.

The Duke of Cambridge criticised Clifford, but other contemporaries sided with him. Sir Henry Bulwer, Governor of Natal, thought he worked as strictly as a Jesuit, adding, 'It is thought he is too much a man of detail to be a good general in the field, but in the office he is the most thorough and the most devoted of men of official business, and he has not spared himself.' A not easily impressed Garnet Wolseley retained Clifford's services when all other Zulu War generals were sent home. In his 1879 journal Wolseley called Clifford 'most zealous and to a certain point a first-rate Qr-Mastr. Genl., but he has no brains'. For a time he became Cetshwayo's gaoler at Cape Town, then acted briefly as administrator of the Transvaal.

He returned to England in 1882 and died worn out by health issues exacerbated by the South African climate. Sir William **Butler**, who had been Clifford's assistant adjutant-general in Natal, wrote later that 'of all the generals I have been brought into contact with, none possessed a personality more lovable, none had a higher courage, a longer sense of public duty, or a greater aptitude for untiring toil'.

CLYDE, FIELD-MARSHAL LORD C. – GREATEST OF MID-VICTORIAN WARRIORS

IT IS, PERHAPS, a sad reflection of our own times that so few people recall the name of Clyde, better known as Sir Colin Campbell. This gnome of a man, with his curly hair and grizzled face, was the veteran of scores of fights, the cautious commander whose assured generalship saved British India during the Mutiny.

He was born Colin Macliver on 20 October 1792 in Glasgow, son of a cabinet-maker. His mother came from richer Campbell stock and Colin adopted the name when an uncle, Colonel Campbell, recommended him for a commission. He served in the Peninsular War with the 9th Foot, notably at San Sebastian where he led a desperate attack known as 'the forlorn hope', was in the awful Walcheren expedition of 1808 and fought the Americans at New Orleans in 1812.

Almost three decades of stagnation followed before Campbell, now serving with the 98th Highlanders, saw action in the First China War. At Chillianwallah in the Second Anglo-Sikh War as a divisional commander, he was censured for leading his brigade from the front, but it was typical of Campbell's courage, and he defended his actions in print. Knighted, he was next sent to the North-West Frontier and led expeditions against the Afridis in 1850, the Mohmands in 1851–52 and the Ranizais and Utman Khel in 1852.

That same year he returned to England and was placed on half-pay. A decade earlier he had declared, 'I am old and only fit for retirement.' When war broke out in the Crimea, however, he was sent to command the Highland Brigade with the rank of major-general. Here his behaviour soon got him noticed by the press and public: he was in the thick of action in the infantry battle that was the Alma and led his immortal 'thin red line' of 93rd Highlanders at Balaklava. Always of a peppery nature, Sir Colin felt, by November 1855, that his talents had been passed over in favour of less competent generals and he resigned his command. Promoted to lieutenant-general in June 1856, he returned briefly to the Crimea and a promised corps, but the war had come to an end.

In 1857, with India in peril, Queen Victoria urged that Sir Colin, one of her favourite generals, should be sent to quell the rebellion. The Governor-General, Lord Canning, had recommended Sir Patrick **Grant**, C-in-C of the Madras Army (and a protégé of Lord **Gough**) to command, but 'Old *Kharbadar*' ('Old Careful'), as 64-year-old Campbell was called by Indian soldiers, seemed 'a safe pair of hands'.

Sir Colin had his critics; one Highland officer thought he was obsessed with money and getting a peerage, concluding: 'A brave man, undoubtedly, but too cautious for India, and too selfish for any place.' 'Sir Crawling Camel' was the sobriquet Campbell soon won in some quarters. His namesake, the administrator Sir George Campbell, wrote that while he was 'pleasant, good-natured', he also 'delayed everything for months, because he would do nothing till he chose'; at Cawnpore 'he dawdled', and the Mutiny 'might have ended early in 1858 if it had not been for Sir Colin Campbell'.   In his defence, it must be said that arriving at Calcutta in August, 1857, the new C-in-C faced a herculean task: revolt was now spread across much of northern and central India. The work of restoring order and defeating the rebels he did, as the Victorian historian Thomas Holmes has written, 'on the whole thoroughly and well'. Campbell's generalship was never spectacular or dashing, but it was competent and achieved with as little loss of life among his troops as possible. Rankers loved the way the old man settled down with them under fire, seemed oblivious to danger and was willing to share their privations. He was, said one Tommy, 'a regular go-ahead fire-eating old cock!'

Campbell's first attempt to relieve Lucknow was a failure; he returned to Cawnpore and there soundly beat the mutineers, reinforced as they were with over 8,000 well-trained troops from the army of Maharajah Scindia of Gwalior. In March 1858 he oversaw the final relief of Lucknow and went on to take charge of operations in Rohilkand, Bundelkand and outlying districts of Oudh. This arduous campaigning took up the rest of the year and went into the next, by which time Campbell's health was suffering. Now raised to the peerage as Lord Clyde, he resigned his command on 4 June 1860.

He had not long to live, dying on 14 August 1863, just a few months after attending the funeral of Sir James **Outram**, who had defended Lucknow. Both lie buried in Westminster Abbey. Eulogies galore were written. Perhaps the best came during his lifetime when an officer who wrote, on hearing the old campaigner was to become C-in-C in India, that 'His presence is worth 10,000 troops.'

COKE, MAJOR-GENERAL SIR J. – GALLANT 'PIFFER'

IN 1849 JOHN Coke raised the 1st Punjab Native Infantry, forerunner of other elite frontier regiments that later became famous as the Punjab Irregular Force – the 'Piffers'.

He was born in 1806, the seventh son of a country parson, and was commissioned an ensign in the 10th BNI in 1827. He served with this regiment for the next two decades and passed several exams in oriental languages. In 1843 the 10th suffered greatly in Sind, helping Sir Charles **Napier** establish control of the place. Two-thirds of the corps died from disease. Coke missed serving in the First Sikh War, being home on leave, but when another war broke out in 1848, he volunteered for active service and managed to get a transfer to the 2nd Irregular Cavalry. His horse was shot from under him at Chillianwallah while leading a battery to the front; later he took part in the pursuit of the Sikhs after Gujerat.

Ten months after raising the 1st PNI, a delighted Napier reported that 'I have seen nothing superior to it in drill – it is admirable ... I am more pleased with this young commander than I can express.' In addition to his regimental duties, Coke was appointed Deputy Commandant of Kohat district in 1850. He led his men in Napier's five-day assault of the Kohat Pass and fought Turi tribesmen in a Miranzai expedition. Later he took part in Campbell's 1852–53 Mohmand expedition and got his first wound, also in the Kohat Pass, in 1853.

A friend, James Fairweather of the 4th PNI, wrote that 'Major Coke was a fine specimen of a frontier officer – tall and dark with a handsome beard sprinkled with grey'. His regiment of Pathans were a wild, unruly lot that he kept in awe with a big stick that he always carried and with which he administered rapid and effective punishment. He was a simple man in his habits and was quite happy to eat from a chair in front of them his dinner. Coke's was a fine regiment and the Afridi orderlies in their rifle green uniforms and high set puggries with a gold fringe hanging down the side of their head looked picturesque figures. One of Coke's maxims on dealing with tribal people was 'first knock him down, then pick him up', which suggests he was a tough fellow.

During the 1857 Bozdar expedition he was wounded in the shoulder and a few months later while leading a sortie at the Siege of Delhi, was seriously injured in the thigh. Less than six months later Coke was back in the saddle again rooting out mutineers in the jungles of Rohilkhand.

John Coke was made a major-general on his retirement in the 1870s. He returned to Herefordshire and became a JP and High Sherriff of his county. This fine old frontiersman died in his nineties during the Queen's Diamond Jubilee celebrations of 1897.

COKE, MAJOR-GENERAL J.T. – RUIN AT SPION KOP

IT WAS JOHN Talbot Coke's bad luck to be one of the officers sent to command on top of the mountain of Spion Kop during one of the bloodiest battles of the South African War. Lord **Roberts** subsequently decided, as Ian **Hamilton** wrote, that Coke had 'hopelessly gone under'. Coke's war diary reveals a general who was not such a duffer.

He was born in 1841, the son of a wealthy Derbyshire landowning family, and entered the army in 1860. A few months after joining, he transferred to the 25th King's Own Scottish Borderers, a corps with whom he would have a long association. In 1866, as a captain, Coke served in the Fenian Raid on Canada, led by Irish Republicans. It was twenty-two years before he next saw active service but in that year, 1888, he led the 2nd Battalion KOSB in operations against dervishes near Suakin and on 22 December at Gemaizeh the regiment played a leading part and Coke was mentioned in despatches.

Various peacetime promotions followed and Coke was commanding in Mauritius, with the rank of major-general, when he was given command of the 10th Brigade formed to fight the Boers in South Africa. He arrived at Spion Kop just before the battle with a bad leg injury. Worse still, the entire battle plan had been given by Redvers **Buller** to Sir Charles **Warren**, one of the most unpredictable of generals. On 18 January 1900 Coke wrote in his war diary: 'Sorry to see Sir C. Warren's force *halted* not half way up the mountains. I really cannot understand the cause of all this delay.' Three days later Coke was told at 5 p.m. that he was to lead the attack that night on the summit of Spion Kop and dislodge the enemy. He pointed out, quite reasonably, that he had been given no time to reconnoitre the proposed route and no guide was available. In his diary he noted: 'I do not like the operation of taking it, and do not see where it will lead.'

Overnight, due to his leg injury, he was replaced by General **Woodgate** as assault commander with his division in support. These British delays simply allowed the Boers to improve their positions on the 1,470ft high mountain, moving precious guns into better positions. Woodgate was mortally wounded during the advance and the situation for the British troops on Spion Kop soon descended into chaos and tragedy. At 9.50 a.m. Coke proceeded to take command. 'The climb was a severe trial of strength,' he wrote, as his reinforcements squeezed up the narrow trail past severely wounded men being carried down in the opposite direction. Coke concluded that too many men were being pushed into the firing line.

Buller now added to the shambles by appointing Lt-Colonel Alex Thorneycroft, already on the summit, to overall command. No one, not least General Warren, thought to tell John Talbot Coke. A critic later wrote that Coke took a nap under a mimosa bush on the way up the mountain. It seems unlikely, but at 60 years old and with a bad leg, he was certainly winded by the climb. Shrapnel fire on his left front was fierce and Coke sent orders to Thorneycroft without being aware that he had been superseded. Both generals begged for better British artillery support. Buller and Warren provided none. At 5.50 p.m. Coke wrote to Warren: 'The shell fire is, and has been, very severe. If I hold on to the position all night is there any guarantee that our Artillery can silence the enemy's guns, otherwise today's experience will be repeated, and the men will not stand another complete day's shelling … The situation is extremely critical.' Later that night he was ordered to report in person to Warren. Trying to respond to this lunatic order Coke found the signaller's lamps had all run out of oil! So he was forced to make a terrifying descent in the dark that took him until 2.30 a.m. A furious Coke declared that General Warren 'should not have taken me away from my command at such a critical moment'. It was too late anyway: Thorneycroft had already given the order for troops to retire from the death-trap.

Coke continued to serve under Warren and was at the Relief of Ladysmith. In December 1900 he was one of the generals sent home by Lord **Roberts**. He died in 1912. His feelings were summed up in his diary: 'Personally I was never in favour of the occupation of Spion Kop, and when Sir C. Warren first spoke to me about it, I replied "We must be careful not to have another Majuba."'

COLLETT, LIEUTENANT-GENERAL SIR H. – SOLDIER AND BOTANIST

VICTORIAN OFFICERS FREQUENTLY displayed remarkable skills in other areas besides soldiering. One such was Henry Collett, who managed to pack an awful lot of fighting into his life and become a celebrated botanist at the same time.

He was born the son of a clergyman at Thetford, Norfolk, in 1836 and entered the Bengal Army in 1855. Within three years he was fighting on the North-West Frontier with his regiment, the 21st Native Infantry, against the Sittana fanatics, returning to Oudh for the final operations against the mutineers. In 1862 he took part in the Khasia and Jaintia expedition on the North-East Frontier and was severely wounded in the foot when attacking a stockade on 2 February. The injury left him with a limp for the rest of his life.

On the Abyssinian expedition in 1868 he met and became friends with Frederick **Roberts**. A decade later Roberts requested Collett as his AQMG in Afghanistan. It was Collett who suggested the enemy's left flank might be turned at Peiwar Kotal on 2 December 1878 by a route over a pass called the Springawi Kotal. Roberts sent him to spy it out, which he did 'admirably', and his suggested approach was used. He accompanied 'Bobs' on the march from Kabul to Kandahar and was rewarded with a CB. C.M. **Macgregor**, Roberts' chief of staff, described Collett as 'One of the best men in the service.'

It was during his service in the Kurram Valley in Afghanistan that Collett began studying plants. In 1886–89 he commanded a brigade in Burma and collected 725 species. He also took part in several punitive operations against Burmese and Karen rebel bands, including a fight at Lwekaw that cost five men killed and eleven wounded. Collett commanded the eastern frontier district during the Chin-Lushai expedition of 1889–90 and in 1891 was given command of the Manipur Field Force sent to punish those who had killed a British Commissioner and Resident. Three columns were despatched, Collett personally leading the one sent from Kohima; Imphal, the Manipuri capital, was taken on 27 April.

Collett was knighted but had decided to retire from the army due to increasing deafness. His botanical magnum opus, *Flora Simtensis*, which lists 1,326 species of the Simla region, was published after his death in 1901. During his lifetime he sent several cuttings of tea roses, azaleas and rhododendrons to Kew Gardens. He was a little man, like his friend 'Bobs', with qualities of command, despite his small stature. A friend remarked after his death that Sir Henry 'constantly reminded me of the late General Gordon'.

COLVILLE, MAJOR-GENERAL SIR H. – SAD ENDING

HENRY COLVILLE'S ENTRY into Kampala as the new British Commissioner for the Uganda Protectorate in 1893 was rather memorable. His horse faltered minutes before he entered the city and deposited Colville in a black pool of reeking mud. Stained and smelly, but 'returning the salute with what dignity I could', the unfortunate officer tried to keep his composure before plunging his head into a basin of cold water.

Later in his career, Colville would be made the scapegoat for mistakes in the South African War, charges that today seem hardly fair. Blunt attempts to clear his name only added to Sir Henry's disgrace. Yet his is a fighting career worthy of re-evaluation.

He was born in 1852, scion of a wealthy family, and entered the elite Grenadier Guards in 1870. When war broke out in the Sudan in 1884 he joined the intelligence department and fought at El Teb and Tamai. He stayed on in Egypt with the British army of occupation and was part of the field force that defeated the Mahdists at Giniss on 30 December 1885. Later he authored the official history of the **Gordon** Relief Expedition.

By 1890 Colville had built himself a reputation as a solid fighting soldier, a respected intelligence officer – and something of an eccentric. His first book (about a tour through Turkey) was cheerily titled *A Ride in Petticoats and Slippers*. He also wrote a musical comedy in 1896. To these interests must be added ballooning, yachting, acrobatics, painting, acting and carpentry. His somewhat odd habits included 'walking on impossibly narrow ledges on high buildings' and 'snap-shotting charging bulls from the front and at very close quarters in Spanish arenas'. As commissioner in Uganda, Colville's aim was to capture the defiant King Kabalega, *mukama* of Unyoro (today Bunyoro). He was unsuccessful, but the ensuing campaign saw quite a lot of fighting and much destruction of crops and cattle. Sir Henry's 15,000 Ganda and Sudanese troops were later accused of war crimes of which he personally was not responsible. It was a bitter war that involved storming the mountain fortress of Musaijamukuru. Realising he could not capture Kabalega in an open fight, Colville next tried to contain his enemy in northern Unyoro by building a chain of forts across the country. Land in southern Unyoro was re-assigned – without reference to the Foreign Office – to friendly chiefs. Despite these policies (criticised even today), Colville's plan was instrumental in causing support for Kabalega to wane (he was eventually captured in 1899). Colville left Africa a victim of fever and returned home in 1894. Four years later he was rewarded by promotion to major-general.

In 1899 he was sent to South Africa to command the Guards Brigade. He was not a popular officer. He had a bitingly sarcastic sense of humour, 'showed himself but rarely, and never inspected his troops'; he liked his officers and men to be well-fed, but otherwise cared little for their comfort or well-being. Officers soon found that Sir Henry's nerves, which had never recovered from Ugandan campaigning, meant 'he could not stand stupid people'. His best friend wrote later that 'he seemed to look upon war as a series of problems which had to be coldly solved by the intellect alone, and upon his troops, as so many pawns to do it with'. Hitherto a jolly man, in South Africa he now seemed 'irritable and nervous'.

Colville got off to a good start and the early deployment of his troops was not at all bad; mistakes were made at Belmont (not his fault) and he controlled his men well at Magersfontein so that the Coldstreams and Grenadiers had only minor losses. In February 1900 Lord **Roberts** moved Colville to command the 9th Division. This force included a division of the Guards and the Highland Brigade. Roberts noted: 'I shall take an early opportunity of finding some more suitable appointment for him, as I do not think he is quite the man to command the two finest brigades in the British army.' Roberts' criticisms grew; he noted Colville did not get along with Hector **Macdonald**, commanding the Highlanders; was slow in chasing the Boers during the advance on Paardeberg; and at Sannah's Post failed to properly assist General Broadwood's cavalry, with a resulting loss of men and guns. In vain did Colville later say of this debacle that he had intended to cut the Boers off at Waterval; officers under him wondered, as one wrote later, why 'he refused to march straight to the scene of the disaster, which was bang in front of us, instead of going on a wild goose-chase'.

Then came the Lindley Affair where 'an ass' called Colonel Sprague of the elite (Irish) 13th Battalion, Imperial Yeomanry, was surrounded. Colville and his staff were confused by Sprague's plea for help, orders sent to Lindley never got through the Boer lines and a bloody disaster ensued – 486 officers and men captured, thirty-eight soldiers killed and 104 wounded. The Irishmen had fought bravely. The jubilant Boers took all the ammunition they needed and burned over half a million pounds worth of supplies. Lord Roberts was furious; he castigated Colville in a report and the Secretary of State demanded his resignation after a court of enquiry (without Sir Henry present) agreed with the C-in-C. A furious Colville refused to resign, and was dismissed. On his way home he foolishly penned an article that suggested Roberts' displeasure was based on the number of the C-in-C's wealthy Irish friends who had been in the 13th IY. Publication cooked Colville's goose and despite an attempt to enlist King Edward VII's help and a debate in Parliament, his career was finished.

He lived another seven years, 'nursing a very sore heart'. Then he found a new hobby – the motor cycle. Whizzing along one day on the wrong side of the road, he was killed in a head-on crash with a motor car. Its driver happened to be Henry Rawlinson (later a Field-Marshal), who happened to have been one of Lord Roberts' staff officers in South Africa.

COTTON, MAJOR-GENERAL SIR S. – NO NONSENSE

SYDNEY COTTON WAS as tough as old boots. In the early Victorian army, where senior officers often took their duties lightly, he was quite the reverse. John Lawrence, Chief Commissioner of the Punjab and an admirer, called him 'a master of all technical details in every arm of the service'.

One of six remarkable brothers who served the empire – two others became generals, while a third, Frank, became an admiral – Sydney was born on 2 December 1792. He arrived in India an 18-year-old cornet with the 22nd Light Dragoons in 1810. His first fighting came seven years later in the Pindari War. In 1822 he purchased a captaincy in the 3rd Foot and served as an aide to his kinsman, General Lord Combermere. The next twenty years saw him soldiering in India, Burma and two spells in Australia where, as commandant of the Moreton Bay penal settlement, Cotton was not afraid to use the lash to keep discipline, but the convicts considered him to be a fair governor.

In 1842 he returned to India and served under **Napier** in Sind. Nine years later he was sent to Peshawar and in 1854 led an expedition against the Mohmand tribesmen on the frontier. The stiff fighting involved taught Cotton that the tactics needed on the frontier were very different from those he had used on the plains. 'Protracted warfare in the mountains has proved to be fatal to success', he wrote. 'There is a sporting phrase which is very applicable to this description of mountain warfare, "In and out clever."'

When the Mutiny broke out Cotton stood firm at Peshawar after the 55th NI mutinied at Nowshera, just 22 miles away, and the 10th Irregular Cavalry refused to act against them. He called a dawn conference and insisted all native cavalry and infantry regiments must be disarmed. Several colonels, proud of their regiments, declared their men would stay loyal, but Cotton was adamant: 'No more discussion, gentlemen! These are my orders and I must have them obeyed.' After this disarmament, Cotton pursued the 55th NI, demanding that 120 of the *sepoys* be blown from the guns. This punishment was considered too harsh by John Lawrence and it was limited to forty of the mutineers. Cotton remained convinced, as he wrote later, 'that the Mutiny was raging to such an extent that no-one ought to have escaped punishment … Sir John's views were humane, but it was not mercy in the end.'

Less than a year later Cotton, now a major-general, led another expedition on the frontier, this time against the Sittana fanatics of the Black Mountain. Using his 'in and out clever' policy of fast attack, delivered without warning and as speedily as possible, his columns advanced on the enemy camp from three sides. Luckily for him (though he did not know it), the *mujahideen* were leaderless as their *amir* had died of fever just days earlier. The fighting was vicious, with no quarter given or asked. Cotton wanted to finish off every last one of the fanatics on the second day, but reluctantly accepted the advice of his political officer, Herbert Edwardes, who counselled retreat. Sir Sydney never quite forgave Edwardes – and the costly Umbeyla expedition required just five years later to once more try and uproot this bed of warlike fanatics was to prove him right.

It was Cotton's last campaign. The grizzled old warrior of 66 years, with his wavy white hair and long Regency sideburns, received further honours, including governorship of Chelsea Hospital. He was given a GCB in 1873 and died the following year.

CREALOCK, LIEUTENANT-GENERAL H. & MAJOR-GENERAL J. – THE WASPS

THE VICTORIAN ARMY contained all sorts of men. Two of the least pleasant generals encountered in these pages are the brothers Henry and John Crealock. Both served in the Zulu War and were widely disliked. Henry Bulwer, governor of Natal, called John North Crealock, assistant military secretary to Lord **Chelmsford**, 'a sort of military wasp and … rather snobbish sometimes'. Elder brother Henry, given command of one of the columns, may have had a lesser sting but seems to have been just as obnoxious.

Henry was born in 1831, John five years later. Aged 17, Henry Hope Crealock joined the 90th Regiment as an ensign; six years later he took part in the Siege of Sebastopol as a captain and was mentioned in despatches for his courage during one sortie. By the end of the war he was DAQMG at headquarters, a post he also held in China in 1857, where he saw fighting at Canton. Recalled to India with his regiment, he took part in various actions against the rebels in Rohilkand. In 1860 he was back in China and won the plum appointment of military secretary to Lord Elgin, British plenipotentiary, witnessing the entry into Peking.

The 1870s saw Henry in military and diplomatic posts in Gibraltar, Russia and Ireland before his departure to South Africa as one of four major-generals sent to assist Chelmsford after Isandlwana. The advance of his 1st Division was so slow that the column became known as 'Crealock's Crawlers'. Apart from minor skirmishes, they saw no fighting. One staff officer remarked that Crealock had 'done nothing, nor attempted anything', acting like 'a feeble young lady'. One officer wrote to Evelyn Wood that Crealock 'is not strong and was never much on a horse', his only abilities being writing 'long letters and keeping an office in apple pie order'. Garnet **Wolseley** had served with Henry Crealock in the 90th Foot. When they met in Zululand he apparently said stiffly to his old comrade: 'How do you do, Sir. You might as well have been marching between Wimbledon and Aldershot as what you have been doing here!' In his journal Wolseley wrote:

> We reached Crealock's column before dark … Just the same vain swaggering snob he has always been. I believe his manner to his Staff & all about him is most disagreeable & his manner to the men, as it always was in the 90th, is offensive. I hate hearing him speak to soldiers as he addresses them as if they were dogs and not men – most of them are more men than he is a man.

Brother John was described by Wolseley, even more harshly, as 'Chelmsford's evil genius'. He had entered the army in 1854 with the 95th Regiment and served at the siege and capture of Kotah in the Indian Mutiny where he was wounded in action. It was at Aldershot in the 1860s as DAAG that he met Frederic Thesiger, later Lord Chelmsford. When Thesiger was sent to command at the Cape he took John Crealock along as his assistant military secretary (in fact he had no other). Crealock loyally served his chief through-out the remainder of the Ninth Xhosa War in 1878 and the Zulu War in 1879. He was slightly wounded in action at the Battle of Gingindlovu.

Problems arose in Zululand because John Crealock, as historians Greaves and Knight have written, was 'arrogant and facetious, protective of his position and jealous of Chelmsford's attention'. One staff officer called him 'swaggering, false, self-sufficient, superficial and flippant'. Wolseley, loathing both Crealocks, said John 'was not a gentleman'. It is alleged by some historians that, after the war, John North Crealock was instrumental in trying to lay the blame for the Isandlwana disaster at the door of the dead Lt-Colonel Anthony Durnford, while safeguarding his own role and that of Chelmsford.

Neither Crealock brother saw active service after 1879; Henry died in 1891 and John in 1895. Both were accomplished watercolour artists; John's Zulu War paintings have been published, Henry's remain in his regimental museum.

DALY, MAJOR-GENERAL SIR H. – DASHING INDIAN ARMY CAVALRYMAN

PREMATURELY BALD, WITH a high, domed head and a dark beard, Henry Daly did not look the typical hero, but he was one of the bravest of cavalry-men. It was his distinction during the mid-Victorian period to command four of the finest Indian cavalry regiments. He survived many battles and wounds, served his country in civilian as well as military capacities and died at the age of 74.

He was born in 1823 in India, according to his biographer, but other sources state 1821 and the DNB says he was born on the Isle of Wight! He was brought up near Ryde by an uncle, Daly's father serving with the Bombay Army, and he arrived in India as an ensign in the 1st Bombay Fusiliers, known as 'the Old Toughs', in 1840. Active service began with the Second Sikh War, where he fought in the siege and capture of Multan and the final battle at Gujerat in 1849. That same year he was told to raise the 1st Regiment of Punjab Cavalry (Daly's Horse). This corps was charged with policing the North-West Frontier districts.

Daly led his men in various forays and campaigns, including the 1851–52 Miranzai expedition under Coke's command. In March 1857, in Harry **Lumsden**'s absence, he was asked to take command of the Corps of Guides, the most elite of the Indian frontier regiments. A few months later the Mutiny broke out and Daly found himself commanding the Guides in one of their most dramatic moments – their celebrated march of 580 miles in twenty-two days wearing full kit, at the hottest time of the year, from Hoti Mardan down to Delhi. When they arrived at the Delhi ridge on 9 June an observer wrote: 'They came in as firm and light as if they had marched but a mile.' A staff officer galloped up to Daly and enquired, 'How soon can you be ready to go into action?' 'In half an hour' was his cheery reply. In the fight that day almost every officer was injured – Quintin Battye mortally – and Daly's horse was shot from under him, while he himself was hit by a spent bullet.

Octavius Anson of the 9th Lancers met Daly that week and recorded in his diary that he was 'a fine, sharp, spirited, good-looking fellow … The Guides require the best of officers, for they are always fighting away in front'. It was said that Henry, a keen huntsman, always rode into battle wearing his velvet hunting cap! Ten days later Daly was severely wounded when a bullet struck him in the left arm (he lost the use of it for the rest of his life). In dark-ness and with just a few of the Guides Cavalry, he had led a gallant charge to save some guns. One participant wrote: 'That charge saved the guns falling into the hands of the enemy. We were in a very nasty position and the enemy were very close to the guns and doing us great damage with their sharpshooters. Daly's charge was a desperate one, right up to the enemy's guns.' Daly, it was generally agreed, should have got a Victoria Cross, but at that time the decoration was not available to officers of the Indian Army (a later application was deemed too late).

Despite his wound, Daly stayed on at Delhi; it was to his tent that the mortally wounded John Nicholson was taken after the final assault. After the death of its founder, Daly was asked to take over Hodson's Horse; he sorted out the regimental accounts and advised that this large corps be split into three regiments. From 1861–71 he commanded the Central India Horse, a promotion that entailed certain political duties, including acting as political agent at Gwalior. So successful was he that Daly was promoted to political agent for Central India. During this time it was said that he hated 'pomp and show', commenting that 'a Political officer who couldn't jump on to a horse and ride 50 miles when duty called him wasn't worth keeping'.

He retired in 1881 and returned to the Isle of Wight and his passion for hunting, married a second time and fathered a son in his sixty-seventh year. While out with the hounds Daly suffered a nasty fall that hastened his end. He died on 21 July 1895 and was buried at Ryde.

DELAFOSSE, MAJOR-GENERAL SIR H. – FORGOTTEN HERO

HE IS NOT remembered with a VC, nor did he look a typical hero, yet few men ever lived who were braver than Henry George Delafosse. He was one of only two officers who, after the dreadful siege at Cawnpore in 1857, escaped a riverside massacre and, half-naked and half-mad, reached the safety of Allahabad. Six years later, in the most savage of all the North-West Frontier campaigns, he played another heroic part fighting at the Crag Picquet in Umbeyla. During his career Delafosse survived a second siege and later a shipwreck, so it might be said that bad luck made him a hero by circumstance!

He was born in 1835, the son of an Indian Army major, was educated partly at the East India Company's school at Addiscombe and entered the Bengal Army in 1854. Three years later he found himself serving with the 53rd BNI at Cawnpore. When his regiment mutinied he entered the weak brick entrenchments with the other soldiers, women and children and took part heroically in the fateful three-week siege. Despite being described as pale and thin, Delafosse performed several acts of gallantry, such as volunteering for sorties or extinguishing the flames of a burning ammunition wagon. Finally the garrison was offered safe passage down the Ganges if it laid down its arms and the commanding officer, old General Wheeler, decided to accept the terms. On 27 June the few remaining British soldiers, escorting several women and children, made for the boats that had been offered to them at the riverside temple called the Satichaura Ghat. Delafosse was one of the first to get to the boats and placed in the lead one with Wheeler. Minutes later, hidden riflemen opened fire as women and children clambered into the boats. Wheeler and almost all the men were killed, and about 100 women and children were taken prisoner (and later cruelly massacred).

Delafosse and colleagues got their boat away from the flames and killing; the party succumbed to fatigue and rebels along the river bank, the craft got stuck on sandbars and at one point they had to swim in the crocodile-infested river for some hours. Eventually Delafosse, another lieutenant, Mowbray Thomson, and two private soldiers reached safety. By this time poor Henry was half-naked, badly sun-burned and temporarily deranged.

A few weeks later he was fit enough to take part in Havelock's attempted relief of Lucknow. This was unsuccessful and Henry Delafosse found himself under siege for a second time. His old comrade Thomson was horrified to see him when Lucknow was finally taken, 'reduced to a most emaciated condition from the continued effects of fever and dysentery'. He received the thanks of the Governor-General-in-Council and decided to return to England on leave with Thomson, but the pair were shipwrecked near Ceylon. Once again they acted heroically and helped the women and children safely to shore through high surf.

Back in India, Delafosse took part in the first Sikkim expedition and on 5 February 1861 his party of soldiers came under fire. It was a minor show and a small taste of what was to follow two years later on India's other frontier at Umbeyla. In this harsh fighting, especially in the morning attack of 20 November 1863 on the Crag Picket led by thousands of *ghazis*, Major Delafosse, commanding a wing of the 101st Royal Bengal Fusiliers, proved once again just how tough he was. Sword in hand, he battled with countless *mujahideen* (I am proud to have in my possession a small, hastily scrawled note by Delafosse asking for reinforcements in that bloody attack).

It was his last campaign and, though he rose in the service, he sadly never wrote any memoirs before he died in India in 1905. A plaque in his memory was installed in All Souls Church, Cawnpore. There, alongside a similar one to his friend, Thomson, it still frames the chancel.

DILLON, GENERAL SIR M. – 'RIPPLING ROT'

AN OFFICER MIGHT serve in any number of Victorian campaigns all over the globe, but such active service did not make him an instant hero or a progressive. Many old warriors grew as fusty with the years as their side whiskers, caked in old-style military values like their favourite crusted port wine. Several of these men gathered around the arch-conservative Duke of Cambridge, C-in-C of the British Army for much of Victoria's reign. One of these was Martin Dillon.

He had entered the army in 1843 and saw an extremely active quarter-century of campaigning. He was in action at the age of 22 fighting the Sikhs in the Second Anglo-Sikh War; two years later he was on the North-West Frontier in the Kohat Pass operations, got to the Crimea after the fall of Sebastopol and then served extensively throughout the Indian Mutiny, being severely wounded in hand-to-hand combat. In 1860 he was sent to China and served as AAG in the march on Peking. This brought him to the attention of Sir Robert **Napier**, who used Dillon as his military secretary in Abyssinia in 1868. The pair worked so well together that when Napier was made C-in-C India (1870–76) he requested Dillon serve him in the same capacity.

Napier was one of Cambridge's favourite officers and in 1878, with the backing of his old chief, Dillon became assistant military secretary at the Horse Guards. He thus played an important role in army administration over the next five years. Hearing the news, the reformer Garnet **Wolseley** was appalled:

> Martin Dillon to be Military Secretary. They might as well have been on the old woman who sweeps the crossing in front of the War Office. She certainly could not have been more garrulous than dear good Martin, now well known as 'Rippling Rot'. His conversation is a bursting diarrhoea of words … without even drawing breath he will discuss a hundred subjects, each totally distinct from the other and his discussion will be as valueless as it is wordy and rapid.

Wanting to return to India after his stint in London, Dillon was given command of the Lucknow and Rawal Pindi divisions 1884–88. Not everyone disliked Dillon. One officer whose opinion differed from Wolseley's was Colonel Henry **Harford** of the Wiltshire Regiment. This veteran of the Zulu Wars owed his appointment on campaign to Dillon's kindness in seeing him after a long day at the War Office. He also served under him in India and described Dillon in his journal as:

a most delightful person, most kind-hearted and courteous who disliked pomp and show, and was a very early riser and hard worker … No one knew when he might turn up. He was rarely seen in anything but mufti and then so shabbily dressed that no one would take him to be who he was. His memory was perfectly marvellous and, although a big man, had the gentlest of voices.

Harford related an anecdote about how Dillon once strolled along with an old soldier, who had no idea he was chatting with a general, and the ranker complained about the meat rations. Arriving at the depot the shocked Tommy found his new pal was the GOC who straightaway inspected the meat, declared it unfit and created merry hell until matters were resolved.

Dillon was made a KCB in 1887, served as an aide to the Queen and GCB in 1902. A proud Irish Catholic officer, Sir Martin died in 1913 and lies buried in Glasnevin Cemetery, Dublin.

DORMER, LIEUTENANT-GENERAL SIR J. – NILE COMMANDER

THE GRANDLY NAMED James Charlemagne Dormer fought in several campaigns, but is best remembered for his service in the Sudan, where he incurred the displeasure of Lord **Wolseley**. If his career was not spectacular, his death was certainly unique among Victorian generals.

A son of Baron Dormer, born in 1834, James joined the 13th Foot aged 19. Within months he was serving in the Crimea and from there went to India, where he won the plum appointment of ADC to Sir Colin **Campbell** in his reconquest of Oudh following the Lucknow campaign. Since Sir Colin liked to be near the action, young Dormer saw plenty of fighting in such places as Agmighar and Gorakhpeer. From India he went into a third campaign, now on staff as AAG and was present at the storming of the Taku Forts and the entry into Peking in 1860.

A long spell of peacetime soldiering followed before he was sent to Egypt as acting chief of staff under Archibald **Alison** at the start of the Egyptian War. He was present at Alison's ineffective small battle at Ramleh on 5 August 1882 and the final battle at Tel-el-Kebir a month later (by which time he was DAG).

In 1884 Dormer was sent to Egypt as chief of staff to General Sir Frederick **Stephenson**, commanding the British army of occupation. While there he wrote to Wolseley at the War Office complaining that his unassuming chief was being sidelined on Sudan policy by the pushy Evelyn **Wood**, Sirdar of the newly formed Egyptian Army, and Evelyn Baring, the head of the government. This letter was instrumental in cementing Wolseley's belief that only British troops could be relied upon to save **Gordon** in Khartoum. At the same time, Wolseley, the kind of man who harboured a grudge, could not forgive Dormer for refusing to support his grandiose plan to approach Khartoum simultaneously with river and land columns. When they met, Wolseley thought Dormer rather soft and refused his offer of employment: 'I impressed upon him the fact that I could have only one Infantry Brigade & could not find employment for more than one Majr. General.' When Dormer dined Wolseley the latter confided to his wife in a letter home, 'I wonder there was no arsenic in it, for I am sure he hates me because I have not included him in the list of those to go up the Nile.' One who did go up the Nile, Charles Wilson, confirmed that Dormer was 'bitter' about being left behind.

The last laugh was Dormer's as he stayed on in Egypt after the failure of Wolseley's mission and commanded the Nile Field Force. At Stephenson's departure he took over command of British troops in Egypt 1887–90.

In 1891 Dormer was sent to India again, this time as C-in-C of the Madras Army. Hunting big game was a passion for all army officers. While out stalking tigers on 3 May 1893, he took an unlucky pot-shot and the beast was able to take its revenge. James Dormer was mauled to death.

DRYSDALE, LIEUTENANT-GENERAL SIR W. – PROUD LANCER

HER MAJESTY'S 9TH Lancers were an elite regiment. History books often allude to Hope **Grant**'s long association with this body of horsemen, but one other fighting soldier who deserves a mention in connection with them is William Drysdale.

The son of an army major, William was educated at the Military Academy, Edinburgh, and gazetted a cornet in the 4th Light Dragoons in 1835. His regiment was soon sent to India where Drysdale was to spend more than a quarter of a century fighting in five campaigns. With the 4th Light Dragoons he served with the Bombay Division of the Army of the Indus in 1839 that marched to Kabul; the cavalry fought no major actions, but suffered terribly as it advanced on Kabul, especially in the crossing of the 60-mile Bolan Pass where Afghan snipers harassed the troops. In 1842 Lieutenant Drysdale transferred to the 9th Lancers and quickly fought his first battle at Punniar, one of two on 29 December 1843 that led to the reduction of the Indian state of Gwalior. That brief war was followed by a pair of greater importance against the Sikhs; Drysdale was in the thick of action at Sobraon, Ramnagar, Chillianwallah and Gujerat. After the final battle the 9th Lancers led the pursuit of the fleeing *khalsa* soldiers, the men 'sticking their lances into them like so much *butter*', a captain vividly recalled afterwards.

By the time of the 1857–59 Indian rebellion, the 9th Lancers were commanded by Hope **Grant**, who had a high opinion of Drysdale, now his second-in-command. In the assault on Delhi he got a bullet through his forage cap and was one of ten officers that day whose horses were shot from under them. Grant wrote in his despatch: 'I have never in the whole course of my life seen so much bravery.' During a two-hour ordeal in which 'Not a man flinched from his post', forty-five of the regiment were killed or wounded. Heat, dust, bad food and fights galore – Drysdale seemed to lead a charmed life. In the action at Bulandshahr on 28 September 1857 the 9th were ordered to charge through the rebel-held town. Five VCs were won, two of them by men who rescued Drysdale when trapped beneath a fallen horse. He was commended for 'conspicuous gallantry'.

Luck seemed to be always on William Drysdale's side. Hope **Grant** recounts a story that when Drysdale was out tiger shooting on one occasion he saw a magnificent bull elephant a short distance away. The beast charged him as Drysdale blazed away with all of his four guns. The effect was negligible and he was thrown a considerable distance, though with no broken bones, by the elephant before it slunk off 'with every appearance of contempt'.

Drysdale commanded the 9th Lancers from 1861 to 1866, when he was promoted to major-general; in 1881 he was made a lieutenant-general and a decade later became colonel of his old corps. He died on 7 August 1900.

DRURY-LOWE, LIEUTENANT-GENERAL SIR D. – LEADING CAVALRY IN ZULULAND AND EGYPT

THE ZULU WAR of 1879, closely followed three years later by the Egyptian campaign, gave a fine role for the British cavalry and led the press to make something of Drury Curzon Drury-Lowe. By the time of his knighthood in 1882 he was the most famous cavalry soldier in England. It must be said that though solid and reliable, with a concern for the men under his command as well as the enemy wounded, Drury-Lowe lacked flair and did not greatly impress his contemporaries. One historian has described him as 'a popular officer and a modest one, not noted for shows of dash or impetuosity.'

He was born on 3 January 1830 at Ashton-on-Trent as Drury Curzon Holden and educated privately. His family were wealthy, his mother being a daughter of Lord Scarsdale and on inheriting an estate in Derbyshire in 1849, Drury's father changed the family name to Lowe. He achieved a BA at Oxford before joining the aristocratic 17th Lancers in 1854 as a cornet. Within two years he had fought at the Battle of the Chernaya, witnessed the storming of Sebastopol, and been promoted to captain.

The 17th Lancers were one of the many regiments sent out to India when news of the Mutiny reached England. The troopers seemed 'very smart indeed' to officers in other corps who had been on campaign longer. Lowe, with 210 men of the regiment, marched 148 miles in 120 hours in pursuit of some of the last rebels under Tatya Tope; at Zirapur on 29 December 1858 the 17th charged and Captain Lowe captured four of Tatya Tope's elephants, though the wily enemy escaped the field.

In the 1860s Lowe changed his name to Drury-Lowe and, after purchasing a majority, was promoted lieutenant-colonel of the 17th Lancers. Among the reinforcements sent to South Africa after Isandlwana were two cavalry regiments, the 1st (King's) Dragoon Guards and the 17th Lancers. Drury-Lowe in fact was no longer with the regiment, having commanded it for twelve years until 1878, but on the day of embarkation his successor was accidentally shot and severely wounded during revolver practice so he agreed, literally on the spot, to take command again as a supernumerary lieutenant-colonel, 'being joyfully welcomed by all ranks'.

In Zululand the general performance of Drury-Lowe did not impress fellow officers. Lord **Chelmsford** was far from happy with him. **Buller** and **Wood** told **Wolseley** that he was 'of no use' and the latter dismissed him as 'a Hyde Park Colonel'. He also suffered a series of physical mishaps; just before Ulundi the British camp was panicked by a false report of attacking Zulus and a soldier ran over a sleeping Drury-Lowe, using his head as a stepping-stone, the hobnail boots cutting his face badly. In the final battle, when **Chelmsford** famously said, 'Lancers out … Go at them, Lowe', the colonel led his men only to be knocked off his horse by a spent bullet. Bruised, he remounted, but missed most of his regiment's moment of glory.

He returned to England, but when war with the Boers broke out in 1881 he was sent back to South Africa to command the cavalry detachments. On arrival at Durban he found the war was already over and General **Pomeroy-Colley** was dead.

In 1882 Drury-Lowe was sent to command the 3,700 mounted troops of the Egyptian expedition. He led them in a splendid charge at Mahsama on 25 August, capturing an enemy camp and bagging some locomotives. Two days later at Kassassin, feeling that his cavalry were being led on a wild goose chase in the desert, he refused to rush to the aid of Gerald **Graham**, but that night the Household Cavalry made a celebrated moonlight charge which scattered the Egyptians. At Tel-el-Kebir the cavalry were resting when the enemy guns opened fire, but Drury-Lowe soon had them in their saddles and racing in a great arc behind the Egyptian lines. He rode with the advanced guard in the celebrated cavalry dash on to Cairo. Once there he was wise enough not to reveal the size of his force to the enemy, ordered the city's commandant and governor to fetch Arabi Pasha and accepted the general's surrender.

Promoted in the press as 'the foremost cavalry leader of his day', knighted by the Queen, Drury-Lowe was made Inspector-General of Cavalry between 1885 and 1890 and in 1892 became Colonel of the 17th Lancers. It was noted, however, that 'no major innovations' took place during his years as cavalry commander. In 1903 he publicly advocated the retention of the lance. It was abolished that year by the reforming Lord **Roberts**. Drury-Lowe died in 1908. One year later, perhaps to the amusement of his ghost and much to Roberts' fury, the lance was reinstated 'not only on escort duty ... but also on guard, during training, at manoeuvres and when so ordered on field service' (a decree that lasted until 1927).

DURAND, MAJOR-GENERAL SIR H. – NOT ONE TO PROVOKE

BRAVE, OUTSPOKEN, TOUGH, inclined to be quarrelsome, unforgiving towards opponents: such a man was Henry Marion Durand. He combined the roles of soldier and administrator most successfully. Today his career is forgotten, though his death occasionally gets a mention as probably the most bizarre among Victorian soldiers.

Durand was born on 6 November 1812, the son of a cavalry officer and at 13 was sent to Addiscombe. He left three years later with the good conduct medal and a commission in the Bengal Engineers. When not digging canals, he seems to have been a swot who made few friends, preferring instead to study Persian and other oriental languages, or go fossil-hunting in the hills.

When the First Afghan War broke out he accompanied the Army of the Indus as an engineer-volunteer and was selected to command the party which was to blow in the Kabul Gate of the great fortress at Ghazni. Under heavy Afghan fire, Durand and a sergeant laid a powder hose but the portfire went out. He had to make a spark using his nails before it caught fire. The massive explosion brought down the gate and adjoining walls. A storming party thought the entrance was blocked, the retreat was sounded, but Durand was able to confirm a path through the rubble and the soldiers returned under 'Fighting Bob' **Sale**. Seventeen officers and men were killed, 165 wounded, but Ghazni was taken with the loss of over 500 Afghan dead. It was a perilous job, an act so brave that Lord **Clyde**, no coward himself, once exclaimed, 'By God, Durand, I would not have done that for my own father!'

This feat of arms made Durand something of a celebrity and he was invited to become private secretary to the new Governor-General, Lord Ellenborough. An energetic man, Ellenborough was on the battlefield at Maharajpore during the 1843 Gwalior campaign, 'utterly regardless as to danger', and Durand was by his side. When Lord Hardinge succeeded Ellenborough as governor-general he offered the young man the plum appointment of Commissioner of Tenasserim.

The weaknesses in Durand's character now started to send his career into freefall. He imprisoned some Europeans for wanton destruction of forest timber, but they were released on appeal and he was removed from his post. When Hardinge (who had been away on leave), tried to set matters right, he got a 'cold' reply from Durand who went into a long sulk. He served as an aide at Chillianwallah alongside Gough, then turned down a whole series of civil and military appointments offered by the next governor-general, Lord Dalhousie. His friend Sir Charles **Napier** wrote scathingly: 'Were I in Lord Dalhousie's place I tell you honestly I would throw you overboard … His desire to serve you has been evident, and in return your answer is little short of insult … If one man insults you, you have no right to insist on an apology from another.' Durand was now thought too 'dangerous' for top political jobs because, in the words of George Malleson, 'He always spoke exactly what he thought, always acted exactly as he believed to be right, regardless of consequences.' He was considering leaving India altogether when he met and impressed Lord Canning, newly arrived as governor-general. The departure on leave of Sir Robert Hamilton allowed Canning to offer his protégé the important political post of Agent for Central India. He accepted and soon found himself based at Indore, a town in Malwa that was also home to the powerful Mahratta prince, Holkar, and his personal army of 7,500 men. Durand had just one local regiment to defend the Residency, British citizens and the treasury. After the fall of Delhi he refused to entrench the Residency, preferring instead to bluff things out, but an increasingly desperate situation finally escalated into open rebellion at 8.30 a.m. on 1 July 1857, when Holkar's 9-pounders started to shell the compound. Thirty-nine British subjects were murdered in the town and Durand was forced to lead a retreat towards Bhopal. 'Of all the bitter bitter days of my life I thought this the worst,' he wrote; 'I would have been thankful if any one had shot me.'

By sheer force of will, bullying when necessary and planning superbly, Durand led a British reconquest of Malwa against an army swollen to over 17,000 rebels. Towns were retaken one by one until his column marched back into Indore on 15 December. Holkar protested his innocence, insisting he had no control over his troops. Hamilton believed him. Durand did not (the start of more acrimony). Holkar can certainly be accused of sitting on the fence, a charge that historian K.L. Srivastava says 'on the whole appears to be true'.

Canning praised Durand for saving 'our interests in India until support could arrive'. His star continued to glow brighter; he was in turn Foreign Secretary to the Government of India, Military Member of the Viceroy's Council and Lieutenant-Governor of the Punjab. On 3 December 1870 Sir Henry entered the town of Tonk on a ceremonial elephant, but was crushed to death when the beast tried to pass through a low gateway. He had proved himself a brave soldier and an able administrator, though, as one contemporary historian wrote, 'he was a dangerous man to provoke'.

EARLE, MAJOR-GENERAL SIR W. – IMPULSIVE AND UNLUCKY

A LIVERPUDLIAN BORN in 1833, William Earle saw early active service in the Crimea at the Alma, Inkerman and the Sebastopol siege. Later he was employed in Canada before winning the choice appointment of military secretary to the Liberal Lord Northbrook during his tenure as Viceroy of India between 1872 and 1876. The two men got along well (Northbrook had once been described by a fellow politician as 'Just a nice, idiotic banker's clerk'), which led to Earle's promotion to major-general in 1880. Noticed by **Wolseley**, he was given command of the lines of communication and base during the advance on Tel-el-Kebir. Earle proved himself to be extremely efficient and in the final battle had his horse shot from under him.

Staff and colleagues liked Earle. He was, said one aide, 'a thorough gentleman', though the waspish Ian **Hamilton** called him 'That old martinet … trying to inculcate standards of military punctilio; dress, deportment and drill'. Nevertheless, he admitted that 'Earle was a bold man who had kept himself in touch with the rank and file and was out for fighting.'

Earle stayed on in Egypt and commanded the Alexandria garrison until the **Gordon** Relief Expedition, when the Duke of Cambridge asked Sir William to lead the advance troops going up the Nile, much to the chagrin of Wolseley, who minuted: 'To select for command of this contemplated expedition General Earle, of whose capacity for command we know literally and absolutely nothing, and whose name is totally unknown to the Army, and will not therefore impress our rank and file with confidence ... is a policy that is incomprehensible to me.' Privately, Wolseley was even more blunt:

> His ideas upon war are childish in the extreme, clever man as he is upon all ordinary routine matters. He thinks that the man who can command well at a field day is capable of commanding in war. Of war he literally [sic] and actually knows nothing. He was at the Alma & at Inkerman, but he lost his head upon both those occasions ...

Wolseley made sure Earle was kept busy at Wadi Halfa, though he was forced to admit that Sir William was 'a very good officer and he should be tried in command of troops under fire & if he showed an aptitude as a leader of men, then upon another occasion he might be made first man'. Later in the campaign Wolseley retracted his earlier opinions and wrote that Earle 'is the most business-like & reliable man I have on the Lines of Commns. – I wish he had been at its head instead of dear puzzle-headed Evelyn **Wood**'.

Earle got his chance for glory when Wolseley gave him command of the river column sailing towards Khartoum. The military historian Christopher Brice has described him as 'a good commander with a degree of tactical nous'. Five days after Earle got word of the city's fall, his army found a dervish *ansar* waiting for them at Kirbekan. Impulsive as always, Earle led a major reconnaissance himself and ended the stiff battle that followed with a spectacular charge of the Black Watch. In typical style, as the shouts and fighting died away, he ran up to a hut known to be full of dervishes and peeped through the window. Instantly he was shot through the head and killed. It was, according to a witness, 'the last shot fired on the field'. Ian Hamilton admitted that Earle, 'always too impetuous in his actions', was also a gallant man. 'He was up against a live thing', wrote Hamilton, 'the Mohammedan faith and he rose to his chance'. The general was buried under a palm tree, the ground for 20yd around 'ploughed up' so as to save the grave from desecration.

Today he is all but forgotten, though he might occasionally be noticed by shoppers and office workers rushing about Liverpool, where a bronze statue of him stands outside St George's Hall.

EAST, GENERAL SIR C. – ALL OVER THE GLOBE

THE CRIMEA, INDIA and its frontiers, Zululand and Burma – Cecil James East saw action in all these areas. He is forgotten today, though he was the senior staff officer present at Ulundi. He was, in fact, a most efficient intelligence and staff officer, both on campaign and at the War Office.

He was born in London on 10 July 1854, educated privately and gazetted an ensign in the 82nd Foot in 1854. He served with his regiment in the Crimea and stayed with them to fight also in the Indian Mutiny, being wounded when part of Windham's force protecting Cawnpore. He transferred to the 41st and later the 57th Foot. Serving in India, Captain East was appointed in 1871 to be AQMG with the Chittagong column entering Lushai country via a southern route. His efficiency was noted by the column's commander, Brigadier **Brownlow**, and he had a mention in despatches for accompanying the 2nd Gurkhas in an attack on the village of Lall Gnoor on 6 January 1872. It was the first time the Lushais had ever seen artillery and the effect of the 7-pounder screw-guns terrified them. East helped drive out the enemy. The campaign was arduous, requiring him to plan all its transport and commissariat arrangements.

When the Zulu War broke out in 1879, Major East was one of the brightest men in Sir Archibald **Alison**'s intelligence department at the War Office. The disaster at Isandlwana saw a number of generals and staff officers sent to help **Chelmsford**, most of whom he did not want, but East came with the blessing of Alison, Brownlow (now resident Indian expert at the War Office) and the Duke of Cambridge, who asserted that he was 'one of the most efficient officers in the army'. Appointed DAQMG, he was one of the last special service officers to arrive and Cornelius **Clery** thought him 'slow, but solid'. East was present at Ulundi but within a couple of days was writing to Alison that 'the Zulu War is now virtually finished'. Before leaving South Africa he wrote to Sir Archibald of the growing discontent with the Boers, commenting perceptively: 'A few companies of infantry have been considered sufficient to overcome them while 20,000 men were necessary to conquer the Zulus!'

Back in London, East returned to intelligence department duties. In August 1880 he authored an important paper, *Memorandum on our Future*

Policy in Afghanistan, in which he argued Russia was too weak and busy elsewhere to attack Afghanistan 'at present'. Not long after reading this document, the foreign secretary ordered a slow retirement of troops out of Afghanistan and refused to sanction retention of Kandahar as a forward base. When the Third Burmese War broke out East was sent to command the 3rd Division. He went on to command various districts in Bengal, Burma and Madras until 1893, when he was appointed governor and commandant of Sandhurst until 1898. One of the cadets who entered and passed out of Sandhurst in those years was Winston Leonard Spencer Churchill. East retired a full general in 1903. He died five years later on 14 March 1908.

EDWARDES, MAJOR-GENERAL SIR H. – PRIGGISH PRO-CONSUL

INTEGRITY, FAIRNESS AND a high moral purpose marked out Herbert Benjamin Edwardes, even as a young man, as someone who would go far. As a lieutenant he told tribesmen on the frontier of India: 'You shall have the best laws that an enlightened people can form for you … You shall be justly ruled, but you shall be free no more.' In the Victorian age his achievements were on everyone's lips, but today he is forgotten, his kind of imperialistic evangelism being distinctly out of favour.

Herbert was born in Shropshire in 1819, the son of a country parson, educated at a private school and King's College, London, before proceeding to India in 1840 as an ensign in the 1st Bengal Fusiliers. During the next five years this 'slight, delicate-looking young man' showed an astonishing aptitude for oriental languages and contributed a series of articles to the *Delhi Gazette* that got him noticed. When the First Sikh War broke out he was made an ADC to Sir Hugh **Gough**. In the first battle at Mudki on 18 December 1845 he was wounded by a ball in the thigh. This prevented him from taking part in the next battle, but Herbert was by his chief's side again at Sobraon on 10 February 1846.

After the war Edwardes became an assistant to Colonel Henry Lawrence, Resident at Lahore. He was instrumental in extending the Pax Britannica along the marches of the North-West Frontier. The tribesmen came to respect him as he conversed fluently in their languages. When a second war with the Sikhs broke out Edwardes marched on the fortress of Multan, fought and won two pitched battles along the way and drove the Sikhs inside the fort. He kept them penned up until a large British army arrived.

Returning to England he found himself feted as a hero. 'Since the days of Clive no man has done as Edwardes', crowed his supporters, though one jealous detractor in the 3rd Light Dragoons complained to his mother back home: 'I was amused to read at your (and everybody else in England) appreciation of that fool Edwardes' performance.' This remark helps explain why opinions on Edwardes were always mixed. Those who worked closely with him came to admire his wide intellectual abilities, the measured diplomatic style and careful way of doing things. 'He rarely put a foot wrong', writes Charles Allen. Yet Herbert had a priggish streak which irritated others. At a first meeting, Henry Daly thought him 'greatly overrated', but later wrote:

> He is subdued and somewhat grave; has somewhat the affectation of dignity … In his early youth he was frolicsome gay and witty; he seems now to have a puritanical conviction that such things are unbecoming. He is a religious man, careful of forms and inclined somewhat to give out his opinions on controversial affairs. He is friendly and polite to me, yet I do not *warm* to him. He is somewhat diplomatic and less straightforward than is pleasant.

During the years 1845–49 Edwardes saw his fair share of adventure and close shaves on the frontier. On one occasion, during a melee, a tribesman placed his long rifle against Herbert's stomach but the *jezail* misfired! In action against the Sikhs, a horseman fired a matchlock at him from 50yd and the ball passed through a shirt sleeve just missing his elbow. His worst injury was self-inflicted: at Multan he hastily put on his sword and pistols and a ball exploded and shattered his right hand. No doctor was with the force and so for twelve days he suffered in agony, his hand stitched up with a packing needle.

Returning to India in 1851 Major Edwardes, now a sombre looking man with a full black beard, took over as Commissioner of the Peshawar frontier district. He was political officer in an 1852 expedition against the Bori Afridis and helped negotiate a treaty in 1857 with the ruler of Afghanistan that was of immense value when the Indian Mutiny broke out a few weeks later. During the great rebellion, Edwardes' presence at Peshawar helped the British keep a tight grip on the Punjab. His last campaign was Sydney **Cotton**'s 1858 expedition against the Sittana fanatics. Edwardes' insistence, as political officer, that the campaign be kept as brief as possible probably encouraged the tribesmen to rise again, with dreadful consequences, five years later.

It has been argued by some that Edwardes' achievements were not recognised after the Mutiny due in part to his zealous Christian evangelism which, following the dreadful bloodshedding years of 1857–59, was seen as a factor in precipitating the rebellion. In 1859 he was made a KCB, but was sidelined to the role of Commissioner at Amballa when he clearly deserved the appointment of Lieutenant-Governor of the Punjab. Edwardes was unhappy and so, his health failing, he returned to England in 1865. In 1866 he was made a KCSI. On 22 February 1868 he was promoted to the rank of major-general and died on 23 December of that year, just 49 years old. His wife later wrote a biography of him, while Edwardes' own book, *A Year on the Punjab Frontier in 1848-49*, remains a classic account of the early days of British rule.

EGERTON, FIELD-MARSHAL SIR C. – VICTOR OF JIDBALI

A TOUGH COMMANDER, Charles Comyn Egerton learned about fighting colonial enemies in the toughest theatre of war – the North-West Frontier of India. He fought five campaigns there as well as serving in the Sudan and eventually put the skills he had learned to good use in Somaliland, where he gave 'the Mad Mullah' a pummelling he long remembered at Jidbali in 1904.

Egerton's father was a respected major-general – later Honorary Colonel of the 89th Foot – who served in the Crimean War. Three of Charles's brothers were also knighted (one an admiral and two as civil servants). He was born on 10 November 1848 and entered the army after Sandhurst as a second lieutenant with the 31st Foot in 1867, transferring to the 79th Foot while in India.

His first campaign was the Second Afghan War, in which he was mentioned in despatches followed by the Hazara campaign 1888. These experiences of frontier warfare stood Major Egerton in good stead when he was appointed AAG in the second Miranzai expedition of 1891. This campaign was necessary to punish sections of the Orakzai tribe, who went on the war path again only days after a first expedition that same year had broken up. Egerton was with the first column when it attacked the village of Tsalai on 17 April. Covered by the fire of No. 3 Mountain Battery, the King's Royal Rifle Corps led the attack but their colonel and three of his men were wounded, along with Egerton and his native orderly. For his bravery he was awarded the DSO, one of the earliest recipients of this gallantry award (it had only been instituted in November 1886).

In 1894, after the surprise attack at Wana on the camp of the commission delineating the Indo-Afghan boundary (later known as the Durand

Line), Egerton was given command of the 3rd Brigade, Waziristan Field Force, sent to punish the Mahsud tribe. Apart from sniping into camp and at patrols, the tribesmen gave the troops only minor trouble. The same was true three years later, when Egerton commanded the 1st Brigade of the Tochi Field Force which marched against the Waziris in response to their cowardly attack on a political officer and his escort. With so much experience fighting Pathans, Egerton felt able to write a tactical study of Indian frontier warfare.

In 1896 he had a short sojourn in the Sudan. This acquaintance with the dervishes proved useful in 1903, when he was sent to British Somaliland to try and quell the uprising of Haji Muhammad Abdullah, known as 'the Mad Mullah'. Egerton's orders in this fourth expedition against the Mullah were to crush him by a huge display of force. He was given almost a whole division, with two infantry brigades and a mounted corps supported by locally raised militias and cavalry – over 8,000 men. His vast baggage train, with all the many commissariat problems encountered in taking an army into a baking desert, included 10,000 camels and 800 mules.

The Somaliland campaign that started in 1892 (and lasted until 1920) was full of bloody encounters. At Jidbali on 27 January 1904 Egerton's army, including 550 men of the King's African Rifles and half a battalion of the Hampshire Regiment, clashed with a dervish *ansar* of 6,000 to 8,000 warriors. Wisely, Sir Charles told his troops to lie down or kneel when the dervishes opened fire. He then replied with forty minutes of artillery and maxim fire which, despite its ferocity, did not stop the warriors from charging the British, drawn up in a single large square, no less than three times; over 1,000 dervishes were killed and 200 taken prisoner while Egerton lost twenty-seven killed (including three British officers) and thirty-seven wounded.

The mullah licked his wounds across the frontier in Italian Somaliand and gave the British a few years of comparative peace. The Home Government was well pleased with Egerton and he was duly made a field-marshal. Honours and peacetime commands followed until his death in 1921.

ELLES, LIEUTENANT-GENERAL SIR W. – HUMBLING HAZARA

WILLIAM KIDSTON ELLES was a soldier whom Lord **Roberts** described, during his tenure as C-in-C India, as particularly efficient. He fought in the Crimea, Indian Mutiny and the Burmese jungles, served as an ADC to the

Queen-Empress in 1881–90 and did a spell as AAG at the War Office, but it was along the Hazara border of the North-West Frontier that was that most impressive work. He served in three campaigns against the tribes of the Black Mountain and in 1891 commanded the large expedition that finally brought a long peace to that turbulent district.

William joined the 54th Foot aged 17, just in time to serve as an ensign in the Crimea in 1854–55. He transferred to the 38th Foot and sailed with it to India in 1857, where it was part of Windham's army at Cawnpore until Sir Colin Campbell re-organised things and Elles found himself in the thick of battle at the second relief of Lucknow. The Indian subcontinent was to remain the theatre of Elles's greatest achievements; there is some confusion as to whether he fought on the Black Mountain at Sittana in 1863, but five years later he was appointed DAAG in the 1868 expedition commanded by Alfred **Wilde**.

Successful in the adjutant-general's department, Lt-Colonel Elles served as AAG at the War Office during the Second Afghan War and the Zulu War. In that role he seems to have got along with both Roberts and **Wolseley** and in 1881 was appointed an ADC to the Queen-Empress.

Back in India a decade later, Elles was given command of approximately 7,500 officers and men, along with fifteen guns, and sent to punish the Hassanzai and Akazai clans of the Black Mountain. Roberts was particularly concerned that the expedition should be a success for two reasons; firstly, the fanatical tribesmen of the area had been a thorn in the flesh of the Raj for over forty-five years (this was the fifth major expedition since 1852); secondly, an expedition sent just three years earlier had failed, due, in Roberts's opinion, to its commander being influenced by his political officers. Elles had two columns and pushed into the territory on 12 March 1891. His reserve brigade was also later called into action as the troops marched up and down the valleys and crags burning villages and fighting several small battles. Elles's main force was withdrawn in June, though a final evacuation did not take place until November. Unpleasant as these punitive expeditions were, they seemed to have had the desired effect: worn out by so much fighting, loss of life, property and crops, the tribes accepted terms and, following a small expedition in 1892, the district was able to settle down to a long period of peace. During the great frontier rising of 1897–98 the district remained surprisingly quiet.

In 1895 Sir William Elles was made C-in-C of the Bengal Army. That same year, he was promoted to lieutenant-general. He died in harness a year later at Naini Tal on 5 August 1896.

ENGLAND, GENERAL SIR R. – 'OLD WOMAN'

GENERALS FREQUENTLY PICK up nicknames from their soldiers; Richard England's was one of the most uncomplimentary – 'old woman'. In his long career he never shone, though he saw a lot of action. He was usually blamed for being over-cautious, though he was also censured for advancing too rashly in the First Afghan War. He was a soldier who seemed embalmed by indecision.

He was the son of a general of the same name, a tough old soldier from County Clare who fought in the American War of Independence and then bought lands in western Upper Canada. Young Richard was born in Detroit (now in Michigan, USA, but then part of Canada) in 1793. He was educated in England and joined the army as an ensign with the 14th Foot in 1808. England was lucky to survive the fever-ridden Walcheren expedition, then served in Sicily in 1810–11, before a period of leave in Canada and marriage. He re-joined his regiment in France just after Waterloo and rose to command them for many years. In 1833 he led them to South Africa where he was given command of the eastern frontier district during the 1836–37 Xhosa War.

In 1839 Colonel England transferred to command the 41st Foot. It was an unlucky time for him: his wife, Anna Maria, died shortly after arriving in India and in 1841 England was told to lead a division of the Bombay Army to relieve British troops besieged at Ghazni and Kandahar. He failed to reach Ghazni in time, but joined Nott at Kandahar as his second-in-command until the end of the war. During his advance the Baluchi tribes were troublesome and during the withdrawal to India via the Bolan Pass, they gave constant harassment. Worst of all, the cranky old General Nott thought England, a Queen's officer, was little short of useless. When England requested the campaign medal for himself and his troops, Nott replied to headquarters:

> General England states that he was at Candahar from the 10th of May to the 10th of August, but as the troops noted by him were not engaged with the enemy during that period, and as they did not fire a shot, I do not think that the fact of their being in the city, can possibly give them a claim to a medal … General England has claimed the 'Candahar medal' – first for the action of the 28th of March when his force was completely defeated, and retreated to Quetta. Secondly – On the 28th of April, in Pesheen, which was a trifling skirmish, of no consequence whatever. Thirdly – For being in garrison at

Candahar ... where they never fired a shot. Fourthly – For what is called the passage of the Kojuck ... where there was no enemy that could possibly have resisted 100 sepoys.

England came away from India, rather surprisingly, with a knighthood, and settled in Bath. In 1851 he was sent to command as a major-general in Ireland. Three years later, his mistakes seemingly forgotten, he was given the 3rd Division in the Crimea. Historians view his career at this point with mixed opinions: Hibbert says he was a 'man of meagre talent and reputa-tion', while another argues that though England had little to do at the Alma, 'his promptitude in sending up his troops at the critical moment to the assistance of hard-pressed battalions' helped salvage the day at Inkerman. Yet an officer in the Crimea called him 'a terrible fool', adding, 'It is quite disgusting to serve under him. He never knows his own mind and it takes him an age to get his Division into position.' Nicknamed by all an 'old woman' because of his caution, when England told commanders that he would keep the 3rd Division strictly in reserve at Inkerman, one of them, old Colonel George Bell, cried out: 'No ... no ... no! No more reserves for me. We had enough of that at Alma.'

In fairness to England, it can be said that he won some respect from the common soldiers during the terrible winter of 1854–55 as he shared many of their privations. He never applied to go home and was 'the last of the original general officers who had accompanied the army to the Crimea to leave it'. He directed the attack on the Redan on 18 June 1855, but cannot be blamed for its failure. On doctor's orders he finally quit the Crimea in August 1855. He was a full general in 1863, and retired in 1877, dying in his ninetieth year on 19 January 1883.

FRANKS, MAJOR-GENERAL SIR T. – DISCIPLINARIAN WITH GUTS

THE EARLY VICTORIAN army had its fair share of martinets and flogging colonels. One of the toughest of these, his cruelty and use of the lash so legendary that he almost precipitated a mutiny on the day of a battle, was Thomas Harte Franks. In his autobiography, Lord **Wolseley** used Franks to exemplify the old-school officer who, though stern, was also brave. Privates, and even officers, serving under Franks learned to admire and fear him. Given a division to command during the Indian Mutiny, he proved to be a remarkably skilful general, one of the best Sir Colin **Campbell** had, but his career, already threatened by ill-health, was ended abruptly when he disobeyed the orders of his C-in-C.

It may be a cliché to describe an Irishman as 'hot-blooded' or 'fiery', but Franks, a son of gentry from County Cork, certainly fitted these monikers. He entered the army as an ensign of 17 years in 1825, joining the 10th Foot, and remained with his regiment for almost three decades, gradually rising in rank. By 1845, when the 10th were stationed in India, Franks had just been promoted to lieutenant-colonel and had never seen a shot fired in anger throughout his whole career. He believed in liberal application of the lash: minor infringements of rules or military discipline met with the use of the bloody triangle or whipping post. Officers also feared Franks as a tyrant and left the regiment. One who joined and served as Franks' adjutant for six years was Henry Havelock (later **Havelock-Allan**), son of the famous general. He wrote that the colonel was 'as vigorous and uncompromising towards his officers as he was in all his dealings with the rank and file'.

Just before the battalion moved into action on the morning of the Battle of Sobraon in the First Sikh War, the colonel, responding to a rumour he had heard, sat on his horse and said, 'Men, I understand you mean to shoot me today, but I want to ask you a favour – let me get in first and don't kill me until the battle is over.' The soldiers took Franks at his word – remember, they had never seen their colonel fight before – but his courage and sheer guts during the fight impressed all who saw him. His horse was blown to bits under him and Franks was slightly injured, but his boys carried him trium- phantly through the battery he had captured. When the Second Sikh War broke out, the 10th Foot were the first British regiment to reach the siege of Multan. Led by Franks, they also performed well at Gujerat.

He had handed over his command and was preparing to go home on sick leave when the 1857 rebellion broke out. Refusing to leave in case his services might be needed, Franks recuperated at Calcutta. In January 1858 Sir Colin Campbell asked him to command a force of nearly 6,000 men and march across north-eastern Oudh driving the rebels before him, then combine with Jung Bahadur's Nepal contingent of Gurkhas and join the main army before Lucknow. Franks, with the temporary rank of brigadier, successfully carried out his instructions and inflicted two severe defeats on the rebel leader Muhammad Hussein Nazim at Chanda and Sultanpur on 19 and 23 February. His whole loss was just two men killed and sixteen wounded. Lt-General McLeod Innes, who won the VC at Sultanpur, wrote that 'The secret of this lay in the formation of his fighting force being not in line but in open skirmishing order.' In other words, Franks made his men difficult targets for the rebels. He 'utterly dispersed the enemy and took thirty four guns, as many as, he laughingly boasted, he had taken at the siege of Multan.' Franks, cap in hand, led the men of his old regiment, the 10th Foot, up to the guns and fought alongside them with his sabre.

Eight miles from Lucknow, Franks decided to disregard his chief's strict instructions to proceed as quickly as possible by attacking the small fort of Dhowara, two miles to the right of his advance, for he feared these mutineers might surprise his baggage train. Refusing to listen to the advice of Havelock and some other officers, Franks sent his troops into attack without using his heavy 24-pounders. The rebels managed to beat off the attack, even wounding McLeod Innes. Franks decided he had to march on and joined Campbell outside Lucknow that same evening. During the final assault on the city Franks's column, now termed the 4th Division, went into action to relieve Lugard's 2nd Division.

Campbell was furious that Franks had not only been defeated at Dhowara, but had also disobeyed him and wasted time. He had intended to give Franks the role in the relief of Lucknow which subsequently went to Sir James Outram. Campbell now refused to grant him another field command. Franks left India and returned home, where he was promoted to major-general, made a KCB and thanked by Parliament, but he was unhappy with the way he had been treated. His health, not good before the Mutiny, was now completely ruined and he died on 5 February 1862.

FRASER-TYTLER, MAJOR-GENERAL SIR J. – ACTION MAN

IN EVERY CAMPAIGN in which he served, James Bannatyne Macleod Fraser-Tytler was always in the thick of the action. As a general he led his men from the front.

He was born in 1821 and entered the Bengal Army twenty years later as an ensign with the 37th Native Infantry. With them he marched to Afghanistan as part of General **Pollock**'s 'Army of Retribution' in 1841. He rushed into a cavalry skirmish in the Khyber Pass against the wishes of Pollock, who reprimanded the young officer and later deprived him of his war medal. In old age Fraser-Tytler said 'General Pollock was right, but it was hard. That was the only medal I really ever wished to possess.'

In the First Sikh War of 1845–46 Fraser Tytler served as an aide to the old warhorse Lord **Gough** and was in the thick of the action at

Mudki, Ferozeshah and Sobraon. Two horses were shot from under him at Ferozeshah as he conveyed the general's orders across the battlefield. In January 1846 Gough appointed Fraser-Tytler to be adjutant of the 9th Bengal Irregular Cavalry ('Christie's Horse'). The 9th fought in the 1848–49 second Sikh War at Chillianwallah and Gujerat, where Lord Gough remarked on 'the intrepidity and intelligence of my old A.D.C'. Following the cavalry disaster at Ramnugar on 21 November 1848, Fraser-Tytler served his old chief again, agreeing to take Gough's orders to General **Thackwell** commanding the cavalry division. He had to swim the Chenab River to reach Thackwell, a feat that so impressed Gough he had Fraser-Tytler made a brevet-major on attaining his regimental rank of captain. According to John Christie, commanding the 9th, the dashing young officer was 'almost constantly in the saddle' during the war and 'daily on outpost duty'.

In 1857 Lt-Colonel Fraser-Tytler was appointed DAQMG to **Havelock**'s column sent to relieve Lucknow. At Fatephur, the first of twelve battles the troops faced as they marched up-country, he rode up to the gunners as the rebels retreated, shouting 'Knock over that chap on the elephant!' A cannon ball duly sent the chief mutineer flying. Havelock admitted, as he approached Lucknow, that 'the only staff officers in my force whom I ever consult confidentially' were his chief engineer, his son and Fraser-Tytler. During the entry into Lucknow on 25 September, Fraser-Tytler, responsible for intelligence, reconnoitred under a heavy fire. When a rush was made for the Charbagh Bridge he rode with the lead troops. His horse was struck by grapeshot but he was unscathed. Then he went on to ensure the enemy's guns were seized by the 90th Light Infantry in a quick charge, directing it on foot, while holding the mane of the commanding officer's horse. A short time later that officer, Colonel Campbell, was mortally wounded and Fraser-Tytler also seriously injured. Sir Robert **Napier** wrote later that 'if Havelock's whole force had the power of conferring the award of the Victoria Cross for general conduct and devoted gallantry they would confer it on Lieutenant-Colonel Fraser-Tytler'.

When war was declared with the small Himalayan country of Bhutan, Fraser-Tytler, now a brigadier, was ordered to command the left column on 15 February 1865. Entering Bhutan, he decided to attack the enemy's strong position crowning the Balla Pass. After sixteen hours' hard march, the *sepoys* of the 18th and 19th PNI rushed the stockade at the summit. This was palisaded to a height of 20ft and backed by a 4ft loopholed wall. Fraser-Tytler said it was the finest charge he ever saw and the C-in-C of India called it 'the most brilliant feat of arms which has ever occurred in Indian mountain warfare'.

Promoted to major-general in 1871, Fraser-Tytler was given command of the Allahabad Division and later Sirhind before retiring in 1879. In 1903 he was made Honorary Colonel of the 12th Pioneers (who had served under him in Bhutan). In 1905 he was given the GCB. Now a venerable old soldier with long white mutton-chop whiskers, he died in his ninety-third year on 2 February 1914, just months before a new age of warfare ended his style of campaigning.

FRENCH, FIELD-MARSHAL LORD J. – HOT-TEMPERED CAVALRYMAN

SOMETIMES REPRESENTED AS a blimpish figure in comparison with Douglas Haig, it is often forgotten that fifteen years before the First World War, during the South African War, where horsed cavalry played a major role, John French was seen as an outstanding general. Short, with a 'heavy-jowled face, bow legs and bull neck', accepted as clever but hot-tempered, he made many enemies in his career and won several admirers.

French was born on 28 September 1852, educated at Harrow and joined the Royal Navy in 1866, but soon found that he suffered from vertigo. He left the service, joined the Suffolk Artillery Militia in 1870 and was commissioned a lieutenant in the 8th King's Royal Irish Hussars in 1874, transferring that same year to the 19th Hussars, with whom he was to have a lifelong association. In 1884 as a major he was second in command of the 19th when they formed part of the desert column in the **Gordon** Relief Expedition. General Stewart, leading the Camel Corps across the Bayuda desert, thought the men of the 19th were 'the very acme of light cavalry'. French was honourably mentioned for his bravery at the Battle of Abu Klea and promoted to lieutenant-colonel. By 1899 he was a major-general and commanding the 1st Cavalry Brigade at Aldershot.

Rather a surprise choice to command the Cavalry Division in the war with the Boers because he was largely unknown to the general public and had 'a comparatively modest service record', French's generalship proved to be one of the few success stories in the campaign. Mistakes were made on several occasions, but he was able to harass the enemy 'with a series of movements of dazzling rapidity and unerring accuracy'. Under his command was the largest mounted division that had ever worked together in the history of the British Army. Even so, French cunningly deceived the Boers into thinking he had more troops than was actually the case, and that the Orange Free State would be attacked from north-eastern Cape Colony. At Colesberg and a host of other battles culminating in his spectacular dash to Kimberley, he led his cavalry with an élan and skill sadly not shown by most generals in the war. An aide wrote later that:

> You only had to look at him to see that he was a brave, determined man … I learnt to love and to admire the man who never lost his head, and on whom danger had the effect it has on the wild boar: he would become morose, furious for a time, harsh, but he would face up and never shirk. He knew of only one way of dealing with a difficulty, and that was to tackle it … If he had once lost confidence in a man, justly or unjustly, that man could never do right in his eyes. He was as bad an enemy as he was a good friend!

One who took time to warm to him was Lord **Roberts**, who told the Minister of War in April 1900: 'French will never be a great Cavalry leader, he is wanting in initiative and has no idea of how to take care of his horses.' Roberts thought French had relieved Kimberley 'in a satisfactory manner', but at Poplar Grove had 'started late and allowed himself to be beguiled by the enemy into fighting a series of rear guard actions … it was much the same at Driefontein and Dewetsdorp … the enemy ought to have caught it if our Cavalry had shown a little intelligent activity'. Four months later, the ice broken, Roberts confided that 'French has improved immensely … He is a man of iron nerves who has learnt how to cope with Boer tactics.'

As the war dragged on through its second year and into a third, it was French's eight mobile columns of cavalry, commanded by such future luminaries as Douglas Haig and Edmund Allenby, that 'scoured' and 'sieved' the northern Transvaal, gradually wearing down the resistance of the Boer commandos. Not surprisingly, French finished the war with a fine service record and the support of men like Lord **Kitchener**. Various promotions followed, including the post of Chief of the Imperial General Staff in 1912. He seemed the obvious choice to lead the British Expeditionary Force in August 1914.

It would be foolish to try to discuss French's First World War career in these pages. They form no part of this book and are amply documented. Suffice it to say that, after the failure at Loos in 1915, he was replaced by his long-term No. 2, Douglas Haig. Sent to Ireland as a tough lord lieutenant, French supported the ruthless Black and Tans and survived assassination attempts. Full of honours, he died on 22 May 1925.

GARVOCK, GENERAL SIR J. – SUCCESS AT UMBEYLA

AN EFFICIENT BRIGADE major in the First Anglo-Sikh War, an excellent aide to Sir Harry **Smith** in his Indian and South African campaigns, it was also John Garvock's good fortune to bring the hard-fought Umbeyla campaign to a close. Success always smiles on victors.

He had entered the army in 1835. As a young officer in the 10th Foot he served alongside the infamous martinet Thomas **Franks**. Garvock was promoted adjutant of the regiment in 1839. During the First Anglo-Sikh War he came to the notice of the fiery Sir Harry Smith, who made him brigade major of his division. The pair formed a lasting friendship (Garvock would later be a pall-bearer at Smith's funeral), and he followed his chief to South Africa as his military secretary, fighting the Boers in 1848 and the Xhosa tribes throughout 1850–52.

Garvock's moment of glory came in 1863 at the height of the hard-fought Umbeyla campaign on India's North-West Frontier. He was selected by the C-in-C, India, Sir Hugh Rose, to replace the physically weakened Neville Chamberlain. He arrived at a crucial moment in the campaign with an army worn out by weeks of vicious close-quarter fighting, but wanting to end the already protracted struggle. Just after his arrival, on 10 December, the Bonair chiefs visited the British camp to parley. Four days later they rejected a peace overture. Rose had sent word to Garvock not 'to attempt any operations until further orders'. Political officers normally erred on the side of caution but, on this occasion, Garvock's advisor, Captain James, realised that the situation with the tribes was deteriorating rapidly in the Peshawar Valley and urged immediate action. Garvock agreed and arranged for his army to move out in three columns and attack the following morning.

Garvock's 7,800-strong columns dislodged 4,000 tribesmen holding the village of Lalu and its conical hill. By the end of a fierce fight the enemy had retreated with a loss of some 400 killed, while the British had suffered sixteen killed and sixty-seven wounded. The general had directed the attack himself from the centre of the line with 'rapidity and vigour', sounding the advance. This was the first clear-cut defeat the tribesmen had experienced in the campaign. Wasting no time, Garvock pressed on the next day to his opponents' chief village. This he did by a careful reconnaissance beforehand and then a movement by his second column to turn the enemy's right flank. During the operation, 200 fanatical *ghazis* swarmed down upon the column under Colonel Turner CB and in the savage hand-to-hand fighting all 200 were killed. The British losses of eight dead and eighty wounded were a testament to the sword blows of their adversaries.

The tribes now agreed to terms quickly and the *ghazi* stronghold of Malka was burned to the ground on 19 December. Garvock was highly praised for bringing the war to a swift close; his honours included a knighthood and colonelcy of the 10th Foot. Back in England he commanded various districts in the periods 1866–71 and 1877–78. He died suddenly on 10 November 1878 while commanding the southern district.

GASELEE, GENERAL SIR A. – DEFEATING THE BOXERS

WITH CLOSE-CROPPED BROWN hair and a splendidly drooping walrus moustache, Alfred Gaselee seems vaguely comical in his photographs, but he was a splendid Victorian soldier. So attuned was he to the requirements of colonial warfare that when he finally got an independent command, leading British troops against the Chinese Boxers in 1900, he was already serving in his eleventh campaign.

He was born the son of a country parson at Little Yeldham, Essex, on 3 June 1844. His dream was to be a soldier and in January 1863 he was duly gazetted an ensign in the 93rd Highlanders then serving in India. Young Alfred set sail and arrived on the North-West Frontier in time to experience some of the fiercest fighting of his life in the Umbeyla expedition. Clearly intelligent, he next applied for the Bengal Staff Corps, was promoted to lieutenant, and in 1867–68 served with the Abyssinian expedition as a transport officer. He was at the storming of Magdala and twice mentioned in despatches. In 1869 he won another mention in despatches in a small campaign against the Bezotis. Promoted captain, he fought in the Jowakai Afridi expedition 1877–78 and was a DAQMG in Afghanistan 1879–80, coming to the notice of Frederick **Roberts**, who took him on the famous march from Kabul to Kandahar. Shortly after the close of the Second Afghan War he served in the Zhob Valley expedition, and seven years later the Hazara expedition. That same year, 1891, he was promoted to lieutenant-colonel.

Transferring to command of the 5th Gurkha Rifles, Gaselee led his men in the 1892 Isazai expedition. Shortly afterwards he was promoted to full colonel and an ADC to the Queen-Empress. In 1894–95 he served with the Waziristan Field Force and was mentioned in despatches for an eighth time. Sir William **Lockhart**, who had served with Gaselee in the previous two expeditions, next offered him command of the 2nd Brigade, Tirah Field

Force, in the 1897–98 frontier war. Mistakes had been made and the campaign was not popular at home or in India, yet Gaselee managed to be one of the few generals who came out of this war with his reputation enhanced. One of his transport officers (later to be a famous general), Hubert de la Poer Gough, wrote during the early days in Tirah that Gaselee 'is a very fussy man and I do not care for soldiering under him at all'. After getting to know his chief better and realise his skills, Gough later admitted that the general was 'a very sound man and a nice one in every way'.

Gaselee was next given command of the Bundelkhand district and then called to Simla to officiate as Quartermaster-General of the Indian Army. While he was there the Boxer Rebellion broke out in China and the legations were besieged in Peking. Sir Alfred was quickly promoted to major-general and sent to command the British forces in a second relief expedition. He arrived at Tientsin on 25 July and made immediate plans for a march on the capital, fully aware of the gravity of the situation and the fact that the first relief expedition had been a miserable failure. Armies of the various nations assembled, especially the French and Russians, wanting to begin the march on 14 August, but Gaselee, who quickly became the commanding military figure in the expedition, 'firmly and courteously' made it plain that the British would start off – alone if need be – ten days earlier. When the United States military supported Gaselee the other nations fell into line.

On the march Gaselee got a message through to the British at Peking – 'Keep up your spirits.' One historian has noted that 'the amiable General Gaselee pushed the advance at a punishing pace, fighting whenever the Chinese offered resistance, then resuming the march immediately, leaving whatever mopping up was necessary to the rear echelon. His tactics were sensibly simple, as was ordained by a multilingual force.' Officers noted Gaselee's compassion for his troops overcome by the intense heat. While other generals and armies treated the local population abominably, he counselled moderation, saying: 'Well, you know, we do not wish to antagonize 350 million Chinese.' It is recorded that when the general reached Legation Street, 'showing on every inch of him the wear and tear of an eighty mile midsummer relief march', he jumped down from his horse at the sight of the first two European women, reverently kissed one of them on the forehead and with tears in his eyes shouted, 'Thank God, men, here are two women alive!' In the days following the Relief of Peking he tried hard to prevent British troops looting or taking reprisals against the Chinese, much to the chagrin of the soldiers of the German Kaiser in particular.

Back home, Gaselee was made a GCIE and promoted full general in 1906; other honours included colonelcy of the 54th Sikhs. This splendid fighting soldier died just at the close of the Great War on 29 March 1918. One obituary noted that his 'grasp of a military situation was instantaneous and accurate and he had the gift of making himself understood and of inspiring confidence in all with whom he came in contact'. More than a half-century later, the historian Richard O'Connor wrote perhaps Gaselee's best epitaph when he said that his 'innate decency still casts a mellow glow on the half-page of history he occupies'.

GATACRE, LIEUTENANT-GENERAL SIR W. – 'BACKACHER'

IN EVERY PLACE of work there are perfectionists. In the late Victorian army no general drilled his soldiers quite so hard, or lectured his officers and men so monotonously, or worked longer hours, or toiled to be a modern super-man quite like William Forbes Gatacre. He was, to all who served under him, always the 'Backacher'.

He was born on 3 December 1843. The son of a Shropshire squire, he entered Sandhurst in 1860 and was duly gazetted an ensign in the 77th Foot in December 1861. Twelve years later Captain Gatacre was admitted to the Staff College and passed out with honours in 1875. Fellow officers recalled him as polite, but noted that he made no close friendships. He nevertheless found time to marry, father several sons and even appear on stage in a production of *Iolanthe*, while stationed at Rangoon. In 1884, after almost a quarter-century of service, Gatacre succeeded to the command of the 2nd Battalion, Middlesex Regiment (as the old 77th were now called).

In November 1885 Gatacre became DQMG of the Indian Army and three years later – after almost thirty years of army service – he finally got to serve on a campaign as chief staff officer to **McQueen** in the 1888 Black Mountain expedition. During his time on the frontier an aide noted, 'Nothing seemed to tire Gatacre, who was the hardest man I ever met. He neither drank, nor smoked, and ate very little.' With the rank of brigadier Gatacre next saw action in the Burmese jungle in 1889–90 during the 'pacification' of the country.

Five years later he was given command of a brigade in the Chitral relief expedition, but the real fighting was already over before Gatacre, 'in his usual tearing hurry', led his 3rd Brigade into the Jandol Valley in pursuit of the rebel chieftain, Umra Khan. Here he got into a furious row with

Bindon **Blood**, who asked him to lead a frontal attack on a fort while he led the cavalry in a sweep to cut off the enemy's retreat. Gatacre fussily refused to co-operate since he was senior in rank (and during this spat Umra Khan slipped away). The historian John Harris described Gatacre, now in his fifties, as a 'lean, long-faced buzz-saw of a man, nagging, fretting, interfering, adjusting, always active and always trying to do everything himself, on his feet at dawn and never stopping until he went to bed.'

In 1898 Major-General Gatacre was given command of the British Infantry Division sent to help in the reconquest of the Sudan under Herbert **Kitchener**. One subaltern wrote home that he was 'a gasbag ... who talked drivel ... and would make a splendid corporal ... the general opinion is that he ought to be locked up.' Kitchener, another uncompromising man with few friends, thought him 'just the right man for the job'. Perhaps the best assessment of Gatacre came from one of his brigadiers, Neville **Lyttelton**, who summed him up as 'brave as a lion, and I never came across such restless and untiring energy. No day was too hot for him, no hours too long, no work too hard. But he was very jealous of authority, he wanted to do everything himself, and was very fond of the sound of his own voice'. Gatacre's greatest moment of glory came at the Battle of the Atbara, when he marched on foot leading his men, sword drawn beneath the Union Jack held aloft by his orderly (who was later killed). When a dervish rushed directly at him, an unfazed Gatacre simply shouted to a soldier, 'Give him the bayonet, lad' and strode on, firing his pistol.

War with the Boer republics in 1899 saw Gatacre given command of the 3rd Division of the SAFF. Onboard ship he was seen pounding out memos on a typewriter and Lord **Methuen** joked that Gatacre seemed to think he would be fighting a second Peninsular War. His search for perfectionism fell apart at Stormberg, the first of three disastrous battles for the British in what became known as 'Black Week'; one of his needless marches led into a Boer trap and the capture of 561 men. Six days after a further disaster at Reddersburg on 4 April 1900, Lord **Roberts** relieved him of his command. When a deeply humiliated Gatacre asked for some explanation, Roberts reply commended the 'Backacher's' honour, courage, energy and zeal, but made it plain that he had 'showed a want of care, judgment and even of ordinary military precautions ...'

His career in tatters, Gatacre left the army in 1903. Job prospects seemed limited. While exploring rubber concessions in Abyssinia in 1906, he caught a fever and died. His last command had been the East of England. It is said that on hearing the news of his death the troops at Colchester barracks hung a banner to the memory of a ramrod general who had been loathed by many and loved by a few. It read: 'Major General Sir William Forbes Gatacre – one of the best'.

GERARD, LIEUTENANT-GENERAL SIR M. – EXPERT CAVALRYMAN

MONTAGU GERARD WAS a well-liked soldier, a British Army gunner in his early days who became an expert on horses and the commander of an elite Indian Army cavalry regiment. His memoirs reveal him to have had a robust sense of humour and (by modern-day standards) an amazing aptitude for killing vast amounts of wild animals. He was also typically self-deprecating about his own remarkable bravery in battle.

He was born in 1842, educated at Stonyhurst and the Royal Military Academy, Woolwich, and commissioned a lieutenant in the Royal Artillery in 1864. Having served in India, he got an early taste of campaigning in 1867 when he was sent to Abyssinia as a transport office and got mentioned in despatches. Prospects of promotion back in India seemed limited in the artillery, so he applied to the Staff Corps and then in 1870 accepted a vacancy in the Central India Horse, a very popular cavalry regiment.

Promoted to captain, Gerard served as brigade major with several brigades during the Second Afghan War seeing plenty of action. On one occasion his horse was shot from under him. His commanding officer reported that in a charge on 30 March 1879, 'Monty', as he was known, 'rendered me the utmost assistance, cutting down a man on my right … We had by this time continued the pursuit to the foot of a small range of hills where Captain Gerard did good work, he and Captain Gwatkin cutting down several men, the former accounting for five or six himself'. Gerard accompanied **Roberts** on his famous Kabul to Kandahar march but wrote later that, '[t]hough universally made so much of, I do not think that, all things considered, it was as risky as Roberts' first advance upon Kabul or as Sir Donald **Stewart**'s march over the same ground three months previously'. He also saw action at the Battle of Kandahar.

By luck Monty got himself onto the staff of Sir Archibald **Alison** ahead of the main expedition and thus was one of the first British officers to land in Egypt in 1882. He fought in the action at Kafr-Dawar and prevented some bluejackets from accidentally firing a cannon at the Royal Marines. Later Gerard was made Quartermaster-General of the Cavalry Division under

Drury-Lowe. He thought the first Battle of Kassassin was 'a curiously mixed-up sort of business', blaming General **Graham**'s 'lack of proper outposts'. He served at Tel-el-Kebir and the cavalry dash to Cairo and was present when Arabi Pasha surrendered. The Egyptian general's demeanour impressed Monty, who described him as 'a well-bred gentleman'.

As he had a knowledge of Russian, Sir Montagu served on several diplomatic assignments in Central Asia and Russia. He was the natural choice to take care of the young Nicholas Alexandrovich (later Tsar Nicholas II) when he visited India. In 1893–95 Gerard served as commandant of the Central India Horse where, despite his easy-going manner, he tightened up the uniform regulations. During the South African War he was sent to Eastern Europe to buy horses. In 1904, on the outbreak of the Russo-Japanese War he was asked to be British attaché at General Kuropatkin's headquarters. The rigours of the campaign were too much for his failing health. He died of pneumonia in Siberia, still 'in the saddle' serving his country, on 26 July 1905.

GILBERT, MAJOR-GENERAL SIR W. – EAST INDIA COMPANY WARRIOR

ONE OF THE best examples of the kind of tough old soldier who spent his life campaigning in India might be Walter Raleigh Gilbert. Field-Marshal **Haines** called him a 'splendid specimen of his class'.

He was born at Bodmin in 1785, the son of a parson, a distant relative of his namesake Elizabethan seadog. In 1800 he joined the 15th BNI as an ensign and by 1810 was a captain. During Lord Lake's campaigns he fought at Delhi, Laswaree, the storming of Agra and the four unsuccessful attacks on Bhurtpore, where he came to the notice of the C-in-C. Three decades of peacetime soldiering followed as Gilbert rose steadily in the Indian Army, commanding the 35th BNI, the 1st Bengal European Fusiliers and finally attaining major-general rank.

Under **Gough** he commanded a division in both Anglo-Sikh Wars and was usually to be found in the thick of the action. On the second day of Ferozeshah he joined in a cavalry charge and at Sobraon he was wounded leading his men up to the Sikh ramparts. In their history of the Sikh Wars, the divisional commanders Gough and Innes noted that **Campbell**'s brigades at the calamitous Battle of Chillianwallah 'proved most disastrous', but 'on the other hand, Gilbert, with difficulties to face of precisely the same kind, manipulated his division with marked success'. Gilbert spoiled his generalship in the final battle at Gujerat when he ordered Penny's brigade to storm the small mud brick village of Burra Kalra. Unbeknown to the troops, the place was filled with Sikh marksmen. In just a few short minutes Gilbert lost 321 killed and wounded. 'He thought that the village seemed to be unoccupied,' wrote historian George Bruce, 'assumed this to be a fact, failed to ask the heavy artillery to knock it down and sent his best brigade pell-mell to be killed and maimed.' After this battle, Gilbert made up for this failure by personally leading 12,000 men in pursuit of the Sikhs' Afghan allies, chasing them all the way to Peshawar. He accepted the formal surrender of the Khalsa army at Rawalpindi, his men forming a gigantic square through which the tearful Sikh soldiers had to pass before laying down their arms – some 20,000 muskets and forty-one heavy guns.

Gilbert was given a KCB in 1846 and a GCB in 1849. He returned to Britain where he was noted, as in India, as a keen rider, huntsman and lover of the turf. He died at a Bond Street hotel in May 1853. His name is all but forgotten, except perhaps at Bodmin, where a 144ft obelisk on the moor above the town commemorates one of its greatest sons.

GLYN, LIEUTENANT-GENERAL SIR R. – 'LITTLE GLYN'

STANDING JUST 5FT 2in in his socks, Lieutenant-Colonel Richard Thomas Glyn commanded the 1st Battalion, 24th Foot, in the Zulu War. The loss of his officers and men at Isandlwana were shocks from which he never fully recovered. He unwittingly almost ended up the scapegoat for the disaster until **Chelmsford** and John North **Crealock** set their sights on a conveniently dead officer. It must be accepted, however, that although Glyn saw his role as a column commander usurped, and his warnings ignored, he seems to have been a rather dull soldier. Perhaps Crealock spoke the truth for once in one of his spiteful gossips when he called him 'purely a regimental officer with no idea beyond it'. He was born at Meerut, India, on 23 December 1831, the son of a 'John Company' officer. His father purchased him a commission in the 82nd Foot in 1850 and five years later this short, stocky but tough young man sailed with his regiment for the Crimea, landing just six days before the fall of Sebastopol. He married, but in 1857 his regiment went off to war again, this time in India. Promoted to captain, Glyn fought at Windham's defence of Cawnpore and Campbell's final assault on Lucknow.

Buying his way up the promotions ladder he acquired the lieutenant-colonelcy of the 24th's 1st Battalion in 1867. Eight years later he embarked with his officers, men, wife and four daughters for South Africa. By this time he was in many respects an archetypal Victorian colonel who would, no doubt, have delighted the Duke of Cambridge. Not for him the Staff College or modern nonsense – he remained an old-style regimental officer who adored fox hunting (having to make do with jackals at the Cape) and kept his own pack of hounds. One of his officers called him 'as good a little man as ever breathed', noting Glyn's hunting obsession amounted to 'monomania'. With a waxed moustache and thinning hair plastered over his balding pate, 'Little Glyn', as Crealock cruelly called him, seems to have been well liked by his subalterns, an unflappable, not especially imaginative officer similar to a score of other colonels of other regiments.

He led the 1/24th to the diamond fields to extinguish a smouldering rebellion in 1876. Then, with the local rank of brigadier, he orchestrated some sweeps against the Xhosa in the Ninth Frontier War. On 13 January 1878 he attacked about 1,000 warriors near the Nyumaga River, cleverly luring the enemy onto the guns of the 24th using his auxiliaries as decoys. This fight showed that, given a chance, Glyn was not a bad strategist and the colonial authorities praised him as 'an excellent, sensible Commander'. He was rewarded with a CB.

When the Zulu War began, he led No. 3 column ostensibly as its commander. His chief staff officer, Cornelius Clery, was unimpressed with Glyn, dismissing him as 'a guileless, unsuspicious man, very upright and scrupulously truthful, yet a slow, not to say lethargic temperament'. Lord Chelmsford's usurpation of many of Glyn's functions very quickly left him 'disinterested and withdrawn'. Reaching Isandlwana an unhappy Glyn suggested that the camp needed to be laagered for safety. 'It is not worthwhile,' replied the general. 'It will take too much time, and besides, the wagons are most of them going back at once to Rorke's Drift.' Detecting Glyn was in poor spirits, one officer commented a short time later that the camp looked 'very pretty though rather extended'. Glyn gave him a hard look, shook his head and said, 'Very.' On the morning of the battle he and his staff rode out of the camp with Chelmsford.

After Isandlwana the little colonel found it hard to come to terms with so many deaths. He wept profusely when the Queen's Colour of the 1/24th, lost in the battle but later recovered, was handed back to him. At the court of enquiry a grim Glyn said very little. 'It is well known to everybody around that Colonel Glyn had as little to do with the disaster as you in London had,' wrote Clery, because under Chelmsford 'he gets anything but encouragement to interest himself much in'.

In 1898, now a lieutenant-general, Glyn was honoured with the colonelcy of his old regiment, now called the South Wales Borderers. In retirement he became 'a sad and stooped little man'. He saw the regiment off to South Africa again, this time to fight the Boers, but died a short time later, on 21 November 1900.

GORDON, MAJOR-GENERAL C. – HERO, MARTYR AND MISFIT

FROM A TWENTY-FIRST-CENTURY viewpoint it is hard to make sense of General Gordon – the supreme Victorian hero. His martyr's death at Khartoum after an epic siege – and here it is worth noting that his fame rests, for once, on having failed, not succeeded – turned him into the perfect Christian warrior of the age.

It is rather comforting to know that those who met him had mixed opinions. Garnet **Wolseley** thought him 'the most remarkable man I ever knew'; Egyptian proconsul Evelyn Baring called him 'a curious character'; the British press labelled him 'the Great Warrior Saint' and 'the Galahad who rode through life in the strength of God'. Disraeli bluntly called him 'a lunatic'; a friend, Wilfred Scawen Blunt, confessed that he was 'less than fully sane'; an officer serving under him exclaimed that he was 'a fearful egotist' and Redvers **Buller** angrily complained that 'Gordon is not worth the camels' required to rescue him. After his death the waspish Lytton Strachey implied he was a drunkard, and other writers have hinted he was a homosexual with paedophilic tendencies. More recently he has been labelled a 'neurotic' who was probably suffering from Asperger's Syndrome.

Charles George Gordon was born on 28 January 1833 at Woolwich, one of six children to Major Henry Gordon, who worked at the arsenal, and his fundamentalist Christian wife. Quite early on, 'Charley', as the family called the tall boy with piercing blue eyes, rejected church-going in favour of his own kind of bible studies. His schooling was unremarkable and his family life happy. His father entered him for the Royal Military Academy, but he was almost thrown out for fighting and what today would be termed bullying. 'While he is in the Academy I feel like I am sitting on a powder barrel', lamented Henry Gordon.

Things improved; 'Charley' was sent to the Siege of Sebastopol as a sapper in 1855 and at the close of the Russian War he blew up its fortifications and docks. He volunteered for the Chinese expedition and, though he later much regretted it, was ordered to assist in the demolition of the

Emperor's Summer Palace in 1860, perhaps the greatest act of vandalism in British imperial history.

Gordon's march to glory was about to begin; in 1863, as a brevet-major, he was given command of a 2,100-strong multinational force soon called 'the Ever-Victorious Army'. Its aim was to smash the Taipings, a vast band of rebels pledging social reform and led by an insane young man who thought himself the brother of Jesus. Wearing a mandarin's costume, carrying only a rattan cane, and refusing cash rewards, Gordon was raised to a Chinese field-marshal's rank as he won victory after victory. The war was one of the most violent of the nineteenth century before Hung Hsiu-Ch'uan, the 'Heavenly King', committed suicide.

The British press, fascinated by this bloody war in far-off China, called him 'Chinese Gordon'. Back home, he was known for his evangelical work at Gravesend where, in 1867, he opened his own school for waifs and paupers. For the next five years he devoted around thirty hours each week to teaching the children. 'How far better to be allowed to be kind to a little Scrub than to govern the greatest kingdoms', he wrote. The War Office did not know what to make of him or his international fame. His requests for service in Abyssinia in 1867 and Ashanti in 1873 went unanswered. Frustrated, resentful, ever restless, Gordon accepted an offer from the Khedive of Egypt to govern his equatorial province. Over the next three years Gordon's efforts to limit the slave trade met with rebuffs, but he did extend Egyptian control of the Nile to within 50 miles of Lake Victoria and increase the ivory trade to pay local administration costs.

After a short spell back in Britain in 1876, Gordon returned to Egypt in 1877 as Governor-General of the Sudan. His tasks included fighting slavers, improving the sanitation of Khartoum, reforming its corrupt local government, guarding the border with Abyssinia while that country's King was 'rapidly going mad', as Gordon wrote. He left in 1880 'not loved, but respected by many as an honest man and resented by many others as an infidel,' says historian Gerald Herman, 'a tool of Egyptian imperialism, or as a destroyer of what had by then become traditional ways of life.'

Back in Britain, 'Charley' was promoted to major-general in 1882 and cold-shouldered by the War Office as his neurotic traits led him to resign for the nineteenth time. As things began to turn ugly in the Sudan and spiral out of control following the rise of Mohammed Ahmed, who called himself 'the *Mahdi*' (the 'Expected One') and preached a bloody *jihad* against the 'Turks' (Ottoman Egyptians), Gordon was planning to go to the Belgian Congo. When an Egyptian army of 10,000 men led by the Indian Army officer Colonel

William Hicks was massacred in the Sudan, HM Government suggested Gordon to subdue the tribes and extricate the Egyptian garrisons, but Baring in Cairo thought it unwise to send a Christian to put down a Moslem revolt. The issue was decided in the press; crusading journalist W.T. Stead of the influential *Pall Mall Gazette* ran the headline 'Chinese Gordon for the Sudan'. The Queen urged the same and Baring reluctantly agreed, but commented drily that he doubted if he could control a man 'who habitually consults the Prophet Isaiah when he is in difficulties'. The night Gordon left London one member of the Cabinet noted: 'He did not seem at all anxious to retain the Sudan; and agreed heartily to accept the policy of withdrawal.' At first Gordon did as he was told; by 11 March 1884 he had evacuated to safety 2,140 Egyptians. His attitude soon changed, and he wrote: 'The Mahdi must be smashed up!' In March he also ominously warned Baring that he would not leave ahead of other refugees – 'How could I look the world in the face if I abandoned them and fled?' Gordon tried to bribe the Mahdi with a beautiful robe. It was returned with a charming letter and the gift of a simple patched shirt, the garb of his warriors. Each man realised that the other was equally dogmatic and implacable. By 20 March some 20,000 warriors had surrounded Khartoum.

Gordon masterfully prepared the city for its siege: he extended its ditch and ramparts, added barbed-wire entanglements, laid out broken glass, buried land mines and drilled the 8,665 defenders who had to man its 15-mile perimeter. To help morale he printed his own bank notes and signed them. In Whitehall and Cairo the politicians and diplomats dithered about sending help and it was not until 12 May that they agreed to act. Gordon sent a letter to Prime Minister Gladstone in which he made clear 'That we will defend ourselves to the last, that I will not leave Khartoum.' Gordon, aware that a relief expedition under his old friend, Garnet Wolseley, was trying to reach him, also knew his position was daily more precarious. On 14 December he closed his journal and sent it down the Nile with the words, 'I have done my best for the honour of my country.' Before daybreak on 26 January (a tiny relief force just hours away) Khartoum was overrun by the Mahdists and Gordon killed (accounts vary).

Today it hardly matters what Gordon was – because he was most of the labels thrown at him and more. He *was* remarkable. He *was* the right man in an age and for a country that needed a Christian warrior to revere. He probably thought he could handle the Mahdi and he overplayed his hand diplomatically speaking. In military terms, he used all his skill as a royal engineer to conduct a strong defence of Khartoum, held out as long as he could, fought to the last and died a soldier's death.

GOUGH, GENERAL SIR C. & GOUGH, GENERAL SIR H. – VC BROTHERS

FEW MILITARY FAMILIES can equal the record of the Goughs. They have produced some remarkable generals, among them the Victoria Cross brothers – Charles and Hugh, nephews of the famous field-marshal.

Elder brother Charles was born in Chittagong on 28 January 1832 and learned Bengali alongside English. Hugh came along a year later. Both brothers were sent to England for their schooling and returned to become East India Company officers. Charles arrived in time to fight with the 8th Bengal Cavalry in the Second Anglo-Sikh War and took part in the actions at Ramnugar, Chillianwallah and Gujerat. By the age of 25 he was a major in the 5th Bengal European Cavalry.

When the great rebellion broke out in 1857 both brothers were destined to become famous as cavalry commanders. Hugh was serving with the 3rd Bengal Light Cavalry at Meerut on that fateful evening, Sunday, 10 May, when the men of his own and other regiments mutinied and marched towards Delhi. He escaped to the European lines with pistol shots and shouts of '*Maro, maro!*' ('Kill him, kill him!') ringing in his ears.

Charles soon found himself serving with the Guides Cavalry and subsequently Hodson's Irregular Horse, where Hugh joined him and became the regiment's adjutant. The Victoria Cross was awarded to Charles for various acts of gallantry between 15 August 1857 and 23 February 1858. These included saving his brother who was wounded, then killing two of the enemy; leading a troop of the Guides in a charge that saw him fighting hand-to-hand combats; killing a leading rebel with his sword in one hand while shooting two of the enemy at the same time with a revolver in the other, and saving the life of an officer by galloping up and killing his opponent.

Hugh was awarded his VC for actions on the 12 November 1857 and 25 February 1858. In the former he led a charge of Hodson's Horse against a vastly superior body of cavalry, while his mount was wounded in two places and his turban sluiced by sword cuts as he fought off three *sepoys*. In an outstanding display of courage at Lucknow, he led another charge against rebel guns, fought a whole series of sword combats, and was shot through his helmet and scabbard until a bullet finally killed his horse and wounded him in the leg.

After the Great Mutiny, both brothers saw action in two relatively bloodless campaigns – Charles in Bhutan and Hugh in Abyssinia. Things were to change with the Second Afghan War 1878–80. Charles commanded the cavalry brigade, 1st Division, Peshawar Valley Field Force during the first phase of the campaign and various brigades during the second half of the war. His cavalry action at Futtehabad on 2 April 1879 was praised by one contemporary historian as 'the most successful engagement of the war'. On 21 December, in the depths of a freezing winter and harassed by a large but unknown number of enemy, he set out on a march from Jagdalak to relieve **Roberts**'s army boxed up at Kabul. Charles Gough, as historian Brian Robson wrote, 'had shown great courage and initiative in undertaking the march', but Roberts and his chief of staff, **Macgregor**, showed little sympathy for his difficulties. Afterwards Roberts refused to use Charles Gough on his famous march to Kandahar. Brother Hugh, also a brigadier, commanded the cavalry of the Kurram Field Force and is said to have been the first to reach the crest of the Peiwar Kotal ridge during the battle. He was wounded in the fighting around Kabul in December 1879, but recovered to command the cavalry in the march to Kandahar and the battle there on 1 September 1880.

Both brothers refused to denigrate Roberts and Macgregor publicly, but within the family it was an open secret that they loathed them. Macgregor once called Charles 'a most useless fellow' and referred to Hugh as 'an ass'. Charles never forgave Roberts for his attitude during the relief march and felt his work had been sidelined. Two decades later, while serving on the Tirah campaign, one of his sons, Hubert Gough, would write to his father that 'I see many are now blaming Roberts entirely for it all, which is true, and I hope that man may yet be shown up in his true colours.' Another son, Johnnie, would also win the VC in Somaliland and both boys became celebrated generals.

After the Second Afghan War, both Goughs held peacetime commands and received various honours. Hugh, a Keeper of the Crown Jewels, passed away in 1909. Charles retired to Ireland and co-authored a history of the Sikh Wars before dying at his country seat near Clonmel in 1912.

GOUGH, FIELD-MARSHAL LORD H. – 'AT THEM WITH THE BAYONET'

IT WAS SAID that Lord Gough commanded in almost as many actions as the Duke of Wellington. Among early Victorian generals he stands supreme – commanding operations in the First China War, the Gwalior War and both wars against the Sikhs. With his Irish brogue, his shock of wavy silver hair and wearing his famous white coat, he was a character on the field of battle. A concern for his troops and total lack of fear under fire made him popular among the ranks. Higher up the chain of command there were frequent grumblings as Gough got older; a tendency to take risks, coupled with his impetuosity and a fondness for frontal assaults at the point of the bayonet, led to the deaths of many a good soldier.

He was born into an Irish military family on 3 November 1779 and destined from birth for an army career. Indeed, at 15, he was adjutant of the 119th Foot! He exchanged into the 78th Highlanders and first saw action with them when his regiment arrived at Cape Town and successfully fought the Dutch for the city. Not long after, he joined the 87th Foot, an Irish regiment, and sailed for three years of warfare in the West Indies. By 1809 he had married, purchased a majority and landed in Portugal, only to have a cannon ball fracture his ribs at Talavera. Two years later, on 5 March 1811, he led his men with reckless bravado at Barossa in capturing the brass eagle of the French 8th Regiment. The 87th were awarded the title of the Prince of Wales Own Irish Regiment and Gough, in recognition of his bravery, was the first officer ever to gain a brevet lieutenant-colonelcy for conduct under fire. At Tarifa later that year, Gough told his men to strike up 'Garry Owen' and repel an attack with the words 'Wherever there is an opportunity the bayonet must be used.' Love of a bayonet charge became his lifelong maxim. By 1813, when he was seriously wounded in the hip at Nivelle, he had commanded a battalion in the peninsula longer than any other officer.

Twenty-eight years of peacetime soldiering followed. Gough was serving as a major-general commanding the Mysore Division of the Madras Army when he was given command of the British Expeditionary Force to China in 1841. Over the next eight years he would fight in four wars and command in sixteen battles. In China a fuming Gough argued for a strong military policy. His hands were often tied by diplomats, but he saw the Bogue Forts captured, Canton capitulate, Chinkiang stormed and Nanking, second city of the Chinese Empire, surrender before the assault of his troops. He was thanked by Parliament, awarded a baronetcy and, on 1 August 1843, made C-in-C, India.

Within a few months a war with the Maratha state of Gwalior led to Gough commanding in another battle, at Maharajpore on 29 December 1843. His army of 6,500 blundered into the 14,200-strong enemy, 'well led and truly gallant', as Gough confessed, but victory was won after an artillery duel at the point of the bayonet. The British lost 790 killed and wounded, including three generals. Luckily for Gough, a second battle at Punniar was fought the same day under Sir John Grey (losses of 217 officers and men) and this double victory ended a war that had lasted less than forty-eight hours, one of the shortest in British history. The Governor-General, Lord Ellenborough, had witnessed the fighting at Maharajpore and soon expressed 'a want of confidence in Sir Hugh Gough who ... does not appear to possess the grasp of mind or the prudence which is essential to the successful conduct of military operations'. Ellenborough added: 'He would do admirably, I have no doubt, at the head of an advanced guard.'

War with the Sikh kingdom of the Punjab broke out in 1845 and a new Governor-General, Lord Hardinge, who had also served under Wellington, agreed militarily to be Gough's second-in-command, though he was his political superior. This situation was delicate: Hardinge described Gough as 'peevish and jealous', though he also admitted him to be 'amiable, kind-hearted & honourably brave ... he does his best and never spares himself.'

Gough was never one for complicated tactics; at Mudki on 18 December his plan was 'to silence the enemy's guns, outflank with his cavalry and then rout them with a bayonet charge'. The battle extended into the night, some of the 872 British losses were the result of friendly fire and the Sikh cavalry almost outflanked their opponents, but Gough could claim the enemy were 'driven from position to position with great slaughter ... our infantry using that never-failing weapon, the bayonet'. The next battle at Ferozeshah ran into a second day and was a costly victory (694 officers and men killed, 1,721 wounded). In all, Gough lost one man in eight. An alarmed Hardinge wrote to the prime minister that Gough had 'no capacity for order and adminis-tration' and 'We have been in great peril, and are likely hereafter to be in greater peril if these very extensive operations are to be conducted by the commander-in-chief ...' No one doubted Gough's courage: on the second day at Ferozeshah he had ridden out in his white coat to draw the Sikh fire on him and away from his soldiers, an act that showed Gough's 'generosity of spirit and irresponsibility', as one historian has declared.

During the final showdown at Sobraon on 10 February 1846 Hardinge advocated a withdrawal unless victory could be guaranteed. Gough snapped back, 'What! Withdraw the troops after the action has commenced and when I feel confident of success? Indeed I will not!' Gough's victory cost him one man in seven, while the Sikhs lost over 12,000 dead and wounded. On 8 March, the Sikh War was brought to an end by treaty at Lahore.

The following year, before leaving India, Hardinge had another spat with Gough over some gossip. He privately called Sir Hugh 'a very shabby fellow' who 'has fallen greatly in my estimation'. Back home, Gough was denounced as 'a reckless savage, devoid of stratagem and military knowledge.' He was hurt and wrote: 'Let the world carp ... Posterity will be my judge.' A grateful Queen, however, gave him a peerage and his pension was doubled to £4,000 a year.

Three months after landing in India the new Governor-General, Lord Dalhousie, committed his country to a second war with the Sikhs. He grandly announced: 'I have drawn the sword and thrown away the scabbard.' Gough, who had been fighting economies in army size and other deficiencies, drily commented: 'Lord Dalhousie is a young man, his blood is very hot, and he speaks of walking over everything. But to walk we must eat.' At Ramnugar on 22 November 1848, Gough fought a 'badly thought-out action'. Two gallant officers, Lt-Colonel William Havelock (brother of Henry), commanding the 14th Light Dragoons, and Brigadier Charles Cureton were killed, the latter reportedly exclaiming before he died, 'My God, this isn't the way to use cavalry!' Critics blamed Gough's Irish temper and impetuosity for the debacle, though his biographer, writing more than half a century later, strongly defended him against these charges.

Then came Chillianwallah with its butcher's bill of 2,357 British and Indian casualties, about one in five of Gough's army. Dalhousie fumed that the C-in-C was the cause of 'the very heavy loss we have unnecessarily suffered and the incompleteness of our success'. Gough argued that he had been forced into action when the Sikh gunners, hidden in dense jungle, opened a barrage on his camp. Several officers, including the Governor-General's Agent, Sir Henry Lawrence, advised against an attack. Gough told Lawrence 'to be silent' and attacked anyway. In the jungle 'each regiment fought a battle for itself'. Dalhousie wrote how 'The Cavalry ... disgraced the name and the colours they carry' by fleeing before the Sikhs 'and never stopped till they were brought up *by the Chaplain* ... who, pistol in hand, declared he would shoot at the first man who passed him!' Chillianwallah might be claimed 'a victory' in public but in reality, 'in any other hands than those of Lord Gough, five times the success would have been obtained at one fifth loss ... Every man in the army ... has totally lost confidence in their leader ...'

Lord Gough offered his resignation, but before Sir Charles **Napier** arrived to supersede him, he met the Sikhs at Gujerat, this time fighting a cautious battle for which he was rewarded with a stunning victory that secured the Punjab for the British Raj. Gough noted that he had won a victory 'not only over my Enemies but over my Country!' Dalhousie felt that he had been instrumental in rethinking Gough's tactics, but was happy to see him leave India a victor. The old soldier landed in England feeling sore at the criticisms levelled at him. Gradually these faded and were forgotten. Over the next nineteen years of his life he became a field-marshal, colonel-in-chief of the 60th Rifles and a Privy Councillor and received many other honours.

Ordinary private soldiers always liked Gough, who died on 2 March 1869 in his ninetieth year. To superiors like Dalhousie, Peel and Hardinge he had always been courteous but exasperating, his tactics rudimentary and risky. Tommies warmed to his obstinate courage and refusal ever to admit defeat. They appreciated how proud he always was of them. True, he had a fondness for cold steel and might at any moment order a bayonet charge, but then, as one sergeant remarked, such things were only natural if an enemy 'got the old man's Irish out'.

GRAHAM, LIEUTENANT-GENERAL SIR G. – CRIMEAN VC AND DESERT GENERAL

GARNET **WOLSELEY** ONCE said of his great friend Gerald Graham that he was 'a man with the heart of a lion and the modesty of a young girl.' Six foot four inches tall, handsome, strongly built, with steel blue eyes and a smart grey-brown moustache, this giant was tactically a weak general, but 'It was an age when qualities of leadership and bravery mattered most and no one ever denied that Graham had these in spades.'

He was born in London on 27 June 1831, a doctor's son, and after attending Woolwich was commissioned into the Royal Engineers in 1850. Sent to the Crimea in 1854, he saw action at the Alma, at Inkerman and in the trenches before Sebastopol. Here on 18 June 1855 he led a ladder party under a storm of musketry and grapeshot. He also carried a wounded officer to safety, despite being a conspicuous target on account of his height, before re-joining the ladder party by walking calmly across the battlefield to the praise of observers. Later that night he went out again, leading a naval brigade 'with remarkable steadiness and gallantry'. Wolseley remarked that Graham was so cool under fire that when touring trenches he would deliberately, lazily and crazily take a short cut right in front of the Russian sharpshooters, and 'it did not occur to him that there was anything unusual in these proceedings'. On the night of 8 July, on duty in the trenches with Wolseley, Graham was severely wounded when splinters from a roundshot struck him in the face. For his bravery at the Redan he was awarded the Victoria Cross.

In the attack on the Taku Forts in the Second China War he was once more badly wounded. The sappers assisting the Royal Marines moved with ladders and bridges as whizzing gingal-balls zipped around them. Gerald explains what happened next:

'Now come on my lads.' Again the best men rise and lift (Pritchard and I and three Marine officers all lay hold). We struggle on a few yards. The shot rattle among the pontoons; men fall away shot, skulking or slipping in the mud ... About this time I got shot in my leg... the ball burying itself in the flesh without cutting the thick serge trousers!

Wolseley, who met his old chum amid the din, put his hand on Graham's thigh 'to get my ear nearer to him'. Without wincing and in an ordinary tone the latter said, 'Don't put your hand there, for I have just had a bullet,' as blood seeped down his leg.

In 1869 Graham was promoted to colonel and from 1877 was on War Office duties until his promotion to major-general in 1881. The following year he joined his old comrade, Wolseley, to command the 2nd Brigade, 1st Division, of Sir Garnet's Egyptian Expeditionary Force. Graham soon came under a different kind of fire – that of ink and print – for his 'loose orders to **Drury-Lowe**, the poor disposition of his picquets and lack of artillery' at the first Battle of Kassassin on 28 August 1882. One of his sternest critics, war correspondent Melton Prior, wrote later: 'had it not been for Drury-Lowe's cavalry charge that small handful of men under General Graham was likely to have met with a similar fate to that which befell our men at Isandlwana.' Montagu **Gerard** was just one of many who accused him of 'having absolutely no proper outposts'. To be fair, it was not Graham's fault that he had so few guns and little cavalry support but, as I have written in my history of the campaign, *A Tidy Little War*, his picquets were poorly organised, the camp had been caught napping and he issued sloppy orders. On 9 September he was caught with his pants down – literally – when the Egyptians marched through the night and mounted a surprise dawn attack. At one point in the morning battle three shells struck the ground a few yards from Graham. 'I think, general, we had better shove on a bit,' said an aide. 'No,' replied Sir Gerald, displaying his characteristic disregard for danger, 'I don't see why we should hurry.'

Graham led his brigade into the trenches at Tel-el-Kebir and stayed on in Egypt after the victory with the army of occupation. In 1884 he escorted his old pal Charles **Gordon** part of the way to Khartoum. A few days later he was sent to the Eastern Sudan after the disastrous Battle of El Teb.

This was to be his theatre of operations for the next twelve months. He fought notable battles at El Teb and Tamai (the latter infamous as the one in which dervishes broke into a British square). A final small battle took place at Hashin on 20 March 1885. Graham's opponent in all of these encounters was the wily Amir Osman Digna, who just happened to be the best exponent of desert irregular warfare that the British ever faced.

On his return to Britain, Graham's exploits were lauded by the jingoistic press but historians, as Brian Robson wrote, hold that he had 'no great talent as a general'. He failed to appreciate the importance of mobility in desert warfare or of maintaining a good staff; he was a poor field commander (especially at Tamai, where he ordered the front face of the square to charge), but also showed little skill 'in those areas where, as an Engineer officer, he might have been expected to be in his element'. Junior officers complained of his 'cold manner', while Lord Wolseley, always ready to throw blame when things went wrong, wrote: 'Graham was not equal to the task, he can fight a Brigade, but he can organize nothing. His plans were bad; they were badly designed and misfortune overtook all he attempted.'

It was Sir Gerald's last campaign. He retired in 1890 and died of a chill on 17 December 1899. He lies buried in the pretty churchyard of Bideford in Devon. Graham once told a friend that he had cherished 'every little bit of sunshine in his life'. It was true, as Wolseley wrote, that Sir Gerald was 'not exactly brilliant', but in the Victorian era his giant physique, cool courage and great good luck had served him well.

GRANT, GENERAL SIR J. – CAVALRY GENIUS AND COMMANDER IN CHINA

IN ONE OF his *Flashman* novels, the author George Macdonald Fraser paints an extremely accurate pen-picture of James Hope Grant, known to all his friends as simply 'Hope'. 'Flashy' says: 'Grant was the best fighting man in the world ... With sword, lance or any kind of side-arm he was the most deadly practitioner that ever breathed; as a leader of irregular cavalry he left Stuart, Hodson, Custer, and the rest at the gate; in the Mutiny he simply *fought* the whole damned time with a continuous fury that was the talk of an army containing the likes of Sam Browne, John Nicholson, and (dare I say it) my vaunted and unworthy self.' Hope Grant was born into a wealthy family in Perthshire on 22 July 1808 (his brother was the portrait painter Francis Grant), inheriting £10,000 (more than £1 million today) at the age of 11 when his father died. A continental education and the cost of soldiering in the elite 9th Lancers meant that twenty years later Captain Grant was poor and on the verge of resigning his commission. Things changed when Lord Saltoun, about to depart for the First China War, realised Grant was an expert on the violoncello (Grant always called it his 'Big Fiddle'). His Grace played the guitar and wanted someone for musical duets! Grant got his first taste of war in the storming of Chinkiang as Saltoun's brigade major, and declared the suffering of civilians, rape and pillage to be 'a dreadful curse'.

During the two Anglo-Sikh Wars he became noted for his courage and expert horsemanship. Men of all ranks respected his courage and simple honesty. His maxim was: 'Act according to your conscience and defy the consequences.' The day after the Battle of Sobraon he walked up to Lt-Colonel Campbell of his regiment and said, 'You know you were very drunk yesterday sir, when you lead us into action. I have come to tell you that if you do not at once undertake to leave the regiment, I shall now put you in arrest and report your conduct.' The colonel was furious. 'Will you indeed ... I now place you in arrest for bringing a false and insulting accu-sation against your commanding officer.' Lord **Gough** settled the dispute, allowing Campbell to retain his command, and Grant apologised – not for charging his superior with drunkenness, but for telling him he should leave the regiment. He had taken a huge risk, but demonstrated that he was a man of the highest integrity.

Promoted to brevet colonel in 1854, Grant commanded the cavalry, including the 9th Lancers, at the Siege of Delhi and the final relief of Lucknow. He was frequently in the thick of the action. Promoted to brigadier, he led mobile columns hunting down rebels until the end of Mutiny opera-tions. Despite his senior command, he sometimes joined in cavalry charges, lived most of his time in the saddle, and despite the arduous campaigning remained remarkably healthy. He also got a reputation for being as tough as he was brave; on one occasion he had twenty-five mutineers executed and on another he flogged fifty British soldiers for looting. The men, when they saw him riding up, used to say, 'Here comes the provost-marshal.'

Garnet **Wolseley** described Hope Grant about this time as 'a tall man of muscle and bone and no unnecessary flesh about him'. Often he got tongue-tied, which made some lesser men call him 'puzzle-headed'. Grant used to laughingly say, 'I am terribly bad-handed at explaining things.' 'His faith in an all-seeing God,' wrote Wolseley, 'who watched over soldiers, was as the very life within him. He tried to serve God with all his might, but detested priestly dogmas ... Death had no horror for him.'

Emerging from the Indian Mutiny as a rising star, Grant was given the local rank of lieutenant-general and sent to China in 1860 as commander of the British troops, though it was whispered he could not read a map. Lord Elgin, British plenipotentiary, remarked how everyone liked Hope's friendly smile, bewhiskered craggy features and Scottish burr. Noticing that a regiment of Sikhs, who had been at Lucknow, grinned when he rode by, Elgin asked Grant the reason. 'Oh, we were always good friends,' he replied. 'I used to visit them when they were sick, poor fellows.'

Grant was confirmed in his rank after the war and knighted. His later service included a spell at Madras as C-in-C and commanding at Aldershot during the Franco-Prussian War. He was raised to full general in 1872, and died on 7 March 1875. In his final moments he seemed to relive the Mutiny again. 'Three times in one day' he kept repeating, a reference to his three attempts with the cavalry to secure the British camp at Delhi on 19 June 1857. His last words are reported to have been 'That position is inaccessible.'

GRANT, FIELD-MARSHAL SIR P. – HOLDING INDIA

SOME YEARS AGO, wandering among the overgrown military monuments in the Brompton Cemetery, I stubbed my toe on the side of a large granite cross forgotten in the long, rank grass. It was the memorial stone to Patrick Grant.

By 8 June 1857 Delhi had been taken by the rebels and the British were hanging on by a thread on the ridge. That day news reached Madras that the C-in-C, India, General Anson, had died. Two days later the Governor-General Lord Canning asked Pat Grant to take command. Until Sir Colin **Campbell** arrived on 12 August, it was Grant who was *de facto* C-in-C. His role in suppressing the Mutiny in those critical two months has long been forgotten or ignored by most historians.

He was the son of a major in the 97th Foot, born in Inverness-shire. He joined the Bengal Army as an ensign in 1820, was made a captain in 1832 and from 1838 to 1854 served in the adjutant-general's department. He won his brevet majority under **Gough** at Maharajpore, where he managed to save a party of wives, including the governor-general's wife, who had been watching the battle on elephants until the beasts stampeded in terror. The incident also introduced Grant to Frances, one of the general's daughters, whom he married a year later. During the Sikh Wars he was an aide to his father-in-law, a very dangerous task as Gough liked to be near the action; at Mudki he was wounded and at Ramnugar he led the cavalry in a futile pursuit of the Sikh general.

After the Second Sikh War, and probably with his father-in-law's help, Grant was made an ADC to the Queen. In 1851 he served on the staff of Sir Charles **Napier** and Colin Campbell in their expedition against the Kohat Pass Afridis. Three years later he was promoted to major-general and then made C-in-C of the Madras Army.

By the time the 1857 rebellion broke out he had served almost forty years in India. He had strong views on the reasons for discontent within the Bengal Army. One of these was a feeling of 'dissatisfaction and distrust' caused by 'a want of officers in whom the sepoy could confide'. Grant also railed against the age of senior officers; at 48 he had been the youngest full colonel in the Bengal Army, but he knew he was a rarity. The affair of the greased cartridges was matter of discontent in the Indian Army for several months before the uprising. Grant examined some of the new cartridges in February 1857 and reported:

> The grease used … is tallow or lard; and there is no doubt whatever that applying the lips to such a substance is opposed to the religious prejudices of natives … I strongly recommend that immediate instructions should be issued prohibiting the issue to native corps of these greased cartridges.

Summoned to Calcutta, there to direct operations as interim C-in-C, India, Grant saw his countrymen besieged at Cawnpore, Lucknow and Agra, the mutineers threatening the camp at Delhi and on the verge of rebellion in scores of smaller outposts between Benares and the Punjab, telegraph links destroyed, not a single field gun available, no horses for artillery or cavalry; no field hospitals had been thought of, or ordnance ammunition prepared.

Quickly Grant championed Henry **Havelock** as the best general on the spot and hurriedly sent him up-country. He asked HM Government for 80,000 European troops to quell the insurrection. The country was scoured for animals – elephants, bullocks, horses – to aid the transport. On 27 June news reached Calcutta of the massacre at Cawnpore, and ten days later of the death of Lawrence at Lucknow. Grant begged to take command of the army before Delhi, but Canning refused him. The arrival of Colin Campbell came as a shock. Canning called Grant 'invaluable', but also wrote privately that 'as a leader in the field Sir Colin inspires me with more confidence'. Not everyone agreed; Lord Dalhousie, an admirer of Grant, wrote that if the government had confirmed him as C-in-C, India, they would have had 'the very best man living' and 'they would have had him on the spot'.

Pat Grant returned to England and was made a GCB and promoted lieutenant-general. Honours, including the governorship of Malta 1866–72 and field-marshal rank in 1874, followed. That year he became governor of the Royal Hospital, Chelsea, and was there twenty-one years later, when he died in his ninety-first year.

GREAVES, GENERAL SIR G. – POMPOSITY AND PRETTY GIRLS

ONE OF **WOLSELEY**'S favourites was Sir George Greaves. He served in various theatres of war and was chief of staff on the 1874 Ashanti expedition. A decade later he was less successful filling the same role at Suakin, where he seems to have been disliked by many. Sir George was also a notorious philanderer with an eye for the ladies.

He was born in 1831, attended Sandhurst and was commissioned without purchase in 1849 into the 70th Foot. Soon after he sailed with his regiment for India and was serving under Sir Sydney **Cotton** at Peshawar when the Indian Mutiny broke out. He saw no fighting as his regiment stayed in the Punjab to secure order throughout the crisis. Things changed in 1858 when he became DAAG with Cotton's expedition to Sitana.

In 1861 Greaves was sent to New Zealand and served with General Sir Duncan Cameron's army as DAQMG. The general sometimes led 'with his sword in one hand and his cap in the other', noted Greaves. He saw fighting as different Maori *pahs* were stormed. He arrived on the morning of 29 April 1864 in time to participate in the attack on the most famous encounter – Gate Pah. Greaves led one of the storming parties into the fort under 'pretty heavy fire', as he wrote later. Reporting back to the general, the pair watched as the Maoris re-took the *pah* just as darkness and a thunderstorm ended operations. Next day the place was found to be deserted.

In 1870 Greaves was made DAAG at Horse Guards where he met and impressed Wolseley. The pair became lifelong friends. Indeed, in his journals, diaries and memoirs, Wolseley was full of praise for Greaves, who did not suffer the brickbats of scorn thrown at other Ring members. During the Ashanti War a lucky Greaves was sent out as chief of staff (after the Duke of Cambridge had vetoed the original proposal) and Wolseley praised his 'most valuable assistance'. He was present at all the major battles. Greaves followed his chief to Cyprus in 1878 and stayed on as acting high commissioner for a few months until returning to India as adjutant-general for 1879–84. The Second Afghan War was in progress. Greaves, newly knighted, did not always see eye to eye with the C-in-C, India, Sir Frederick **Haines**, who opposed aspects of Lord Lytton's forward policy. The Viceroy called him 'able and energetic', but also told Frederick **Roberts** of the problems Greaves was making in his desire to be chief of staff: 'Hence it is the incessant endeavour of Genl. Greaves, to get the entire virtual control of military operations, little by little, through the C-in-C, into his own hands, and he chafes at any authority which stands in the way of this result.'

With the help of Wolseley, Greaves got himself appointed as chief of staff of the Suakin Field Force in 1885. He had wanted to command, but Wolseley plumped instead for Gerald **Graham**. An officer of the expedition – albeit a junior one, Ernest Gambier-Parry – described Sir George as a 'short, sharp-featured individual, with a pompous and rather disagreeable manner, a loud voice, a quick temper, and a sense of his own importance which defied everything. He was not popular and he seemed generally to be absorbed in that wonderful thought, 'I am'. A short answer was all you ever received from him, and one which often fell short of ordinary courtesy'. Greaves continued to rise in the service, returning to India where he was appointed C-in-C of the Bombay Army in 1890. He fully expected to be made C-in-C, India, in succession to Roberts. This post went instead to Sir George **White**, a junior to Greaves who resigned his command in 1893 'bitterly disappointed'. Written not long after he retired, Sir George's memoirs say little of campaigning but are replete with Society tittle-tattle. No book by a Victorian general is more full of references to 'beautiful', 'very handsome' and 'very pretty' women. This roving eye for the ladies was well known; after the death of his wife in 1880, Sir George took as his mistress Julia Venour, wife of a surgeon in the 15th Hussars. They married twenty-eight years later, but not before he had lived in a ménage-à-trois with a Mrs Rochfort-Boyd and her husband! Greaves died in 1922 at almost ninety, his autobiography published posthumously.

GRENFELL, FIELD-MARSHAL LORD F. – AFRICA MAN

SOME OFFICERS SEEMED to spend all their best years serving in the same part of the world. Francis Grenfell saw a lot of campaigning and commanded in some battles – all in Africa.

He was born in 1841, the son of a wealthy copper mining magnate, and in 1859 purchased a commission in the 60th Royal Rifles, reckoned to be one of the most expensive regiments in the British Army. In 1873, the last year that purchase was allowed, he bought a captaincy. His career stagnated and he was in the process of resigning from the army when an offer came to serve on the staff of General Cunynghame at the Cape. He accompanied his chief on the bloodless expedition to quell the Diamond Fields disturbances, and first saw real fighting at the Battle of Quintana, 7 February 1878. He could have taken overall command, being the senior officer present, but opted instead to command just the cavalry. He cleverly led his men out to fire at and taunt some 4,000 Galekas and Gaikas who, incensed, pursued the horsemen towards Quintana Fort. They were thus drawn into the range of British artillery and, 'after a plucky rush, broke and retired, followed by my men'.

At the start of the Zulu War, Major Grenfell found himself on the staff organising things at Pietermaritzburg. As soon as word reached him of the battle at Rorke's Drift, he galloped there with a small relief column on 23 January 1879. Later in the war he said goodbye to the Prince Imperial on the fateful day of his death. 'Take care of yourself, Prince, and don't get shot.' Louis Napoleon replied, pointing to Captain Carey, 'Oh no! He will take very good care that nothing happens to me.' After Carey rode in 'agitated', Grenfell was one of the party which found the Prince's body, 'stripped of everything except one sock … assegaied in seventeen places …' In the square at Ulundi, with the Zulus advancing, Grenfell thought, 'Had any panic occurred, we should have been lost, but the men stood well to their rifles.'

The Transvaal War of 1881 ended before Grenfell arrived to be DAQMG. He had better luck acting as AAG in Egypt in 1882, where he saw more action at Tel-el-Mahuta and Tel-el-Kebir. The day after the last battle, despite the intense heat, he insisted on taking a water cart to the thirsty Egyptian wounded, a most decent act. Grenfell stayed on in Egypt as second-in-command of the new Egyptian Army. In 1885 he was made its Sirdar in succession to Evelyn **Wood**. He controlled the Nile lines of communication during the Sudan War and in the final battle at Giniss on 30 November led a division under General **Stephenson**, though the latter credited him with the victory. Grenfell was in total command at the Battle of Toski on 3 August 1889, when his troops pounded and charged a Mahdist army sent to invade Egypt.

In 1892 Sir Francis ceased to be Sirdar, but he returned to Egypt to command the British army of occupation in 1897–98. The new Sirdar, Herbert **Kitchener**, had served under him at Toski and was extremely apprehensive that Grenfell had been sent to replace him. Grenfell was aware of this and treated the neurotic Kitchener with kid gloves. In 1908 Sir Francis retired from the army, having become a field-marshal that same year. He died on 27 January 1925 and is buried at Beaconsfield. To the end of his days he disliked several changes made by the Esher Committee in the 1900s, arguing that the abolition of the post of C-in-C was a mistake. In his memoirs, published shortly after his death, he also prophesied a second war with Germany.

GREATHED, MAJOR-GENERAL W. – BRAVE BENGAL SAPPER

THE GREATHEDS CAN be very confusing for anyone studying the Siege of Delhi, for there were three brothers there: Hervey was the popular Civil Commissioner attached to the forces; Edward, called a 'funk-stick' or a 'fool' by some, commanded the 8th Foot; and the youngest was William, a Bengal Engineer.

Born in 1826, William Wilberforce Harris Greathed entered the Military Academy of the East India Company at Addiscombe in February 1843, joining the Bengal Engineers twenty-two months later. Young and impulsive, Greathed saw action at the Siege of Mooltan in the Second Sikh War. When the city was finally stormed he was the first officer through the breach. He also served under Lord **Gough** in the final battle at Gujerat.

He was at Allahabad working as a consulting engineer to the East India Railway when the mutiny broke out. Summoned to Agra by the lieutenant-governor, he was asked to take despatches to Meerut through country swarming with rebels and thieves. He returned and did the journey again; on the first trip he was the first traveller to get through from 'down country' and no other European survived the route for four months after his second trip. A historian has described him at this time as 'witty, dashing and quick-tempered'. Army friends used to tease him about his pre-mutiny job as a 'consulting engineer' by calling him 'the insulting engineer' (a typical Victorian joke).

From Meerut the athletic Greathed set off to meet General Barnard's column heading towards Delhi. He found them at Alipore and took part in the battle at Badli-ka-Serai that forced the rebels back from the British on Delhi ridge, directing the left attack. In a sortie on 9 July he and a fellow officer found themselves surrounded by rebel *sepoys* and escaped by hacking a path out with their swords. During the siege he was a strong spokesman for action. He concocted a plan to blow up the bridge of boats over the Jumna, but the plan misfired spectacularly. When the big attack came William and a fellow engineer constructed their No. 2 battery near the city's Kashmir

Gate, the pair sustaining themselves in the heat by drinking pints of claret! In the assault on 14 September sapper Greathed accompanied the No. 2 attacking column that included his brother Edward's regiment. Within minutes of the pair shaking hands and wishing each other good luck, a bullet smashed into William's right arm and passed round his ribs under the skin.

He made a full recovery and at Lucknow was directing engineer under Colonel Robert **Napier**. The latter was fond of Greathed and took him along as an aide in the Second China War. He was present at the capture of the Taku Forts and entry into Peking. His was the signal honour of bringing home to England the war's despatches. From 1861 to 1865, now a lieutenant-colonel, William was Assistant Military Secretary at Horse Guards. In the 1870s he returned to India but his days of fighting were over; the climate exacerbated his ill-health, though he commanded the Royal Engineers inspected by the Prince of Wales on his Indian tour. Greathed left India in 1876, was promoted to major-general and died on 29 December 1878. During his lifetime he had been honourably mentioned in despatches no less than eighteen times.

HAINES, FIELD-MARSHAL SIR F. – COURAGE AND CAUTION

FREDERICK PAUL HAINES' greatest few hours were at the Battle of Inkerman, but his hardest fought times came twenty-five years later when he tried his best to exercise caution and common sense during the Second Afghan War. He is forgotten today, but deserves to be remembered.

He was born on 19 August 1819, the son of a commissary-general who had served with the Great Duke. He trained at Sandhurst and was gazetted an ensign with the 4th Foot in 1839. Through an old family friend Haines met Sir Hugh **Gough** and was appointed an aide in 1844, just in time to serve alongside the old warrior in the First Sikh War. At Mudki he was twelve hours in the saddle carrying orders for his chief; at Ferozeshah he was wounded in several places after delivering an order to the artillery. He slept all night on a gun limber, his wounds perfunctorily dressed by a fellow officer, and next morning suffered an agonising gallop on the gun. Two days later a large iron grape-shot was extracted from his groin!

By April 1846, Haines was sufficiently recovered to resume his duties as military secretary to Gough – and able also to join in his peacetime passion of cricketing. When the Second Sikh War broke out, Haines was by Gough's side in all his battles. In 1849 he went back to England and the following year was made a brevet colonel for his Indian services, despite only having the substantive rank of captain. It was as a captain that he now joined the 21st Foot. When the Crimean War broke out he sailed with his regiment as part of Sir George **Cathcart**'s division.

Haines was at the Battle of the Alma, but his real day of glory was at Inkerman on 5 November 1854, where, after the death of Colonel Ainslie, he commanded his regiment in the defence of the stone barrier in front of the 2nd Division. The fighting was fierce for several hours, many officers and men were killed, but Haines kept his head, throwing out flanking forces to prevent encirclement. In the words of Christopher Hibbert, 'by a display of astonishing courage, energy and skill [Haines] was able to beat back every attack until the pressure on his heroic but diminishing troops was relieved by a new force'.

Less than two years later, Colonel Haines was invited to return to India to serve as military secretary to his old friend Patrick **Grant**, son-in-law of Lord Gough and C-in-C, Madras. He was with Grant through the trying days of the Great Mutiny, but in 1860 moved to Ireland as DAG, becoming a major-general in 1864 before returning once more to India to command the Mysore Division. Here his fondness for cricket got him into hot water. as generals were not supposed to play 'undignified' games. A very brief stint as QMG at Horse Guards led to his appointment in 1871 as C-in-C of the Madras Army. A firm favourite with the Duke of Cambridge, his appointment as C-in-C, India, followed in 1876.

Relations between Haines and Lord Lytton were good for the first few months (indeed, even at their worst, they were always courteous to one another), but soon the Viceroy began to think his army chief was, in the words of a modern historian, just an 'unintelligent mediocrity'. The new C-in-C, India, took exception to the influence exerted on the Viceroy by Colonel **Colley**, his military secretary; Haines neatly described George Colley as 'the finest theoretical soldier I have ever met', a superb back-handed compliment. The forward policy of Lytton and Colley was not something to which Haines was opposed; his biographer noted that 'he was in thorough sympathy with its aims, though he not infrequently disapproved of its methods'. To be precise, Haines and Lytton locked horns over the value of the Kurram Valley as a base for operations against Kabul, the need for immediate preparations and the number of troops to be employed. In the early stages of the war Haines complained of the power exerted by Major Cavagnari, the political officer, and later in the war he was prevented from taking the field himself, though he did visit the front line during both the 1878 and 1880 campaigns.

The second phase of the war gave Haines many headaches, with the disaster at Maiwand and **Roberts**' struggles at Kabul and need for reinforcements, followed by his arduous march to meet the Afghans in battle at Kandahar. At headquarters he was also in danger of being manipulated by George **Greaves**, who saw himself as a quasi-chief of staff. Maiwand, in particular, was laid at Haines' door and he admitted that too many hopes had been pinned on the Afghan commander, Ayub Khan, not advancing on Kandahar, or being unsuccessful against General Burrows' troops. In his fine history of the war, the late Brian Robson is critical of Haines, though he seems not to have read the C-in-C's biography (I base this assertion on the bibliography in *The Road to Kabul*), where it is shown that Sir Frederick frequently alluded to the weakness of the Kandahar garrison and the dangers it would face if Ayub Khan moved his army in that direction. The new Viceroy, Lord Ripon, said that 'Ayub has cried wolf, wolf, so often, he will never come.' A depressed Haines told a friend that 'Lord Ripon has misquoted the fable. Ayub is the wolf; we are the heedless shepherds ... for Ayub will come, we shall have a disaster, and I shall be hanged for it.'

By the close of the war Haines could write: 'I only sit at my table and do the best I can ... those who are on active service are the Heroes of the day.' In 1881 he returned to London after almost sixteen years' continuous service in India. His parents, wife and brothers were all dead and so he became resident at his Pall Mall club. He lived on until 1909, the British Army's senior field-marshal, dying in his ninetieth year, one of the last survivors of the First Sikh War. The innate decency of Haines, an old-style gentleman, was made clear by one of the wreaths at his funeral, which bore the inscription: 'From the Bugler who gave you a drink of water on the field of the Alma and whom you did not forget when he was in trouble forty-four years later.'

HAMILTON, GENERAL SIR I. – SLICK 'JOHNNY'

'A NICE FELLOW' is how Douglas Haig described Ian Standish Monteith Hamilton, known to his friends as 'Johnny'. He was liked by everyone, from stern-faced Kitchener to portly King Edward VII, from dapper Earl **Roberts** to egotistical Churchill. Well, almost everyone: Redvers **Buller** called him, with good reason, 'a dangerous advisor', General Lord **Methuen** said he was 'mad' and Prime Minister Asquith once described him as 'feather-headed'. By 1902 this energetic, cheery, hugely intelligent officer was a shooting star considered to be one of the best commanders emerging from the Boer War. Yet this tall, thin, effete man with twinkling eyes was also a terrible gossip, conceited and smug. When such men fall they usually do so from great heights.

He was born on Corfu, the son of a Scottish army officer stationed there, on 16 January 1853, attended Sandhurst, graduated in 1872 and joined the 12th Foot. Eighteen months later he transferred to the 92nd (Gordon) Highlanders, his father's old regiment, then serving in India.

A major event in his life occurred in July 1879, when 'Johnny' disturbed some Afghan raiders near the British camp in the Second Afghan War; General Roberts invited him for a glass of sherry and was so impressed with the young subaltern that Hamilton soon found himself gazetted as an aide to General Massy commanding the cavalry brigade. At the Battle of Charasiab on 6 October he charged with the 5th PC and later wrote: 'The dust clouds of the Chardeh Valley – the 5th Punjab Cavalry – red pugar-rees – blue swords flashing; the galloping line, and I also galloping with that sensation of speed which the swiftest motor car can never impart … Dust, shouts, shots, clash of steel …'

The Gordons were soon off to the Transvaal for a war with the Boers and Hamilton found himself trudging up Majuba Hill with George **Pomeroy-Colley**. When the enemy started swarming over the top, bumptious Johnny, who thought it was foolish not to entrench, asked the general if he could lead a charge. Colley told him to wait a little longer. Next moment, the general was shot dead and many soldiers were killed or caught escaping down the hillside. Hamilton, his left wrist shattered by a bullet, was taken prisoner. He was later recommended for a VC, but considered 'too young' to receive the honour.

Luckily for him he was selected to be an aide to Roberts in his role as C-in-C of the Madras Army. The War Office refused after six months to confirm him as assistant military secretary, despite two campaigns, wounds and mentions in despatches. Hamilton blamed Redvers **Buller** – the start of a mutual loathing – whom he termed the 'evil genius' of the Wolseley Ring. With six months' leave owing, he decided to try and join the **Gordon** Relief Expedition. In Egypt a surprisingly human Buller wired that 'You may attach Hamilton to the Gordons.' Johnny toiled up the Nile with the river column, was near General **Earle** when he was killed at Kirbekan and took charge of his burial.

Back in India, on Roberts' staff, Hamilton became the youngest colonel in the army. He showed a rare talent for staff work and followed his chief to Burma during the 1885–86 period of pacification. Roberts treated him like a second son. Hamilton confessed later that he owed Lord Roberts 'militarily everything' and thought him to be 'the best soldier of his age'. After Roberts left India, Johnny stayed, serving on the staff of the Chitral relief expedition and then being given a brigade of the Tirah Field Force in 1897. In Tirah he befriended a young subaltern called Winston Churchill.

In 1898, after twenty-five years in India, Hamilton took over command of the School of Musketry at Hythe. On the eve of the South African War he was AAG at the War Office and was sent out to the Cape with Sir George **White**. In one of the early battles, Elandslaagte, he commanded the 7th Brigade with the local rank of major-general and was once again recommended for a VC after rallying his men under fire and choosing exactly the right moment for a final attack (ironically, he was rejected this time because of his seniority). He served in the Siege of Ladysmith, led the Mounted Infantry Division in Roberts' march on Pretoria and was promoted to lieutenant-general. He left South Africa with his chief in 1900 but returned exactly a year later to be Kitchener's chief of staff (on Roberts' recommendation).

Roberts never doubted Johnny's skill as a general and was intensely loyal. He told the war minister that Hamilton was 'quite the most brilliant Commander I have … He takes infinite trouble in matters of detail and knows his work thoroughly … I would select him before all others to carry out any difficult operation.' **Kitchener**, too, worked harmoniously with Hamilton, trusting him to deal with messy business like the Breaker Morant affair.

The only problem with 'Johnny' Hamilton was that he could be a cruel gossip, using his influence with both Roberts and Kitchener to cloud or poison their opinions of fellow officers, and he played a major role in blackening Buller's name (and, to a lesser extent, White's). To an influential journalist he wrote: '*Buller is no use*. He is, indeed, far *far* worse than use-less.' He snitchingly told Roberts that Buller attributed 'dishonest motives' to him. In another letter he called Buller a 'deadly enemy'. His views of the war and those conducting it, for good or ill, were relayed to London society, the press and politicians. It is difficult, for all his accomplishments, attributes, charm, intelligence and wit, not to find Hamilton a rather conceited man at the end of the Boer War, at least based on his correspondence – he almost seems to be smirking in some photographs.

The part of his life for which he is best known, a period still filled with controversy, falls outside the scope of this book, and still lay several years ahead in 1902. Hamilton would live on until 1947, a venerable old warrior by then, but for the last thirty-two years of his life he never held another command and is still remembered, unjustly, most say, as the general who in 1915 commanded the tragic Gallipoli debacle.

HARRISON, MAJOR-GENERAL SIR R. – ESCAPING BECOMING THE SCAPEGOAT

RICHARD HARRISON WAS an intelligent officer who served on several campaigns, and almost found himself made a scapegoat for the Prince Imperial's death in the Zulu War.

He was born on 26 May 1837, the son of a wealthy parson, and educated at Harrow. During the Crimean campaign the War Office offered public schoolboys direct commissions and Harrison decided on a life in the Royal Engineers. He volunteered, was accepted and was soon en route to the Crimea, but the war was over before he got there, so, after a spell on Malta, Richard landed in India, where the great rebellion had broken out. He served under Robert **Napier**, chief engineer, took despatches to James Outram and made reports to Colin Campbell. He served in Walpole's column at the Ruiya debacle (where Brigadier Adrian Hope was killed) and joined the C-in-C in his pursuit of the Oudh rebels.

In the China War of 1860 young Richard served under Gerald **Graham**. He was in one of the assault parties at the Taku Forts and counted sixteen dead Chinese around one of the enemy guns. At the looting of the Summer Palace he was appalled by the avarice of the French. In the 1860s he served in Canada and visited the USA during the Civil War (almost getting shot for a spy).

After Isandlwana, the bright Harrison was one of the royal engineers sent to assist Lord **Chelmsford**, but he found himself transferred to the headquarters staff as AQMG. When the Prince Imperial of France, serving under him, was killed while on patrol, some senior officers said that Harrison had provided an 'insufficient' escort and he was censured by the Duke of Cambridge. Luckily he had many defenders – Redvers **Buller** told the Queen he was not to blame, Cecil **East** called him 'a most excellent officer' and **Wolseley** promoted him.

Harrsion next did some scouting for Wolseley as the latter prepared a little war against Chief Sekhukhune of the BaPedi. In 1881 Harrison took a spying trip to Egypt in the company of his wife, ostensibly as tourists, but in reality trying to gain as much intelligence as possible. In the 1882 war he assisted General **Earle** on the lines of communication and fought at Tel-el-Kebir, where he took the Egyptian Commissary-General prisoner. He served again with Earle in the Sudan, but sickness forced him to leave before his chief's death at Kirbekan.

In July 1888 Harrison was made a major-general. Later he was governor of Sandhurst and made a KCB. He retired in 1903 after forty-nine years' service, published his memoirs in 1912 and lived on in pleasant retirement at Brixham until his death in 1931 aged 94 years, one of the last survivors of the Indian Mutiny.

HART-SYNNOT, MAJOR-GENERAL A. & HART, GENERAL SIR R. – THE 'NO-BOBS' BOYS

ARTHUR (HE PREFERRED to be called Fitzroy) and Reginald Hart were two of the soldier sons of General Henry Hart, creator of *Hart's Army List*. Both brothers became famous for their coolness under fire and their refusal to duck from whizzing bullets. Younger brother Reginald twice won the silver medal of the Royal Humane Society for saving lives, as well as gaining a Victoria Cross in the Second Afghan War. Fitzroy charged at Ashantis, Zulus, Egyptians and Boers with the same disregard for danger and was nicknamed 'No-bobs' by his soldiers. His fame rests on the disastrous handling of the Irish Brigade at Colenso in the South African War. Unlike many other generals, he was not recalled after this poor show but went on to lead columns until the end of the campaign.

Fitzroy was born in 1844, Reginald four years later; the elder Hart left memoirs (Reginald only produced some dull works on tactics and sanitation), but curiously, while mentioning his father, wife and sons, he omits any mention of his famous VC-winning brother. This is especially odd since both brothers served in senior posts in the Egyptian War 1882 and must have met on campaign; there seems to be an imputation of sibling rivalry (and it is worth mentioning that Fitzroy failed to pass the exam to become a royal engineer while Reginald succeeded, so perhaps some jealousy existed).

At just 13 years old, Fitzroy entered Sandhurst and passed out three years later. General Hart then seems to have had a change of heart (sorry!) and considered him too young to be a soldier, so he was sent back to school, failed to enter Woolwich, did the whole Sandhurst course for a second time and was finally gazetted an ensign in the 31st Foot in 1864. Both brothers did well at the Staff College. Fitzroy passed out in 1872 and was delighted a year later to be chosen by **Wolseley** as a special service officer on his Ashanti expedition. He commanded the Sierra Leone Company of Russell's Regiment, seeing action at Amoaful and Ordahsu. In 1878 he volunteered again for special service in Zululand and served with the Natal Native Contingent as part of Pearson's column. On 22 January 1879 he bravely led a charge against Zulus near the Nyezane River, supported by a few white non-commissioned officers and a Naval Brigade detachment. 'Hart, on horseback, was first among the Zulus who then gave way and retreated', wrote Greaves and Knight. Pearson was besieged at Eshowe and Hart, now with **Chelmsford**'s column, fought at Gingindhlovu. He wrote of the approaching Zulus:

> No whites ever did, or ever could skirmish in the magnificent perfection of the Zulus ... they bounded forward towards us from all sides, rushing from cover to cover, gliding like snakes through the grass, and turning to account every bush, every mound, every particularly high patch of grass between us and them, and firing at us, always from concealment. If total concealment were possible, we should not have seen a Zulu till he reached our trench ...

In the meantime, Reginald had been awarded a medal by the President of the French Republic for saving a drowning man at Boulogne and when the Second Afghan War broke out he served with the 2nd Division, Peshawar Valley Field Force. In fact, on 31 January 1879, as his eldest brother was by the banks of a river in Zululand, Reginald won a VC by running 1,200yd to the rescue of a wounded native *sowar* of the Bengal Lancers lying in a river-bed exposed to heavy fire. Hart reached the man and drove off the enemy until help arrived.

In 1881 Fitzroy applied a third time for special service and was appointed AAG and QMG of the Natal Field Force under Evelyn **Wood**, but saw no fighting. Things changed in 1882, when both Harts saw action in Egypt; Fitzroy went with Wolseley to be DAAG at headquarters, later being sent on intelligence duties, was wounded in the elbow at Kassassin and was responsible for the line of advance of the 2nd British Brigade in the night march to Tel-el-Kebir (he deliberately asked to serve with them as he thought they would see the heaviest fighting). Reginald, a major like his brother, served as ADC to General **Graham**, commanding the same brigade, and was at his side in all the major battles.

Fitzroy now had seventeen years of peacetime soldiering, including a stint commanding the 2nd battalion of the East Surreys in India. On the same continent Reginald won a second RHS medal for saving a man in the Ganges. In 1897 he commanded the 1st Brigade of the Tirah Field Force. Whilst attacking an Afridi village, bullets flying everywhere, he came across Horace **Smith-Dorrien**, who wrote: 'We were lying down in the position we had secured, but I had to stand up to salute him. He gave me a warm greeting, hooked his arm in mine and insisted on walking up and down discussing the art of war, in spite of my protests that we provided the sole mark for the

enemy to aim at. It was some time before I could manoeuvre him into a position of safety. Why neither of us was hit I do not know, but I came to the
conclusion that a too brave General might not be a very pleasant companion.'

The younger Hart saw no more active service after Tirah though he was
C-in-C, South Africa, 1912–14. It was there, on 15 December 1899, that
Fitzroy led the Irish Brigade at Colenso. He was previously commanding
at Aldershot and there is an unintentionally very funny line in *Celebrities of
the Army* (published in 1900) that it would have been 'simply impossible' for
him to command there unless he was an 'up-to-date soldier'. Hart's ideas on
up-to-date soldiering were shown at Colenso. **Buller** later claimed that Hart
marched his men beyond the position he had allotted to them. A messenger
sent to help untangle this mess was delayed (meantime the Irishmen fell into
a bloody trap by the banks of the Tugela). Hart said Buller lied: the native
guide supplied to him had led his troops to the wrong spot to cross the river
and then ran off when the firing started, while the instructions given him
clearly read that he was to 'force the passage of the Tugela', which he tried
to do. Amid the recriminations and mud-slinging after the battle, one thing is
clear – Buller's maps and orders led to all kinds of confusion that day.

Hart cannot be excused, despite his bravery, for being irresponsible and
stupid. He glares out of photographs, a proud man, with a finely twirled
moustache. That morning he had given his troops half an hour's parade
ground drill, then made them advance in close formation quarter-column
(he refused a suggestion to open up the line), in clear daylight, on the open
veldt, towards a wide salient – described by Thomas Pakenham as 'like putting your head in a noose'. When the Boers opened fire, Hart, brave as ever
and declining to retreat, thought it would be best if the men charged. He
walked calmly among the flying bullets and shrapnel. 'If I give you a lead,
if your General gives you a lead – will you come on?' he asked his men. The
Irish lads responded with a cheer and many went to their deaths. General
Lyttelton, whose brigade came up to support the inevitable Irish retreat,
wrote that 'The choice of Hart to conduct the main attack was very unfortunate.' In a letter to his wife, Lyttelton bluntly called him 'a dangerous lunatic'.

Hart failed to see that he had done anything wrong, despite a dressing
down from Buller that quite upset him. 'Please God I shall survive it and prove
my ability', he wrote to his wife. The battle at Hart's Hill near Ladysmith
in February 1900 proved that he learned nothing from Colenso: he flung
more close formations and companies into the firing line without hesitation.
Indeed, one might have expected him to be in the batch of generals culled by
Roberts and sent home. It seems that the C-in-C and **Kitchener** respected

Hart's courage and rated his desire to attack above the dithering of some of their other commanders. In December 1901 Kitchener told Roberts (via Ian Hamilton) that he placed Hart's abilities higher than **Barton** or **Rundle** and some other generals, 'saying that under certain exceptional circumstances, he might come out unexpectedly strong, and do a big thing …' He served to the end of the war, leading columns in the Orange River Colony and Orange Free State, and also relieving colonial troops besieged at Wepener.

Fitzroy married and added a Synnot to his name. He died in May 1910. Reginald outlived him for twenty-one years, dying at Bournemouth in 1931.

HAVELOCK, GENERAL SIR H. & HAVELOCK-ALLAN, LIEUTENANT-GENERAL SIR H. – SOLDIERS FOR CHRIST

IT IS ALL too easy, after a span of more than a century, to fail to comprehend just how important a part religion played in the lives of many Victorian officers. They were soldiers of the Queen, but many saw themselves as servants of Christ doing his good work. The epitome of this kind of warrior was Henry Havelock, whose death at Lucknow was a kind of epiphany for some Victorians. His son, a Victoria Cross winner, tried hard to emulate his father, but fought a constant battle with the demons of madness.

Havelock senior was born on Easter Day 1795, son of a Sunderland shipbuilder. He grew into a youth of just 5ft in height who, at 19, hoped to become a lawyer until, in that year, the family fortunes crashed. Following his elder brother, William, into the army, Henry was commissioned into the Rifle Brigade in 1815. Influenced by his commanding officer, Harry **Smith**, he started to learn not just pipe clay, but the finer details of tactics, strategy and military history. Transferring to the 13th Foot, Henry sailed for the East with his regiment in 1823. Two things happened on the voyage: firstly, he made the friendship of his senior officer, Major Robert **Sale**; secondly, he came under the spell of an evangelical lieutenant, James Gardner, who loaned him books of religious essays until Havelock found his Saviour. It was a life-changing experience.

When the First Burmese War broke out in 1824 Havelock volunteered and was made DAAG of the army. No chaplain had been sent with the troops, so Henry started prayer meetings. One night an outpost was attacked and word was sent to General Archibald Campbell. When he was told most of the available troops were drunk, he replied: 'Then call out Havelock's saints, they are always sober and can be relied upon, and Havelock himself is always ready.' After the war Henry expanded his proselytising alongside temperance work. It was clear to him that sober soldiers made better fighters.

Not being rich, his climb up the promotional ladder was agonisingly slow; by 1838 Havelock had just received his captaincy, without purchase, when the Afghan War broke out. He set out as an aide to General Cotton, commanding the Bengal Division, and was at Ghazni and the entry into Kabul. When Sale, now a general, was sent to hold Jellalabad, he took Havelock and the 13th with him. The defence of the town, which held out against tribal attacks, was one of the better features of a humiliating war. Havelock organised much of the resistance and urged Sale to hold out when all hope seemed lost.

A year later, at Maharajpore, in the short Gwalior War, Henry on horseback led a wavering Indian regiment into battle, then galloped straight at the enemy guns to inspire his men. At Mudki in the First Sikh War the same horse, 'Feroze', was killed under him. He survived his next battle unscathed, but at Sobraon had another horse killed, the cannon ball striking his saddle just an inch from his thigh. During the war Havelock made the friendship of the Governor-General, Lord Hardinge, who had him promoted to DAG of the Queen's troops at Bombay. Before he left India, Hardinge remarked that Havelock was 'Every inch a soldier, and every inch a Christian.' When the Second Sikh War broke out, chafing that the Bombay Army was not involved, and mourning the loss of his brother William, killed in battle, Havelock got a leave of absence and was on his way to the Punjab before being sent back with a flea in his ear by Lord **Gough**, who disliked any protégés of Harry Smith.

In 1855 Havelock was promoted to AG of the Queen's troops in India. It was the perfect job for a man with a rigid sense of discipline. A supporter of the lash when necessary, he made it plain that the Queen's officers 'were individually responsible for every breach of discipline that might be committed under their orders'. His inspections demonstrated he was a rigid yet just martinet. When the Persian War started in 1856 he was offered a divisional command and, in his own words, 'Old as I am, I did not hesitate a second.' He found his chief, James **Outram**, to be 'kind as he is brave, skilful and enterprising'. It was a relatively bloodless war and Havelock landed back at Bombay on 29 May 1857 to hear the astounding news that the Bengal Army had mutinied.

He set off to join the C-in-C, but on the way met Patrick **Grant**, who was tasked with finding a general who could march up-country and conquer. Havelock made it clear in a memo that he distrusted all native regiments. 'Mutineers,' he wrote, 'must be attacked and annihilated'; whole regiments 'deemed guilty' were to be promptly executed. When they reached Calcutta, Grant introduced Havelock to Governor-General Earl Canning with the words, 'My Lord, I have brought you the man!' Opinions were mixed, however: the Indian press called him 'an old fossil', and Lady Canning wrote: 'No doubt he is fussy and tiresome, but his little, old, stiff figure looks as active and fit for use as if he were made of steel.' One Mutiny participant wrote that Havelock's 'sour discipline' made him 'unpopular with his soldiers to an extraordinary degree', while another who served him closely noted, 'He was always well-mounted, and a good rider, quick of speech, too, and ready for retort,' but 'sterner and more severe than is generally understood.'

A legend was born as this tough, white-haired little general began his march. He had a moveable column of barely 1,200 Britons and 300 Sikhs. They left Allahabad on 7 July destined to relieve Cawnpore and Lucknow. In a host of battles (four in the first nine days), Havelock refused to be rushed or risk his troops unnecessarily. Back in England news of his victories were as manna from heaven. He was lauded as the greatest Indian general since Clive. As the fights grew and the death toll rose, Havelock told his men they were 'the strength and prop of British India in her severest trial'. On 15 September, before the advance on Lucknow, Outram arrived as senior general but offered, with humility, to serve under Havelock. Unfortunately, Sir James did not keep his word and began issuing his own orders or countermanding Havelock's, creating, perhaps accidentally, a divided command. Havelock, who respected Outram greatly, refused to make waves. The hard-fought entry into Lucknow, followed two months later by Campbell's first relief, exhausted the wiry little man, who had been sick for weeks. He died in his son Harry's arms at 9.30 a.m. on 24 November 1857 with a smile on his face. His last words were, 'Harry, see how a Christian can die.'

The younger Havelock always revered his father's memory, but he knew he was a different kind of man. He had the courage of his father, he even tried to emulate him as a Christian, taking public baptism in 1859, but he was impetuous with a fierce pride and temper that won him a reputation as one of the most eccentric men in the army. Father and son had argued much in the boy's youth when he had alternated between fits of depression and hyper-activity. Troubled by psychosis, he bore deep grudges and for many years treated his mother as an enemy.

Harry was DAQMG on the staff of his father in Persia, aged 26 years, then stayed by his side with the moveable column. When his father recommended him for a VC – 'in the last action, [he] placed himself in front of the 64th Foot, right opposite the muzzle of a 24 pdr. gun which scattered grape into our ranks' – Harry was appalled, thinking it would make him look 'ridiculous' to be honoured thus (but he got the medal). Later in the war he was recommended for a bar to his VC by Outram for saving his life on two occasions. After his father's death Harry was DAAG to General **Franks'** column in central India.

Five years later he saw more fighting in New Zealand as DAQMG of the Queen's troops. He was present in at least four of the main fights and commanded at a skirmish near Waiari.

Gradually his eccentricities asserted themselves; in a rage, he once flattened a sergeant with a billiard cue, while his loathing of the arch-reactionary Duke of Cambridge was such that when the pair met at an Aldershot parade Havelock handed an aide his sword, saying he could not be trusted with it. Highly intelligent, Harry was a champion of army reform, especially mounted infantry. **Wolseley** called him 'the finest soldier of his time', but admitted his friend was 'curiously mad'. Another friend wrote that Sir Henry's problem was that he feared nobody and did not know how to channel his reckless temper.

In 1880 he added the name of Allan in compliance with a cousin's will. Shortly after, he retired from the army, only to pop up in Egypt in 1882 as an 'observer', apparently without telling his wife. He *walked* across the battlefield of Tel-el-Kebir after his horse toppled him off in a trench. Next he entered Parliament as a Liberal MP for the Durham miners (they adored him). In 1897 he set out to investigate the situation on the Indian frontier. Typically, he rode ahead of his escort and went missing on 30 December. The last entry in his diary read; 'A lovely morning – got them all up – as fit as a fiddle.' A few days later his body was found, stripped but not mutilated, shot by an Afridi.

HILLS-JOHNES, LIEUTENANT-GENERAL SIR J. – VC-WINNING ANGLO-INDIAN

JAMES HILLS (THE Johnes was added in 1882 on his marriage to heiress Elizabeth Johnes) won his Victoria Cross in the Indian Mutiny fighting alongside his fellow Bengal Horse Artilleryman, Harry **Tombs**. He became a close friend of Frederick **Roberts**, who always called him 'Jemmy', and they served together in four campaigns.

'Jemmy' (some said 'Jimmy') was born at Neechindipore, Bengal, on 20 August 1833, the son of an indigo planter and his Italian wife. After being sent to Edinburgh and Addiscombe, young Hills returned to India in 1853 with a commission in the Bengal Horse Artillery. This elite regiment with blue and gold uniforms were referred to as 'the Red Men' because of the scarlet mane that hung from their brass mounted Roman-style helmets.

Throughout the Mutiny 'Jemmy' served with the 1st Brigade, 2nd troop, commanded by the dashing Harry Tombs. On 9 July 1857 Hills was trying to get two heavy guns into position when he and a small cavalry escort were attacked by about 120 rebel *sowars*. In the melee the cavalry support and guns were swept away. Hills, wanting to give his men time to load, charged single-handedly to meet the enemy. 'He cut down the first man he met', wrote General Hughes, struck a second, and was then ridden down horse and all. Men and horses thundered over him as he lay on the ground, groping for his sword, which had been struck from his hand. Recovering his sword, he struggled to his feet, much hampered by his heavy cloak which was soaked with rain. Three men charged at him. He wounded the first with his pistol, seized the lance of the second and wounded him with his sword, but was then thrown to the ground by the third man, who was on foot. He was about to be killed when Tombs rode up and shot the rebel dead. The two men were walking to a mound to see what was happening when they saw a mutineer advancing carrying Hills' pistol. He also turned out to be an expert swordsman; the fellow parried blows from both British officers, then broke Hills' guard and drove the sword deep into his skull (apparently with minor brain damage), and parried another thrust from Tombs before that officer drove his sabre through the trooper's body.

Hills recovered from his wound and fought alongside Tombs for the rest of the Mutiny – at the assault on Delhi, the capture of Lucknow, Bareilly and a score of other fights. Lieutenant Hills was made a captain in 1862, then brigade major, northern division, Royal Artillery, Bengal, 1862–69. During this period he commanded an 8in mortar battery at the capture of Magdala fortress in Abyssinia. In 1871–72 he commanded a mountain battery in the Lushai expedition, was awarded a CB and was made brevet-colonel.

When the Second Afghan War broke out, Hills served in the first phase with **Stewart**'s Kandahar Field Force as AAG. During the second part of the war he made an epic journey to join Roberts, who wrote, 'Although I had no employment for Hills at the time, there would be plenty to do at Kabul, and I was delighted to have such a good soldier with me.' Once the Afghan capital was reached Hills was made military governor; subsequently he commanded the 1st Division of the Kabul Field Force, being responsible for the defence of a section of the Sherpur cantonment perimeter when it was attacked by the Afghans.

The waspish Charles Metcalfe **Macgregor** grew to admire Hills and wrote that 'He is a much more very sensible man than Bobs, and a thousand times more honest,' adding, 'he has not a high opinion of Bobs, and agreed with me, he has not a particle of independence of character.' It is hard to know what to make of Macgregor's statement – was he exaggerating as usual, did Hills really find Roberts 'very weak', or was he agreeing with Macgregor to humour him? Roberts certainly rated 'Jemmy' as one of his closest friends and in South Africa twenty years later he accompanied the C-in-C in a private capacity from Kronstadt to Diamond Hill. In 1879 Hills, who had a thick head of snowy white hair cut all over about an inch deep, acquired a new nickname. Macgregor wrote: 'Jimmy Hills came in looking very well. I could not help thinking as he sat at breakfast with white hair all standing on end how like an enraged mongoose he looked, indeed, they call him the 'infuriated mongoose'. After the war Hills was given a KCB. He was promoted to lieutenant-general in 1886 and retired two years later. In 1893 Hills-Johnes became a GCB and in his old age honours included honorary colonelcy of the 4th Welsh Regiment. He died on 3 January 1919.

HOME, SURGEON-GENERAL SIR A. – VC-WINNING MEDICAL MAN

ON 25–26 SEPTEMBER 1857, as Havelock's soldiers battled their way towards the Lucknow Residency, no less than four VCs were won by medical men. In the case of Anthony Dickson Home, this did not just involve caring for the sick and wounded under fire, but also commanding and fighting in his own mini-siege, which lasted twenty-two hours.

Home was born in 1826 and entered the Army Medical Department as an assistant surgeon in 1848. Six years later he followed the 8th Hussars to the Crimea in the same capacity, later working at the base hospital at Scutari. He later transferred to the 13th Light Dragoons and in 1857 moved again to the 90th Foot. With his regiment he set sail for China that year but, on receiving news of the Indian revolt, the 90th were sent to join **Havelock** in his advance on Lucknow.

In his memoirs Home, with all the humility of an old soldier, refused to give details of the incident which won him the coveted cross of honour.

He and his assistant surgeon, Bradshaw, had set off to help two other doctors, Jee and McMaster of the 78th Highlanders, whose column of wounded was trapped behind enemy lines. In their progress Home and Bradshaw collected their own party of injured and dying men. Coming under attack from a large body of rebels, Bradshaw was able to get away with twenty men on covered litters known as 'doolies', but Home's doolie bearers ran away and he and just a few men took shelter in a house while the poor patients outside were massacred. The rebels then set fire to the house and Home had to conduct a retreat to a shed a few yards away, where he spent almost a whole night and day leading a spirited defence; three of four wounded officers with him were killed and only six were left when help finally arrived.

In the 1860 China War, Home was present at the attack on the Taku Forts and tried to aid the enemy wounded after the battle. In the 1860s he was stationed in Canada and visited Washington during the Civil War. More campaigning followed in New Zealand in 1863–64. His last war was Ashanti in 1873, where **Wolseley**, his old friend from the 90th Foot, insisted on using him, describing Home as 'one of, if not the cleverest' doctors in the army. He arrived six weeks ahead of the main troops and by the time of the march up-country, like so many others, he was down with fever (there is an irony here – unlike Wolseley, Home did not believe in the efficacy of quinine). Consequently he was sent home, though **Brackenbury** later wrote that 'his personal exertions had been conspicuous'.

It appears that as Home grew older he also grew gloomier. While PMO with Wolseley on his Cyprus Mission in 1878 the couple had several arguments; in his journal Sir Garnet wrote that Home 'has become so melancholy that one feels inclined to look about for your undertaker after he has addressed you'. Sir Anthony did not retire until 1886, by which time he was serving as PMO to the British troops in India. He lived another twenty-eight years in Kensington, where he died on 10 August 1914.

HORSFORD, GENERAL SIR A. – OLD-SCHOOL

BARREL-CHESTED, BEWHISKERED ALFRED Hastings Horsford was the kind of man approved of by the Duke of Cambridge, the reactionary C-in-C of the British Army for much of Victoria's reign. Horsford was a regimental man – Rifle Brigade through and through – brave, intellectually blinkered and just the type of gentleman to be HRH's military secretary in the 1870s, unlike that upstart **Wolseley** and his ring.

Born at Bath in 1818, Horsford went to the Royal Military Academy and then into the Rifle Brigade in 1833. He served with them in the Seventh Xhosa War in 1847 and commanded the 1st Battalion in the Eighth Frontier War in 1852. When the Rifle Brigade went to the Crimea so did Horsford, now a colonel, leading his green jackets at the Alma, Inkerman, Balaklava and Sebastopol. Perhaps his biggest fight was at foggy Inkerman, where he and his men fought many small battles of their own before reinforcing **Haines**. At one point, Horsford and 140 of his 'green flies', as the Russians called his men, kept up such a concentrated fire that they had their enemies running for their lives, the wounded begging for mercy on their knees. Sent to India to command a brigade on the outbreak of the Great Mutiny, Horsford served in Oudh under **Clyde**, marching and fighting rebels all over the province as far north as the Nepal frontier.

On his return from India, brigadier Horsford was made DAG at Horse Guards and so impressed the Duke of Cambridge that he was recalled in 1874, now a major-general, to serve as his military secretary. The pair got along famously. The Duke's rival, Garnet Wolseley, complained that Horsford was 'civil' but not 'generous' in company. Sir Alfred retired but did not live long after, dying on 13 September 1885.

HUNTER, GENERAL SIR A. – THE FIGHTING MAN'S SOLDIER

ARCHIBALD HUNTER WAS never happier than when in command of troops in action, something he did superbly. He was dashing, energetic, good-humoured, impulsive and popular with his men. Fellow officers also found him to be, at times, rash, tactless and, as he got older, increasingly irrational in behaviour. Lord Edward Cecil, who served with Hunter in the Sudan and South Africa, described him as 'a real live Cromwellian, brutal, cruel, licentious, religious, brave, able, blunt and cunning'. A recent historian has written that Hunter 'was a no-nonsense soldier, devoted to his service, a realist who had a tendency to speak his mind at times, a man's man who thought nothing of taking his Abyssinian mistress with him to Cairo'.

Hunter was proud of his lowland Scot ancestry, but actually born in London on 6 September 1856. Following Sandhurst he was gazetted to the 4th Foot in 1874. A decade of peacetime soldiering left him profoundly bored and so in February 1884 he joined the newly reformed Egyptian Army. This corps offered him increased pay, prestige and, best of all, a chance of active service. Soon Archie was getting noticed; his defence of the fort at Kosheh near Wadi Halfa won him the newly instituted DSO in 1886. Three years later he led his battalion to acclaim at the Battle of Toski. The Sirdar, Sir Francis **Grenfell**, noted that Hunter was 'a strict disciplinarian and at the same time universally popular'. When Grenfell was replaced by **Kitchener** as Sirdar it fell to Hunter to become his right-hand man, or 'sword-arm', as some said, leading the Egyptian Army in battle.

In 1896 Hunter was made a major-general, supposedly the youngest in the British Army since Wellington. During the 1896–98 reconquest of the Sudan he led his troops superbly. He was a loyal subordinate to Kitchener in public, though often having good cause to disagree and rage against him in private. He was less than happy with the Sirdar's tactics at Omdurman (and thought if the dervishes had attacked on the night before the battle, they would probably have won). He also defended his Egyptian and Sudanese battalions against charges of brutality inside Omdurman after the battle.

After Omdurman he was made a KCB. Wanting a change from Egyptian service, he was happy to be assigned to the Quetta Division in India in May 1899. Before he could take up this appointment, the South African War broke out. Hunter arrived at Cape Town weeks ahead of Buller with instructions to be Sir Redvers' chief of staff. **Buller** telegraphed that Sir Archibald might assist Sir George **White**, who was in command of the Natal troops. The result was that Hunter got bottled up in Ladysmith along with his chief and 12,000 soldiers. White proved to be a reckless and increasingly demoralised general as the siege dragged on and Hunter proved 'indispensable', capturing Gun Hill on the night of 7 December 1899, the 'life and soul' of the town's defence, much to Sir George's chagrin. He was, in the words of Thomas Pakenham, 'the main prop of Ladysmith's defence, a heart and nerve that had never faltered, despite White's feebleness'.

After Ladysmith's relief Hunter was made a lieutenant-general and led various columns in pursuit of Boer commandos. Lord **Roberts** thought him an 'excellent' and 'reliable' general. One trooper wrote: 'He has a way of looking at you, no matter who you are, Tommy or officer, or what not, with a wonderfully kind expression, as if he felt the most friendly interest in you. And so he does; it is not a bit put on.' During the hunt for De Wet in 1900, Hunter broke his collarbone but found himself commanding three divisions in a fortnight's campaign which forced the surrender of General Prinsloo, with the capture of '4,314 prisoners, two million rounds of ammunition, three of the guns taken at Sannah's Post, much livestock and, perhaps best of all, more than 4,000 ponies'. After South Africa Sir Archibald saw no more campaigning, though he was made a full general in 1905, and given an Indian command. In 1910 he was sent to Gibraltar as governor, acted rashly and discourteously towards the locals and was forced to resign in 1913. During the First World War he commanded at Aldershot until 1917. Hunter resented not being given a field command and retired in 1920. He was briefly an MP before his death in 1936. Perhaps his greatest compliment came from Prime Minister Asquith in 1916, who said that Hunter 'had won the Battle of Omdurman, in spite of Kitchener, and defended Ladysmith, in spite of White'.

HUTTON, LIEUTENANT-GENERAL SIR E. – 'CURLY' OF THE MI

EDWARD HUTTON'S REGIMENTAL history says that he 'did more for Mounted Infantry in raising, training and leading it in the field than any Officer in the British Army'. That is all true, but there is much more to Hutton, known by his friends as 'Curly', than just mounted infantry.

He was born on the 6 December 1848 at Torquay and as a young man taught at Eton before deciding on an army career, which began with the purchase of a commission in the 60th Rifles in 1867. He served in the Zulu War with the 3rd Battalion and was mentioned in despatches for his performance at Gingindhlovu. The brilliant skirmishing and the bravery of the Zulus under fire impressed Hutton, who wrote that his own men were 'awfully frightened … we officers had enough to do to keep the men cool'.   His experience with mounted infantry really got going in 1881, when he commanded a squadron created during the Transvaal War. The following year in Egypt, on Archibald **Alison**'s staff, he was allowed to form his own mounted infantry corps; he led them successfully and had a horse shot from under him at the Battle of Tel-el-Kebir. In the 1884–85 Sudan campaign he again led the mounted infantry and had by now started to lecture on the subject.

Though not a major member of the Garnet Ring, he had the support and encouragement of Lord **Wolseley** in all his mounted infantry endeavours. At his suggestion Hutton commanded HM forces in New South Wales 1893–96. In 1898, with the rank of major-general, he was put in charge of the Canadian militia. When war with the Boers broke out Hutton dragged an unwilling Canadian government into the fray by publishing mobilisation plans. Sir Wilfred Laurier, the premier, announced his country's refusal to send contingents to South Africa, but due to Hutton's actions he was forced to bow to political pressure. Hutton was recalled, but quickly sent to South Africa to command a 1st Brigade of Mounted Infantry.

Lord **Roberts** told the War Minister Lord Lansdowne that Sir Edward was 'inordinately conceited and talks too much', but 'is a man I feel confidence in and he has managed several difficult affairs with considerable skill. I believe his troops do not like him, but they trust him as a Commander.' In actuality, Hutton handled his mounted infantry well at Vet River, Brandfort and Doornkop. John **French**, commanding the cavalry, disliked Hutton and called him 'an ass', but Lord Anglesey noted in his cavalry history how, 'on at least two occasions', Hutton's mounted infantry showed that they possessed mobility superior to the cavalry.

After the war 'Curly' played an important role as the first commander of a united Australian Army. Despite early involvement in the First World War, he was relieved of his command in April 1915 due to a riding accident. He died in 1923.

KEANE, LIEUTENANT-GENERAL LORD J. – LUCK OF THE IRISH

ROUGH, GRUFF JOHN Keane was the Irish general who commanded the ill-fated Army of the Indus which invaded Afghanistan in 1838. Despite logistical and tactical mistakes, he got his forces to Kabul, placed a pretender on the throne and secured for himself a peerage before the war turned into the British Army's greatest disaster of the century.

He was the second son of Sir John Keane, 1st baronet, an Irish MP. At just 11 years old young Keane joined the 60th Regiment as an ensign. Twenty years later he was commanding a brigade in the Peninsular War. He saw action in Martinique and at Vittoria, the Pyrenees, Nivelle, the Nive and Toulouse, his bravery being rewarded with the Army Gold Cross with two clasps. Promoted to major-general, he was second-in-command at the Battle of New Orleans in 1812 and was wounded twice that day. In peacetime he acted as Governor of Jamaica 1827–29 and in 1833 was made C-in-C of the Bombay Army.

Keane's appointment to command the Army of the Indus as a Queen's officer was resented by many 'John Company' soldiers; the outspoken William Nott, left to protect the rear at Quetta, wrote that Keane's promotion was 'a dirty job' that had 'paralysed and nearly given a death blow to the enterprise'. Sir John was also a hot-blooded Celt who offended evangelical soldiers such as Major Henry **Havelock** with 'an open parade of private vices and affected coarseness of language' which, hinted the Christian soldier, were 'a cloak for darker features of his character.'

Just before the storming of Khelat the hardbitten Nott had a fiery falling-out with Keane when the latter insisted Sir William should serve under Major-General **Willshire**, an officer he considered his junior in rank. 'Your conduct is very extraordinary in an officer of your rank,' Keane told Nott. As tempers rose Keane bellowed, 'You insult my authority.' When Nott responded that 'I trust I have left no ill impression on your mind,' Keane replied, 'Ill impression, Sir! I will never forget your conduct as long as I live!'

Luckily Keane had a defender in the Governor-General, Lord Auckland, who told a contemporary, 'Do not let what you know of his temper tell against him. He has done admirably well.' In fact, from the very start of the expedition Sir John was anxious to try and bring the Bombay and Bengal columns of his unwieldy army together and press on with speed towards the Afghan capital. He re-organised the army command structure (even if it was a slap in the face for Nott) and when the Baluchis rose and caused transport problems, he appointed a brigadier of the day 'who had to report personally to the Commander-in-Chief before going off duty'.

Keane has been oft-criticised for his fast march from Kandahar to Ghazni, the mighty fortress which he attempted to breach without the support of heavy guns. In fairness, it can be argued that his errors were very largely due to the interference of political officers and bad advice from gunners, the latter assuring him that Ghazni could be taken without siege artillery. 'Being bold, breezy and confident', as the historian Norris wrote, it was a lucky Keane who watched his troops capture Ghazni – 'one of the most brilliant acts it has ever been my lot to witness', the general wrote after crying tears at the sight.

Nott and Keane never patched things up; the politicals loathed him too and one carped to Sir William that the C-in-C's 'plan of operations has been injudicious throughout'. One later defender of the general is the historian J.A. Norris, who noted that with his rough temper and habit of swearing like a trooper, Keane was 'a good officer but not a great gentleman'. The fall of Ghazni on 23 July 1839 was the last battle on the road to Kabul and Keane soon returned to India to be made Baron Keane of Ghazni and Coppoquin (County Waterford). He had not long to enjoy his peerage, however, dying on 24 August 1844.

Keane was no fool and in fact he was a perceptive man: on the journey back to India from Kabul, he had told young Henry **Durand**: 'Mark my words, it will not be long before there is here some signal catastrophe!' Prophetic words indeed.

KELLY-KENNY, GENERAL SIR T. – WISE OLD WARRIOR

ALONG WITH A handful of generals – Ian **Hamilton**, Neville **Lyttelton**, Archibald **Hunter** – Thomas Kelly-Kenny was one of the few to emerge from the South African War with his reputation intact. Considering that he was almost made a scapegoat for the losses at Paaredeberg and Poplar Grove in 1900, this was no mean feat.

Born plain Thomas Kelly (he took the second surname Kenny under the will of a maternal uncle who had fought at Waterloo) at Kilrush, County Clare in 1840, he was raised a staunch Catholic and later became a close friend of William **Butler**, the general from County Tipperary. In 1858 Kelly was gazetted to the 2nd Foot as an ensign without purchase, but within two years had a lucky break when he was appointed an ADC to the senior general in South Africa. A year later he proceeded to China as orderly officer to Brigadier Jephson, who took the 1st battalion of the 2nd from Cape Town to join the expedition. Thomas saw action at Sinho – where he was mentioned in despatches – the taking of Tangku and the Taku Forts. In 1867, while serving with his regiment in India, Kelly volunteered for service in the Abyssinian expedition and was later commended for his 'zeal, energy and ability' commanding a division of the transport train. In 1874–75 he studied at the Staff College. After twenty-four years with the 2nd Queen's Royal West Surrey Regiment he was appointed its lieutenant-colonel. The 1890s saw Kelly-Kenny promoted further to major-general and holding various appointments, including AAG at the War Office and inspector-general of auxiliary forces and recruiting.

After the failures of 'Black Week' in 1899, Kelly-Kenny was ordered to South Africa as Lt-General commanding the 6th Division. It must also be said that Kelly-Kenny had not seen any real fighting in forty years. Roberts' early assessment was that Kelly-Kenny was 'nervous and over-cautious'. The truth was that he was intelligent, careful in his planning and not ready to sacrifice the lives of soldiers needlessly.

Despite outranking **Kitchener** at Paardeburg on 18 February 1900, Roberts made it plain that he expected Kelly-Kenny to take orders from his junior general as if they were from the C-in-C. Kelly-Kenny was wise enough to realise that Roberts did not trust him. He confided in his diary that Kitchener was 'recklessly impatient'. A well-made plan to fence in the Boer general Cronje and his camp was over-ruled by Kitchener, who advocated a brutal frontal assault. What then followed was later described in the official history as 'chaos'. Kelly-Kenny bewailed in his diary that he

got 'No written orders of any sort. Kitchener only sends verbal messages
…' The British losses were the most severe of any day of the war – 303
officers and men killed, 906 wounded. That night Kelly-Kenny wrote:
'Awfully sad. Poor fellows' legs being amputated, it sickens one with war.'

Three weeks later, on 7 March, Roberts himself tried to re-enact
Paardeburg at a place called Poplar Grove, using improved tactics. The Boers,
as historian Thomas Pakenham has written, refused to behave 'like well-bred
pheasants'; the British cavalry, 'practically starving' and 'beat', as one officer
wrote, were too slow to trap the enemy, while Kelly-Kenny's infantry, with
barely half a water bottle per man, were similarly hesitant to attack (he later
admitted that he would have driven his men harder if he had realised the
Boers' low morale at this point). Three days later Kelly-Kenny trounced the
Boers at Driefontein. In his memoirs Horace Smith-Dorrien praised Kelly-
Kenny for leading the 6th Division 'in the very best style' at this fight.

Lord Roberts was now starting to re-evaluate his fellow Irishman.
He wrote in August 1900 that Kelly-Kenny:

> has done very well … He is careful, painstaking, and showed coolness, steadi-
> ness and resource, when our railway line was cut early in June. He looks
> after his men and sick and wounded, and knows all that is going on in his
> Command. He is probably not a brilliant Commander, but can, I believe, be
> trusted to carry out whatever he is told to do.

Roberts lobbied in 1901 for Kelly-Kenny to be made a KCB (he was raised
to GCB three years later in 1904). In 1902 Ian Hamilton reported to his old
chief that 'Kelly-Kenny is doing remarkably well, and has thoroughly justified your choice.'

On his return from South Africa, Sir Thomas was made Adjutant-
General; he retired in 1907 and one later award was the honorary colonelcy
of his old regiment. He passed away on Boxing Day 1914, and was buried
in Hove Cemetery.

KEYES, GENERAL SIR C. – 'KEEK SAHIB'

FEW OFFICERS SPENT their entire career in an area so confined as the
North-West Frontier of India, but Charles Patton Keyes served there from
1850 to 1878 in every major frontier campaign as well as several minor expeditions. In his autobiography, *Listening for the Drums*, Ian **Hamilton** singled

out Keyes, known as 'Keek Sahib' to friend and foe alike, as the epitome of the fighting frontier generals who led their men into battle sword in hand.

He was born in 1823 and joined the 20th Madras Native Infantry twenty years later. Bored in that relatively peaceful presidency army, he volunteered, and was accepted, as a subaltern in the newly formed 1st Punjab Native Infantry. This regiment, led by the tough John **Coke**, was part of the nucleus of the Punjab Irregular Force (called 'the Piffers'), later better known as the Punjab Frontier Force. Keyes first saw action in the 1850 expedition against the Kohat Pass Afridis. Three years later, within the space of a few days in April, he served against the Shinranis, fighting a rear-guard action that won him a mention in despatches, then rushed a stockade at the head of his men in a second expedition, this time against the Kasrani tribe. In 1860 the 1st PNI were sent to Miranzai as part of Neville **Chamberlain**'s expedition against the Mahsuds. During severe fighting on 4 May the tribesmen launched a charge downhill right up to the British guns. Captain Keyes, sword in hand, engaged the leading warrior. 'As they closed in single-handed combat the sound of battle died away on both sides,' wrote Major-General Elliott. Keyes finally cut down his opponent and the Mahsuds fled with the 1st PNI in such hot pursuit that they captured the main breastwork. Keyes found himself once more lauded in despatches and the talk of the force.

Promoted to major, Keyes became one of the heroes of the hard-fought Umbeyla campaign in 1863. Perhaps his toughest fight was on 30 October when he and his men, who had defended the Crag Picquet through the previous night, were driven out in a dawn attack. He re-formed the regiment and re-took the Crag, killing more than fifty of the enemy in savage hand-to-hand fighting. In the words of Ian Hamilton: 'As Keek Sahib ... topped the crest three men fired at him: the first bullet knocked the sword out of his right hand, the second bullet completely shattered his left hand, the third bullet making two holes through his *poshteen* or sheep-skin coat, only grazed his side.' Keyes lost three fingers in the fight, while thirty-nine other officers and men were wounded and thirteen killed. Almost on the last day of the war, while the British were burning the stronghold of the enemy, tribesmen launched a sneak attack on the camp. This was admirably defended by troops under Keyes command.

The year 1869 saw Charles Keyes leading his men in expeditions against the Orakzais and Kabul Khel Waziris. Promoted to brigadier and given command of the Punjab Frontier Force, Keyes next led a relatively bloodless expedition against the Dawar tribe of Waziristan in 1872.

His biggest command was the Jowaki Afridi expedition of November 1877 to January 1878. This winter campaign, much of it fought in freezing rain and bitingly cold winds, involved 2,090 troops in several small columns. It had become necessary and was deemed urgent after the Afridis had slaughtered a small party of British infantry. Keyes (aided by his fellow brigadier Charles Ross) was able to punish the tribe by burning villages and crops until the Afridis finally submitted after the Amir of Afghanistan refused to help them.

Keyes was subsequently made a KCB, left the frontier and commanded at Hyderabad, before retiring in 1884. He was made a general in 1889. During the 1870s he had argued at a conference on the Waziri problem for military control of the frontier, not civilian management. He opposed dual control – the traditional British policy – and if the army was not given a free hand he recommended the frontier be controlled entirely by the police under civil management.

Charles Keyes died on 5 February 1896 in Ireland. He and his wife, Katherine, had raised a large family; the most famous of his children was Admiral of the Fleet, Roger, 1st Baron Keyes, one of the heroes of the Boxer Rebellion and First World War; another son, Adrian, also served as a naval commander in the Great War, while Terence became a celebrated political officer in India; a fourth son, Charlie, charged with the Guides Cavalry at the Malakand in the year after his father's death, but was killed in 1901 by Nigerian cattle thieves while on secondment to the West African Frontier Force.

KITCHENER, FIELD-MARSHAL LORD H. – 'K OF K'

IN THE GOLDEN summer of 1914 the writer Sir Osbert Sitwell observed Kitchener at a London soiree: 'He sat there as if he were a god,' noted Sitwell:

> A large square frame, with square shoulders, square head, square face, a square line of hair at the top of a square forehead … he plainly belonged to some different order of creation from those around him … And you could, in the mind's eye, see his image set up as that of an English god, by natives, in different parts of the Empire which he had helped to create and support, precisely as the Roman Emperors had formerly been worshipped.

The media helped Kitchener rise astonishingly fast to the rank of general, then beyond to that of military supremo, a giant who seemed to be the very epitome of British might. Journalists such as G.W. Steevens of the *Daily Mail* labelled him an automaton 'to be patented and shown with pride …

hors concours, the Sudan Machine'. It was true that he was aloof, brusque, dour, even brutal to subordinates. His Sudan intelligence chief, Reginald Wingate, complained of Kitchener's 'boorish insults'. A recent historian noted how he 'detested failure, weakness and even sickness in others – and himself. He also did not aim to be popular amongst the troops but in time they came to revere him.' A distraught Archibald **Hunter**, who was forced to work closely with Kitchener as Sirdar, once railed that

> he is inhuman, heartless, with eccentric and freakish bursts of generosity, spe-
> cially when he is defeated: he is a vain, egotistical mass of pride and ambition,
> expecting and usurping all and giving nothing; he is a mixture of the fox, Jew
> and snake and like all bullies is a dove when tackled.

There was another side to Kitchener, too, equally remarkable, for he was also highly strung at times, prone to depression, sensitive to perceived slights, a man who found it difficult to show his true emotions or inner feelings. The stern soldier who seemed to have little pity for the thousands of dervishes wounded after Omdurman was also the man who tenderly grew orchids, loved interior design and was happiest playing with his gun dogs. The great warrior and automaton venerated by the masses in the press, was the same man who wrote to a friend from the Sudan campaign of his 'continual anxiety, worry and strain … I feel so completely done up that I can hardly go on, and wish I were dead'.

Those who had to deal with Kitchener on a daily basis, such as his aides, realised he was an extraordinary man. One of them called him 'a queer cus-tomer', but added that he was 'a long-headed, clear-minded man of business with a wonderful memory'. Later the same aide declared that he was 'a rum 'un and a ripper. He is as hard as nails and as cool as a cucumber … Here he is an absolute autocrat, does exactly what he pleases, and won't pay any attention to red-tape regulations and … There is very little correspondence except by wire and in the field almost every order is given verbally'. He could have added that Kitchener seemed incapable of delegating even simple tasks, kept a very small staff and followed a strict routine which meant at least three hours of work before breakfast. His drinking was temperate, his uniform spot-less, and he would go into a rage if anyone touched his papers.

Herbert Horatio Kitchener was born in Ireland on 24 June 1850, the son of an eccentric lieutenant-colonel. After an education partly on the continent, where the family went to live for the sake of his mother's health, he entered the Royal Military Academy at Woolwich in 1867. Here he met his lifelong hero, Charles **Gordon**. In 1870 young Kitchener served as a volunteer with a French field ambulance during the Franco-Prussian War. Twelve years later he was serving in Cyprus, where he absconded and took part in spying missions during the early stages of the Egyptian War before a furious superior ordered him back. His abilities as an orientalist made him a natural choice as one of the first recruits to the new Egyptian Army in 1883. During the **Gordon** Relief Expedition he was engaged on intelligence duties and deeply shocked by the death of his hero, a loss he vowed to avenge; from 1886 to 1888 he was Governor-General of the Eastern Sudan, led a small expedition against the dervishes, made a tactical error and was wounded in the jaw. The next four years saw him as Adjutant-General of the Egyptian Army before his surprise appointment as Sirdar.

When a chance came for an advance up the Nile, a jubilant Kitchener grabbed it (dancing a jig in his night clothes when he got the news). His advance to Omdurman was a masterpiece of logistics. Superiors, such as Prime Minister Lord Salisbury and Lord Cromer, the British Envoy in Cairo, respected a soldier 'who did not think extravagance was the handmaid of efficiency'. Each step of the way was part of Kitchener's master-plan to bring the dervishes to battle in the vicinity of Omdurman. He succeeded and gained a peerage.

Kitchener was a lucky commander in many ways: his great fame developed at a time when the British Empire was its apex and the jingoistic press most fervent. To the masses he became the perfect hero at a time when one was needed. The fact that he re-took the Sudan at a modest cost in money and British lives, while avenging the national shame of **Gordon**'s death thirteen years earlier, simply added gloss to the image. This success story was also helped in no small part by fast-action maxim machine guns and repeating rifles facing natives armed only with spears and a belief in God. A criticism of Kitchener expressed after Omdurman, and also recently, is that 'he was never a confident general, and being an engineer meant that he had not studied strategy and tactics fully'. On the Kerrari Plain outside Omdurman, after the first phase of the battle, he carelessly led a dash for the Mahdist capital before the main dervish attack had been delivered; at Paardeberg in South Africa, the one chance he had to fight a big battle against an intelligent foe, according to his biographer, Sir Philip Magnus, 'he charged bull-headed, and suffered a humiliating defeat.' The historian Thomas Pakenham has noted that, for a time after Paardeberg, wags remarked that Kitchener was not 'K of K' but 'K of Chaos'.

Lord **Roberts** barely knew Kitchener before he joined the old general as his chief of staff in South Africa. Surprisingly, they got along very well;

Kitchener called his chief 'splendid' and Roberts told the war minister that 'I have never been served more efficiently than by Kitchener, and on no single occasion has there been the slightest friction between us ...'

After Roberts' departure from the Cape the war dragged on two more years, into a guerrilla phase. Kitchener was blamed for blockhouses and Boer deaths in the infamous concentration camps. It was a tough war, but he showed skill in launching numerous small columns to chase the Boer commando units, in developing a blockhouse system and internment camps aimed at depriving the enemy of material and physical support, and in creating new fighting units composed of former Boer combatants. He was partly responsible for the high death rate in some of the camps, but did what he could to remedy matters when the situation was pointed out to him. In 1902 he also had to fight a different kind of battle, against Sir Alfred Milner, the British High Commissioner who wanted to impose a tough settlement on the Boers. Kitchener wanted a conciliatory policy and, luckily, won the argument.

During the Edwardian period Kitchener's fame and prestige grew as he served in India as C-in-C and then secretary for war in 1914 (the first soldier to be in the cabinet since 1660). By then, even he had come to realise his popular appeal to the masses, to understand that he was a legend in his own lifetime, and that fighting and saving the British Empire 'often called for abilities beyond the battlefield and Kitchener had those'. His death aboard *HMS Hampshire* in 1916, struck by a mine, came as a profound shock to the nation in the middle of a terrible war – and a genuine loss because, despite all his faults, Lord Kitchener worked unceasingly for his country and its army right to the end of his days.

LAWRENCE, LIEUTENANT-GENERAL SIR G. – A RIGHT GOOD FELLOW

GEORGE ST PATRICK Lawrence was the eldest of a remarkable trio of brothers, though his services are eclipsed by those of siblings Henry, who died commanding at Lucknow in its famous siege in 1857, and John, who rose through the civilian service to become viceroy. George nevertheless had a career that saw him imprisoned or held hostage no less than three times during the disastrous first Afghan War, followed by five months' captivity in the Punjab during the Second Sikh War. During the Indian Mutiny his duties as a political officer had to be combined with more active soldiering when it was his lot to stifle revolt in Rajputana.

Descended from good Ulster stock, the Lawrence boys were the sons of Lt-Colonel Alexander Lawrence, an East India Company soldier who had led the storming of Seringapatam in 1799. George, his third son, was born in Ceylon on 17 March 1804 and sent to Ireland for his education followed by the HEIC's seminary at Addiscombe. He arrived in India on 10 September 1821 and was posted to the 2nd Bengal Light Cavalry. Seventeen years later Captain Lawrence and his regiment were deputed to join the Army of the Indus proceeding to place Shah Shuja on the Afghan throne. Early on, Lawrence was selected as military secretary to the British Envoy (senior political advisor), Sir William Hay Macnaghten. Many of the mistakes made by the British at Kabul were laid at his door; the C-in-C, India, Sir Jasper Nicholls, complained of his 'total want of forethought and foresight', while General Nott dismissively wrote: 'It has always appeared wonderful to me how Government could have employed so very weak a man. I fear that his three years' doings cannot be retrieved, and that our blood must flow for it.' In recent accounts of the war, William Dalrymple and Edmund Yorke have both made much of Macnaghten's shortcomings.

In his memoirs, written in 1874, Lawrence made a spirited defence of 'the man I loved and revered as a father … a skilful politician and a most distinguished statesman, but above all, an upright, high-minded, chivalrous gentleman … a victim to his own rectitude of purpose and unbending sense of honour.' For, in Lawrence's exciting tale, it is Macnaghten who is the hero and the military command, represented by ailing General Elphinstone and foolish Brigadier Shelton, who are responsible for the disasters. Macnaghten urged military action countless times, did not trust the Afghans, and wanted the British troops, as did Lawrence, to move into the old citadel overlooking the city where they could, with luck, have held out through the winter until the snows melted.

When Sir William was treacherously murdered at a parley with the Afghan chiefs, Captain Lawrence was by his side. In the ensuing tumult he was luckily taken to safety by a friendly chief and held prisoner for a few days. On his release Lady Sale, one of the garrison wives, described him as 'looking haggard and ten years older from anxiety'. During the terrible retreat from Kabul the women were in Lawrence's care. He was taken prisoner by the Afghans, one of a small group of hostages, and forced to watch the killing of the British-Indian troops and camp followers (more than 16,000 souls); only one man, Dr Brydon, reached Jellalabad alive. 'Thus perished our Cabul army,' wrote Lawrence, 'sacrificed … to the incompetency, feebleness and want of skill and resolution of their military leaders.'

In due course Lawrence and his fellow prisoners were released by returning British troops bent on vengeance. He returned to India and a well-earned leave. In 1846 he was appointed British Resident and political agent for the frontier districts based at Peshawar. Under him were such future luminaries as Herbert **Edwardes**, Harry **Lumsden** and Reynell **Taylor**. One aide at this time called him 'brisk, jolly ... capable of great deeds in a crisis by his pluck, talent, honesty and decision'. When the Second Sikh War broke out in 1848, Lawrence and his family were taken prisoner. Though guarded night and day he was treated with respect by the Khalsa warriors and used as the negotiator during peace talks after the Battle of Gujerat; when released by the Sikhs and allowed to cross the Sutlej to parley with the British, he honourably returned to their camp to carry on the deliberations.

In 1850, when the Afridis attacked engineers building a road through the Kohat Pass, killing twelve and wounding eight, Lawrence acted as political officer with the expedition under Sir Colin **Campbell** that was sent to punish the tribe. Ill health then made George ask for a transfer and he got the plum appointment of Political Agent for Rajputana. Sir Charles **Napier** about this time called him 'a right good soldier, and a right good fellow'.

During the Mutiny, raised to the rank of brigadier, Lawrence was for a time in both civilian and military control of Rajputana, an area of 10,000 square miles and with 10 million inhabitants. He acted quickly to protect the treasury at Ajmeer, but had to contend with risings at Aboo, Indore and Kotah, though on the whole the district remained peaceful. In 1860 he was made a CB and the following year a major-general. He retired in 1864, was made a KCSI in 1866 and lieutenant-general in the following year. His memoirs were published in his seventieth year and a decade later he passed away at his home in London.

LITTLER, LIEUTENANT-GENERAL SIR J. – FIGHTING MAHRATTAS AND SIKHS

DURING THE FIRST fifty years of the nineteenth century John Hunter Littler became one of the best fighting generals in the Indian Army, described by historian Donald Featherstone as 'an experienced, trustworthy and capable soldier, daring, resolute and self-reliant'.

He was born in 1783, scion of an old Cheshire family. Luckily, his maternal grandfather was a director of the HEIC, so it was without much difficulty that the young man was made an ensign in the 10th Bengal Native Infantry in 1800. On the way to India a French privateer captured Littler's ship and he was set adrift in a small boat, but was rescued and reached his regiment. During the Second Mahratta War the dashing Lieutenant Littler saw action; more fighting followed at the capture of Java in 1811.

In 1812 he was promoted to captain. There then passed thirty years of peacetime soldiering as Littler, rising with purchase, became colonel of the 36th BNI. In 1841 he was promoted to major-general and two years later joined the 12,000-strong army under **Gough** sent against the Mahrattas of Gwalior. He commanded the left of the British line at Maharajpore; he and both his brigadiers, Wright and Valiant, were wounded as they charged the enemy's front line of twenty-eight heavy guns, the general also having his horse shot from under him. One of his aides, Luther **Vaughan**, said he was one of the kindest officers he ever served under.

The next year Littler was made a CB and given command of the frontier district at Ferozepore with 7,000 men. When war with the Sikhs broke out, he cleverly avoided a confrontation with the Khalsa warriors and drew them deftly towards Mudki where he knew they would meet the main British army. His skirmishing and adroit manoeuvring, done with 'great skill', meant that Littler missed the first battle of the war at Mudki and was late arriving on the field of Ferozeshah for the second encounter. Fighting did not begin, after an artillery duel, until 4 p.m. on the shortest day of the year. The British advance was precipitated prematurely by Littler's division, which was decimated, with 185 officers and men killed and wounded in ten minutes. A private wrote that 'our men fell like rain, in perfect rows on the ground', while Littler thought the whole business was 'awful' and furiously blamed one of his brigadiers for allowing his men to charge too soon and then, without consulting him, letting them retire.

He fought no more battles, but was given the GCB. He went on to serve on the Governor-General's Council where he opposed setting up colleges for Indian females, as Lord Dalhousie joked, because 'he thought that a smattering of English would lead them to immoral habits!' By 1852 he was reporting that 'Poor old Littler is so broken and frail that I could not have been savage with him even if I wished to.' Shortly afterwards Sir John returned to England and died in Devon on 18 February 1856. He is buried with his ancestors in Cheshire.

LOCKHART, GENERAL SIR W. – INTERESTING ENIGMA

FEW SOLDIERS SERVED in so many North-West Frontier expeditions as William Lockhart; in 1897–98 he had command in the biggest expedition ever mounted against the frontier tribes. His reward was promotion to C-in-C, India, yet he remains an interesting enigma, largely forgotten today. A recent brief biography, useful for outlining his family background, adds no letters, diaries or other correspondence to help us know more.

William was born at Milton Lockhart, Lanarkshire, the son of a laird-parson, on 2 September 1841. He joined the EIC army as an ensign in the 44th BNI in October 1858, but was attached to the 5th Fusiliers in pursuit of mutineers. A year later he transferred to a cavalry regiment, the 14th Bengal Lancers. His superiors first noticed Lockhart during the Bhutan War of 1865, during which he conducted an important reconnaissance. In 1867 he was appointed an aide to Brigadier Merewether in Abyssinia and saw his first battles at Arogee and Magdala.

Within a few months of returning to India from the Dark Continent, William set out on what was to be the first of many punitive frontier expeditions; as DAQMG of the 2nd Brigade of the Hazara expedition he led another vital reconnaissance. Eight years of peacetime soldiering followed, during which he began raising a family with his young wife. The most notable incident of these years was his part in rescuing two women from an upturned boat in 1869. This won him the bronze medal of the Royal Humane Society. Possibly bored by the lack of adventure, but more likely at the instigation of the Indian Army intelligence department, to which Lockhart was increasingly connected, he went to Sumatra where the Dutch were having difficulties subduing the locals. He took part in the assault on Lambada, displayed his customary gallantry and won the Dutch campaign medal. One side effect of this cruel war was malaria in the fever-ridden Dutch camp, an ague that plagued him for the rest of his life.

When the Second Afghan War broke out in 1878, much to his irritation, Lockhart was attached to the QMG's department at Simla but, following a resumption of hostilities in 1879, he was first sent as Road Commandant in the Khyber Pass and then joined **Roberts** as his AQMG at Kabul. On 'Bobs" staff Lockhart formed a lasting friendship with a fellow Scot, the acerbic Charles **Macgregor**, who called him 'flabby and uninteresting' in one of his nasty diary entries, but vowed to help his pal's career when writing in a better mood. Everyone in the mess during that bitter winter at Kabul appreciated William's cheery disposition and Macgregor noted he was a better man in the field than in the office.

By the close of the Afghan War it was clear that Lockhart was a rising star. He was made chief of the Indian Army's intelligence department based at Simla. He was an active supporter of the 'forward policy' on the frontiers (much to the annoyance of intelligence chiefs back in Whitehall. Historian William Beaver has noted that the Simla men were known in the Indian Army as the 'Mutual Laudation Society', a clique that took care of their own, membership of which was seen as a stepping-stone to greater things). In 1885 Lockhart was chosen by Viceroy Lord Dufferin to be his envoy on a delicate fact-finding mission to Chitral, an attempt to spread British influence into the higher valleys of the Hindu Kush. On his return, the government praised him for the 'firmness, temper and discretion' he had displayed 'in circumstances of unusual difficulty and hardship' and the 'high value' of the intelligence he provided.

Within weeks Lockhart was back in the field again. This time it was as commander of the Eastern Division in Upper Burma, where operations were underway to extend British rule. A contemporary later wrote, 'If there had been more Lockharts in command of brigades, the final pacification and settlement of the country would have taken less time to complete.' Returning to England, he was made a CB and assistant military secretary at Horse Guards.

In late 1890 Lockhart jumped at the chance of seeing active soldiering again when he was offered command of the Punjab Frontier Force. In January 1891 he led his first expedition, commanding three columns that attacked the Orakzais of the Miranzai Valley. A second expedition, also led by Lockhart, was necessary three months later to finally cow this recalcitrant tribe, who had attacked workers building a chain of forts – Lockhart, Gulistan and Saragarhi – on the ridge leading into Orakzai territory. A year later, following another expedition to the Black Mountain led by Major-General **Elles**, Lockhart led a bloodless Isazai Field Force to the same region after a peace treaty was broken. In 1894–95 he led three columns into Mahsud territory in Waziristan to punish those who had attacked a delimitation commission fixing the frontier between Afghan and British territory. Resistance, as in Lockhart's previous three expeditions, was minimal. Things were about to change spectacularly.

1 Frederick Ernest Appleyard

2 Geoffrey Barton

3   *George Bourchier*

4   *James 'Buster' Browne*

5 *Charles Henry Brownlow*

6 *William Francis Butler*

7 *Frederick Carrington*

8 *George Cathcart*

9 George Nicholas Channer

10 Cornelius Francis Clery

11 Henry Hugh Clifford

12 John Talbot Coke

13 *Henry Collett*

14 *Henry Edward Colville*

15 Henry Hope Crealock

16 Henry Dermot Daly

17 William Drysdale

18 Henry Marion Durand

19 William Kidston Elles

20 Richard England

21 Alfred Gaselee

22 Charles John Stanley Gough

23 *Patrick Grant*

24 *Francis Wallace Grenfell*

25 Frederick Paul Haines

26 Arthur Fitzroy 'No-Bobs' Hart-Synnot

27 *James 'Jem' Hill-Johnnes*

28 *Arthur Dickson Home*

29 Edward Thomas Henry 'Curly' Hutton

30 Thomas Kelly-Kenny

31 Charles Patton 'Keek Sahib' Keyes

32 Robert Cunliffe Low

33 Harry Burnett Lumsden

34 Charles Metcalfe Macgregor

35 Herbert Taylor Macpherson

36 Frederick Francis Maude

37 Hugh McCalmont

38 John Carstairs McNeill

39 Frederick Dobson Middleton

40 William Charles Francis Molyneux

41 *Charles James Napier*

42 *Henry Wylie Norman*

43 William 'Hellfire Jack' Olpherts

44 Charles Henry Palliser

45 Arthur Power Palmer

46 Robert Phayre

47 Henry Hallam Parr

48 Harry North Dalrymple Prendergast

49 James Maurice Primrose

50 Abraham Roberts

51 Robert Gordon Rogers

52 Robert Henry 'Fighting Bob' Sale

53 Henry 'Hawk`s Eye' Somerset

54 Frederick Charles Arthur 'Old Ben' Stephenson

55 *Donald Martin Stewart*

56 *William Penn Symons*

57 *Reynell George Taylor*

58 *Joseph Thackwell*

59 Harry Tombs

60 Frederick William Traill-Burroughs

61 Alexander Bruce Tulloch

62 John Adam Tytler

63 Charles Warren

64 Edward Robert Prevost Woodgate

In 1897 the North-West Frontier erupted in flames. Lockhart, stricken by old maladies in England, was on sick leave when the Waziris and Afridis rose, the Khyber forts were sacked and it looked as if Peshawar might be threatened. Hastening back to India he found himself at the head of a sizeable army of two divisions, each with two brigades – a total of 44,000 combatants – to chastise all who had risen in revolt and especially to traverse and put to the sword the heartland of Afridi territory, the Tirah Valley, a sacred area which the tribesmen had kept secret from the eyes of unbelievers. The campaign, by far the largest fought by the Queen's army on the Indian frontiers, has been more scrutinised than others. It began in October and Lockhart was well aware his troops would have to fight and survive in the bitter Himalayan winter. He expected – and got – a gruelling campaign in which the tribes avoided pitched battles in most cases and contented themselves in expertly picking off their enemy, using stolen British rifles, with deadly accuracy. While Indian Army regiments fought very well on the whole, mistakes were made by the less experienced British Army commanders who had no previous knowledge of frontier warfare. This resulted in a couple of massacres beyond Lockhart's control. The only pitched battle of note – the storming of the Dargai Heights – infuriated Lockhart, who censured the commanding general who had placed lookouts on the surrounding hills prior to the fight, then removed them, only for the enemy to take their place!

Sir William was seriously ill for most of the campaign and many decisions were taken without his full consultation; his chief of staff, William **Nicholson**, was a dogmatic man not liked by subordinates. Hubert de la Poer Gough, later a general, wrote home: 'Lockhart has been very seedy the whole time & his staff, Nicholson in particular, have not done anything to help make things run smooth or even seen to anything themselves.' Gough thought the reconaissances were disastrously mismanaged 'in spite of Lockhart's reputation'. Colonel Haughton, 36th Sikhs, who was dead before the end of the campaign, wrote on 16 January 1898: 'Things would have been better managed if Sir W. Lockhart not been in such bad health. He has constantly been down with fever, diarrhoea & I believe has been really ill all the time ...' Sir William's plan for the invasion of Tirah was 'sound but it almost failed to get off the ground'. It saw the tribes punished, their villages, including those in the Tirah Valley, destroyed and crops and fruit trees burned as a lesson of reprisal. The tribesmen followed the British throughout their withdrawal, picking men off with fearful accuracy using the new smokeless-powder rifles. Tirah alone cost the lives of 287 British and Indian soldiers, with a further 1,524 wounded and ten missing before the coming of peace.

The difficulties of the Tirah campaign, and the sigh of relief in government circles when it was over, made Lockhart a celebrity. In 1898, after a
visit to London where he was feted, he was appointed to succeed Sir George
White as C-in-C, India. He did not have long to enjoy this well-earned
promotion. His old health problems flared up in January 1900 and two
months later he was dead. He lies buried in the Fort William military cemetery at Calcutta. There are memorials to him at Rawalpindi and in St Giles
Cathedral, Edinburgh. By all accounts Lockhart was liked and respected.
A fine epitaph was written by Colonel Thomas Holdich, who had helped
Lockhart demarcate part of the frontier. He extolled: 'A careful adviser, a
faithful friend, a genial and kindly companion whose unswerving honesty of
purpose was never to be doubted for an instant – such was Lockhart.'

LOW, GENERAL SIR R. – FIGHTING TO CHITRAL

OF ALL LATE Victorian campaigns, the most romantic, at least in the eyes
of the jingoistic press, was the relief of a small garrison besieged high in
the Hindu Kush at a remote fort in Chitral. Commanding the main relief
column which had to contend with the aggressions of man and nature along
the way was an officer who is totally forgotten today – Robert Cunliffe Low.
    Born on 28 January 1838, son of General Sir John Low of Fife, Robert
joined the 9th Bengal Cavalry as a cornet in 1854. During the Siege of Delhi
in 1857 he was one of Archdale **Wilson**'s aides, took part in the second
relief of Lucknow and the operations in Central India. He won his second
war medal fighting in the 1863 Umbeyla expedition as the commander of a
troop. A long spell of peacetime soldiering followed until the Second Afghan
War; at first Low did duty in the Bazar Valley, but later joined **Roberts**' staff
in Kabul as Director of Transport. This post was hastily appointed when
another officer failed in the task. 'Bobs' was impressed by Low, who became a
specialist in transport matters, and remained in this line of work at war's end.
In 1886 he was promoted to brigadier and sent into the field in Upper Burma.
Here he stayed for two years as general commanding the Mandalay Brigade.
He was mentioned in despatches and on his return to India was made a KCB.
    This slim, white-haired man of stern countenance, expert at compiling an
efficient transport team, seemed ideal to lead an army on the difficult route
to Chitral in 1895. He had three infantry brigades, two regiments of cavalry,
four batteries of mountain artillery and detachments of sappers and miners –
some 15,000 men – under his command. The fort at Chitral had been under

siege for a month when Low's army set off. They forced their way up the Malakand Pass into the mountains fighting tribesmen fearful of this encroachment on their sacred lands, had a pitched battle near the Panjorka River and then slogged through the snows in twelve days to relieve the trapped garrison.

It is unclear to what extent Low was really an adept general since he was well supported by some excellent officers, including a frontier hardened chief of staff, Bindon **Blood**. During operations at the Malakand, where Low was all for attacking early and at night, Blood tried to curb his chief's impetuosity and argued for an attack the next day. When bad weather settled the issue Low was not amused when Blood said, 'Isn't it fortunate that the Almighty intervened?' (Later the general owned up to his mistake).

This successful little war pleased just about everyone except the tribesmen who vowed vengeance. Low was made a GCB and in November 1896 promoted to lieutenant-general. Two years later he was given command of the Bombay Army. He died in August 1911 and, after a few newspaper obituaries, slipped gently into obscurity.

LUGARD, GENERAL SIR E. – STEADY AS A ROCK

OVERLOOKED IN HIS own lifetime, Edward Lugard was a brave and efficient general who campaigned widely in Asia and deserves better recognition. His services in the Indian Mutiny, sadly ignored, were exceptional. Lugard also looked like a warrior – tall and prematurely bald, with a shiny pate, handsome white sideburns, a bristling moustache and goatee beard.

He was born in Chelsea on 8 May 1810, the son of a soldier, entered Sandhurst and joined the 31st Foot in India in 1828. Fourteen years of peacetime soldiering followed before Lieutenant Lugard followed his regiment as part of **Pollock**'s avenging army into Afghanistan. During an expedition against the Shinwarris near the Khyber Pass he had his horse shot from under him and received a favourable mention in despatches. When the First Sikh War broke out Captain Lugard served as DAAG under Sir Harry **Smith**, who became a lifelong friend. Edward was slightly wounded in the first battle at Mudki, then more seriously by a bayonet thrust to his knee in the next fight at Ferozeshah. He recovered sufficiently to be by Smith's side at Aliwal and was commended by his general, who wrote: 'a more cool, intrepid and trustworthy officer cannot be brought forward.' So impressed was Smith by Lugard's bravery at Sobraon that he had him raised to a brevet majority on the battlefield and championed his friend as

AAG of HM's forces in India. Throughout the Second Sikh War Lugard served on Lord **Gough**'s staff as acting AG of the British regiments and was present at all the battles.

After the Sikh Wars, now a lieutenant-colonel and a CB, Lugard moved to Simla in his AAG role. In 1854 he was appointed DAG of the Bombay Army and an aide-de-camp to the Queen. When the Persian War broke out in 1856 he joined the expeditionary force under Outram as his chief of staff. Shortly before the Battle of Khushab on 8 February 1857, Sir James **Outram** was stunned by a fall from a horse. He gave the credit for a British success that left 700 Persians dead on the field to Lugard, to whom he 'owed everything'. In a despatch he praised Lugard's 'zeal and exertions through-out the campaign'. Nor was he alone: Brigadier John Jacob, a harsh critic of Outram, wrote: 'I find Col. Lugard one of the most excellent men and best soldiers I have ever met with – able, energetic, cool-headed and methodical – it is evident to me that his presence alone has saved this army from some great disaster.' Noting Lugard's style, Outram told the Governor-General Earl Canning that he 'sees into all departments, but so kindly in his deport-ment to all officials that all cheerfully attend to his suggestions'.

When the Mutiny broke out Lugard was soon appointed Adjutant-General in India, partly at the insistence of Sir Colin **Campbell**, who rated him highly. During the second relief of Lucknow, Sir Colin gave him com-mand of the 2nd Infantry Division; according to Campbell it fell to Lugard and his troops to meet the 'sternest struggle' of that battle. Lugard was sin-gled out for 'the greatest credit' in these operations. Following the capture of Lucknow he was given command of the Azimghur Field Force and sent to deal with Veer Koer Singh, a wily rebel chieftain who had defeated one British army. Between them, Singh and Lugard played a dance through Bihar, but finally Sir Edward re-occupied Jagdispur and chased the rebels through thick jungles, recapturing two howitzers on 23 April 1858 and finally defeating them with 'great slaughter' on 4 June.

After twenty-five years' continuous service in India it was hardly surpris-ing that this hot weather campaigning took a toll on Lugard's health. He returned to England, his campaigning days over, but from 1861–71 was under-secretary of state for war and served as president of the commission on the abolition of army purchase. In 1867 he was made a GCB and he became a full general in 1872. He died in 1898 and lies buried in Kensal Green Cemetery beside his two wives. Despite being a tough commander, friends also noted his 'keen sense of humour'. One of Lugard's nephews, Frederick, rose to become conqueror of Uganda and northern Nigeria, the last great pro-consul-warrior of the British Empire.

LUMSDEN, LIEUTENANT-GENERAL SIR H. & LUMSDEN, GENERAL SIR P. – FRONTIER BROTHERS

HARRY AND PETER Lumsden saw more fighting than most men; they proved themselves instrumental in dealings with the wild frontier tribes. Harry's achievements are well-recorded, but Peter's are less so. Harry, the elder by eight years, known to friends from his youth as 'Joe', was a born leader of men, one of the most important warriors on the North-West Frontier. Younger brother Peter, no less courageous, saw much campaigning in staff appointments and took part in major frontier missions.'

'Joe' was born during a gale aboard an East Indiaman on 12 November 1821. His father was a celebrated Bengal Horse Artilleryman. It was thus hardly surprising that the son, nominated for an HEIC cadetship, was gazetted an ensign in the 59th BNI in 1838. Quickly qualifying as an interpreter, he accompanied the 33rd BNI in this capacity when General **Pollock** invaded Afghanistan in 1842. Young Lumsden saw plenty of action and seemed to enjoy every minute of it. He served with his own regiment four years later at Sobraon against the Sikhs. His regiment lost seventy-three killed and wounded and when a ball sliced through his foot 'Joe' laughed it off: 'If you hear of an old boy wishing for a cure for corns just recommend him to have a musket shot sent through them.'

After the First Sikh War 'Joe' was chosen to be one of the assistants to Henry Lawrence, the new British Resident at Lahore. A wise and influential man, Lawrence gathered about him a group of young officers, all of whom would find fame as paladins on the frontier. Early in 1847 came Lumsden's greatest moment, when he was chosen to raise a Guide Corps to police the frontier districts. 'It will be the finest appointment in the country,' he told his father, 'being the right hand of the army and the left of the political. I am to have the making of the new regiment all to myself.' Within a few months Lumsden's Corps of Guides were carving themselves a formidable reputation. Dressed in a dung-stained, dust-coloured uniform called 'khakee', its soldiers – a mix of hardy Pathans, Gurkhas and Sikhs – walked fast and rode faster.

'Joe', an expert horseman, practically lived in the saddle. He was a first-rate shot, an excellent (left-handed) swordsman, who expected his officers to display the same skills. He laughed, lectured and punished his native troops in their own languages, and they adored him. He was always down to earth, bluff and cheery. The men nicknamed him 'Cease Firing' because he would whack anyone with his Irish shillelagh if they continued to shoot after he had given the order to stop. Lumsden led his new regiment at the Siege of

Multan in 1848 and was at the head of the cavalry that pursued the Sikhs after the Battle of Gujerat. That same year – 1849 – he led the Guides in an attack on the Utman Khel Afridis, the first of numerous frontier expeditions the regiment would serve in over the next century. Similar campaigns followed in 1850–52 before he took a well-earned leave.

In 1855 'Joe' returned to India and his Guides. Two years later he was sent on an important diplomatic mission to Afghanistan aimed at restoring the troubled relations with that country. With him rode his younger brother Peter, who had missed the Sikh Wars, but been an aide to General Abraham **Roberts** (father of 'Bobs') on the frontier, and seen action in four small expeditions against Afridis and Mohmands. The Afghan Mission took the Lumsdens away from India while the Mutiny was at its height. 'Joe' missed the excitement of leading his men at Delhi and a host of other fights, as well as the deaths of many comrades. Yet the mission was vitally important, convincing the Afghans not to invade India and throw in their lot with the rebels. A contemporary soldier noted that 'from the time it entered Afghanistan to the last day of its departure' the mission was 'in jeopardy'.

Peter Lumsden did, in fact, take part in the final stages of **Rose**'s Central India campaign as his AQMG, sharing in the pursuit of Tatya Tope. In 1860 the brothers were in separate wars – 'Joe' leading his Guides against the Waziris and Peter as QMG in China. It was while in the Orient that the younger Lumsden had an amazing escape from death when a small boat he was in capsized 5 miles out to sea. A storm was raging, the night was dark and lit by flashes of lightning and there were high seas, but he somehow managed to swim to shore. Once there he collapsed exhausted on the sands. Next day he could get no help and so walked along the shore in just a shirt, his feet badly blistered, until he found a small boat and rowed to within the British lines, where his dishevelled appearance created quite a stir. Five years later, he served in the Bhutan expedition as a lieutenant-colonel.

The year 1860 marked the end of 'Joe' Lumsden's campaigning days and he became political agent at Hyderabad, one of the plums of the political service, before retiring in 1869. He made his home in Scotland and died there in 1896. Brother Peter meanwhile continued to rise in staff appointments, including both AG and QMG of the Indian Army. In 1876 the C-in-C, India, Sir Frederick **Haines**, wrote that 'General Lumsden's frank and genial manners at once inspires confidence.' Possibly Haines trusted Lumsden too much. This at least was the view of historian Colonel H.B. Hanna, who singled out Peter as one of three men instrumental in misleading the bellicose Viceroy, Lord Lytton, into thinking that a new war with Afghanistan would be a walkover. Haines wanted Lumsden to have the job of frontier commissioner or lead the Kurram column into Afghanistan. Intensely jealous of **Roberts**, who got both roles with Lytton's backing, it has been suggested that Lumsden deliberately caused his rival transport problems in retaliation. During 1884–85 Lumsden served on the Afghan Boundary Commission, but resigned when war clouds loomed again during the Penjdeh Incident. For the decade 1883–93 he served on the Council of India as a venerable elder soldier-statesman before he too, like his brother, retired to Scotland. He lived for twenty-two years after Harry's death, dying on 9 November 1918 – his eighty-ninth birthday.

LYTTELTON, GENERAL SIR N. – SMART GRASS-SNAKE

DURING THE LAST two decades of the nineteenth century, on campaign in Egypt, the Sudan and South Africa, one of the few soldiers whose careers moved solidly upwards was Neville Gerald Lyttelton. Several historians have pointed out how his snide comments to the press about Redvers **Buller**, his chief in the Boer War, contributed to the destruction of that officer's reputation, though Lyttelton had few good words to say about any of his fellow generals. During the Edwardian era his career rose, but his star ceased to shine.

He was born on 28 October 1845 at Hagley, the Worcestershire home of the 4th Baron Lyttelton, went to Eton and was gazetted to the Rifle Brigade in 1865. He was quickly sent to join the 4th Battalion in Canada, where he took part in a bloodless campaign against Irish Fenians along the Quebec-United States border. Sixteen years of peacetime soldiering followed in Ireland, India and England, including a spell in the 1870s at the War Office, where he was an aide to the reforming Liberal War Minister, Hugh Childers (the Liberal leader, Gladstone, was Lyttelton's uncle and godparent).

In 1882 Captain Lyttelton at last saw real action at Tel-el-Kebir, where he was an aide to Sir John **Adye**, chief of staff on **Wolseley**'s Egyptian expedition. He subsequently became a member of Wolseley's reforming 'ring'. Impressed by Neville's clear intelligence and cool head, his career upwards was shepherded by the likes of Wolseley and Evelyn **Wood**. Lyttelton was serving as assistant military secretary at the War Office in 1898 when he was given command of the 2nd British Infantry Brigade in **Kitchener**'s final march to Omdurman. Relations with his divisional commander, William **Gatacre**, were not, as Lyttelton confessed, 'altogether pleasant':

he thought the general's bombastic speeches were 'sad stuff' and the man too keen on the sound of his own voice. Kitchener's dispositions prior to the battle Lyttelton assessed as 'dangerous and if we had been attacked in the night the consequences would have been serious'. In print he later defended British troops against accusations that they had killed injured dervishes after the battle, claiming that it happened 'in just a few cases, as some of the wounded began shooting at our men …'

Given command of a brigade at Aldershot in 1898, Lyttelton went to South Africa in command of the 4th Division. Lord **Roberts** summed him up as 'not brilliant, but he is a gentleman and tactful'. After the reverses of 1899–1900 'Bobs' did not quickly change his opinion, but gradually Lyttelton emerged as the most likely successor to Kitchener by war's end.

In his memoirs Lyttelton claimed to have witnessed Redvers Buller begging Wolseley not to send him to South Africa. Perhaps this clouded his judgement (though the pair had not been friends when Buller was AG at the War Office), but he quickly became leader of a whispering campaign. He complained that Buller's 'lack of enterprise' was 'deplorable' and confided to the impressiona- ble *Times* reporter Bron Herbert that the old man had lost his nerve and would fail to relieve Ladysmith. After Spion Kop, Herbert wrote that Lyttelton, 'the soundest brigadier here', had exclaimed, 'My faith in Buller is shattered. Don't tell anyone this.' Not that Lyttelton had much good to say about other commanders: **Barton**, **Coke** and **Woodgate** were all 'incapable' and **Hart** plain 'mad'. This hatred was mutual: one staff officer noted how 'The Divl. Leaders all crab each other … they are all at loggerheads.'

Lyttelton fought a good war, helping to extricate Hart's soldiers from a death-trap at Colenso, organising a vital turning movement on the Boer left at Spion Kop, defeating the Boers at Monte Cristo (and almost get- ting shot in the head during the fight). Sir Alfred Milner, the British High Commissioner, liked and championed him so that he became C-in-C, South Africa, after the peace treaty. His rise continued with promotion to chief of the new Imperial General Staff in 1904 (with full rank of general in 1906).

In his memoirs Lyttelton wrote that he felt that his work on the IGS helped prepare Britain for the First World War and was the most important of his career. History has felt differently; Edward Spiers wrote that Lyttelton in these years was 'feckless, malleable and failed to lead the Army Council', a view supported by a secretary of state who declared him to be an 'empty head' that 'simply rattled'. In 1908 he moved on to be C-in-C, Ireland, before holding the post of Governor of the Royal Hospital, Chelsea for almost two decades. It was here that he died on 6 July 1931, in his eighty-sixth year.

MACDONALD, MAJOR-GENERAL SIR H. – THE TRAGEDY OF 'FIGHTING MAC'

NO SOLDIER IN this book rose so high and then fell so far as Hector Macdonald. His courage was beyond dispute, his intelligence as a soldier obvious in battle, his rise from the lowest rank to Olympian heights as a darling of the popular press remarkable, and his ultimate fall from grace shockingly horrible.

Facts have become blurred amid the legend that was 'Fighting Mac's' life, but he was born at Rootfield, a small croft rented by his father on the Black Isle in Easter Ross, on 4 March 1853. After a rudimentary education in the nearby village school at Mulbuie he left, aged 13, to work as a stable boy in Dingwall, and then tried his hand as a draper's assistant. While based in Inverness he joined the Highland Rifle Volunteers, a militia unit, 'with enthusiasm'. On 11 June, without telling his God-fearing parents, Hector accepted the Queen's shilling and signed up as a private soldier in the Gordon Highlanders.

Soon he was off to India and a decade of rising steadily through the ranks, so that by 1879 he was a colour-sergeant. On 15 October the 26-year-old Scot was mentioned in despatches for having fought off an Afghan charge on a detachment of Gordons and 3rd Sikhs. He was commended for 'excellent judgment and boldness ... energy and skill' by his general, Frederick **Roberts**. Barely three months later, to the delight of the men of his company who carried him shoulder-high, Macdonald was promoted to sub-lieutenant. For a ranker to become an officer was uncommon, but not infrequent in the Victorian army – but for that man to rise upwards, to succeed on a modest income (when even junior officers needed £200 per annum to survive and a 'gentleman' was expected to be worth at least £1,000 a year), took determination, ambition and guts.

Before the Second Afghan War ended Macdonald had led his men in the fierce fighting at Kabul, then accompanied Roberts on his celebrated march to Kandahar, where the new lieutenant commanded the left flank of the Gordons in the savage hand-to-hand battle that ensued on 1 September 1880. A year later the Gordons were off to South Africa and another war – this time against the Transvaal Boers. Here Hector was one of the 180 Gordons who followed General **Pomeroy-Colley** to the top of Majuba Hill. When attacked by the Boers he was told to hold the southern spur with just twenty men. The Boers soon reached the top and many British soldiers fled, but Macdonald held out to the last, deigning surrender, hurling rocks at the enemy, with just five shots left in his revolver when the Boers overpowered him. When a man tried to steal his sporran, Hector kicked him in the stomach. Boer General Joubert returned Macdonald his sword, upon whose blade a fellow officer in Afghanistan had had inscribed the message: 'A man who has won such a sword should not be separated from it.'

Eight years later a strapped-for-cash Macdonald decided to join the newly reformed Egyptian Army, where British officers could expect an increase in pay and better promotion. There was also a good chance of seeing active service. A journalist, T.P. O'Connor, captured the essence of Macdonald in his Egyptian years (along with the class bias he faced all his life) when he wrote: 'He was one of those men who ought never to have appeared out of uniform. He gave you the strength and splendid manliness and bulldog power, but there was nothing of distinction in his air, in his manner or in his dress. He just looked a Tommy in his Sunday clothes, which is not Tommy at his best.' Macdonald led the 11th Sudanese Battalion at Gemaizeh in 1888 and Toski in 1889. In the former battle he had a hard time keeping his men in line and swore at them in Gaelic. Drill, something he loved, became a fetish as he worked to transform his corps into an elite unit. He, too, was becoming a 'character' – a risen-from-the-ranks officer and media fodder. He was, wrote the press, 'so sturdily built that you might imagine him to be armour plated under his clothes ... He has been known to have fever but never to be unfit for duty.' The finest day of Macdonald's life came on 2 September 1898, when he led the 1st Brigade, Egyptian Division, at the Battle of Omdurman. 'The cockpit of the fight was Macdonald's', wrote the war correspondent G.W. Steevens. To meet the brunt of the dervish attack in the second phase of the battle, 'he moved his front through a complete half-circle, facing successively south, west and north. Every tactician in the army was delirious in his praise.' Over drinks and out of earshot of the Sirdar, Sir Herbert **Kitchener**, cheeky officers such as Winston Churchill said that it was Macdonald who had really won the battle.

Hector returned home a conquering hero; there were banquets, public honours, a CB from a grateful sovereign who made him one of her ADCs. It is this public esteem, coupled with the man's undoubted courage and skills as a soldier, that makes what followed within three years all the more tragic. On his way to India in 1899 news was received that Andy **Wauchope** had been killed at Magersfontein. Macdonald seemed the perfect popular choice to replace him at the head of the Highland Brigade in South Africa. It turned out to be a short war for 'Old Mac' as he was wounded in the left foot at Paardeburg and forced to take a long convalescence. During this period rumours began circulating that he was having a homosexual relationship with a Boer prisoner. Both Kitchener and Roberts were aware of the rumours – and that is all they remain, unsubstantiated in official records. Roberts may also have known that Macdonald had also a wife and son back home. 'Mac' was posted to India but here, as Roberts wrote, there were further 'grave suspicions' of his behaviour. Perhaps to squash the rumours, Macdonald asked for and got a posting to Ceylon where he landed in March 1902.

What happened exactly during his eleven months in Ceylon is unclear and open to interpretation, especially since he antagonised the wealthy planter community and shouted at the governor, Sir Joseph West Ridgway. He was recalled to London to see the C-in-C after 'grave, very grave, charges' were brought against him. Those charges are shrouded in gossip, but it seems he was caught exposing himself to four schoolboys in a railway carriage. Macdonald may also have had some kind of homosexual affair with two teenage sons of a prominent burgher. Ridgway, a former Bengal Army officer with impeccable credentials, wrote that 'Some, indeed most of his victims ... are the sons of the best-known men in the Colony, English and native ...' In the twenty-first century such charges against a prominent general would be bad enough, but at the dawn of the last century they were simply horrendous.

Clearly Macdonald hoped that he could clear his name sufficiently to be allowed a posting elsewhere by talking with Roberts, his old mentor. Yet when the C-in-C heard his story – and if any transcript of what was said between them was made, it has never been found – it was clear that 'Bobs' thought the only way a 'gentleman' could carry on was to return to Ceylon and face his accusers at a court-martial. In Paris on 25 March 1903, on his way back East, Macdonald saw with horror an American newspaper headlining his story (up to that point it had been avoided by the British press). He went to his room, 105, in the Hotel Regina and, after carefully tidying his things, took out a small revolver and blew his brains out.

To this day no one can be certain of the charges, or of what passed between Roberts and Macdonald, or of the major-general's innocence or guilt. This much, however, can be said: Ridgway thought the charges very serious; his possible bias against Macdonald has to be considered in the light of Roberts's views, which can be discerned by his 1901 memo on courts-martial in which he said that he very much opposed officers having to face them, 'unless I feel tolerably certain that a conviction will follow [my italics]. An acquittal or reprimand, in my opinion, does harm as it puts those who have ordered the court-martial in the wrong by showing that an erroneous view of the case has been taken by them.' Having stared into the man's eyes and listened to Macdonald refute the charges, it is clear the C-in-C did not like what he heard and considered the general, a soldier he had promoted from the ranks, to be guilty of sexual crimes.

MACGREGOR, MAJOR-GENERAL SIR C. – THE INDIAN ARMY'S MEPHISTOPHELES

IN THE 1880S the most influential general writing on the defence of India and propounding a 'forward policy' was not **Roberts** but a close associate, Charles Metcalfe Macgregor. 'Associate' is a better word for him than 'comrade' since Macgregor was decidedly waspish and bitter about almost all his colleagues, and particularly so in the case of Roberts. In time, despite considerable skills as a historian, geographer and staff officer, Macgregor felt that his talents were side-lined, which may have been the case as he made enemies in high command.

Charles was born at Agra on 12 August 1840 where his father, a gallant officer invalided after the capture of Bhurtpore in 1825, ran a bank. Educated in Scotland, and then at Marlborough, a fellow student later recalled him as 'reserved with all … his whole mind was towards the army'. He duly succeeded in joining the HEIC army as an ensign in the 57th BNI just in time to see the mutiny break out at Firozpore. For the next two years Macgregor was busily engaged and seemed to take an unhealthy delight in killing. After the capture of Delhi, he admitted in a letter: 'I have filled my room here with loot – nearly everything I have got is plunder …' He fought particularly bravely at the second relief of Lucknow and was commended in despatches for engaging a leading mutineer in single combat. A brother officer saw 'Mac' drive his sword through a rebel's body, his features 'exceedingly wild and happy'. He seemed to make a habit of capturing guns and at Daryabad in 1858 charged the rebels in one incident, capturing yet another cannon, his horse being killed and himself severely wounded. Despite being courageous, Macgregor knew his own weaknesses: 'If it were not for my temper, I would get on well with everyone; but I cannot curb my temper as I would: it will break out now and then and get me into trouble.'

In 1860 Charles volunteered for the China War. 'I shall have another chance of the Victoria Cross. Fancy Lieutenant Macgregor V.C.' He almost won the thing he coveted most in the world leading a troop of irregular cavalry, spearing his man, saving the guns again and getting hit with no less than five slugs at point blank range – three in the chest and two in his face. Despite a visit from the C-in-C in China, Sir Hope **Grant**, 'and the general opinion in camp that I deserve the Cross', Macgregor quarrelled with his regimental commander, who refused to sanction his application. He was bitterly disappointed and cheered himself up by grabbing more loot in Peking.

Back in India, Charles joined the 10th Bengal Cavalry but admitted that 'I scarcely ever make a friend, as I am so difficult to please.' His luck changed somewhat with the 1864–65 Bhutan War, in which he got the post of brigade major with one of the invading columns and, later, DAQMG. In an attack on a stockade on 15 March 1865 he led a charge and was wounded again by a bullet that struck his left hand. Like his earlier wounds it seemed to heal in remarkably quick time. Two years later he was off on campaign again as AQMG of the cavalry in Abyssinia and saw action, though at a safe distance.

The year 1869 saw two events of significance: in February he married Frances, the impressionable 18-year-old daughter of Sir Henry **Durand**, a major Raj figure who had the power to help his son-in-law; that same year he was asked to compile a *Gazetteer of Central Asia* for the intelligence department. Created in collaboration with other brainy soldiers, such as William **Lockhart**, this epic opus won Macgregor a CB in 1879, and illuminated him as a geographer of merit. He was also instrumental in setting up the Royal United Service Institution of India and took up photography to assist in his topographical studies. Compiling over 170 intelligence reports, memoranda and articles, travelling to remote corners of Baluchistan and other places, Macgregor became a major proponent of the forward school of frontier policy, arguing for the acquisition (and retention, after the Second Afghan War started) of Herat and Kandahar.

Busy in the Quartermaster-General's department at Simla during the first phase of the Afghan War, Macgregor joined Roberts as his chief of staff when an army was assembled to avenge the death of the British Resident at Kabul. A real snake in the grass, 'Mac' appeared on the surface to serve his chief loyally, but his diary is full of bitter criticisms and at times he seems to have been positively disloyal. He was now 'a big bluff gruff man', as one junior officer called him. Macgregor, who had jet black eyebrows beneath greying hair and a Napoleon beard, himself admitted that he looked like an operatic Mephistopheles. He was with Roberts at Kabul and Kandahar. Later he was given command in an expedition against the Marri tribesmen of Baluchistan.

Macgregor's reward for Afghan services was a KCB and promotion to QMG in India, which meant control of the Indian Army's intelligence department. In 1884 he wrote *The Defence of India, a Strategical Study*. This book incensed the Liberal government at home because it argued clearly that 'there can never be a settlement of the Russo-Turkish Question until Russia is driven out of the Caucasus and Turkestan'. Some historians, such as Adrian Preston, have much praise for the book, while others like William Trousdale are less kind. During this same period Macgregor authored a massive official history of the Second Afghan War, but this was considered so controversial that it did not appear until 1908, long after his death, in an expurgated version.

By 1885 Macgregor had enough enemies to find himself excluded from further promotion and his talents were sidelined into command of the Punjab Frontier Force. He did not have long to enjoy this more active role as Bright's Disease and a weakened heart forced him to take a long convalescence. His first wife had died less than four years into their marriage, but in 1883 he had married again to a younger woman. It was with her that he enjoyed the warm weather of Cairo and there that he died in his sleep following an operation for an abscess of the liver on 5 March 1887. His body was taken to Scotland for burial. Lady Macgregor oversaw a lengthy hagiographic biography, while Roberts delivered a eulogy in India, unaware of the slanderous diary, which was published ninety-eight years later. One soldier who had been allowed to view it in 1923 had written: 'His own egotism and self-seeking and the way he writes about Sir F. Roberts are in the worst taste … the man on whom the book reflects the least credit is Macgregor himself.'

MACINTYRE, MAJOR-GENERAL D. – LUSHAI VICTORIA CROSS WINNER

ON 4 JANUARY 1872 the Pax Britannica was being extended along the north-east frontier of India as the British fought the warlike Lushai tribe. The village of Lagnoora was under attack, flames and smoke leaping into the sky as timbers crackled in the heat. Leading the charge 'up the steep and rugged hillside', urging his men on, then being the first to climb the 9ft high stockade as the enemy fired at him with a hail of musket balls, spears and poisoned arrows, was Major Donald Macintyre. Undeterred, the officer jumped over the stockade and set off into the smoking inferno. So impressed was his commanding officer (the next subject in this book) Herbert

Macpherson VC, 2nd Gurkhas, that he recommended Macintyre for the VC. This was later approved, along with a brevet lieutenant-colonelcy and the thanks of the Indian government.

Macintyre had been born in 1831 at Kincraig, Ross-shire, was educated at Addiscombe and entered the HEIC army serving with the Gurkhas in 1850. Almost immediately he saw action in the two 1852 expeditions against the Afridis, then helped raise the 4th Gurkha Regiment during the Mutiny. On several occasions he was employed protecting the eastern frontier hill tribes from Rohilkand rebels.

Six years after winning his VC, Donald led the 2nd Gurkhas with the Khyber column on the invasion of Afghanistan and later in the expeditions to the Bazar Valley. He retired from the Bengal Staff Corps in 1880 with the rank of major-general and died on 15 April 1903.

MACPHERSON, LIEUTENANT-GENERAL SIR H. – DEPENDABLE VC SOLDIER

IN AN OBITUARY after his premature and sudden death, one newspaper eulogised Herbert Macpherson as second only to Frederick **Roberts** in the Indian Army's estimation. If this was so, then it was for a short time only and in India only; at home in Britain he was decidedly less well-known. More recently one historian has called him a 'plodding' general of no extraordinary distinction. This may have been true, but Macpherson was also, as Roberts knew, a solid, wise, dependable soldier who in battle rarely put a foot wrong.

Herbert entered the army aged 18 years in 1845, under the command of his father, Colonel Duncan Macpherson. His career, however, was carved out in the 78th Highlanders. He saw action with them in the night battle of Khooshab in Persia and also at Mohummerah. A year later Herbert was thrust into the maelstrom of the Mutiny and saw his fair share of fighting with **Havelock**'s relief column marching to Lucknow. He was wounded, though not severely, fought at Lucknow, assisted Colin Campbell as a brigade major and was wounded a second time. His bravery in leading a charge of men to secure 'two brass 9-pounders at the point of the bayonet' on 25 September 1857 led to the supreme honour of a Victoria Cross.

In 1868 Herbert served in the Black Mountain expedition, then three years later fought on India's north-eastern frontier against the Lushais. In 1878, when the Second Afghan War broke out, he was given command of one of Sam **Browne**'s two brigades forming the Peshawar Valley Field Force. His handling of troops was not spectacular, yet adequate enough to win him a senior command under Roberts in the second phase of the war. At Charasiab he led the rear-guard in a controlled march towards Kabul, meeting heavy attacks from large bodies of tribesmen with charges of the 67th Foot and 28th Punjab Native Infantry. In the Chardeh Valley operations in December 1879, when Roberts' army was threatened by no less than three Afghan armies, Macpherson was sent out to face not 2,000 foes (as his chief wrongly told him), but five times that number. He narrowly averted disaster, as Rodney Atwood has written, 'by his initiative and speedy march'. Later in the war, at the Battle of Kandahar, his 1st Brigade broke the enemy in one charge as Macpherson led them from the front as 'cool as a cucumber', in the words of participant George White.

He was promoted to major-general and the press started to notice Macpherson's name when he led the immensely popular Indian Contingent to Egypt in 1882. They only saw real action at Tel-el-Kebir, but fought bravely, and Macpherson's firm command of his regiments, their discipline and brilliant Indian Army organisation (they had adequate transport when the British Army units were floundering in the sands) drew much admiration.

In 1885 Macpherson was made C-in-C, Madras. Shortly after the capture of Mandalay that year it was felt that a cool, steady commander was needed in Burma to replace **Prendergast**. Macpherson set off, but caught a severe fever en route and died at Prome on 20 October 1886. His old comrade and former commander, Frederick Roberts, wrote to the Viceroy, Lord Dufferin: 'This is terrible news about poor Macpherson. I was afraid from what I had heard that he would not be able to stand the climate but I never anticipated his dying. We had seen a good deal of service together, and I feel very sad at his death.'

MALCOLM, LIEUTENANT-GENERAL SIR G. – DASHING HERO OF THE BOMBAY ARMY

A TRUE INDIAN, George Malcolm was born in Bombay on 10 September 1818 and, after an English education, returned to his presidency and served it faithfully for forty years. In that time he carved out a Raj legend as a dashing cavalryman.

Aged 19, young George joined the 1st Bombay Native Infantry; within a year he was serving as deputy assistant commissary-generals with the Bombay Division of the Army of the Indus. He was present at Ghazni and the entry into Kabul. During 1840–2 he was very active, commanding out-posts of the Sind Irregular Horse in eastern Kutch, where the Baluchis were a constant thorn in the British side. Shortly after being made a full lieuten-ant in 1840, at the head of a detachment of the Sind Horse, Malcolm joined the troops sent to relieve Kahun in Baluchistan. Here he got mentioned in despatches when troops had to force the Natusk Pass against fierce Marri tribesmen. The ensuing fight saw 179 British and Indian soldiers killed and ninety-two wounded.

In 1843 Malcolm tried a civilian appointment for six months, but it was not to his liking. He was by now a protégé of the celebrated black-bearded commander of the Sind Horse, John Jacob. He re-joined his chief and the regiment fighting at Shadadpur and Shahpur during **Napier**'s conquest of Sind. In 1847 there was a spat when Malcolm applied to command one of the two Sind Horse regiments without discussing the matter with Jacob, but the business was cleared up and the older man, who held his friend in high regard, does not seem to have been angered by this attempt 'to filch from his command one of his regiments', but actually commended him on the excel-lent discipline of those he led. Malcolm proved this at the Siege of Multan in 1848, then took the Sind Horse to glory at Gujerat on 21 February 1849 in a charge against Afghan cavalry supporting the Sikhs. It was a chance to settle old scores from a decade earlier as he rode with just 243 sabres to face 1,500 horsemen but, as he wrote later, his troops 'sent the Afghans to the devil'.

Seven years later Malcolm served in Persia, this time leading the Southern Mahratta Horse, though his unit was one of the last to arrive and the first to leave, being required to settle an insurrection in the Deccan. This was followed by a much greater conflagration – the mutiny of the Bengal Army. When the well-drilled troops of the Nizam of Hyderabad threatened to take war west of his dominions into the Bombay Presidency, it was Malcolm, with small detachments of the Southern Mahratta Horse, various infantry and some artillery, who barred their path. He captured the fortified village of Halgalli on 29 November 1857, punished the Mahratta rebels at Dharwur, then led his little army against the Raja of Nargund, who threatened to raise the whole Southern Mahratta country. The Raja was confident that he could lead the British into a trap, but when his men saw Malcolm's mounted troops they wavered. He led his men in a charge and they scattered only to be cut down. The survivors re-grouped in the strong old fortress. Malcolm was unbothered by the apparent need to storm the place. 'Give them a quiet night and they will save us the trouble,' he said. Sure enough, by next morning the rebels had fled. His success at Nargund extinguished revolt in that part of India.

In 1867, now a major-general, he was sent to Abyssinia in command of the 2nd Division guarding the lines of communication. It was a final war for Malcolm, who reached the rank of full general in 1877. He lived on another two decades and died in August 1897 while another major war was raging on the Indian frontier.

MAUDE, LIEUTENANT-GENERAL SIR F. – A VICTORIA CROSS IS DEAF TO COWARDICE

VICTORIAN GENERALS SUFFERED all kinds of maladies. Some, like Evelyn **Wood**, were famously deaf. Another who was hard of hearing was Frederick Maude, though it hardly stopped him, like Wood, from winning a Victoria Cross or being a good commander in Afghanistan.

He was 18 when he joined the Buffs in 1840 and soon sailed for India, where his regiment saw action at the Battle of Punniar in the Gwalior campaign. Here on 29 December 1843 Maude's horse was shot from under him while he served as adjutant of his regiment.

He won his Victoria Cross twelve years later in the Crimea during the final fateful assault by the British of the Redan. Lt-Colonel Maude had been given command of the ladder party of the 2nd Division composed of men of the Buffs. His citation read: 'Having entered the Redan, he with only nine or ten men, held a position between traverses and only retired when all hope of support was at an end, himself dangerously wounded.' Shortly afterwards he was made a full colonel, reaching the rank of major-general in 1868 and commanding a division in India 1875–80.

At the time the Second Afghan War broke out the Viceroy, Lord Lytton, described Maude as 'intelligent and energetic but very deaf and hot-tempered'. He was thought by at least one fellow officer to be 'the handsomest man he ever saw' and C.M. **Macgregor** called him 'a fine soldierly old fellow'. He seems also to have been wise enough to listen to his troops, both British and native: an Indian Army officer, Captain O'Moore Creagh, wrote that Maude impressed the soldiers 'By his kind manner and the sympathetic way he spoke to them', thus gaining 'the confidence of every man in the battalion'.

During the war Maude served as second-in-command to Sam **Browne** with the Peshawar Valley column entering Afghanistan. Earlier that year Maude had been told he would command any division marching through the Khyber, so it was 'to his credit' that he agreed to serve under Browne.

He showed a healthy distrust of his political officers and in the Bazar Valley advance issued a 'no prisoners' order advising troops that any tribes-men caught stealing, or even suspected of such things, were to be shot on the spot. 'This order seemed to have the desired effect for things went along very smoothly', noted Private H. Cooper of the 1st Battalion, 5th Northumberland Fusiliers. It was unfortunate for Maude that Sam Browne's command – indeed, the whole performance of the PVFF – was sharply criticised by Lytton, who turned on all its officers. He now called Maude 'a mediocre man whose want of tact and temper was not relieved by any apparent military talent'. Historian Brian Robson considered Maude one of the losers of the campaign, a man who had 'proved himself a competent commander and … might have been a better choice than Browne for com-mand of the Khyber force'.

Maude's Afghan War journals have recently come to light. They reveal 'a soldier's soldier … who failed to get on with politics, the politicals, and poli-ticians, most significantly the Viceroy himself'. Maude felt he knew as much about the tribes as Browne: 'I also was face to face with the Mohmands and Khyberres, throughout the winter, perhaps more so than Browne.'

He was shuffled off to command at Rawalpindi. In 1885 he was placed on the reserve list and made a GCB the following year. Like the previous subject in this book, he died in the summer of 1897. Many tales had been told about Maude's deafness. I conclude with this gem: on one occasion in Afghanistan a Highland piper was placed at his side during dinner and commenced playing. After a time the rest of the officers were sick of the wailing pipes and so one of them approached Maude and asked 'Do you like the pipes, sir?' Maude ignored him and went on eating. The man asked a second time. Again, Maude ignored him and seemed completely oblivious to the screeching. So the man went up to Maude's ear and bellowed into it, 'Do you like the pipes, sir?' Maude turned to him and replied, 'Thank you, but I'll stick with cigarettes.'

MAURICE, MAJOR-GENERAL SIR J. – PENMAN AND RING MEMBER

TODAY JOHN FREDERICK Maurice is best remembered, in the words of Adrian Preston, as Lord **Wolseley**'s 'lifelong friend, apologist and amanu-ensis'. It is sometimes forgotten that this controversial historian and military theorist also saw his fair share of fighting.

He was born on 24 May 1841, eldest son of the social reformer John Denison Maurice. Following Sandhurst, John was commissioned into the Royal Artillery in 1862. Eight years later he entered the Staff College and there won a special prize for an essay of field manoeuvres, beating another entrant, Garnet Wolseley, whom he cheekily quoted in his treatise. Wolseley did not forget him and four years later, when selecting staff for the Ashanti expedition, he offered Maurice the post of his private secretary. On the campaign Wolseley thought him 'the worst man of business I have ever had to deal with. He is like a woman, never on time', but confessed Maurice was also 'a dear good fellow' who nursed him through a bout of malaria (as he did an attack of erysipelas on the way to Egypt in 1882). After the war, Maurice wrote his own account (though it sold few copies).

John next spent a spell in Canada, then the Intelligence Department, before joining Wolseley again in Zululand as an intelligence officer. During the short but violent Sekhukhune campaign he took part in the final storming of the enemy's 'Fighting Kopje' and was shot in the chest at the entrance to a cave. He continued to lead his men, despite the wound, causing Wolseley to joke: 'Now I know the value of Maurice – to lead forlorn hopes.' Wolseley castigated Maurice on one occasion in Zululand as 'utterly unbusinesslike, untidy, erratic and excitable … completely useless as a staff officer'. During the 1882 Egyptian War, Major Maurice was DAAG on the headquarters staff and present at all the battles by Wolseley's side. In 1887 he wrote the official history of the war, a book that was remarkably brief and distinctly favourable to his chief. Maurice's last campaign was the **Gordon** Relief Expedition, but the rigours of the desert took their toll and he was sick for much of the time.

He returned from the Sudan to become professor of military art and history at the Staff College. Here he proved to be an excellent teacher. Famously absent-minded and argumentative at times, Maurice continued to write numerous articles including articulate support for 'a British, rather than an Indian-based, strategy of imperial defense'. In 1895 a biography of General Hamley, one of the divisional commanders at Tel-el-Kebir, which was highly critical of Wolseley, was published. A furious Maurice leapt to his chief's defence in print. He sarcastically dismissed Hamley the night before the battle 'wrapped in swaddling and nursed across a march'. Maurice was asked to co-write and edit the official history of the South African War, following the death of its initial author, but the level of political censorship on the project so appalled him that he retired following completion of the third volume (of a total of four). He died in 1912. In some respects, he was the most loyal of Wolseley's celebrated 'Ring', having authored histories of the Ashanti, Egyptian and South African wars, all favourable to his mentor and friend.

McCALMONT, MAJOR-GENERAL SIR H. – JESTER OF THE GARNET RING

WHEN SELECTING OFFICERS for his celebrated 'Ring', Lord **Wolseley** sought a mixed bunch. They were not just brilliant theorists, like Colley, or excellent staff officers, such as **Butler**. He also wanted damned good fighters, and one of these was Hugh McCalmont, a top-class cavalryman, though not the brightest of the bunch.

Scion of a wealthy Irish landowning family, Hugh was educated at home by governesses until being sent to Eton at 11. Small and wiry, he proved to be a bit of a scamp. When it came time to go to university he was rejected – much to his delight, as it interfered with riding to hounds – so he bought himself a cornetcy in the elite 9th Lancers. A year later he spent almost £100,000 in today's money in purchasing a lieutenancy.

Bored by Irish hunts, Hugh decided to apply for leave to join Wolseley's Red River expedition. He duly found his way to Canada and presented himself, pointing out that he played the piano as accompanist to General Sir Hope **Grant** on the cello! Wolseley had a soft spot for his old commander and read his letter of introduction. He had no need for a pianist, but thought McCalmont's 'wet bob' Eton skills might be put to good use, so he was told to join a party of militia. It was a bloodless campaign and at its close Wolseley honoured McCalmont by giving him the despatches to carry home (this usually resulted in a promotion or pecuniary reward). Hugh got as far as St Paul, Minnesota before he made, by his own admission, a 'bad blunder' and dropped the despatches into a United States mailbox. The C-in-C, Canada, was furious and Wolseley none too pleased either. While other Red River officers were promoted, McCalmont got no reward at all save a medal.

A forgiving Wolseley agreed to take McCalmont with him to Ashanti in 1873. Hugh had bombarded him with requests and apologies for his Red River mistake. As things turned out, he quickly went down with fever and had to return home. Wolseley had been warned before setting out that McCalmont was 'not strong enough for the job' and that 'an ailing A.D.C. is the devil'. Indeed, the first real fighting that McCalmont ever saw was in the Russo-Turkish War.

In 1878 Sir Garnet went to Cyprus and he once more took McCalmont as an aide. The pair hurried on to South Africa after the Isandlwana disaster. Hugh led some patrols in the hunt for Cetewayo, but at last he got involved in some real action in the storming of Chief Sekhukhune's stronghold on 27 November 1879. He wrote:

> It was about the best ten minutes possible. Going up the koppie, one savage as nearly as possible got me; how that shot missed I cannot make out. I pinned him with my revolver; and there were some others … We had very hard work … The tents were struck at 2.30 a.m. and the fighting began at 4 and lasted till midday.

The British troops were criticised for their behaviour in the Transvaal by William Russell, a famous war correspondent, but Wolseley laid the blame at McCalmont's door for putting a snake one night in the journalist's bed!

Within six weeks, back in London, McCalmont agreed, on Wolseley's advice, to apply for more leave and try and see some action in Afghanistan. He went at his own expense, presented himself to Charles **Macgregor**, and was permitted to take part in an expedition against the Marri tribesmen. It all turned out to be relatively bloodless or, as McCalmont put it, 'fell flat'. His fortunes were soon to change – he was sent in 1882 to Egypt as DAQMG of the Cavalry Division. This meant he could experience a real war with another hard-drinking, hard-swearing comrade – Baker **Russell**. The pair charged through the Egyptian camp at Mahsama, where McCalmont admitted, 'Well, we killed every man jack of them except one, and I saved *his* life. I saw he was unarmed and shouted not to kill him. He was holding on to my leg like grim death.' He had another charge with the Household Cavalry at Kassassin, this time by moonlight, slashing and cutting down Egyptian infantry. A few nights later the pair rode towards the Egyptian lines at Tel-el-Kebir quaffing champagne from a large bucket.

During the 1884–85 Sudan War it was a joy for McCalmont to find himself second-in-command of the Light Camel Regiment but his 'atrocious luck' to be 'out of everything'. He seemed to be everywhere yet always missed the fighting by a whisker. This simple old cavalryman did have one last fight to enjoy. Side-stepping regulation-obsessed General **Dormer** in Cairo, he found his way to Suakin in December 1888 just in time to take part in a dervish attack on the town. Most of the fighting took place in a long trench that ran for three-quarters of a mile some 800yd outside the main defences. It was a bloody battle of screaming men, smoke and pain.

With superb understatement McCalmont later recalled how he had 'mingled through the throng and it was a scene one would not readily forget'. After it was over, the dead lying in hundreds, he breakfasted on some fine champagne.

Hugh offered his services during the South African War as a commander. Roberts, probably wisely, ignored them and gave him the Cork Command. He was placed on the retired list in 1906. He enjoyed his old age – painting, travels, playing music, his large family – until his death on 2 May 1924.

MCCASKILL, MAJOR-GENERAL SIR J. – ODD IRISHMAN

CONSIDERED A MILDLY eccentric yet kindly general, John McCaskill was one of the senior battlefield fatalities of the First Sikh War.

He joined the army as an ensign with the 53rd Foot in 1797 and saw action that very year at Porto Rico and St Lucia in the Caribbean. Twenty years later he fought in the Mahratta War as was present at the siege and capture of Satura and the storming of Sholapur. Somewhat erratically, McCaskill leap-frogged through regiments grabbing promotions; by June 1835 and after four exchanges he was serving with the 9th Foot and sailed to join them in India. Two years later he was a colonel by brevet and local major-general.

In October 1842 McCaskill led his Norfolkmen to Afghanistan as part of **Pollock**'s avenging army, but en route he was chosen to command the 1st Infantry Brigade. A tough old bird, Pollock liked the way McCaskill controlled his men and entrusted to him all four infantry brigades with the full rank of major-general. After capturing Jellalabad his troops fought in several actions and finally, at war's close, they were sent to destroy the last enemy stronghold at Istaliff. This attack was planned by McCaskill's adjutant-general, Henry **Havelock** and the old general waited for news of its success sitting under a tree with a basket of fruit. Finally a messenger from Havelock rode up and gave him the news of Istaliff's fall. McCaskill was remarkably unconcerned and simply replied, 'Indeed, will you take a plum?' The town was set on fire, the inhabitants driven into the bitterly cold snow-clad mountains. One source claimed: 'Every male past puberty was killed and many of the women raped.' The matter was brought before parliament, but McCaskill replied that 'only one-third of the town was destroyed by fire' and that he knew of 'a single instance only of the mal-treatment of a woman', adding that inhabitants who begged for quarter 'were in every case protected', answers that make clear McCaskill was being extremely disingenuous.

After the war and with a KCB, Sir John returned to the 9th Foot until conflict with the Sikh Kingdom erupted in 1845. He was appointed to command the 3rd Infantry Division in the Army of the Sutlej. At Mudki on 18 December the right and centre divisions were commanded by **Gilbert** and **Smith**, the left by McCaskill. His men were the last to trudge into a battle on a dusky, almost dark, afternoon with the fog of war hanging all around them. Sir John, on horseback, stationed himself at the head of his division and set off in the gloom only to be mortally hit by a grapeshot squarely in the chest. It was a fitting end to a long career. He is commemorated by a memorial in St Andrew's Church, Ferozepore.

MCNEILL, MAJOR-GENERAL SIR J. – HERO OF TOFREK

JOHN CARSTAIRS MCNEILL won a Victoria Cross in New Zealand but his fame, if he is remembered at all today, rests on his command against ferocious dervishes at Tofrek in 1885.

Born on 29 March 1831, the son of a soldier, he was educated at Addiscombe and gazetted to the 12th BNI. This regiment mutinied in 1857, part of it at Jhansi on 6 June and the rest at Nowshera five days later. McNeill became an aide to Edward **Lugard** and saw much fighting.

Returning to England, he transferred into the 48th Foot as a captain, then was off to New Zealand where he became an aide to a fellow Scot, General Sir Duncan Cameron. Attacked in the bush by some fifty Maoris, a mounted McNeill refused to leave a wounded private soldier. The man declared that 'he owes his life entirely to Lieut.-Colonel M'Neill's assistance, for he could not have caught his horse alone, and in a few minutes must have been killed'. McNeill's reward was a VC.

Returning to Europe, McNeill next commanded the Tipperary flying column sent to quell Fenian disturbances in Ireland 1866–67. The following year he set sail for Canada as military secretary to the governor-general. It was during this period that he joined the Red River expedition and became a member of **Wolseley**'s select circle of officers. He returned from Canada in 1872 and the following year set out for West Africa as chief of staff on the Ashanti expedition. During the fighting at Esamano in October – an action full of smoke, burning huts, cries and confusion – McNeill arrived by Wolseley's side shouting: 'An infernal scoundrel out there has shot me through the arm.' Looking down, Wolseley saw that muscles and tendons stood out from McNeill's wrist 'like strands of an unravelled rope's end'. The wound was a bad one, Wolseley telling his wife: 'He bled so profusely that my clothes & waterbottle were dried with his blood: he is a man of the right sort, for he took the wound like a soldier, although the pain was excruciating.'

Back home, McNeill became an equerry to the Queen, who liked him a lot, and an ADC to the C-in-C. When war broke out in Egypt in 1882, McNeill joined Wolseley for a third time; he accompanied the Queen's son, the Duke of Connaught, who was commanding the Guards Brigade. That same year he was promoted to major-general.

In March 1885 he joined Gerald **Graham**'s army at Suakin as commander of one of the three infantry brigades sent to quell the dervish *amir*, Osman Digna. A junior officer described McNeill:

> as of middle stature, somewhat stout, and with a round, red, good-humoured face ... He has a quick, sharp way of asking questions, and a somewhat 'stand-off' manner with strangers, though when you know him there was no pleasanter companion or kind-hearted friend. He possessed also an attractive manner and a cool, quiet way of taking things ... He looked as though he had the constitution of a giant and as if he could go through with anything.

The same writer also caught a sense of McNeill's weaknesses – 'He was always perfectly self-satisfied and even when things went against him he acted as though it was all *couleur de rose* and rather a good thing for him.'

On 21 March 1885 McNeill set off to build a *zariba* some 6 miles from Suakin. With him went 3,300 troops, some 1,500 transport animals and about 5,000 camp followers. McNeill later wrote privately:

> We also speculated on the great probability of being attacked, but I was never told the morning we started ... that Osman Digna had distinctly declared that the first lot that came out were to be rushed. The certainty of attack, however, was so much on my mind ... that I told everyone I thought the convoy was too large and that I did not think it fair to make one responsible for it ... I took every precaution and halted short of the distance ordered. If I had to do the same thing again, I should not alter in the least the arrangements ...

By noon the British battalions were lying down in the biggest square as fatigue parties helped the Royal Engineers construct *zariba*s. McNeill, 'not oblivious to the possible danger', had two-thirds of his men close to their stacked rifles or standing-to. Without warning, at 14.40 p.m., when the *zariba* thorn hedge was largely complete – within a mingled mass of stores, animals and men – thousands of dervishes attacked its weakest corner. For twenty minutes it was bloody mayhem, until the 'Cease Fire' was sounded. McNeill had lost 141 soldiers killed and 155 wounded, along with 501 camels and 157 camp followers. Historian Brian Robson wrote that McNeill acted competently at Tofrek, but was caught out by the dash and ferocity of the Mahdist attack. It might be argued that, with the benefit of hindsight, he should have taken cavalry with him. Contemporary critics bemoaned the fact that he had no artillery, but Robson doubted this would have been much help in the thick mimosa scrub. The whole Suakin expedition swiftly came to a close and McNeill wrote that he was glad to be rid of 'this ridiculous and cursed performance'.

Back home, the storm of controversy continued and the Queen wrote to Wolseley and complained of the 'unjust slur' cast upon one of her favourite generals. As the years rolled by the royal family pressed more honours on McNeill, who became a handsome white-haired and moustachioed figure, his long face set off by dark eyebrows. He was made a GCVO and a KCMG. He was still in the royal service, as an extra equerry to King Edward VII, when he died at St James's Palace on 25 April 1904 in his seventy-third year.

McQUEEN, LIEUTENANT-GENERAL SIR J. – DISPLEASING 'BOBS'

A COMMANDANT OF the Punjab Frontier Force, hero of many hand-to-hand combats in the Mutiny and a true warrior, McQueen seemingly had a fast-track career to the highest command in India. It all was within his grasp until he incurred the displeasure of Frederick **Roberts**, who punished him cruelly.

John Withers McQueen was born in Calcutta on 24 August 1836, the son of a chaplain, was educated in Scotland and returned to the land of his birth with a cadetship in the HEIC army, serving first in the 27th BNI before joining the 4th PNI. He served with these hardy frontier soldiers throughout the Mutiny and was recommended – unsuccessfully – for a Victoria Cross for his heroism at Delhi, where he led the attack on the Palace. Armed only with a sword and revolver, when a native challenged him, McQueen instinctively knocked him down with his fists. He also served with the 4th PNI in two expeditions against the Kabul Khel Waziris and the Mahsuds in 1860. In April of that year he became second-in-command of his regiment while still only a substantive lieutenant.

In 1870, though just a captain, he was given command of the 5th PNI and remained with them until 1883. During the Jowaki Afridi expedition 1877–78 he was mentioned several times in despatches. In a memorandum on frontier warfare, Frederick Roberts noted in 1878 that 'it requires a very good regiment, and a very good Commanding Officer, such as the 5th Punjab Infantry under Major McQueen to be of use in this sort of war.' Roberts selected McQueen and his men to serve under him in both phases of the Second Afghan War, including the siege at Sherpur and the famous march from Kabul to Kandahar. In 1881 he led his regiment against the Mahsud tribe once again, was appointed an aide to the Queen, and promoted full colonel.

The grooming of McQueen continued when, in 1886, he was made Commandant of the Punjab Frontier Force. In 1888, with the temporary rank of major-general, McQueen was given command of an important expedition intended once and for all to settle the Black Mountain tribes. On 10 October Roberts wrote to McQueen:

> I cannot tell you what a relief it was to get your telegram of the 9th instant, and to hear that you had reconsidered your decision about withdrawing from the Black Mountain. I fully appreciate your difficulties, but ... I consider it absolutely necessary that the military programme should be carried out to the fullest extent ... We shall never have a chance again of dominating the Black Mountain tribes and we should do it in thorough good style and completely.

McQueen, as events unfolded, did not follow his chief's wishes, but listened instead to the instructions of his political officers. His reasons remain unclear, but three years later it became necessary to launch another Black Mountain (Miranzai) expedition. On applying to command it he got a withering rebuke from his old friend of thirty-seven years. Roberts told McQueen that his 1888 conduct 'was not such as would justify me in recommending you for a position which might any day entail your being again required to exercise command on service'. With this letter, McQueen's hopes of rising higher and of seeing any more active service were dashed forever.

He gave up the PFF command in 1891 and retired back to England. His eldest son, Malcolm, was killed in the South African War. McQueen lived on until 1909 and is buried at Wimbledon.

MEIKLEJOHN, MAJOR-GENERAL SIR W. – HARDY FRONTIER SOLDIER

WILLIAM HOPE MEIKLEJOHN was the commanding officer at the Malakand Fort on the North-West Frontier of India in 1897 when large numbers of tribesmen attacked the fort continuously for almost a week. Adding extra drama – and, one must assume, a fair degree of stress – to Meiklejohn's difficulties, his infant daughter Meg was with him in the fort and without her mother.

Meiklejohn was born on 26 June 1845, the son of the Scottish parson at St Andrew's Church, Calcutta. After an education at Rugby School, young William returned to the land of his birth and joined the Bengal Infantry in 1861. By 1865 he was serving as a lieutenant in the 20th PNI, a regiment he would be associated with for more than thirty years. He saw his first action in the 1868 Hazara expedition, was promoted captain in 1871 and was mentioned in despatches for his services in the 1877–78 Jowaki Afridi campaign. The war services continued: the 20th served with the Peshawar Valley Field Force during the first phase of the Second Afghan War and Meiklejohn was also second in command of the regiment at Tel-el-Kebir in the 1882 Egyptian War.

Twelve years later, back on the Indian frontier, Meiklejohn took a leading part in the fight at Wana when the Afghan boundary commission was attacked in the early hours of 3 November 1894. Hordes of Mahsud tribesmen, led by mullahs and fanatical *ghazi* warriors, streamed into the British camp. Colonel Meiklejohn quickly formed two companies and set to work, his men meeting the tribesmen at the point of the bayonet as the officers used revolvers and swords. He then led his regiment in pursuit of the Mahsuds for 11 miles before returning to camp.

In 1896 the colonel left the 20th PNI and was given command of the Malakand Brigade at its outpost on the road to Chitral. He was also responsible for a nearby fort at Chakdara which guarded the Swat River Valley. On the night of 26–27 July 1897, thousands of tribesmen attacked the British camp at Malakand. With cool understatement, Meiklejohn called the attack 'sudden and severe', confessing in a letter to his wife (away at Murree) that in the fierce hand-to-hand fighting the officer standing next to him was severely wounded, 'the bullet having passed through my left gaiter. My orderly was killed. Altogether we had a hot time.' He omitted to tell her that he had been struck on the neck by a sword but, fortunately, the stroke was weakly delivered.

On that first night, the garrison lost twenty-four killed and thirty-five wounded. Meiklejohn wisely evacuated the Malakand north camp, concentrating his troops in a smaller area known as the 'Crater' and a ridge close by. He proceeded to supervise the defence, hard pressed by the tribesmen, from the vantage of the precipitous fort where his 4-year-old daughter, in the care of a sergeant's wife, was blissfully unaware of the danger. Gradually the fighting died down as the enemy realised the futility of their attacks. Bindon **Blood** arrived on 1 August to assume command of a field force. Meiklejohn had already determined to relieve Chakdara, whose garrison was in a perilous state and had sent a message – 'Help us.' The colonel, now appointed brigadier by Blood, fought his way through to Chakdara as the tribesmen fled up the Swat Valley. He subsequently commanded the 1st brigades of the Malakand and Buner Field Forces sent to punish the tribes.

On 19 March 1900 Meiklejohn was promoted to major-general. He also won a CB and was made a CMG. He commanded at Lucknow and Derajat before his sudden death on 1 May 1909. The last survivor of the Malakand siege – little Meg – had a hearty life and died in 1977.

METHUEN, FIELD-MARSHAL LORD P. – HONOURABLE FELLOW

FOR SOME HISTORIANS, Lord Methuen, lean and tall with a walrus moustache, has seemed, like **Warren**, to represent all that was bad about British generalship in the South African War 1899–1902; it is true that the war minister wanted him sacked, Lord **Roberts** demoted him and he became the first – and only – British general to be captured by the Boers. While not absolving him of all faults, Baring Pemberton, and especially Stephen Miller, are two dissenters who have reassessed Methuen's career and deemed him to be not quite such a duffer. The general had no illusions himself – 'There must be a scapegoat,' he wrote sadly following the Battle of Magersfontein, 'so I must bear my fate like a man, holding my tongue.'

Paul Sandford Methuen was born on 1 September 1845 at his family's seat, ivy-clad Corsham Court, Wiltshire. After Eton he purchased a commission from Sandhurst in 1864 in the Scots Fusilier Guards. Family connections saw the young Paul climb up the promotion ladder, carefully watched over by the CO of the 2nd Battalion, Frederick 'Old Ben' **Stephenson**, who 'loved Methuen as a son'. A decade later Captain Methuen was accepted for special service and served under Evelyn **Wood** in the Ashanti War, where he was tasked with stopping the desertion of Wood's irregulars, which he blamed on a poor transport system – 'As it is the poor devils have no one to look after them, to see they get paid and rationed.' Suffering from fever and dysentery, Methuen nevertheless fought bravely at Amoaful. He was impressed by Wood's strong character, **Brackenbury**'s intelligence and, above all (and rather ironically), Redvers **Buller** – 'A splendid soldier, entirely without fear and a dear practised head ...'

After passing out of the Staff College, the fast-rising Methuen got married and proved a useful military attaché in Berlin. In 1882 **Wolseley** recalled him to serve as his press censor on the Egyptian expedition: he was present at Tel-el-Kebir and next day, along with his close friend, Francis **Grenfell**, was compassionate enough to take a water cart to the hundreds of wounded Egyptian soldiers lying in the sun. A senior officer about this time noted how Methuen, 'with all the temptations of a life of pleasure, lives entirely for his duty, works hard, and far more for others than himself'.

In 1884 Methuen raised a volunteer corps of gentlemen in London, designated 'Methuen's Horse', and supported Warren's Bechuana expedition, but it was a bloodless affair. He returned to South Africa in 1889–91 as DAG before returning to England, where his father's health was failing. In September he duly succeeded to the barony and in 1892 became commander of the Home District. Five years later, almost on a whim, and perhaps as a 'last hurrah', he sailed for India and was press censor on the Tirah expedition. He got on well with his chief, William **Lockhart**, whom he described as 'quite quiet, very determined and as simple minded as a child ... he has Ben Stephenson's charm and Buller's firmness.'

When war broke out with the Boers, Lt-General Lord Methuen was given a division, including the Guards Brigade, and on 10 November he was ordered by Buller to relieve the besieged town of Kimberley. Almost immediately he had a 'victory of sorts' at Belmont, and another at Graspan, both utilising the flanking movements associated with Roberts and the night marches of Wolseley. A third battle at Modder River was another victory, but Methuen suffered a casualty rate of 7 per cent; faulty maps, poor communications and weak reconnaissance were partly to blame. Methuen's choice of a frontal assault was justly criticised.

Then came total disaster at Magersfontein. Methuen must bear the brunt of the blame for, once again, poor reconnaissance, an early barrage that alerted the Boers to the British plan, an unwise night march, and faulty deployment and use of his reserves. British casualties amounted to 902 (compared with 236 Boers), and the Highland Brigade was decimated.

Somehow Methuen stayed on despite his mistakes. Roberts thought him not entirely to blame for the errors, yet made sure he was given less responsibilities. 'He has certain good qualities', noted the C-in-C. 'He is careful about his men and about his transport, and since I have been in this country he has carried out satisfactorily the minor operations which have been entrusted to him.' Indeed, Methuen performed better; at Hartbeestfontein in February 1901 he carried out a 'brilliant' (Official History) attack on 1,500 Boers with a much smaller force, part of his 'superb feat' (Miller) in moving towards Klerksdorp. Sadly for the general, he came up against an ever better soldier, Jacobus De la Rey, who, on 7 March 1902, smashed Methuen at Tweebosch. The general fought bravely, being wounded twice in action, but was captured along with 204 others, with a loss of sixty-eight killed and 121 wounded. The Boers captured six guns and a lot of supplies. When Kitchener heard the news his mood was so black that he locked himself in his bedroom and would not come out for two days.

Tweebosch did not end Methuen's career, and in fact it positively enhanced it; he was praised for fighting with so few men in the Western Transvaal, along with his high standards of personal courage, humility and modesty. De la Rey told Christian de Wet that Methuen's bravery 'was beyond praise'. Back home in 1905, Methuen was given command of the Eastern Counties district. He then returned to South Africa for a fourth time in 1908 as GOC and worked hard to reconcile Boer and Briton. In 1912 he returned to Britain as a field-marshal and during the Great War succeeded Rundle in 1915 as Governor of Malta, where up to 3,000 soldiers were treated at a time in the various hospitals. He died in 1932. An obituary called him 'a perfect knight who never swerved a hair's breadth from the path of truth and honour, and would never believe evil of another man.'

MICHEL, FIELD-MARSHAL SIR J. – WISE OLD BIRD

IN HIS LATER years, with his shock of white hair and a droopy moustache, John Michel looked the epitome of a sweet old gentleman, but as a warrior he had seen a good deal of fighting and commanded in a number of actions on three continents.

He was born in 1804, educated at Eton and commissioned into the 64th Foot in 1823. Every step of Michel's career was taken by purchase and he had the good fortune in 1835 to be appointed an aide to Sir Henry Fane, C-in-C, India, a post he held until 1840.

Michel then bought a colonelcy in the 6th Foot and led his men to South Africa, where he was a prominent commander in the Eighth Xhosa War. Sergeant McKay of the 74th Highlanders has left us a vivid impression of Michel and his men:

> A rag-a-muffin, devil may care lot of Irish boys formed the 6th Foot ... They were commanded by an experienced, able officer, who was a father and friend to them – Colonel Mitchell [sic]. This day was the first time I had ever seen him, and he was busily engaged in pointing a gun which was loaded with shell at a group of Kafirs in the valley. His shirt sleeves were turned up to his elbows, his wide-awake cocked on one side, strong blucher boots on his feet and a pair of corduroy trowsers [sic] on his legs. He appeared to be the beau-ideal of an able campaigning commander, willing to brave the difficulties and dangers of the campaign with his men, upon the same fare and clothing. How men do delight to serve under such commanders ...

During this war of ambushes and attrition, with many tough marches through the bush, Michel proved himself a steady pair of hands, especially during the 1851 invasion of the Waterkloof.

In 1858 it was Michel's lot to command in the last major campaign of the Indian Mutiny – the search for rebel leader Tatya Tope, whom the British held partly responsible for the Cawnpore Massacres. Starting out on 13 September and leading the 2,000-strong Mhow Field Force, the old general kept up a furious pace, refusing to let his soldiers fire rounds at the retreating foes if it might delay his advance. He finally forced a battle on some 5,000 rebels at Mungrowlee on 10 October capturing six guns, but 2,500 mutineers led by Tope escaped and Michel had only ninety cavalry to pursue them. This pursuit with many small actions went on into 1859, but Michel could never quite corner his wily quarry. Tatya Tope was eventually caught in an ambush and duly hanged at 4 p.m. on the parade ground at Sipree Fort on 18 April 1859. During this campaign Michel got Evelyn Wood his brevet majority and recommended him successfully for a VC.

There was seemingly little rest for Michel, who was sent to China the next year as commander of one of Hope **Grant**'s two divisions. He then moved on to Canada as commander of HM's forces in British North America. It was a time of Irish Fenian agitation and Michel played a key role in organising the militia volunteers to meet the invasion from across the United States border. During the 1860s and 1870s Michel was one of the main champions of Garnet **Wolseley** and was not frightened to tell the

Duke of Cambridge of the young man's talents. After his Cape frontier and Indian Mutiny service Sir John was considered to be one of the best exponents of irregular warfare, and the historian Adrian Preston suggests that Wolseley listened intently to the old soldier's advice.

The period 1875–80 saw Michel as C-in-C, Ireland. While there he wrote a letter of advice to the future Lord **Chelmsford**, who was setting off to fight the Xhosa in a ninth frontier war. 'No plan or operation of yours can in any way circumvent the Caffre,' he wrote. 'He is your master in everything.' He advised that flanks should be covered, use of mounted infantry encouraged and night attacks best avoided. Michel concluded with the prophetic words: 'Yours, my dear Thesiger, is a command of great danger to your reputation.'

In 1885 this sensible old man reached the rank of field-marshal, dying less than a year later, aged 81, at his home in Dorchester on 23 May 1886.

MIDDLETON, MAJOR-GENERAL SIR F. – DEFEATING THE METIS

'A PONDEROUS MAN, both physically and mentally', was how George Stanley, doyen of Canadian historians, summed up Frederick Dobson Middleton. Certainly in photographs and contemporary cartoons, Middleton stares out at us as a seemingly blimpish figure not unlike the walrus in a Teniel drawing. He found Canada and Canadians not much to his taste – though he married one – but no one ever doubted his physical courage and he had several problems to overcome when defeating the Metis, who caused the 1885 North-West Rebellion.

Born on 4 November 1825, Frederick, third son of a general, was educated at Maidstone Grammar School and Sandhurst. He entered the army on a commission without purchase in 1842 serving with the 58th Foot. For a brief time, two years later, he was an officer at the notorious penal colony of Norfolk Island, the *ne plus ultra* of the British Empire where the lash was king, but within months he was off to New Zealand. Just 19 years old, Middleton was mentioned in despatches for his gallantry at the capture of one Maori stronghold and again for helping to repel an attack on Wanganui during the First Maori War.

In 1848 he was transferred to the 96th Foot in India as lieutenant and he was gazetted a captain four years later. In 1855 Frederick commanded a troop of cavalry during the Santhal Rebellion and, back home, transferred again to the 29th Foot. He returned to India and was twice recommended for the Victoria Cross as a staff officer during the Mutiny. He did not win the coveted bronze medal, but instead got his brevet majority. During this war, along with **Havelock-Allan**, he was an innovator of using infantry on horseback. The 1860s saw Middleton, always in financial straits, trying to improve himself via musketry exams at Hythe and Staff College exams at Camberley. He went with the 29th to Canada 1867–70 and 1874–84 was spent at Sandhurst, first as its executive officer and then as commandant; by now he was a colonel and a CB. One of his students later recalled him as 'a kind-hearted but explosive disciplinarian with a huge moustache. He always used to become much excited at the annual inspections by the Duke of Cambridge, and use to race about giving contradictory orders at the top of his voice.'

Perhaps it was his French-Canadian wife who urged him to think of Canada again, for Middleton, wife in tow, arrived in Quebec in July 1884 to take up the $4,000-a-year post of general officer commanding the Canadian militia. Newsmen reported him as 'red-faced, very short and friendly'. The job seemed in many ways a cosy little number. On 23 March 1885, however, word reached Ottawa that Metis leader Louis Riel – the same man who had caused the 1870 Red River expedition – had seized hostages near Batoche and formed a provisional government of the north-west. Middleton was told to organise his militia and crush the rebellion in what would be the Dominion's first real campaign.

No fool, Frederick realised that logistics posed his biggest problem. 'These scoundrels have just selected the time when the roads will be almost impass-able,' he wrote, 'the river the same ...' Determined to smash the insurrection before it spread across the prairies, Middleton rushed his militia recruits across Canada and met the enemy at Fish Creek on 24 April. The battle was a draw, with the general exposing himself to enemy fire in an attempt to encourage his troops, six of whom were killed and forty-nine wounded (including both his aides) – one-seventh of his entire force. The whole busi-ness now disheartened him; the militia behaved as if 'they were going out on a picnic'. When he heard that a subordinate had foolishly attacked the camp of Chief Poundmaker of the Cree tribe at Cut Knife Hill, putting the Indians on the warpath, Middleton called this Canadian officer 'as inex-perienced as his troops'.   On 11 May the government troops defeated the Metis at Batoche (though the attack had little to do with Middleton). Riel surrendered on 15 May and the Cree followed suit one month later. In a report and later articles Middleton somewhat enlarged his role and sug-gested an 'omniscient wisdom' over the campaign. Yet it can also be said, in the words of historian Desmond Morton, that 'he had ignored bad advice, overcome obstacles and prevailed'. His rewards were great – $20,000 from a grateful Canadian government, a knighthood from the Queen and a British pension of £100 a year.

By the war's end the recriminations started; the Canadians found Middleton to be pompous and the fact that no honours other than a medal were offered led to fury. This was not his fault, rather that of the deliberate policy of the defence minister, Adolph-Phillippe Caron, but it was Sir Frederick who got the blame. By now, he thought Canada 'the country of vain, drunken, lying & corrupt men'. It was a bad choice of words, especially 'corrupt', since Middleton was soon embroiled in a scandal regarding furs stolen from a Metis trader. The local press thundered that he had 'degraded his high position, disgraced the uniform of a British officer, and hurt our ideal of an English gentleman'. In a *Parting Address to the People of Canada*, the general now made things worse by rebutting his accusers and naming officers he had proposed for honours. The fact that the honours had never been handed out stirred up more wrath. 'Poor Middleton made an awful muck of it,' wrote Caron.

Back in England, the public admired a hero who had smashed the slimy French-Canadian rebels, the press defended him against Canadian slurs and a grateful monarch allowed him to become Keeper of the Crown Jewels. It was at the Tower of London that Middleton died without warning of a sudden heart attack, on 25 January 1898.

MOLYNEUX, MAJOR-GENERAL SIR W. – FIGHTING XHOSA, ZULUS AND EGYPTIANS

BORN IN 1845, William Molyneux was an officer of the Cheshire Regiment who has left us one of the most vivid accounts of the Xhosa, Zulu and Egyptian wars. He was gazetted an ensign in the 22nd Foot in December 1864 and then had sixteen years of peacetime soldiering. During this period he did courses in musketry at Hythe and passed through the Camberley Staff College. In 1874 he served as an aide to Colonel Thesiger (the future Lord **Chelmsford**) at Aldershot and found him to be 'the best and kindest-hearted man I have ever known'. Work in the Intelligence Department followed (Thesiger did not approve), before Molyneux was lucky enough to accompany his chief to South Africa as an ADC. Here he witnessed several skirmishes in this last and most pathetic of the Xhosa wars.

Not long after his return from the Cape, news of the Isandlwana disaster reached England. Molyneux immediately volunteered to return to South Africa, where he took up staff duties. He was present at the Battle of Gingindlovu when a Zulu missed shooting him by a whisker (the fellow was killed for his pains). Shortly afterwards Molyneux's horse was killed from under him, throwing William into the mud. He was at the relief of Eshowe, one of the party that found the Prince Imperial's assegaied body and finally fought in the British square at Ulundi.

He was serving as brigade major at Aldershot when Wolseley's Egyptian expedition was announced. Molyneux managed to get himself appointed as DAA and QMG to the 1st British Division. He spent much of the war galloping across hot sands delivering orders. He had a particularly galling time on 28 August 1882 when he was sent to hurry up **Drury-Lowe**'s cavalry to assist Gerald **Graham** under attack at Kassassin. General Drury-Lowe refused to hurry, calling it 'inadvisable', and Molyneux had to ride off again to tell General Willis commanding the 1st Division. Later that night, he had to ride back again and found the cavalry all carousing after their celebrated night victory; at the Second Battle of Kassassin, Molyneux was trapped under fire in the middle of the action for some time; on the night of the march to Tel-el-Kebir it was Molyneux's job to keep the troops in correct formation and alignment. He was standing next to Willis during the actual battle when a bullet narrowly missed him and struck the old general on the left shoulder.

Molyneux returned to South Africa a third time to assist Charles **Warren** in his bloodless Bechuanaland expedition before he retired as a colonel in 1885. He was promoted to major-general and published an excellent book of wartime reminiscences in 1896. He died two years later and is buried in the Chelsea and Kensington Cemetery at Hanwell.

NAPIER, GENERAL SIR C. – RASCALITY IN SIND

THE VICTORIAN ARMY had no generals to compare with Charles Napier – small and wiry, with a large beak of a hooked nose, a mass of long, untidy hair and a scraggly beard, more a bantam fighting cock than a man. Big in all things, Napier was a man of hyperbole and also of action: passionate about women, passionate about life, surrounded by a brood of brothers, some also generals, others admirals, one a splendid writer and apologist for Charles. 'His prejudices were fierce, his scruples few,' wrote Philip Mason.

'But the fiery and romantic imagination which enhanced his appeal to the troops also persuaded him, after the event, that he had always been right.' An historian of Sind has written that Napier was 'a man of contradictions; he was capable of great generosity and small-minded parsimony, of humility and unbounded conceit. His military orders reflected both honour and justice. Worshipped by his men, he was often despised by his peers.'

The Napiers have provided scores of soldiers over the years, their blood spilled across Europe and the Empire. Charles was born on 10 August 1782, first-born of five sons and three girls; his father was reputed to be the best-looking officer in the army. A small, short-sighted and sickly child, Charles at just 12 years was commissioned as an ensign in the 33rd Foot, a regiment commanded by the man destined to be the Iron Duke. By 1805 the boy had matured into a major with the 50th Foot, though barely out of his teens, serving in Portugal where he took part in the famous retreat to Corunna. In 1808 he was hit by a musket ball above the ankle, bayoneted in his side and back, sabred on the head, had some of his ribs broken, then was taken prisoner – all in one battle. Released in time to fight at Busaco in 1810, a bullet buried smashed his nose and lodged in his jaw. Two surgeons cut out the ball but so damaged Napier's nasal passages and palate that for the rest of his life he suffered feelings of suffocation.

He fought the Americans in the War of 1812, but missed being at Waterloo three years later (excitement came on the journey home from Belgium when he was almost drowned at Ostend). During the long years of peace that followed Napier had a happy spell in 1822–30, governing one of the Ionian Islands, acquiring a young Greek mistress and fathering two illegitimate girls (whom he adored for the rest of his life). He was knighted in 1837 and the next year he was given command of the Northern District of England. This was the period of Chartist agitation and Napier's sympathies were with the common people. He described the mill owners as 'uncontrolled despots'.

Living frugally, short of cash, he grudgingly accepted command of the Bombay Army in 1841. The new governor-general, Lord Ellenborough, was a man after Napier's heart, 'outspoken, brilliant, headstrong and contemptuous of bureaucratic folly'. The pair got along famously. In August 1842 Ellenborough told Napier to take command of all troops in Sind. This independent territory, ruled by a set of violent *amir*s, had been a thorn in the British side during the recent Afghan War, its fierce Baluchi tribesmen preying on caravans and attacking supply lines. From the start Napier adopted a policy of antagonising the *amir*s. He also wrote in his journal: 'Charles

Napier! Take heed of your ambition for military glory, you had scotched that snake, but this high command will, unless you are careful, give it all its vigour again. Get thee behind me Satan!' Ellenborough at a stroke removed all political officers from Sind. The chief of these, James **Outram**, who was suspicious of British intentions, agreed to stay on as a 'commissioner' to try and push through a new treaty with the *amir*s that he considered odious. The die was cast; soon Napier and Outram would be bitter foes over what was to follow. Only one *amir* refused to sign the treaty, but it was excuse enough for Napier to march on Hyderabad. When, on the night of 14 July 1843, tribesmen attacked the Residency, Napier was able to use this as a further pretext for intervention (Outram felt the *amir*s were not to blame). Battle was joined at Miani on 17 February. It was a massacre: the British lost just sixty-three killed while the Baluchis, facing concentrated firepower, had over 6,000 slain. A month later, at a second battle Napier defeated 26,000 Baluchis with a British loss of just thirty-nine killed and 231 wounded. Sind was his.

Few small nineteenth-century British wars were as controversial; there was the question of Napier's colossal £70,000 in prize money; the legality of the whole business; deliberately misleading despatches; and the enmity of Outram. The chairman of the HEIC thought the war 'expensive and impolitic', Henry Lawrence agreed with Outram that Sind should be restored to its *amir*s, and Mountstuart Elphinstone, a senior Raj statesman, 'likened Ellenborough's behaviour to that of a bully who, having been knocked down in a street brawl [i.e. Afghanistan] returned home to pummel his wife [i.e. attack Sind], which was a reasonable analogy'. Napier's own view of things can be found in his journal six months earlier: 'We have no right to seize Scinde, yet we shall do so and a very advantageous, useful, humane piece of rascality it will be.'

It must be said that Napier worked hard for four years to bring justice and better administration to his pet province. In 1847 he led an expedition against robber tribes in the Cutchi Hills. Returning to Britain, now lionised, he was not long at home when the call came to return to India and supersede Hugh **Gough** as C-in-C following the disasters of the Sikh wars. Charles set off again in 1849 and soon confronted a new governor-general, Lord Dalhousie. At first all went well. Charles wrote 'I like Lord D. so much', and Dalhousie said, 'I never had a more agreeable inmate in my house.' Reform of the Indian Army was on the cards, but the pair could not agree which way to go. Soon the recriminations started: Napier called his chief 'a petulant man, cunning and sly', while the governor-general was offended by a letter 'so insulting, both to my office and myself personally that I should be justified in proceeding to extremities with him'.

Napier took part in a small campaign against the Kohat Pass Afridis, but the rift with Dalhousie was great. Two years after leaving London he was back home again. In 1853 he caught a chill at the funeral of the Duke of Wellington and died on 29 August. During his last hours a relative tried to cheer him by waving flags carried at Miani and Hyderabad above his bed.

NAPIER, FIELD-MARSHAL LORD R. – CONQUEROR OF ABYSSINIA

THE INDIAN ARMY produced many fine engineers in the nineteenth century, men equally adept at constructing a canal as sapping a fortress. Pre-eminent among them was Robert Cornelius Napier, chief engineer in many battles and finally, as a commander, conqueror of Abyssinia.

He was born at Colombo on 6 December 1810, the son of an artillery officer who died when Robert was just a baby. After Addiscombe he went on to Chatham to study as a royal engineer and arrived in India in 1828. Seventeen years of peacetime soldiering followed, during which period Robert honed his craft and demonstrated his knowledge by designing and constructing new barracks at Umballa, considered the most spacious and healthy in all India.

When the First Sikh War erupted, Napier was so anxious to see action that he rode 150 miles on one horse in three days and went straight into battle at Ferozeshah. During the confused fight, he somehow got attached to the C-in-C's staff, had two horses shot from under him and saved the life of Pat **Grant**. Next day he spiked every Sikh gun he could find and helped convince Hugh **Gough** not to retreat, but to hold his ground. Three years later, when the Second Sikh War started, Napier was chief engineer at the Siege of Multan. Herbert **Edwardes** was impressed by this man who 'to encourage the gunners … laid and helped to work them (the guns) himself'. On 12 September 1848 he was struck by a cannon ball and had to rest for several weeks.

Next Robert was off to the North-West Frontier, where he took part in the 1852 Black Mountain expedition as a volunteer; he commanded the right column and led his men over a 9,000ft crest without mishap. Eleven months later he served against the Jowaki Afridis and was told the successes of the expedition were mainly due 'to his ability and exertions'.

Napier was returning to India when the Mutiny broke out. He met James **Outram** in Calcutta and agreed to serve as his military secretary, but in reality was chief engineer and chief of staff. The fighting as they approached Lucknow was, Napier wrote, 'desperate'. In one combat, he broke his sword on a mutineer's head and when meeting Campbell's relief column, he was shot through the thigh. After Outram finally parted from Napier he eulogised him as 'the brave soldier, the able and scientific officer, the upright man and the warm friend'.

Napier was next given command of the 2nd Brigade of the Central India Field Force. The campaign was a tough one, but Napier wrote to his mother: 'You must not be anxious. Generals are hardly ever killed ...' Using Gwalior as a base he led countless pursuits of the rebels; in December 1858 he wrote that he had been 'fortunate enough to out-general them yesterday ... We took six elephants and killed several leaders ... and we shall eat our Christmas dinner in peace.'

Robert had little time to dwell on his promotion to major-general and the knighthood that came with it before being sent to China in 1860 to command one of Hope **Grant**'s two divisions. He was present at all the main actions, but found dealing with the French allies to be most challenging. He wrote: 'I sincerely hope that this is the last Gallic alliance that we shall have – it has been a most unfortunate one and has hampered us in every way.'

He returned to India and was made a military member of the Viceroy's Council; 1863–65 saw him president in council before taking over the Bombay command. When, in the summer of 1867, it became apparent that an expedition might have to be sent from Bombay to free British prisoners held in Abyssinia, the governor turned to Napier for advice. He was simply asked for professional guidance, but in less than a fortnight had produced a memorandum that covered all aspects of sending an expedition. Back at the War Office, inundated with generals offering their services, the Duke of Cambridge had the sense to realise that the complex logistics of sending an army into the Abyssinian highlands required an engineer officer to lead it. Napier got the job and immediately made clear his plans would not be influenced 'by some misplaced economy'. It did, indeed, turn out to be an expensive expedition, but Napier had to get his 20,000 men to the Abyssinian coast by sea, form a base camp, then march across mountains and deep ravines before fighting a battle on the plain beneath the royal stronghold of Magdala. This was successfully stormed on 13 April 1868 with a loss of just one officer and nine men wounded. The Emperor Theodore was killed and his young son placed under Napier's protection.

It was a hugely popular war with the British press. Napier was raised to the peerage and granted a pension of £2,000 a year. He went on to command in India, then was Governor of Gibraltar, before finally being made Constable of the Tower. In these later years there was a rivalry with **Wolseley**, who 'denigrated the cost and conduct of Napier's Abyssinian Campaign, to which Napier retaliated by barring Wolseley's ambitions to succeed Thesiger (**Chelmsford**) as Adjutant-General in India'. The historian Adrian Preston has noted that Napier, a champion of Chelmsford and **Roberts**, was 'a severe critic of Wolseley's generalship both in Egypt and the Soudan'. Lord Napier died in harness on 14 January 1890. One old comrade said that he had no faults save a refusal ever to see wrong in any man he liked.

NICHOLSON, FIELD-MARSHAL SIR W. – 'OLD NICK'

IT CAN HAPPEN that a general is respected by his peers but not much liked. A cold fish was William Gustavus Nicholson, epitome of the thinking man's soldier, of whom one war minister wrote 'he was born to be a lawyer, and if he had gone to the Bar, he might have become Lord Chancellor.' Yet he saw action in several campaigns.

The son of a Yorkshire landowner, William was born in 1845, passed out of Sandhurst as the best cadet of his year and was duly commissioned into the Royal Engineers in 1865. His war service began fourteen years later when, as a captain, he served under **Roberts** in Afghanistan, including the Kabul to Kandahar march. Three times he was mentioned in despatches. Serving next under **Wolseley**, he went to Egypt and arrived in time to see more action at Tel-el-Kebir. Back in India he was AAG, Royal Engineers 1885–90. He saw more campaigning under Roberts again, this time in Burma, gaining another mention in despatches and a brevet lieutenant-colonelcy in 1887.

Between 1890 and 1893 Nicholson was Roberts' military secretary. It has been suggested that he helped his chief write his epic and bestselling autobiography. Roberts learned to respect Nicholson's extraordinary brain and the clear way he examined knotty problems, such as the cost of frontier defence. In 1891 he became a CB and a colonel.

Six years later William got as close as he ever did to commanding in a campaign when DAG and chief of staff to an ailing General **Lockhart** in Tirah. Due to his chief's sickness, Nicholson had a free hand to make many decisions and was blamed by some for mistakes which, it was whispered, a healthy

Lockhart would not have made. One participant wrote that Nicholson 'never seemed quite the right man for frontier warfare … and he had never held any executive military command. The mysteries of "picquets, perimeters and patrols" were a closed book to him'. On one occasion, crossing the Sampagha Pass, Nicholson rode to a viewpoint and sat in full view of the enemy. 'Don't be a fool, Nick, get off that pony!' yelled Lockhart. 'Yes, yes sir,' replied Nicholson. A bullet zipped through the helmet of an Indian orderly holding his bridle while, to the amusement of other staff officers, he slowly dismounted. In his memoirs Brigadier Ernest Maconchy recalled Nicholson at Maidan in Tirah acting in a high and mighty manner while Lockhart lay sick with fever. After a heated exchange, he told Maconchy 'to take no orders except through him'. The dreadful retreat from Tirah, with rear-guard mistakes, ambushes and much confusion, was partly due to Nicholson's failure to understand the essentials of frontier warfare.

Knighted after his return to India, Nicholson next accompanied Roberts to South Africa, again as his military secretary. This was a post more to his liking and in February 1900 he was made Director of Transport. He was also at the battles of Paardeburg, Poplar Grove and Diamond Hill among others. His abilities as a theorist coupled with a keen analytical brain made him the perfect desk general in the Edwardian era. He went to Manchuria as an observer in the Russo-Japanese War, was appointed QMG at the War Office in 1905, a full general in 1906 and in April 1908 got the top plum of Chief of the General Staff, the new professional head of the army. His promotion to field-marshal came three years later.

By now it was said of 'Old Nick' that 'he had a good cheek and had never been known to turn the other one'. Ian **Hamilton** saw him as a 'venomous enemy', an accusation fully realised after the Dardanelles disaster when Nicholson, as head of an investigating commission, damned his former comrade's generalship. He died in 1918, just weeks before the end of the First World War, accepted as one of the great military theorists, though not much liked on a personal level.

NORMAN, FIELD-MARSHAL SIR H. – ABLE INDIAN CAMPAIGNER

HENRY WYLIE NORMAN, calm, cool, orthodox, well-mannered, was one of the most able Raj generals. He knew all aspects of his profession and was helped by a photo-retentive memory.

Born in 1826, son of a travelling merchant, he had a lonely childhood, then went to Addiscombe and arrived in Bengal to join the 1st NI in 1844. The following year he transferred to the 31st NI and served with them as their adjutant at Chillianwallah in 1849 and again at Gujerat, where his regiment lost eleven men killed and 132 wounded. He made the friendship of Brigadier Colin Campbell, who asked him to temporarily serve as his brigade major at Peshawar. He served under Campbell and **Napier** in the expedition against the Kohat Pass Afridis, where he gallantly led a small party up a mountain to rescue four wounded *sepoys* and bring them to safety, an act that won praise from his superiors. After Campbell's departure from Peshawar, he stayed on as AAG to Abraham **Roberts**, again leading troops against the Ranizais in March 1852, the Mohmands in April (where he took part in a rout with 600 troops that sent 6,000 tribesmen fleeing) and the Afridis in May. In 1855 Norman took part in the suppression of the Santhal Rebellion, though he thought fighting these poorly armed and primitive tribesmen was unworthy of his profession.

At Delhi on 8 June 1857 he was riding beside the Adjutant-General, Colonel Chester, when the latter man was struck and killed by a cannon ball. Norman now became the besieging army's AG. He supported the sick Archdale **Wilson** as commander, frequently getting exposed to enemy fire himself, and dealing with the discipline of a demoralised force. The whole army on Delhi ridge came to admire Norman's exertions, the officers realising that he was the man to smooth over difficulties, not least the dispute between those who wanted an instant attack and the cautious Wilson. Officers frequently turned to Norman when orders were needed. Observing him during the siege, the war correspondent William Russell described the adjutant-general as 'a sort of steam-engine, made of bones, flesh (very little of that), blood and brains.' It is worth pointing out that while officially only a lieutenant Norman frequently held sway over his superiors 'by force of energy and intellect'.

After Delhi he joined Greathed's column moving up-country to join Campbell as his Adjutant General. On the way the mutineers surprised the British at Agra. Norman was in the fort having breakfast, but he hastily galloped to the action, shouting out orders at the top of his voice. 'Our blood was up', he later recalled, and he despatched two rebels with a sword belonging to Campbell and shot a third. He survived the Lucknow assault without injury, but at Bareilly on 5 May 1858, a roundshot killed his horse and grazed his foot, a narrow escape 'giving me no end of a nap'.

Returning to England, it looked as if Norman might take up duties at the Horse Guards, but he was recalled to India as DAG under the new C-in-C,

India, Sir Hugh Rose. Norman went on to become secretary to the Indian government in the Military Department and a member of the Viceroy's Council 1867–77. During these years he pushed through his reforming scheme to create a Staff Corps for the Bengal Army. He left when it was clear his opinions on frontier defence did not meet with the approval of the bellicose Viceroy, Lord Lytton. 'Our best course is to remain within our frontiers', warned Norman, but his warning went unheeded. His golden years saw him as a colonial governor, in Jamaica 1883–88 and Queensland 1889–96. In 1901 he was made Governor of Chelsea Hospital and on 26 June 1902 promoted to field-marshal. A stroke affected his movements a year later and the end came on 26 October 1904.

'Admired and universally praised, Norman appears to have combined intelligence and application in his duties with a capacity to excel without offending those whom he surpassed', writes the historian Peter Stanley. There are memorials to Norman at Chelsea, in St Paul's Cathedral and, perhaps the one he would have liked the best, in the old cantonment church at Delhi.

O'CONNOR, MAJOR-GENERAL SIR L. – VC SERGEANT WHO BECAME A GENERAL

A LEAN, HANDSOME young man, O'Connor from Roscommon enlisted as a private in the 23rd Foot in 1849, aged 17 years. He was a sergeant in 1854 when his regiment landed in the Crimea. It was in the first battle that O'Connor rushed under withering fire to plant the Queen's colour of his regiment on the heights of the Alma. The effect galvanised the other soldiers, who rushed to his support. Despite injuries, he refused to part with the flag until the battle was over. Sir George **Brown**, a tough martinet but a brave man himself, was so impressed by O'Connor's courage that he told him in front of his assembled comrades that he would be recommended for a commission. While in hospital, Luke was told that he had also been chosen to receive the new honour of the Victoria Cross. This was pinned on his breast by Queen Victoria at a great parade in Hyde Park on 26 June 1857. By this time O'Connor had also distinguished himself in the attacks on the Redan at Sebastopol, getting shot through both thighs in the assault of 8 September 1855.

The 23rd embarked for China in 1857, but were needed en route in India. O'Connor was present at the defeat of the Gwalior rebels outside Cawnpore, the assault on Lucknow and several minor actions. He was promoted to captain in 1858 and took part in the 1873–74 Ashanti expedition as a major.

It was rare for an enlisted private soldier to make it as an officer and even harder to rise to become a general. In 1884, to O'Connor's great pride, after thirty-five years with the 23rd Foot, now called the Royal Welch Fusiliers, he took command of the 2nd Battalion. He retired in 1887 with the rank of major-general and was knighted in 1913. He died in London two years later in his eighty-fourth year.

OLPHERTS, GENERAL SIR W. – 'HELLFIRE JACK'

PHOTOGRAPHS OF WILLIAM Olpherts show a tall man with a mass of straggly hair thinning to baldness as the years rolled by. What is remarkable is the frown displayed in all these pictures. Olpherts became known throughout the army as the epitome of the dashing soldier who, beyond exceptional courage, was excitable, obstinate, proud and fierce-tempered. These idiosyncrasies stifled his career somewhat, though his good friend Robert **Napier** once remarked that in a tight corner he would sooner have Olpherts drunk by his side than a dozen other men sober.

He was born in Donegal of Protestant Irish stock in 1822 and entered Addiscombe in 1837. He passed out two years later with a commission in the Bengal Artillery. In 1842 Olpherts fired his guns for the first time in earnest when he quelled a native insurrection in the Saugor district. The next year he commanded a light field battery in the Gwalior War. This was followed by service in Sind under Charles **Napier** fighting hill brigands. He wrote that Napier was 'by far the finest soldier I ever came across ... he was the only man I served *under*'. In 1853, still only a lieutenant, he took part in the expedition against the Kohat Pass Afridis.

In May 1852, with a captain's appointment as orderly officer at Addiscombe, Olpherts sailed for England. He was a 'stickler for discipline' at the academy, but also demonstrated a good nature beneath his fierceness, donating an annual prize for the most athletic cadet. When war broke out in the Crimea he volunteered and was sent to Turkey to help raise irregular cavalry units. He served in the Kars campaign, a sideshow of the war, and was later bitter that his Turkish services were never acknowledged (possibly because he saw no real fighting).

Olpherts returned to India 'thoroughly disheartened'. Fifteen months later, the Great Mutiny erupted. He joined **Havelock**'s army at Cawnpore and fought with them into Lucknow. He won his Victoria Cross on 25 September 1857 charging with the 90th Foot to capture two guns, then galloping back

under severe fire and bringing up the limbers and horses to carry off the ordnance. His comrades selected him to receive the medal. One Victorian historian
wrote that Olpherts won his VC thirty times over. Lord **Wolseley** wrote later:

> His battery was a sort of military curiosity in every way. His gun-carriages were
> very old, and always on the verge of absolute dissolution; and as for his harness,
> it seemed to be tied together with pieces of string. First came dear old Billy him-
> self, clad in garments he had used in the Crimean War, a fez cap and a Turkish
> grego, the latter tied round his waist with a piece of rope. About fifty yards
> behind him came his well-known battery sergeant-major in a sort of shooting
> coat made from the green baize of a billiard-table; then a gun, every driver flog-
> ging as hard as he could … Some of the spokes had gone; they all rattled.

Olpherts got his nickname 'Hellfire Jack' because of his strong language and
hot temper. He displayed both early in the campaign when facing rebellious
Sikh soldiers, exclaiming, 'I don't know what they mean but by God they shall
know what I mean – fire!' Olpherts called himself 'an old smooth-bore muzzle
loader hopelessly behind the times'. Perhaps so, but Robert Napier thought
him the bravest man he ever met. It seemed as if Olpherts never knew fear
and had a charmed life, despite charging with his guns in countless actions.
When kept back from the fighting by Campbell during the final assault on
Lucknow, 'Billy Olpherts was jumping mad', recalled one of his troopers.

In 1858, besides his VC, Olpherts got the brevets of major and lieutenant-
colonel simultaneously, as well as being made a CB. A year later he served as
a volunteer in **Chamberlain**'s campaign against the Waziris. It was Billy's
last fight. He commanded various districts of India, but became convinced
that his fire-breathing reputation prevented him from more rewarding commands. He was probably correct – known as a difficult man to deal with,
sometimes contemptuous of civilian authority, he reached full general rank
in 1883, was knighted three years later and made Colonel Commandant
of the Royal Artillery in 1888. One story told of the old general concerned
an injury he sustained on a parade ground. The medical officer was hastily
summoned and the man, who had been relaxing, grabbed his shirt and coat
and was still doing up the buttons when Olpherts shouted out, 'Arrest that
officer! How dare he come before his C.O. improperly dressed!'

'Fighting Jack' died on 30 April 1902 at his home in Upper Norwood.
A gun carriage, escorted by X Battery, RHA, took him to his grave in
Richmond Cemetery. Suddenly the sky turned black and the heavens rolled
thunder. Olpherts would have applauded the jest.

OUTRAM, LIEUTENANT-GENERAL SIR J. – BAYARD OF INDIA

IN HIS LIFETIME, and rather to his annoyance, James Outram was known as 'the Bayard of India'. The irony of this epithet, not lost on Outram, was that it had been accorded him by Charles **Napier**, a man who became his worst enemy. Noble as Outram was, his outspoken manner created foes. He quarrelled with those he thought corrupt, was sacked on occasions, and yet was one of India's finest political officers.

He was born on 29 January 1803, the son of a rich Derbyshire engineer. Orphaned at barely 2 years of age, James was raised in Scotland and set out for India in 1819 as a cadet in the 23rd Bombay NI, a corps he was associated with for thirty-six years. Sent to police the wild Candeish country, a lawless area of proud Mahratta nobles and savage Bheel tribesmen, Outram created a 900-strong Bheel Corps and pacified the region in ten years.

When the First Afghan War started he was sent to conclude a treaty with the *amirs* of Sind before joining **Keane**'s staff as a political officer. He returned to Sind as Resident in 1840 and worked hard to protect General Nott's line of march via the Bolan Pass. Outram advised Nott to ignore any orders from weak General Elphinstone at Kabul. 'Attack the enemy on every occasion', he urged Nott. So outspoken was he on the governor-general's retirement policy that at the end of the war Lord Ellenborough gave him no reward and then slyly removed him from his Sind post. He was 'a Charlatan', declared the Governor-General; 'no soldier ... owes his reputation to newspaper puffs.' Outram stayed on to help Napier, advising strongly against any British seizure of Sind. When the Hyderabad Residency was attacked by over 7,000 Baluchis he led a spirited retreat to the safety of a river steamer. The subsequent war appalled him; he labelled Napier a liar in print and called him 'mad' in public.

In 1844 Outram went on special service in southern Mahratta country, taking part in the storming of the fortress of Samanghur on 13 October. He was then asked to deal with a rebellion in the Western Ghauts. His reward was promotion to Resident at Baroda, but he was forced to resign in 1852 when he spoke bluntly to the Governor of Bombay about corruption in his presidency. An outcry in Britain sent him back to India nineteen months later as Resident at the Court of Oudh. James was instrumental in encouraging the HEIC to annex the territory and was appointed chief commissioner before being selected by Prime Minister Lord Palmerston to command a military expedition to Persia. He had with him just 5,000 troops. It was a short war with brief but effective fighting. Outram was made a lieutenant general and got the GCB for his services. He had been sick for much of the campaign with acute rheumatism, though the Governor-General, Lord Canning, thought he might improve if he stopped smoking twenty-four cigars a day.

He arrived back in India with the Great Mutiny in its third month and was reinstated in his Oudh post. Setting off to join **Havelock**, he told the general: 'I shall accompany you only in my civil capacity as Commissioner, placing my military services at your disposal, should you please, serving under you as a volunteer.' It was high-minded stuff, probably well-intentioned, and won him much praise but, in reality, Outram was soon issuing his own orders or countermanding Havelock's, 'so that no one in the force knew actually who was commanding', wrote the old general's son. Not everyone liked Outram: Lady Canning thought him 'a very common looking little dark Jewish bearded man, with a slow hesitating manner ... He is not the least my idea of a hero.' Most officers though found him 'very clever and amusing', a giver of dinner parties and cigars.

After the celebrated siege at Lucknow, which Outram conducted with skill, also taking part in several fights such as the sorties on 24 and 25 February 1858, he was created a baronet and given a special pension of £2,000 a year. One historian has written that his demands for a VC 'show a conceit and a desire for self-glory that make sickening reading'. Various honours followed, though not the bronze medal he coveted. Worn out by his exertions, overweight and a heavy smoker, Outram died in the south of France on 11 March 1863. He was buried in Westminster Abbey. Now, 150 years on, we can see that he was not a true bayard – a perfect knight – but alongside his faults stood a first-rate administrator, a man of integrity and moral courage, and a brave soldier.

PALLISER, MAJOR-GENERAL SIR C. – INEFFECTIVE CAVALRY COMMANDER

CHARLES HENRY PALLISER was typical of a good many generals not included in this book in that he was gallant, served in several wars, and yet was an ineffective commander. He was born at Devonport in 1830, son of an artillery officer, and joined the 63rd Bengal NI, in 1847. Six years later he was severely wounded in action against the Shiranis while serving as adjutant of the Sind Camel Corps on the Derajat frontier. During the Indian Mutiny he served with the 13th Irregular Cavalry and later the

Benares Horse, was at the first relief of Lucknow and fought in the defence of the Residency under Outram. Always in the forefront of the action, Palliser was wounded three times in 1857–58. During the Oudh campaign he joined Hodson's Horse, initially serving with the 1st Regiment, then being appointed to command the 2nd Regiment in 1859, a post he held for the next twenty-one years.

Palliser campaigned in Abyssinia in 1868, and in 1878 was given command of the cavalry brigade of the Southern Afghanistan Field Force. He continued under Donald **Stewart**'s command during his march to Kabul. Unfortunately for Palliser, the cavalry had a very sticky time of it at the Battle of Ahmed Khel: the 19th Bengal Lancers were decimated in a massive charge by 2,000 enemy horsemen, though the 2nd Punjab Cavalry on the left flank were more successful in dispersing the Afghans. 'Some of the cavalry did not do very well', wrote Stewart tersely in his diary. Under scrutiny from Simla, the authorities asked Sir Donald if Palliser 'was fit for a command and he gave an ambiguous answer', wrote the malevolent Charles **Macgregor**, 'He knows and says Palliser is quite unfit and he ought to have said so.' Palliser remained in Afghanistan until Stewart left in August 1880. He was knighted and took over the Sialkot Brigade in 1881, but retired the following year. Twelve years later he was given the GCB and died on 22 November 1895.

PALMER, GENERAL SIR A. – COMMANDER-IN-CHIEF, INDIA

THE LAST VICTORIAN C-in-C of the Indian Army was also one of its least remembered, yet Arthur Power Palmer fought in eight campaigns and well deserves a place in this book. Tall and distinguished-looking with a slim moustache curled at the ends, Palmer was a cavalryman down to his spurs. He was born in India on 25 June 1840, the son of a captain in the Bengal Army. His service began three months before the Great Mutiny as an ensign in the 5th Bengal Europeans; a year later he joined Hodson's Horse and served with the 2nd Regiment for four years before transferring to the 10th Bengal Cavalry for seven years and the 9th BC for a further nineteen years.

Palmer fought in several Mutiny cavalry actions including Nawabganj, was adjutant of his regiment in Abyssinia, served in the Dafla expedition on India's north-east frontier 1874–75, fought alongside the Dutch at Achin in 1876–77 and fought in the first phase of the Second Afghan War.

In **Roberts**' famous battle at the Peiwar Kotal in 1878 the young Palmer was the first officer to reach the crest, leading his Turri tribal irregulars. The war services continued thick and fast; Palmer commanded his regiment to Suakin in 1885. The 9th Bengal Cavalry had not seen action in the recent Afghan War and wanted to cover themselves in glory. On 20 May 1885 at Hashin the regiment had a stiff fight in **Graham**'s fruitless and messy little battle where two squadrons were surprised when dismounted by an onslaught of dervishes. Palmer also played an important role in the Chin Hills expedition in 1892–93.

During the Tirah expedition in 1898 Sir Arthur was asked to succeed an ailing William **Lockhart** during the final weeks of the war. On one occasion Palmer almost lost his life when one of the spurs of the long cavalry boots he insisted on wearing got wedged in the narrow upper-floor entrance of an Afridi tower-house that the sappers were about to blow up. From 1900 to 1902 he served as C-in-C, India. His adjutant-general, Horace Smith-Dorrien, called him 'a popular and fine leader ... calm and imperturbable'. In truth, Palmer was just an interim C-in-C, according to Smith-Dorrien, and knew it. He was never confirmed in the post and his years were peaceful apart from a Waziristan blockade and the selection of Indian regiments to serve in the Boxer Rebellion.

Palmer died unexpectedly in London on 28 February 1904. He is buried in Brompton Cemetery. A few years earlier he had married and left two infant daughters; when his wife also passed away a short time later, the children were adopted by Smith-Dorrien and his wife, a niece of the Palmers. In his memoirs, General Smith-Dorrien called Palmer 'one of the most delightful men I ever met'.

PARR, MAJOR-GENERAL SIR H. – ALL OVER AFRICA

SIR HENRY HALLAM Parr came from a long line of military men – of seven generations and eighteen males, thirteen joined the army, two were killed in action, five were wounded and four died in service. Henry was born in 1847, educated at Eton and, after Sandhurst, was gazetted in 1865 to the 13th Light Infantry. Nine years of peacetime soldiering led to him being offered the position of military secretary to Sir Bartle Frere, South Africa's Governor in 1877, while serving in Natal with his regiment. Parr found Frere to be 'gentle and kindly' on the surface, yet also a man of 'courage, iron will and exceptionally steady nerves' who 'read most men like an open book'.

During the 1877–78 Ninth Frontier War, Captain Parr was appointed colonial military secretary – army liaison with the colonial authorities. When the Zulu War broke out, he served as an aide to **Clery**, who was chief staff officer of the 3rd column. On the day of Isandlwana a lucky Parr was one of those who accompanied **Chelmsford**. That night he recalled the soldiers returning to camp with fixed bayonets advancing nervously, 'men and horses stumbling and falling over tents half upset, broken wagons, dead bodies of soldiers and of Zulus, dead oxen, dead horses, dead mules, burst sacks of grain, empty ammunition boxes, articles of camp equipment.' Later, at Rorke's Drift, he took charge of a burial party. He recalled the soldiers' dogs coming back after the battle, 'one by one, thin and poor, but seemingly overjoyed to be among the red coats again. Most of them were cut with assegais'.

In 1881 Parr returned to South Africa on **Pomeroy-Colley**'s staff, but the Transvaal War was over by the time of his arrival. He was then invited to organise and train a battalion of mounted infantry. A year later, in Egypt, he was able to continue as commandant of a mounted infantry corps. All went splendidly at first, but Parr was hit in the fight at Tel-el-Mahuta on 24 August 1882. 'The bullet was as civil as possible,' he wrote, 'struck my right leg clear of the knee and went clean through.' He was sent home but returned again to Cairo six weeks later to command the new Egyptian mounted police. On 11 January 1883 he accepted command of a regiment in the re-formed Egyptian Army. During his khedival service he was for a time commandant at Suakin and was mentioned in despatches for his gallantry at the Battle of Tamai. The dervishes, 'literally hundreds', charged the main square 'stabbing and doing much execution', wrote Parr. He tried to bring up the reserve ammunition while his nervous horse 'was snorting at the dead and swerving from the bullets till one could hardly sit upon him'. During the Nile expedition in 1885 Parr was appointed second-in-command of the Egyptian Army, then promoted to brevet-colonel and an ADC to the Queen. During **Grenfell**'s absence he was acting Sirdar, issuing orders to Herbert Kitchener at Suakin in his operations against the Mahdists.

Recurring health problems caused Parr, with much regret, to quit his Egyptian assignment in 1888. Rejecting several offers, he re-joined the 13th to command their 2nd Battalion. In 1894 he became Assistant Inspector-General of Ordnance at the War Office, becoming a major-general in 1898. Health issues made him decline the offer of a brigade in the South African War. He decided to retire in 1902, but was delighted in 1910 to be appointed colonel of his old regiment. He died on 4 April 1914 and is buried in the small upland churchyard of Bourton in Dorset. Among the eulogies one officer recalled him simply as 'the smartest man I ever knew.'

PHAYRE, GENERAL SIR R. – NO JOY IN SHERBET

THE ONLY GENERAL – indeed, one of the few soldiers – serving in the Second Afghan War who had also fought in the first one almost four decades earlier was Robert Phayre. He deserves to be remembered in military history as the commander who had a tougher time than 'Bobs' in marching to the relief of Kandahar, but his achievements were sidelined by **Roberts**' media circus. A man with a notoriously hot temper, Phayre also tried to work as a political agent, but his less-than-charming manner – and a glass of sherbet – ended that career.

Phayre was born on 22 January 1820, educated at Shrewsbury and joined the 25th Bombay NI as an ensign in 1839. A year later he was made lieutenant and fought in action against the Baluchis earning a mention in despatches. In 1843 he fought at Miani under **Napier** and was severely wounded by a musketball in his lungs, which earned him a further mention in despatches. Robert joined the quartermaster-general's department, serving in Sind and the Mahratta country, then the expedition to Persia. During the Mutiny he was QMG of the Bombay Army.

By 1867 he was a lieutenant-colonel and was sent to Abyssinia as Robert **Napier**'s QMG. One historian of the war has called him 'a man of boundless energy'; the contemporary press reported that Phayre was a noted geographer and explorer, keen on hill-walking and 'able to cover the most difficult country on foot at a speed which quickly reduces young officers half his age to a state of exhaustion'. Abyssinians called him *Fitaurari* or 'Advanced Guard Commander' as he surveyed hitherto unmapped country. During the march Phayre suggested a route over the Amba Alaj Pass which proved so disastrous that, in the words of Darrell Bates, 'Napier continued to use Phayre for reconnaissance, but after this he always travelled with the leading party himself.'

During this period, Phayre's brother had been carving out a name for himself as an administrator in British Burma. Perhaps this is what encouraged him to apply for a career change and join the Political Department. Following in **Outram**'s footsteps in the 1870s, he served first as Superintendent of Sind and then Resident at Baroda. It was unfortunate for Phayre that the *Gwaekar* of Baroda, Malhar Rao, was acknowledged to be the worst ruler in India – flogging women, using forced labour in his palace, torturing subjects who opposed him. He needed very careful handling, but Phayre was, in the opinion of his superiors, 'tactless and overbearing'. Matters came to a head when Phayre accused Malhar Rao of trying to poison him by putting diamond dust and arsenic in his glass of sherbet. Hushing up the scandal, the government quickly got rid of Phayre, who decided to return to military duties. A commission of inquiry could not agree on the murder plot evidence, but the *Gwaekar* was removed anyway, not for the attempt on Phayre's life, but his 'incorrigible misrule', a rare occasion of British intervention in a native state.

During the second phase of the Second Afghan War, Phayre found himself commanding the line of communications between Quetta and Kandahar. He was the obvious choice to replace **Stewart** at Kandahar but, according to historian Brian Robson, the Viceroy thought him 'deficient in tact, good temper and sober judgement', preferring instead to give the command to James **Primrose**. The Baroda affair led to whisperings that Phayre could not get on with political officers or native rulers. Donald Stewart agreed with Roberts that Phayre 'might go off the rails' if given the Kandahar command. The Maiwand disaster changed everything. Two columns were now ordered to march towards Kandahar – Roberts from Kabul and Phayre from Quetta. There was a strong feeling in some military circles that if the two armies arrived at the same time, any battle with the Afghans 'must be a success'. Roberts, in particular, seemed intent on snatching the glory for himself, the new Viceroy, Lord Ripon, was suspicious that Phayre had the same thoughts and wags termed the march of both armies as 'a race for the peerage'. Phayre had a tougher time than Roberts; his transport was strung out and took longer to concentrate, a delay which gave the tribes time to gather and harass him along the route. He arrived at Kandahar after his rival's signal victory over the enemy, though he conducted his march with skill and his troops had fought nobly. His reward was simply a knighthood and a return to his old duties on the line of communications.

This tetchy old warrior, with his heavily receding forehead and white walrus moustache, commanded the Mhow Division between 1881 and 1886. He was made a full general in 1889 and officially retired in 1895, dying two years later.

POLE-CAREW, LIEUTENANT-GENERAL SIR R. – LIKABLE 'POLLY'

EVERYONE SEEMED TO like Reginald Pole-Carew, known to his friends throughout the army as 'Polly'. Good-looking and courteous, he also proved himself to be an adept field commander. He was born on May Day in 1849 and, after a public school education, enlisted in the Coldstream Guards in 1869. His big break came ten years later, when 'Bobs' chose him as an aide in the Second Afghan War. Even the waspish Charles **Macgregor**, **Roberts**' chief of staff, respected Pole-Carew and wrote that he was 'very nice, handsome and has seen lots of dissipation in London'. During the march from Kabul to Kandahar, Roberts wrote to his wife, 'Polly Carew is, I am afraid, far from well ... He is such a nice, well-plucked fellow that I am quite concerned about him.' 'Polly' soon rallied with all the vigour of the perfect school prefect and in 1882 accompanied the Duke of Connaught to Egypt, serving as his orderly officer with the Guards Brigade at Tel-el-Kebir.

Returning to India, Pole-Carew became assistant military secretary to Roberts, one of the team of young men invariably treated as sons by Lady Roberts. Another of these bright officers was Ian **Hamilton**; he and 'Polly' became lifelong friends, the latter serving as Hamilton's best man at his Calcutta wedding. When Roberts was sent on campaign to Burma, 'Polly' went too and at times even slashed a path through the jungle for his chief with his sword. He got a CB and shortly after was gazetted a brevet-colonel before returning to England to command a battalion of the Coldstreams.

In April 1900 Pole-Carew got command of the 11th Division of the South Africa Field Force. Four months later Roberts confidentially told the war minister that he was 'active, intelligent and looks carefully after his men ... I think he will do extremely well'. Two years later 'Bobs' was less kind, and privately told **Kitchener** that Pole-Carew could not be trusted with an independent command since he 'has not sufficient self-reliance or military acumen to be left to himself'. Harsh words. The split was so deep that after the war Pole-Carew told Maurice, when writing the official history, that he did not expect Roberts to say anything good about him. 'Polly' had, on the whole, fought a good war and was instrumental in capturing Koomati Port, where 3,000 Boers had been made to take refuge in Mozambique. A high point had also been the Battle of Diamond Hill in 1900, where Hamilton commanding the British right, and Pole-Carew the centre, had charged together in 'a glorious scrimmage' and won.

In 1901 'Polly' married Beatrice, daughter of the Marquess of Ormonde. It was the society wedding of the year. He was 51 and she was less than half his age. Gossips like Winston Churchill and his mother thought the new bride 'foolish', but Lord Minto told Lady Randolph Churchill 'she's lovely' and 'about Genl. Polly ... I am very fond of him'. In 1903 Pole-Carew was given a command in Ireland. He later retired to his Cornish estate and died on 19 September 1924.

POLLOCK, FIELD-MARSHAL LORD G. – THE HAND OF RETRIBUTION

CAREFUL IN HIS planning, calm in his aims, cold-blooded in the execution of his military duties, George Pollock was the cruel hand of retribution on the Afghans for their massacre of an entire British army. Indeed, so successful was he in inflicting fire and sword on them in 1842 that it seems a shame he had not been at Kabul two years earlier instead of the inactive and pathetic officers who caused the deaths of so many fine men.

He was born on 4 June 1786, went as a youth to the Royal Military Academy Woolwich and was commissioned into the Bengal Artillery in 1803. Within a year he saw his first action at the Battle of Deig, fighting the Mahrattas. A few months later he served at the Siege of Bhurtpore. A spell of staff roles was followed by more war service in Nepal. In 1824 he was appointed a lieutenant-colonel and, despite being ordered to take sick leave, he managed to serve with distinction in the First Burmese War and was rewarded with a CB.

Two decades of peacetime soldiering followed until he was ordered to relieve Jellalabad. One officer wrote: 'General Pollock, if not a Napoleon, is superior to any general officer I have yet chanced to meet in these regions.' He was a man renowned for his calmness and discipline under pressure. He was told to move quickly on Jellalabad, but refused to be rushed as he waited for reinforcements of artillery and cavalry. When he left Peshawar on 5 April 1842 he entered the dreaded Khyber Pass and took it cleverly by breaking his army into three columns and turning breastworks on the hills via his flanks. The Army of Retribution then sat at Jellalabad for two frustrating months due to a lack of camels. When they finally marched towards Kabul, his troops earned their reputation for ruthlessness, butchering many Afghans, burning villages, destroying houses and crops. The army stayed briefly in the Afghan capital, but long enough to burn the Grand Bazaar on 9 October, just before the return journey.

When questions were asked in parliament about troop excesses, Pollock defended the actions of his army, though less forcibly than General **McCaskill**, and there was a degree of shilly-shallying in his replies. He claimed press reports were 'unfounded', yet admitted that he was not much surprised if his troops had committed some war crimes under the provocation of a treacherous and brutal enemy. He said that the inhabitants were given two days' warning to remove their personal property before the burning of the Kabul Bazaar.

The historian J.A. Norris thought Pollock a fine general though the destruction at Kabul 'unfortunate'. William Dalrymple calls him 'precise, ruthless and doggedly efficient'. It is worth remembering that he was under orders to inflict on the city 'some lasting mark of the just retribution of an outraged nation' before marching back to India. Levelling the bazaar, a national monument and principal place of commerce, was certainly effective (and is remembered by Afghans to this day).

Pollock saw no more war service, but he served as a military member of the Governor-General's Council in the 1840s and lost a son in the First Sikh War. He went on to become a director of the HEIC. He retired in 1870, senior officer of the Royal Artillery and a field-marshal. A year later he was made Constable of the Tower. His baronetcy came in 1873 shortly before his death on 6 October. He lies buried in Westminster Abbey. His brother Frederick also won a baronetcy and was a memorable judge and Lord Chief Baron of the Exchequer.

POMEROY-COLLEY, MAJOR-GENERAL SIR G. – FLAWED GENIUS

GEORGE COLLEY (HE added the Pomeroy in 1880) is dimly remembered today as the general who took his troops up a hill, waited for the enemy and got killed in the ensuing debacle, 'stretched out exactly as a Knight in a cathedral, upon the flattened summit of Majuba'. He remains the worst example during the Victorian period of a brilliant mind totally unfit for a field command. Even his memoranda, lauded in its day, now seems suspect since Colley appears to have been the *éminence grise* behind Lytton's plans to invade Afghanistan in 1878 and **Wolseley**'s oft-criticised dissolution of the Zulu kingdom in 1879.

During his lifetime Colley was simply 'a genius'; he passed out of the Staff College in just ten months instead of the usual two years with the highest marks ever awarded up to that date, wrote the influential article 'Army' for the 1875 edition of the *Encyclopaedia Britannica*, was a gifted water-colourist and an ornithologist of repute. Evelyn **Wood** spoke for many contemporaries when he called him 'the best instructed soldier I ever met'.

Born in 1835 into a wealthy Anglo-Irish family, George was gazetted an ensign in the 2nd Foot in 1852. Eight years later, as a captain, he was present at the capture of the Taku Forts in China and the looting of the Summer Palace (he grabbed some fine silks). Thirteen years later he was serving as a professor at the Staff College when Wolseley invited him to join his expedition to West Africa. Colley took on the daunting task of reorganising the transport; threatening floggings, burning villages when necessary, he was everywhere along the lines of communication. One war correspondent wrote: 'To Colley it is due that Coomassie was taken when it was.' He returned from Ashanti probably the only officer who could call this pestilential campaign 'fun and a pleasant three months trip'.

Less than a year later he accompanied Wolseley, who now considered him the most gifted member of his 'Ring', to South Africa as colonial treasurer. In 1876 he accepted the post of military secretary to the new Viceroy of India, Lord Lytton. Members of the Viceroy's Council noted how Colley, always silent at such meetings, seemed to be Lytton's 'real military mentor'. Gradually he came into conflict with the C-in-C, India, General **Haines**, who described him as 'a greatly over-rated man'. Colley's *Memorandum on the Military Aspects of the Central Asian Question* has been referred to by one historian as 'the charter of Lytton's defence policy.' His influence over the Viceroy's Afghan War plans was so strong that a visitor noted how the pair seemed to think 'they could direct the whole detail of the plan of campaign from Simla'.   It must have been with some reluctance that Colley left India in May 1879 to assist his old chief, Wolseley, in Zululand. Sir Garnet thought him 'a man in a thousand' and wanted him as his chief of staff. It has been suggested by several modern historians that Wolseley's plan to rule Zululand through compliant chiefs instead of a British Resident – a policy that has been bitterly condemned as 'disastrous' – was concocted by Colley. Adrian Preston wrote: 'The settlement in its final form uncannily resembled that which Lytton originally intended to impose on Afghanistan ... To this extent, therefore, the settlement would appear to be Colley's rather than Wolseley's in inspiration.'

In India Colley had met and married the ambitious Edith Hamilton. Daughter of a general, pushy Edith urged him on to greater things – and greater risks. On Wolseley's departure from the Cape in April 1880, his protégé took over as Governor of Natal, High Commissioner for South-Eastern Africa and C-in-C Natal and the Transvaal.

Within weeks war clouds began to form above the Transvaal where the Dutch-Boer inhabitants seemed intent on re-establishing an independent republic. The situation was exacerbated by the brutish tax collections of the local administrator, Owen Lanyon, one of the lesser lights of the Wolseley Ring, who thought the locals were 'mortal cowards'. Colley, too, underestimated the Boer capacity to fight. War broke out on 16 December, but the slow-acting general did little until 28 January 1881, when he tried to assault the pass over the Drakensburg Mountains at Laing's Nek. His frontal assault was repulsed with 197 casualties. Eleven days later, at Ingogo, he lost a further 150 men.

On 16 February Colley received instructions from London to offer an armistice with the Boers and 'avoid effusion of blood'. Given some latitude to act as he felt fit, he decided on a final battle at Majuba Hill, wishing to retrieve his own honour and that of his country. His use of a mixed force of 402 officers and men has been much criticised. One elite regiment might have been better. Colley, it seems, wanted all his units to share in his anticipated victory. The result was a little army that lacked cohesion. When his men reached the top of Majuba after an eight-hour climb on 26 February, Colley failed to tell them to entrench and remarked, 'We could stay here for ever.' By daybreak, 450 of the enemy were storming the heights while a further 150 blocked any retreat. In the early afternoon, surrounded by the enemy, Colley was killed. British troops fled pell-mell down the hill, ninety-two officers and men were killed, 131 wounded, fifty men captured and two missing. Boer losses were a trifling two dead and four wounded.

George Pomeroy-Colley's mistakes were later ascribed to 'over-confidence'. To this day no one is absolutely clear why he thought it necessary to take his small force up to the top of a hill and await the enemy. The final words can be left to one of the campaign's officers, Percy Marling of the 60th Rifles, who wrote:

> He was a great hand at making speeches and writing despatches, and a more charming and courteous man you could not meet. I heard an old officer who had seen considerable service say after the Battle of Ingogo that he ought not to be trusted with a corporal's guard on active service ... everybody was sorry about Colley, he was a most lovable person, but his death was a most fortunate thing for him, and as someone said, for the Natal Field Force too.

PRENDERGAST, GENERAL SIR H. – PROBLEMS ON THE ROAD TO MANDALAY

AFTER HIS FUNERAL a friend of Harry Prendergast called him 'one of the very noblest men who ever lived'. Winner of a Victoria Cross when only 23 years old, he went on to command the Burma Expeditionary Force in 1885 and conduct a carefully planned, relatively bloodless campaign of conquest, overthrowing a dynasty and adding a new territory to the empire, only to see his achievements demeaned in print. He died with this chip still on his shoulder.

Harry was born on 15 October 1834, son of a Madras civil servant, went to Addiscombe and entered the Royal Engineers as a lieutenant in 1854. Two years later he served as a sapper at the Battle of Mohumerah in Persia. But it was the Mutiny which became his testing ground; Prendergast, now a lieutenant in the Madras Engineers, served with the Deccan and Malwa Field Forces in Central India, getting shot through the ribs at Mundisore on 21 November 1857. This incident, during which Harry saved the life of a fellow officer, won him a VC. He campaigned under Hugh Rose at Jhansi and the Battle of the Betwa. His life seemed strangely charmed – he was shot again, at Ratghur, this time in the arm, and at the Betwa he took a sword wound in the upper arm that severed his biceps, a second cut which almost removed one thumb and a third which sliced his index finger.

In 1867 Major Prendergast led three companies of Madras sappers to Abyssinia. He was present at Arogee and the storming of Magdala. In 1878 he led sappers to Cyprus. He missed out on the Afghan War, being a Madras man, but was promoted to QMG of his presidency army. In 1882 he was promoted and assumed command on the Burma frontier. Three years later the Viceroy, Lord Dufferin, gave Prendergast command of the 10,000-strong Burma Field Force. He was told to secure the Burmese King and his capital with as little bloodshed as possible. The army steamed up the Irrawaddy in a flotilla and the 1,100-strong garrison of Gwe-Gyoun-Kamyo was taken almost without a casualty. The nearby Minhla fort was a tougher nut to crack and cost the lives four British killed and twenty-eight wounded along with about 210 of the enemy. George **White**, one of Prendergast's officers, thought he was advancing 'in too great a hurry … There was no hospital ship up, and a great want of medical arrangements'. Prendergast, however, had been told by Dufferin to advance swiftly. The general wisely refused to overrate his success. He also told his soldiers not to fire on any Burmese who were not in uniform.

Around 3.30 p.m. on 29 November 1885, King Theebaw of Burma and his Queen were marched down the palace steps to a waiting boat and exile. The couple had been given practically no warning and their removal came as a profound shock to the Burmese. Frederick **Roberts** thought Prendergast had wrapped up his little campaign very well. 'At Ava and in his dealings with Theebaw he showed not only forebearance but firmness and decision,' wrote Roberts. 'A more excitable commander might have precipitated matters and brought on a collision, the result of which would have been great bloodshed and quite possibly the flight of the King.' 'Bobs' went on to criticise Prendergast for a degree of naivety in his dealings with the press and 'insufficient backbone' to firmly punish his provost-marshal. The two scandals he was referring to had rocked Mandalay: a *Times* correspondent, E.K. Moylan, deported on Prendergast's orders, revenged himself with poisonous articles that led Lord Randolph Churchill in London, the architect of the war, to turn against the general. Matters were not helped by Major Hooper, the 'camera-mad' provost-marshal, taking pictures of rebels at the moment of their death by firing squad, an act which appalled the Viceroy by its inhumanity, not to mention lack of good taste, causing Dufferin to write: 'Daily I become more convinced of the perfect unfitness of General Prendergast for his position in Upper Burma.'

A solution was needed – and found. Prendergast, despite protestations, was raised to lieutenant-general and ordered out of the country. It came as a shock to Sir Harry and he never recovered from this disgrace. Even Dufferin thought the act, done at Churchill's insistence, was shabby. Besides which, as White remarked, 'He is such a nice man, everybody likes him.' Years later, salt was rubbed in Prendergast's wounded pride by an official history full of distortions and inaccuracies (it even got the year of the campaign wrong). He returned to England and, despite several official dinners, was ignored by the Queen who normally saw her returning victorious generals. Instead, he was passed over for C-in-C, Madras, and given the political appointment of Resident at Travancore and Cochin. He went on to be a successful Resident at Mysore and then Baroda before his retirement in 1891. Sir Harry died at his London home on 24 July 1913, still smarting over his treatment at Burma and the slurs on the men he was proud to have commanded. He is buried in Richmond Cemetery.

PRIMROSE, GENERAL J. – DISASTER AT KANDAHAR

THIS BOOK IS not simply a roll call of Victorian heroes. Each man was different: some remain famous; most are forgotten; several proved themselves masters of irregular colonial-style warfare; many had a moment of glory. A few in this book saw their careers end in ignominy, the result of a battlefield mistake. One of these was James Primrose.

He was born in 1819, joined the army in 1837 and saw his first action serving with the 43rd Foot in the Eighth Xhosa War in South Africa. A few years later he fought in the Indian Rebellion at Kirwi and several other Central Indian engagements. Fast forward two decades and Primrose was a major-general and cosily commanding the Poona Division. Everything changed when he was ordered to take over from Donald **Stewart** at Kandahar. The historian Leigh Maxwell described Primrose as 'outwardly a well-knit soldierly figure ... but he was not healthy physically'. The Viceroy was aware of this but – under pressure from London, where the Duke of Cambridge, C-in-C of the British Army, was complaining that all senior posts in Afghanistan seemed to have been taken by Indian Army officers – thought Primrose was worth an appointment. Lord Lytton refused to sanction Robert **Phayre**, with his short temper and indelicate way of handling political officers. He was just on the verge of offering the appointment to Robert **Bright** when the Governor of Bombay cabled that Primrose was in his opinion quite fit and also a tactful man.

Until the Maiwand disaster changed things, Primrose certainly seems to have acted cautiously. Following that massacre, and with the Afghans preparing to lay siege to Kandahar, he started to panic. Aware that **Roberts** and Phayre were marching to his relief, but possibly wanting to win his moment of glory, Primrose sanctioned a poorly devised attack on the Afghans at Deh Kwaja, a village just outside Kandahar. He found himself up against a resilient enemy and Brigadier Brooke, Primrose's second-in-command, was shot and killed by a bullet in the neck during the fierce fighting. Remonstrations followed and the general refused to send out more troops and had the buglers sound retreat, 'thereby informing friend and foe alike that the sortie had failed'. When the senior Royal Engineer, Colonel Hills, begged to take some men to support the retreat, Primrose shouted: 'It is all your doing.' An indignant Hills fired back: 'I am damned if it is. You have done everything I told you decidedly and strongly was not to be done – bombardment, small force, separate attacks, and the wrong end of the village, and you never informed me of all these changes. I told you, moreover, that it was no child's play, this sortie, and that if you did take it up, it must be carried out thoroughly and with every available man.'

This affair destroyed Primrose's career. Both Roberts and Stewart felt he needed to be replaced, the latter writing to his wife: 'General Primrose should have taken out his whole force, and gone himself in command. There may have been good reasons for acting as he did, but I can't see them.' C.M. **Macgregor**, Roberts' waspish chief of staff, felt Primrose should have been court-martialled. A recent historical verdict on the Deh Kwaja sortie is that it was 'desperate and foolish', a 'mini-Maiwand' with the loss of 226 officers and men.

An official rebuke was James Primrose's mild punishment. He was recalled, his career in tatters, though he was raised to lieutenant-general before his death in 1892.

PROBYN, GENERAL SIR D. – VICTORIA CROSS COURTIER

DURING THE INDIAN Mutiny no officer exemplified the dashing irregular cavalryman quite so well as Dighton Macnaghten Probyn VC. When his soldiering days were over, he carved out quite another career for himself as a respected and important member of King Edward VII's household.

He was born on 21 January 1833 and joined the 6th Bengal Cavalry in 1849. Almost from the start he served in the irregular cavalry units of tough frontier warriors: from 1852–57 he was second-in-command and adjutant of the 2nd Punjab Cavalry, a fine regiment led by Sam **Browne**. Probyn served with the 2nd PC in the 1857 Bozdar expedition before going with his regiment to the Siege of Delhi. So many were his gallant moments during the rebellion that his Victoria Cross was awarded for 'continual daring', in particular a fight near Agra when Probyn was surrounded by half a dozen of the enemy and killed two in combat before his own men re-joined him. On a later occasion he singled out a standard-bearer and, in the face of a number of mutineers, killed the man and took his standard. What is more remarkable is that earlier that same day he had been in action and received a wound on the wrist in another sword-fight. Major-General W.A. Watson, who knew him well, described Probyn as 'tall, dark, bearded, exceedingly handsome': a superb horseman, his features set off by the coloured turban of his regiment, a thick Afghan coat with cheerful silk scarves at the neck and waist, his hand in a long leather glove resting on a curved sword which he used in action with deadly effect. After the Mutiny the stalwart major served with his regiment in the Second China War, before more frontier campaigning in Umbeyla, where he was mentioned in despatches. In 1866 he became a colonel and four years later was promoted to major general.

In 1872 a new career began when Probyn became Equerry to the Prince of Wales. He was so liked by 'Bertie' that for fourteen years from 1877 he served as his comptroller and treasurer. The Queen was impressed by the way Probyn got her spendthrift son's accounts in order. Honours fell thick and fast; full general in 1888, Privy Counsellor in 1901, Keeper of the Privy Purse 1902–10, Extra Equerry to the new King, secretary of the Royal Victorian Order and so on. In 1904, much to Sir Dighton's delight, he was appointed Colonel of the 11th (King Edward's Own) Lancers (Probyn's Horse).

By this time Probyn's jet-black beard had turned snowy white and he had let it grow almost down to his waist. This Methuselah of the court was somewhat stooped but still a tall, dignified and commanding old man. Visitors noticed the highest award for bravery worn on his breast. He died on 20 June 1924 at Sandringham and is buried in Kensal Green Cemetery. The town Probynabad in Pakistan was named after him. Large farmlands there are still connected with his regiment. His VC was bought by an anonymous bidder at auction in 2005 for £160,000.

ROBERTS, LIEUTENANT-GENERAL SIR A. & ROBERTS, FIELD-MARSHAL LORD F. – CREAM OF THE INDIAN ARMY

ABRAHAM ROBERTS AND his well-known son Frederick form a remarkable pair of Indian Army soldiers. Between them they served in nine campaigns and over eleven decades of service to their country. The father is obviously less well-known, while his son, the subject of several books and numerous articles, is one of the most important British soldiers of the nineteenth century.

Roberts senior was born in 1784, son of a rector-architect who designed both the Protestant and Roman Catholic cathedrals in Waterford. He joined the local militia in 1801 and two years later got a cadetship in the Bengal Infantry, joining the Bengal Europeans, a corps he stayed with for many years (serving as its colonel when it later became the 101st Royal Bengal Fusiliers). Almost immediately upon his arrival in India young Abraham set off on campaign against the Mahrattas though he did not fight in any major battle. This came nine years later in the arduous Nepal War. Roberts served as adjutant with the 13th BNI and was praised for his behaviour in fights at Peacock Hill on 27 December 1814 and Birluku Tebee on 2 April 1815.

Twenty-three years of peacetime soldiering followed before the invasion of Afghanistan. Brigadier Roberts was given command of Shah Shuja's Levy, a 6,000-strong army of tribesmen intended by the British to keep their puppet on the Afghan throne. A Queen's officer, Brigadier Dennie, lambasted these troops as 'raw ... worse than worthless ... he has not a single subject or Afghan amongst them! – his army being composed of camp followers from the Company's military stations ...' Abraham led his troops bravely at the storming of Ghazni, but once Kabul was reached he became a vocal critic of the British envoy, William Macnaghten, and of local army decisions. He thought the site of the British camp was 'very unfortunate', being 'commanded in two places' and at the mercy of the Afghans who were 'expert thieves and assassins'. Complaints to the governor-general saw Roberts relieved of his command in December 1840. The historian Fortescue commented that:

> The policy of raising native levies to check the Afghan nobles had resulted only in mutiny on the one side and bitter discontent on the other ... Nominally General Roberts was in command of Shah Shuja's forces ... but Macnaghten insisted on keeping every detail of control in his own hands ... He kept from him all knowledge of the movement of troops on the frontier; he intercepted from him the reports even of regiments which were unquestionably under Roberts command; he would listen to no warnings ... In vain Roberts remonstrated and protested.

The next time Roberts had a chance to command in action was twelve years later on the North-West Frontier and by then he was joined by his son. Frederick was born at Cawnpore on 30 September 1832. His father had been desperate for him to become a lawyer or clergyman, but his heart was set on being a soldier. Not being able to afford a Sandhurst education, Abraham sent the boy to Addiscombe, where he gained a commission in the Bengal Artillery. At first glance he seemed an unlikely candidate for any army, being just 5ft 3in tall, blind in his right eye and plagued by stomach problems. But he was sturdily built and in time displayed an incredible inner toughness coupled with a street-wise intelligence, a friendly manner and the ability to be a team player.

Father and son had a few precious weeks together at Peshawar before Abraham left India in 1853, worn out by five decades – with only two spells of home leave – in the Indian climate (he died in 1873). Young Fred was described by a fellow officer around this time as 'a dapper little fellow ... smart as paint' and, apparently, a skilled waltzer. 'Little Bobs' returned to his battery. He proved adept at learning all aspects of his job and worked closely with his men. This interest in and sympathy for the common soldier was something he never lost and it would help to shape his legend. He also showed a knack for ingratiating himself with the right people and so impressed the QMG at a luncheon that in 1855 he was invited to join his department. Leap-frogging up the promotions ladder via staff appointments, seeing lots of campaigning along the way, would be Roberts' route to fame. He also began to demonstrate a massive ego, letting slip no opportunity of advancing his name or career. During the Indian Mutiny, as a member of the QMG's staff, he was ever in the thick of things, especially at Delhi and Lucknow. He met all the great names in the army and made sure they remembered him. Along the way, on 2 January 1858 at Khudaganj, he galloped after some mutineers, captured a standard and cut down his foe, winning the Victoria Cross.

Back home, he married Nora, daughter of a Black Watch officer. She would, it was later gossiped, extend a baleful influence over her husband's personnel choices and 'toughen up' some of his military decisions. With Nora at his back, Frederick now began moving up the promotions ladder: he was sent to report on the situation in the Umbeyla campaign, served as AQMG in Abyssinia and organised the expedition to the Lushai Hills where, on 25 January 1872, he was able to command troops in his first, albeit small, battle, leading Gurkhas to attack a stockade.

The springboard to Robert's fame was the Second Afghan War. Luck played a large part in his career, and he was fortunate to be commanding the Punjab Frontier Force and thus be in the perfect position to be given one of the three columns invading Afghanistan in 1878. He was doubly fortunate that his Kurram column was the best-equipped. On 2 December he defeated a superior Afghan army at Peiwar Kotal with a flanking movement, dividing his smaller army in a manoeuvre that broke the traditional rules of war. This victory ensured the success of the British invasion. After the murder of Sir Louis Cavagnari at Kabul on 3 September 1879, the Kurram troops were reactivated and designated the Kabul Field Force. Marching into the country Roberts met the Afghans with his 6,000 men and eighteen guns near Charasiab on 6 October and out-witted them with another flanking movement. Besieged at Kabul by 50,000 of the enemy, things reached a crescendo in a dawn attack by the Afghans on 23 December. Roberts kept his cool and sent out the 5th Punjab Cavalry and some artillery in a long sweeping movement to surprise the Afghans on their flank. It worked and he secured Kabul with a loss of ninety-six officers and men killed and 299 wounded.

The southern Afghanistan apple-cart was upset on 27 July 1880 by the disaster at Maiwand, the Indian Army's own Isandlwana. Roberts hastily assembled a flying column of 273 British officers, 2,562 British and 7,151 Indian troops plus eighteen guns and set off to relieve endangered Kandahar. The 300-mile march completed in twenty-three days, with 'gentlemen' of the press in tow (since Roberts always had time for war correspondents), became the defining event that established his fame. It mattered little that 'Kabul to Kandahar' was free of fighting – the march demonstrated British pluck after the awfulness of Maiwand. 'Bobs', as Kipling was soon to immortalise him, naturally won the battle at the end of it all (though he collapsed afterwards).

He returned to England a major-general, a KCB and a hero. A special medal in the shape of a star was even permitted for the Kabul to Kandahar participants. The period 1885–93 saw Roberts as C-in-C, India, and for four months in 1886–87 he led forces in the pacification of Upper Burma. By now he was accepted as the leading Indian Army general and major thinker on all things Asiatic, stemming from his belief that the races of northern India were more 'martial' than those of the south and that a Russian invasion of British territory was imminent and best met on the Kandahar-Ghazni-Kabul line.

The sheer cost of Roberts' Indian defence plan saw it sidelined back in Britain where, newly created Baron of Kandahar and Waterford, he was promoted to field-marshal in 1895 before being sent to Ireland as C-in-C. By now the leading thinkers in the army had formed into two main groups – Roberts and his 'Indians' and **Wolseley** and his 'Africans'. When war broke out with the Boers again in 1899, 'Bobs', who had never seen fighting in South Africa, was not slow to offer his services. He wrote early on to the war minister in case **Buller** or **White** were 'incapacitated', continued to express misgivings about the former and, a week before Colenso, placed his 'services and … experience at the disposal of the Government', while demanding 'supreme command'. After the reverses of 'Black Week', he had his way.

Having arrived at the Cape commanding the largest army the British ever used in a colonial war, he set out defeating the Boers in a lengthy and elaborate flank march on Bloemfontein, Pretoria and Johannesburg. In the opinion of historian Andre Wessels, 'Roberts proved that he was a good strategist, although he out-manoeuvred the Boers, rather than defeated them.' Some of his moves were bold, but he 'under-estimated the Boers' determination to continue to fight'. He also made one crucial mistake: by allowing his enemy to escape south of Johannesburg on 28–29 May 1900, so as to avoid street fighting or the destruction of the gold mines, 'he probably added nearly two years to the duration of the conflict'. According to Thomas Pakenham, this was the most serious British strategic mistake of the whole war.

Roberts left South Africa in December 1900. By then he had also demonstrated a ruthlessness in his make-up: firing a whole clutch of generals and sending them home; beginning the process of driving Boer women and children into barbed-wire camps. For there was a dark side to Roberts away from all the charm, the singing of comic songs by the piano, his twinkling eyes and genuine concern for the common soldier – a cold capacity to castigate or destroy officers he found deficient, a willingness to do whatever necessary to win. In Afghanistan he had not hesitated in executing forty men loosely suspected of being involved in Cavagnari's death, so now in South Africa if burghers would not surrender 'they and their families will be starved'.

Regarded by many as the best Victorian general, Roberts was also the last C-in-C of the British Army and even after the abolition of that post in 1904, he worked tirelessly for reform, not least his belief in conscription and preparations for a coming European conflict. In 1914, with the splendid title of Colonel-in-Chief of the Empire, the 82-year-old warhorse went to see the Indian troops in France. He caught a chill at St Omer and died on 14 November. His funeral truly marked the end of an epoch and he lies buried in St Paul's Cathedral, close to his rival Wolseley.

Most contemporaries liked him, though Wolseley, who did not deny Roberts' abilities on the battlefield, thought him a 'snob' and 'a cute little showman'. He was unquestionably more human and easy for troops to relate to than Kitchener or Wolseley. We will leave the last word to Ian **Hamilton**, who had reason enough to be grateful to his old chief. He wrote:

> Lord Bobs had the most equable, well balanced, commonsense disposition imaginable. The men knew he was a fighter; they knew he could harden his heart … He combined moral and physical courage … It took him a lifetime to touch everyone but by the end he had pretty well brought it off.

ROGERS, LIEUTENANT-GENERAL SIR R. – THE FIGHTING 20TH

A MAXIM OF the Duke of Cambridge, C-in-C of the British Army 1856–95, was that officers served the institution best by staying with their regiments. Many of them did and a goodly proportion were rewarded close to retirement with promotion to major-general rank. This book cannot accommodate many of them, brave as they were and exciting as some of their careers were. I have selected two who both displayed great gallantry, saw much action and had the same first and last names, though completely unrelated – one each from the Indian and British armies of the Queen-Empress.

Robert Gordon Rogers was born on 19 April 1832 in London and joined the Bengal Army as an ensign at 16 years of age. He missed the Mutiny, serving as commandant of the Arracan Battalion on the north-east frontier (though still just a lieutenant), and after some transfers found his way into the 20th Punjab Native Infantry in 1861. The regiment, commanded by the dashing Charles **Brownlow**, needed a second-in-command.

A journal surfaced a few years ago written by a surgeon who served with the 20th for just two years, 1868–70. He claimed that Rogers was unpopular, but there may have been some bias in these writings. Robert seems to have been a strict man, but also a courageous one, and Brownlow praised his 'efficient management' of the men. Rogers was mentioned in despatches for his bravery at Umbeyla 1863 and the Black Mountain expedition 1868. In the former campaign he showed special gallantry during the fighting around the Crag Picquet on 20 November when 5,000 of the enemy brought fire on the British from surrounding hills as a further 1,500 tribesmen prepared to charge. According to Captain Charles Stewart, 5th PNI, Rogers directed the mountain battery in its shelling before a 'great rush' of warriors. During the hand-to-hand fighting the 'last man to come in was Major Rogers of the 20th P.I., who was helping to carry a wounded man of his regiment'. In a letter to his mother written the next day, Rogers said the enemy could have been beaten but for the 'utter cowardice' of a British officer who caused a panic. Using the flat of his sword, Rogers hit Europeans and natives over the head in a vain attempt to make them stand and fight until someone pushed him down a steep slope. He got to his feet to see a *ghazi* rushing at him with shield and sword:

> I at once fired at him, but bruised and shaken as I was, missed – he turned on me & I again missed him at not five paces. He, however, turned and bolted thinking one barrel of my revolver, which he then saw, might roll him over. A sepoy of ours shot him dead.'

In 1872 Rogers succeeded Brownlow as commandant of the 20th PNI and remained its colonel for eleven years. It is fair to say that by the end of that time, having served twenty-two years in total with the regiment, and having earned several more mentions in despatches, that the men liked and respected him. On a rare furlough to England in 1882 he even wrote a special letter describing the place to his subardar-major, Mauladad Khan, one of the most decorated soldiers in the Indian Army. Rogers led the 20th against the Afridis in 1876, 1877 and 1878 and against the Afghans 1878–80. He was proud when it was chosen as one of only three infantry regiments to form part of the contingent sent to Egypt from India in **Wolseley**'s expedition. He told his sons that the regiment charged at Tel-el-Kebir 'in splendid style ... as the Egyptians ran like hares'. He then led the 20th on 'a devil of a march' towards Cairo. He wrote:

> I have had longer, but taking heat, dust, flies etc., never a more tiring one – and not even one of our followers fell out ... glad was I on searching the railway refreshment room to get a bottle of beer ... gladder was I when I had seen to the men and to lie down on a wooden bench with my helmet as a pillow and sleep soundly as fighting horses and cursing Britishers would allow.

In 1881 he was made a CB and also an ADC to the Queen-Empress. He joined the Bengal Staff Corps the next year, bidding farewell to his regiment, was knighted and retired in 1897. He passed away at his home in Bath in 1918.

ROGERS, MAJOR-GENERAL R. – TAKU FORTS VICTORIA CROSS

ROBERT MONTRESOR ROGERS won a VC for gallantry in China. Nineteen years later he had to display the same courage against the Zulus at Kambula. He was born in 1834 and joined the 44th Foot twenty years later. Within a year he was off to fight in the Crimea and saw action at the Siege of Sebastopol. When the China War broke out his regiment was sent and during the attack on the Taku Forts at Sinho he swam the stagnant muddy ditch under heavy fire with two others, Lieutenant Lenon of the 67th Foot and Private MacDougall of the 44th. While Lenon forced his sword and some bayonets into the mud wall of the fort, Rogers climbed up and entered through an embrasure, the first Briton to gain entry. Six VCs were won that day (including by Rogers' two comrades) in an attack that cost seventeen British dead and 184 wounded.

Though severely wounded in the fighting which followed, Rogers recovered to wear his coveted bronze cross and enjoy promotion to captain. In 1873 he became a major and transferred to the 90th Light Infantry. At Kambula on 29 March 1879 his men fought splendidly, holding a corner of the British square and losing forty-four killed and wounded during the battle. Evelyn **Wood** VC described Rogers' efforts as 'sterling' in a speech on 14 June 1880 and went on to say: 'No regiment could fail to be influenced by the steady guidance and well-tried courage of my loyal supporter, Major Rogers VC, who commanded the corps throughout the Zulu War.'

In 1880 Rogers was given a CB and became a lieutenant-colonel when the 90th moved to India. The old war wounds from his Chinese and South African exertions had taken a toll on his health. He retired, was raised to major-general rank, and died on 5 February 1895.

ROWLANDS, GENERAL SIR H. – VC HERO AND VACILLATING COMMANDER

HUGH ROWLANDS WAS a brave Welshman who won a VC in the Crimea but over two decades later he proved to be an ineffectual commander against the BaPedi and Zulus while commanding in the Transvaal.

He was born on 6 May 1828 at Llanrug near Anglesey, educated at Beaumaris and joined the 41st Regiment as an ensign in 1849. After a short peacetime service he sailed with them to the Crimea in 1854. At the Alma he led his men steadily up the heights, 'under a heavy fire of shot and shell from a battery on a high hill'. A few weeks later, at the Battle of Inkerman, Captain Rowlands heroically charged the enemy several times and on one occasion saved the life of his colonel who was surrounded by Russians. He was severely wounded in the arm in the same fight. His rewards were immediate promotion to brevet-major and, a short time later, investiture of the newly instituted Victoria Cross, the first Welshman to win the coveted medal.

Twenty-four years of peacetime soldiering followed in India and other places before General Thesiger, who had served in the Crimea, remembered the highly decorated Rowlands and requested him as one of his ADCs in South Africa. There he accepted the new post of inspector of colonial forces. Rowlands soon found himself in a tricky political position, trying to appease Thesiger on the one hand, and Theophilus Shepstone, administrator of the newly annexed Transvaal, on the other. In August 1878, as commandant of the Transvaal Forces, Rowlands was instructed to begin operations against the wily BaPedi chieftain, Sekhukhune. Thesiger wanted this native threat neutralised before he invaded Zululand. Shepstone had the 'greatest confidence' in Rowlands, but his expedition failed disastrously, 'due to lack of resources and the difficult conditions'.

Thesiger was furious and never forgave Rowlands. A rare defender was his deputy, Captain C.L. Harvey, who called him 'a soldier all over, a practical man, eager to do his duty'. Most other soldiers felt differently: Redvers **Buller**, who commanded the Frontier Light Horse in the campaign, thought Rowlands 'quite useless. He cannot make up his mind to anything, sitting on his behind … a charming man he is too, so nice, but I would rather be cursed by someone who wanted to do something.' Another officer wrote home that Rowlands 'made an awful mess of his business. He failed utterly and completely and worse still, rather humiliatingly for our name and fame. He not only did not take Sekhukhune's place, but he did not even try to take it.'

When the Zulu War broke out a still bitter Lord **Chelmsford** (as Thesiger now became) sidelined Rowlands' efforts in northern Zululand, making him serve under Evelyn **Wood**, his junior in the service. John North **Crealock**, Chelmsford's military secretary, admitted 'we have not put much confidence in Rowlands of late', while the Cape governor, Sir Bartle Frere, wrote: 'I wish Wood had Rowlands' regiment without Rowlands.' Despite leading a number of forays against Zulu outposts, Rowlands was damned as a field commander by Chelmsford, who even wrote to Wood congratulating him 'on getting rid of Rowlands'.

After the war, Rowlands was given a hero's welcome on his return to Wales, but his fighting days were over. He continued to rise in the service, holding various commands, retired in 1896 and died on 1 August 1909. He is buried at Llanrug, close to his birthplace. His biographer, W. Alister Williams, provides a strong defence of his hero, making Mansfield **Clarke** the scapegoat for errors in command during the first British Sekhukhune expedition. But it must be said that by failing to defeat the BaPedi, Rowlands made the British Army look weak in the eyes of other native peoples, as well as the Boers, at a delicate moment in South African history, while he seems to have been, as the Swazi agent Captain Macleod noted, 'a very nice fellow, but very vacillating'.

RUNDLE, LIEUTENANT-GENERAL SIR H. – 'LESLIE TRUNDLE'

HENRY MACLEOD LESLIE Rundle, who was always known to his friends as 'Leslie', certainly did not lack bravery: as a young man he demonstrated his pluck against the Zulus and Boers, then went on hazardous missions in the dervish-infested Sudan. Years later, after a decade of staff work, he proved a disappointment as a field commander in the South African War.

The son of a naval officer, Leslie was born on 6 January 1856 and entered the Royal Artillery in 1876. Within five years he had gained several mentions in despatches. First came the Zulu War, where he supervised one of the two hand-cranked Gatlings used on the north face of the British square. The machines fired 200–300 rounds a minute, cutting swathes through the Zulus, but they jammed six times as bolts dropped on the ground (a defect probably caused by cranking too fast). Two years later Lieutenant Rundle was posted to N/5 Battery as part of the garrison of Potchefstroom in the Transvaal. When the Boers besieged the town he became a leading light in its defence with his two 9-pounders and forty-three soldiers. The siege, one of the mini-epics beloved by the Victorians in their small wars, lasted ninety-five days. Despite the town's encirclement by the enemy, Rundle put on a good show, his gunners frequently knocking out targets, so that by the end of it all he was acclaimed something of a hero. He was wounded in the siege, but fit enough a year later to command another battery at Tel-el-Kebir.

Egypt and the Sudan would remain Rundle's base for the next sixteen years. On 1 January 1883 he joined the re-formed Egyptian Army, one of its earliest recruits. During the 1884–85 Sudan War he served as a spy and junior assistant to the enterprising Herbert **Kitchener**, who described him as 'a charming fellow'. Their Abaddeh Field Force was a motley collection of 1,500 Arabs from various tribes who gathered intelligence on the Mahdists across the baking desert between the Nile and Red Sea. Rundle was often left at Korosko to organise things while Kitchener went on reconnaissance. He was exasperated: 'You cannot control this work from the end of a telegraph wire … Do you intend returning? If so, when?' By the end of 1885, Major Rundle had been mentioned several more times in despatches. Over the next six years he was closely involved with the operations of the Sudan Frontier Field Force, commanded the mounted troops at Saras in 1887 and the artillery at Toski in 1889, winning the DSO and getting a lieutenant-colonelcy. When the reconquest of the Sudan got under way in 1896, the Sirdar of the Egyptian Army, Herbert Kitchener, made his old friend chief of staff. Behaving much as he had done a decade earlier, Kitchener refused to delegate even simple tasks and left Rundle back at headquarters. The latter did manage, however, to be by his chief's side at Omdurman.

In December 1898, now a major-general, Rundle left Egypt and returned home to command the south-east district. On the outbreak of the South African War he temporarily replaced **Clery** as DAAG before sailing to the Cape to command the 8th Division of the SAFF. There he soon found himself serving under his old comrade, Archibald **Hunter**, in the hunt for De Wet. During **Roberts**' great advance in May 1900 there was a reverse at Senekal, with a loss of 180 men, when Rundle failed to pull off an attack. This earned Roberts' displeasure: 'Rundle has incurred a heavy loss for no purpose … he is not a commander to be trusted.' Three months later, Roberts castigated him:

> He was never tried as a Commander in Egypt – He was Chief of Staff to Kitchener, and Chief of Staff to a man like Kitchener with a comparatively small force had probably but little to do. He has failed twice in this Country as a Divisional Commander. He failed to fight at Dewetsdorp when he ought to have fought, and he went out of his way to fight on the Senekal-Bethlehem road when he ought not to have fought.

Ian **Hamilton** wrote over a year afterwards that Rundle was 'one of the great failures' of the war. Kitchener, it was said, felt his old friend was 'of very little use now, and will never be of any use to the army hereafter'.

Nicknamed 'Leslie Trundle' for his slow, cool way of dealing with things, Rundle spent the latter part of the war in the Orange Free State. In 1905 he was raised to lieutenant-general. He spent a happy six years from 1909 as Governor of Malta before his retirement in 1916. His sister had married Reginald Wingate, intelligence chief in the Sudan, and Sirdar after Kitchener. He and Rundle had been rivals in those days, but in old age they became good friends before the latter's death in 1934.

RUSSELL, GENERAL SIR B. – FIGHTING CAVALRYMAN

NO SOLDIER IN this book, especially among cavalry officers, quite fills the role of a fighting general like Baker Creed Russell. Indian mutineers, war-like Ashantis, fierce BaPedis and mounted Egyptians all were chastised by him. There was nothing subtle or clever to his soldiering, or his generalship in command. Baker liked to lead from the front and get into the action, even as he got older, but soldiers trusted him. Russell proved an excellent field commander in the second Sekhukhune campaign, while in Egypt he led one of the great Victorian cavalry charges.

He was born in Australia on 11 January 1837, the son of an infantry officer, joined the 6th Dragoon Guards in 1855 and embarked for India. Baker was at Meerut on 10 May 1857 when the Great Rising started. At Karnaul near Delhi he took part in his first cavalry charge and, three weeks later, he took command at Gungaree when three senior officers were killed. He went on to fight notably at Bareilly and then in lots of minor actions during the 1858 pursuit of Tatya Tope.

In 1862 Russell transferred to the 13th Hussars, a regiment he would go on to command, turning it into one of the finest light cavalry corps in the British Army. Soon it became known as 'the Baker's dozen'. One of its junior officers, Robert **Baden-Powell**, called Russell 'the beau ideal of a fighting leader'. One historian has noted that:

> He bawled out his orders in a gravel voice that could wake the dead and did not suffer fools gladly but his magnetic larger-than-life personality led men to obey him without question … On the parade ground woe betide any junior officer whose actions annoyed Sir Baker. Like an old wild boar [which, with his huge moustache, he much resembled], he would gallop up to the unfortunate individual and give him a tongue-lashing.

But Russell 'cared little for the drill-book, had an instinctive soldier's eye for where his men should be in a fight', and they, in turn, would have followed him to Hell if need be.

In 1873 Major Russell was selected to join the Ashanti expedition. On the voyage out to West Africa he and Garnet **Wolseley** became lifelong friends. Wolseley respected Russell's fighting skills and 'jolliness'. Later in the campaign, after the irregular 'Russell's Regiment' had seen action, Wolseley succinctly noted his friend's weaknesses when he wrote in his journal: 'He is rather impetuous & does not obey orders as strictly as I should like when he is near the enemy. He is one of those men who when they think they have a chance of having a fight on their own hook, almost invariably bring it on no matter what orders they may have received to the contrary.' After the war Russell was rewarded with a brevet lieutenant-colonelcy. Three years later, he accompanied Wolseley to Cyprus and, not long after, to Zululand. He was kept busy in the hunt for Cetewayo, but his real chance to shine came in the Transvaal, where Wolseley allowed Russell to be field commander in the second British expedition against the BaPèdi. He led 1,800 Europeans and 2,200 natives in the attack on Chief Sekhukhune's *kraal* and his strongly defended redoubt, a rocky hill known as 'the fighting kopje'. Russell divided his forces into four columns and after a bloody fight the *kraal* and *kopje* were both stormed and taken. Wolseley insisted on sharing the honours with Russell who, as usual, led from the front, losing a horse shot from under him during the attack.

Made a KCMG, Sir Baker joined Wolseley three years later for the invasion of Egypt. This time he commanded the 1st (British) Cavalry Division under **Drury-Lowe**. He led the charge through the enemy camp at Mahsama on 28 August 1882. Three nights later in the desert near Kassassin he had perhaps his finest moment – white-coated, sitting high in the saddle, he thundered out the command, 'Household Cavalry, charge!' In this moonlight melee he led 450 cavalrymen at the Egyptian guns and infantry, had yet another horse killed under him, but picked himself up and despatched two or three of the enemy with his sabre. Tel-el-Kebir, followed by the cavalry dash on Cairo, were his last tastes of war. The Duke of Cambridge, who disliked all 'the Wolseley Gang', prevented Sir Baker from joining his chief during the **Gordon** Relief Expedition. Instead, the old warhorse was sent to command in places like Aldershot and Bengal before his eventual retirement.

He died on 25 November 1911. He was perhaps the antithesis of **Brackenbury**, the intellectual soldier. He had tried to live truly by his own maxim, that it was a cavalry officer's duty to 'look smart in time of peace and to get killed in war'.

SALE, MAJOR-GENERAL SIR R. – 'FIGHTING BOB'

THE STORMING OF the fortress at Ghazni was at its height. As Captain Kershaw of HM's 13th Regiment stepped gingerly into the breach and amid a mass of rubble, dust, shouts, screams and confusion he came across the burly figure of his commanding officer, in scarlet coat and gold braid, rolling across the ground locked in a deadly embrace with an Afghan. Both men's hands were tightly clasped around the handle of the Afghan's scimitar. The brigadier, the same man who had led the assaulting party, politely asked Kershaw to 'do him the favour to pass his sword through the body of the infidel'. The captain obliged, but the Afghan continued to fight until his opponent smashed in his skull. The victor – not a young man I might add, but 56 years of age – was 'Fighting Bob' Sale.

The early Victorian army was commanded by generals with the ethos of the Napoleonic Wars fresh in their veins. They rode into battle at the head of their troops, and a good officer was prepared to die in front of his men. It set an example. Robert Sale was this kind of officer. He was brave but not brilliant; one authority has written that his men 'loved him for his courage which often bordered on foolhardiness'. He exemplified the fighting generals who covered themselves in glory and wounds and, rightly enough in his case, died on the battlefield.

Born in 1782, Sale joined the 36th Foot at 13 years of age, transferring to the 12th Foot and going to India as a lieutenant with them in 1798. He fought at Seringapatam and served under Wellesley. Promoted captain in 1808, Sale was engaged in Harris's operations against the Rajah of Travancore 1808–9. In 1810 he went on the expedition to Mauritius and three years later was promoted to major. He transferred to the 13th Foot and would be connected with them for the rest of his life. He led the 13th in all the actions of the First Burmese War up to the capture of Rangoon, and in one fight killed an enemy commander in single combat, cutting the man almost in two. Later, in another engagement, Sale was severely wounded in the head.

Decimated by disease in Burma, Sale's battalion of the 13th was increased by men described as 'the sweepings of the London jails' and, in the words of a fellow officer, 'in a frightful state of insubordination'. Now known as 'Fighting Bob' due to his courage in Burma, Sale liberally applied the lash to these soldiers. On the parade ground he let the men fire blanks at him and shouted, 'Ah, it's not my fault if you don't shoot me.' This kind of 'jovial challenge', combined with Sale's genuine concern for the welfare of his troops, led to them becoming 'mere babies' in his hands, though their chief affection, as a contemporary remarked, was for 'Bob's' refusal 'to behave himself as a General should do. Despite his staff's protests, he used to ride about two miles ahead of his troops, and in an action would fight like a private.'

Awarded a CB, Colonel Sale was given command of the 1st Bengal Brigade of the Army of the Indus in 1838. He personally led the storming of Ghazni and foolishly called for retreat too soon, but this error was overlooked after the citadel was taken and his personal bravery duly acknowledged. He was knighted and given the local rank of major-general. While at Kabul he was joined by his wife, Florentia, and their 20-year-old daughter. Sale was next tasked with clearing the lines of communication with India and occupied Jellalabad on 12 November 1841 after heavy fighting. This soon developed into what was called 'a siege' but, in reality, was a close investment of the town. He had 1,500 men against an Afghan army of around three times that number. Provisions were low and Sale's troops had just 120 rounds of ammunition per man. Luckily for the general, who was 'brave if, at times, pedantic', his officers included 'a veritable array of talent' led by Henry **Havelock**, his long-term adjutant and friend. Gradually the energy and innovation of Sale's team began to flag, and he was considering surrender when news came of Pollock's advance.

Later Sale rode through hostile territory to rescue his wife and daughter from their ten-month captivity. 'All hearts were full,' wrote one of his officers, 'hardly anyone could speak.' Sale was congratulated. 'The gallant old man turned towards me and tried to answer, but his feelings were too strong; he made a hideous series of grimaces, dug his spurs into his horse and galloped off as hard as he could.' The Victorians loved sieges; Sale was given a GCB and a special medal was struck for the Jellalabad defenders.

Three years later, when war broke out with the Sikhs, the red-faced and chubby Sir Robert was made QMG of Her Majesty's forces. If he had ever yearned for death in battle, his wish was now granted. It was at Mudki on 21 December 1845, the first battle of the Anglo-Sikh Wars, riding with his staff, that a grapeshot took off one of Sale's legs. He died that evening, a by-word in the army for physical courage. Florentia, one of the great *memsahibs*, saw her diary of the Afghan War become a bestseller when published. She had even been shot in the wrist during the retreat. She was granted a pension of £500 a year in light of Sale's record and her own conduct as a prisoner of the Afghans, but outlived him by fewer than eight years, dying at Cape Town in 1853.

SANDHURST, GENERAL LORD W. – INTELLIGENT AND HAUGHTY

WILLIAM ROSE MANSFIELD, later 1st Baron Sandhurst, was given one golden opportunity during the Indian Mutiny to prove himself a good field commander, but he bungled it badly. He was chief of staff and confidante to Colin Campbell throughout the campaign, exercising more control over Mutiny operations than is generally realised. He later proved to be also an intelligent C-in-C, India. It was a shame that Mansfield/Sandhurst always displayed, besides a sharp brain, a marked superciliousness that made many officers dislike him intensely.

He was born in Hertfordshire on 21 June 1819, grandson of a general in the American Revolutionary Army. After Sandhurst he joined the 53rd Foot in 1835, serving in both Anglo-Sikh wars and commanding his regiment in the 1848–49 campaign, notably the pursuit of the enemy after Gujerat. He also saw action in Campbell's 1850 expedition against the Kohat Pass Afridis. It was here that the pair formed a long friendship. In 1855 Mansfield was made military advisor to the British ambassador at Constantinople and accompanied him to the Crimea during the war.

Returning to India, Mansfield was chosen by Campbell to be his chief of staff. Their relationship was extraordinarily close. Mansfield later told a colleague that 'The ordinary official reserve between superior and subordinate never existed between us.' There is a famous photograph of them together, Mansfield sitting, while Campbell stands. Sometimes people assume the seated man is the C-in-C because Mansfield seems to dominate as he stares at a document while crooking a long finger in his chief's direction, like a Latin master dissecting his scholar's prep. Besides the C-in-C, few people liked Mansfield, though Lieutenant Lang of the engineers, after meeting him for the first time, described him as 'a neat, gentlemanly, quiet, courteous officer, and, I should think, shrewd and clear-sighted'. Everyone knew Mansfield was clever. They just did not like his manner: Charles **Macgregor** found him to be 'dark, Machiavellian, very knowing'; the war correspondent William Russell noted how 'he is obliged to wear glasses or spectacles, the use of which, combined with the cut of his lips, the *pose* of the head, which is thrown back with the chin forwards, gives General Mansfield an air of *hauteur* – some people say superciliousness'; Garnet **Wolseley** thought he had 'a cold, calculating and logical train of rare quality', adding bluntly, 'no one liked him'.

Critics could not deny that Sir William was a first-rate chief of staff, writing his chief's orders clearly and working non-stop to defeat the mutineers. He was also a reformist who told a commission in 1858 that 'tight jackets and shakos should be forgotten forever'. In his writings Mansfield demonstrated an intelligent understanding of the Mutiny's causes and the defects of the Bengal Army.

At Cawnpore on 6 December 1857 he was told by Campbell to block the line of retreat of the Gwalior Contingent, a huge army of rebels. Notoriously short-sighted, this action, in which his bungling allowed most of the rebels to escape, led the Victorian historian Thomas Rice Holmes to quip that 'he did not possess the eye of a General'. A rare defence of his actions is found in the writings of another Mutiny historian, George Forrest, who pointed out that Mansfield had followed the orders of Campbell, which were to avoid pursuing the enemy through 'the enclosures and houses of the old cantonment' and, despite criticisms at every level of his 'blunder', the chief was full of praise for his assistant's conduct. Mansfield did things carefully but slowly. Unhurried in his judgements, refusing to rush in his decisions, it now seems clear that Campbell's dilatory manner in pursuing the overthrow of the rebellion, widely criticised at the time, owed much to his chief of staff's advice and influence over him.

After the Mutiny the old, tired Campbell, now Lord **Clyde**, and the much younger Mansfield had a falling-out. Clyde wanted his assistant to command in the China War, but Sir William refused to leave India, thinking he would be next in line for the plum role of C-in-C, India. He was not (it went to Sir Hugh Rose), but in 1865 he got his wish. He had five relatively peaceful years in command before leaving India in 1870 to be C-in-C, Ireland. In 1871 he was raised to the peerage as the 1st Baron Sandhurst and made a privy councillor. Despite his relative youth, he seems to have had bad health for many years and died in 1876 just two days after his fifty-seventh birthday.

SARTORIUS, MAJOR-GENERAL R. – VICTORIA CROSS ASHANTI WINNER

REGINALD 'REGGIE' SARTORIUS was one of a rare pair of brothers who both won a Victoria Cross – his came in Ashanti, though he behaved with pluck in three other campaigns too. He was born on 8 May 1841, son of an admiral, entered the Bengal Cavalry in 1858 and within days was fighting mutineers at Azimghur. The town was invested, but Sartorius volunteered to carry despatches through the enemy lines, and was successful, though he was wounded twice and had a lucky bullet pass through his cap.

In 1864 he served in the Bhutan War, but it was his part in the Ashanti campaign ten years later that made him, for a few weeks, a national hero. 'Reggie' was serving with a column under Captain Glover RN that had set out to approach the Ashanti capital, Kumasi, via the River Volta. On 10 February 1874, commanding a small party of twenty native soldiers, each man armed with just forty rounds, Sartorius set off to find **Wolseley**'s army, believing it to be just a short distance away at the capital. He soon found out that the general had burned Kumasi and set off back for the coast. Kofi Karikari, the Ashanti king, was said to have vowed vengeance. To make matters worse, Sartorius discovered the distances he had been told were all wrong and were in fact much longer. Avoiding pitched battles surrounded by a warlike enemy, he reached the blackened capital and marched briskly on with the Ashantis watching to catch up with Wolseley on 12 February – 'a most remarkable march of fifty-three miles through the heart of the enemy's country, often surrounded or threatened, without provisions, and without having fired a single shot or lost a man of his small escort.' A Victoria Cross was suggested, but Sartorius's trek did not seem to be covered by the terms of the award, so he was given one for saving the life of one his soldiers at Aboogoo on 17 January.

Raised to major and created a CMG, 'Reggie' Sartorius saw his last fighting five years later in the Second Afghan War. His younger brother, Euston, serving with HM 59th Regiment, won a VC leading an attack on a hill held by fanatical tribesmen, making the Sartorius boys, along with the Goughs, two of the only four pairs of brother who have ever won the VC 'Reggie' became a colonel in 1886 and major-general in 1895, retiring two years later. A keen yachtsman, he died suddenly of a heart attack at Cowes on 8 August 1907.

SMITH, LIEUTENANT-GENERAL SIR H. – 'BRAGGADOCIO'

IT WAS AN old soldier fighting in South Africa who nicknamed Sir Harry Smith 'Braggadocio'. Fiery, impulsive, brave yet egotistical, the moniker seems apt. He impressed some contemporaries, who lauded the 'hero of Aliwal', and several pubs were named after him. Others were less kind: one Cape settler labelled him uncouth and offensive, but noted he treated his officers just as badly, swearing at them in front of the men. The wife of another colonist agreed, adding that 'this hot-headed and most generous of governors', despite all his faults, 'was ready to cover you with kindness' in a better mood. Historians have not been impressed: to Meintjes he was 'a grotesque'; Harrington thinks him 'bungling' and Mostert describes him as 'a disturbingly mercurial personality … a crass, foolish, posturing man but not a cruel one … a mixture of crudeness, menace, humane perception, kindness, silliness and frivolous behaviour.'

Harry was never sure of the date of his birth, but it was probably 28 June 1787. He was born at Whittlesea in Cambridgeshire. Aged 16, this doctor's son became an ensign in the local yeomanry and at a review in 1804 so impressed William Stewart, one of the founders of the Corps of Riflemen, that he offered the boy a commission in what had become the 95th Regiment (known after 1816 as the Rifle Brigade). Soon Harry was off on his first campaign – the disastrous expedition to Monte Video. Here he learned Spanish as a prisoner and returned to Europe in time to join

Moore's celebrated retreat to Corunna. He reached England safely, but a skeleton, 'literally covered and almost eaten up with vermin ...' He quickly returned to the Peninsular War and saw a great deal of fighting, though the action he always remembered best was Badajoz in 1812, where he saved a beautiful young *señorita*, Juanita de los Dolores de León, from rape. The pair became lovers and were quickly married. Juanita would follow Harry in most of his adventures and give her name to a town – Ladysmith.

In 1814 the British, fighting another war with the Americans, burned the civic buildings of Washington. Smith was one of the lucky forty who enjoyed a fine meal hastily left by President Madison's wife at the White House. Afterwards they torched the place. Harry was honoured by bringing home the despatches. At Waterloo, two horses were wounded under him but he himself remained unharmed. Afterwards he became a brevet lieutenant-colonel and got a CB. His Waterloo and Peninsular War medals commemorated no less than thirteen battles.

England, Nova Scotia, the West Indies – peacetime soldiering bored Smith. In 1829 he and Juanita set sail for South Africa, where he spent nearly six uneventful years as AQMG until late December 1834, when news reached Cape Town that the Xhosas had invaded the colony in force and a sixth frontier war had started. Given full military and civic powers by the governor, Smith raced to the action. The war developed into a duel between him and Hintsa, paramount chief of the Gcalekas, whom Harry variously described as 'a very fine fellow' and a 'shuffling scoundrel', depending on his mood. The drama reached its climax on the day Hintsa tried to escape from Smith's 'protection'. Harry was almost 50 but he galloped after the chief, throwing his pistols at him as they galloped abreast, and dodging an assegai. Finally he managed to drag Hintsa off his horse when his own beast refused to stop. After Smith heard the chief had been killed he refused even to bury the corpse decently, using the lame excuse that he 'had no tools', but kept his enemy's assegai and some bracelets. The base killing (some whispered murder) of the great chief shamed Smith for a while, but it was forgotten. The war degenerated into a guerrilla phase and was finally wrapped up to Harry's satisfaction. The colonists considered him a hero. Never one to waste time with modesty, the victor gave himself full credit for punishing a people he patronisingly referred to as 'children', 'barbarians' and 'contemptible enemies'.

In 1840 the Smiths bade farewell to South Africa and sailed for India, where Harry was to be AG of HM's soldiers. He fought alongside **Gough** in the 'one-day war' at Maharajpore, but his moment of glory – perhaps the

high point of his fighting career – came at Aliwal on 28 January 1846. Here
he was alone in command and able to defeat the Sikhs in what he called 'a
stand-up gentlemanly battle', with losses of just 145 killed and 3,000 of the
enemy slain. One trooper noted there were tears in the general's eyes as he
rode among them murmuring, 'God bless you, my brave boys, I love you.'
Smith had much praise heaped on him for his careful co-ordination of all
services. 'I have read the accounts of many a battle,' wrote his mentor, the
Duke of Wellington, 'but I never read the account of one in which more
ability, energy and experience has been manifested than in this.' Smith, ever
boastful, told his sister: 'I have gained one of the most glorious battles ever
fought in India.' This balloon of pomposity was pricked six years later by
Governor-General Lord Dalhousie, who wrote:

> Sir Harry Smith is treated with ridicule or worse. His entire suppression of the
> facts of the affair of Buddiwal just before Aliwal, where he was shamefully sur-
> prised – lost all his baggage, many of his sick and followers, and was saved from
> utter rout only by the cavalry … is regarded with great contempt … In short,
> while all admit him to be a gallant, dashing soldier, he has no military reputa-
> tion in India. There his apotheosis in England created unmitigated disgust.

Harry ended his Sikh War at the 'brutal bull-dog fight' of Sobraon where,
on five occasions, he grabbed regimental colours and planted them forward.
His cane was shot out of his hand, but he was miraculously unscathed. The
Sikhs defeated, Harry returned home with a baronetcy 'of Aliwal' and a fat
sum in prize money.

Soon he was back to the Cape as governor – a surprise appointment
– where it was hoped he might bring a Seventh Frontier War to an end.
The war spluttered out and in 1848 the governor declared sovereignty
over the Orange River territory. This resulted in a battle with the Boers at
Boomplaats. Smith talked of enemy losses of forty-nine killed and 'upwards'
of 150 wounded. His enemies admitted to just nine killed and five wounded
(Smith's losses were seven killed and forty-five wounded).

In December 1850 an eighth Xhosa war broke out. Smith ordered all adult
male colonists to serve in his militias and sent a force deep into the Xhosa
heartland of the Amatola Mountains. This was to be the biggest and ugliest
of the frontier wars. At times he had three brigades and seven columns harassing the natives, who managed to create some spectacularly bloody ambushes.
Gradually the Colonial Secretary in London, Lord Grey, grew increasingly
sceptical of Smith's bombastic false despatches. By late 1851 Grey thought

British losses were 'very serious' and admonished Smith: 'I am forced to believe that no real advantage has been gained over the Kaffirs.' On 14 January 1852 he accused Smith of failing to show 'foresight, energy and judgment', and told him 'the conduct of the war should be placed in other hands.' Harry and Juanita returned to England and, as usual, he had many supporters, but his fighting days were over. He died of angina pectoris on 12 October 1860. Twelve years later his devoted wife also passed away. Both are buried at Whittlesea.

In fairness, his generalship against the Sikhs, fighting somewhat in the European manner, was largely successful. He had more problems conducting irregular warfare in the bush, yet he also stamped his strong personality on the events of the sixth and eighth Xhosa wars. His play-acting before the locals – white and black – coupled with boasts and rash assurances made to settlers and politicians alike, made him seem, in time, merely foolish to all of them.

SOMERSET, LIEUTENANT-GENERAL SIR H. – FIGHTING THE XHOSA

IN 1966 THE writer Dorothy Rivett-Carnac published a sympathetic biography of Henry Somerset, the aristocratic soldier who participated in every Xhosa war from 1819–1852. She remains his only champion – Noel Mostert dismisses him as lazy and unintelligent, while John Milton goes so far as to call the general 'Bluff, good-natured, stupid', with a 'long-standing reputation for asinine incompetence'.

Henry was born on 30 December 1794, son of Lord Charles Somerset, Colonel of the 101st Foot. Hereditary Dukes of Beaufort, the Somersets were a large clan and one of Henry's younger uncles was Lord Fitzroy Somerset, later to be better known as the Crimean War C-in-C, Lord Raglan. Shortly before his seventeenth birthday the boy was given a cornetcy in the 10th Hussars. The war against Napoleon raged across Europe and Henry fought at Vittoria and other battles as the French were pushed across the Pyrenees. Transferring to the 18th Light Dragoons in 1814, he joined his uncle, Lord Robert Somerset, who commanded the 1st Cavalry Brigade at Waterloo, where his nephew had no less than two horses killed and three wounded as he carried orders across the battlefield.

As a young man Henry had a mass of reddish hair. Soon this started to recede and turn a snowy white. With mutton-chop whiskers, his large Beaufort nose and his high domed forehead, Somerset looked a blimpish character, though he always sat high and erect on any horse. In 1817 Henry married his childhood sweetheart and a year later the pair sailed for the Cape of Good Hope, where his father was governor. When war broke out with the Gaika tribe in 1819, Henry found himself campaigning on the Cape frontier. Unlike European warfare, this was 'a silent hideous game of hide-and-seek with death as the penalty when faltering vigilance earned the quick flight of an assegai'. Gradually Henry came to know and respect the tough British and Boer colonists who lived on the edges of Xhosa tribal territory. He was also introduced to the various chiefs.

Appointed frontier commandant with his own regiment, the newly raised Cape Mounted Riflemen, Somerset became a regular fixture known to the natives as 'Hawk's Eye', a reference to his beaky profile. His 'generalship' under the patronage of his father was undisputed for many years. It was finally tested and found wanting in the Sixth Frontier War. Mostert has written: 'The Xhosa rolled forward unhindered towards Port Elizabeth and Uitenhage, as though bound for the Cape itself ... and Henry Somerset, supposedly the most experienced mind in frontier matters ... had not the slightest idea what to do.' By now he had become 'an amiable pleasure-loving man of limited intelligence who liked, in his easy moments, to be all things to everyone.' Colonists found him charming and hospitable and he showed sympathy with the Xhosa in periods of drought or cattle loss. Somerset's 'blundering' helped provoke the Sixth Xhosa War, while his 'military incompetence' led to the worst disaster in the seventh war when a column was ambushed on 11 April 1846. This failure was only partly erased by his success at the Battle of the Gwanga two months later where 300 Xhosa were slain. One noble aspect of Somerset was a natural kindness and concern for the welfare of his troops (it was hinted he had fathered a few). One soldier wrote that he was 'the beau ideal of a cavalry officer of the "old regime" ... His bronzed complexion and fine features well contrasted with his large moustache which, with his hair, was snowy white. He had a fine seat on a horse ... on his white charger ... quite a picture.'

Polite to his face, carping behind his back, Harry **Smith** called Somerset 'Colonel Ass' and once wrote that 'he never wounded a Kaffir, no, nor ever frightened one'. As the years rolled by he became a fixture on the Cape frontier landscape, endured only because he had been there so long and, in theory, knew more about the tribes than any man alive. In October 1852, after thirty-three years in South Africa, Major-General Somerset and his family left the Cape for Bombay. In 1860, now a lieutenant-general and KCB, he and his wife returned to England. Two years later, while inspecting the 25th King's Own Borderers, of which he was colonel, Somerset caught pneumonia at Gibraltar. He lies there in the military cemetery.

STAVELEY, GENERAL SIR C. – EFFICIENT ORGANISER

CHARLES WILLIAM DUNBAR Staveley was an old-school officer and comrade of the C-in-C, the Duke of Cambridge. He proved himself a brave warrior as a young man and in Abyssinia in 1867–68 re-organised a shambles of an army into a fighting machine.

He was born in France in December 1817, the son of a general, and was commissioned a second lieutenant in the 87th Regiment in 1835. Ten years later he transferred to the 44th Foot as a captain. While serving in Canada he was an ADC to the governor-general and proved such an adept draughtsman that his sketches were used to help settle the Oregon boundary dispute. He served briefly as his father's secretary at Hong Kong before embarking with the 44th for the Crimea in 1854.

Staveley served at the Alma, and at Balaklava acted as an aide to HRH the Duke of Cambridge (a service that would prove useful when Prince George became C-in-C). Promoted brigadier in 1860, Staveley commanded the 1st brigade of **Michel**'s division in China and was present at the capture of the Taku Forts. At the close of this war he was retained in China as commander of British troops and in 1862 took part in operations against the Taiping rebels. When asked to recommend an officer to lead the Imperial Chinese Army he named Charles **Gordon**, with whom he had served in the trenches before Sebastopol and to whom he was related by marriage.

In 1865, while serving in India, Staveley was given command of the 1st Division of the Abyssinian Expeditionary Force. The historian Myatt called him 'energetic and capable'. Landing on the beach at Zula in Abyssinia, where the entire transport and commissariat operations had broken down, Staveley quickly took charge. 'Everything was going wrong, disorder ruled supreme', wrote the war correspondent George Henty, who considered the general's arrival 'most providential'. Once things had been put in order at Zula, Staveley hurried to the front, where the transport train was in a mess. He sensibly deputed infantrymen as mule leaders and got things moving again through the mountains. Throughout the war he was **Napier**'s wise right arm.

It was Staveley's final campaign, though he did not retire until 1883. He died at his Cheltenham home on 23 November 1896 and is buried in the Brompton Cemetery, West London.

STEPHENSON, LIEUTENANT-GENERAL SIR F. – 'OLD BEN'

SELF-EFFACING, DILIGENT, HONOURABLE – all qualities that can be applied to Frederick Stephenson, who fought in the Crimea and China before commanding forces in Egypt. During the **Gordon** Relief Expedition he bravely pitted himself against **Wolseley**, opposing the latter's Nile route in favour of a dash across the desert from Suakin. He would also command in the final battle of the 1885 Sudan War.

The son of a general, Frederick was born on 17 July 1821 and at 16 joined the Scots Fusilier Guards as an ensign. When the Crimean War broke out Stephenson, now a lieutenant-colonel, went with his regiment and saw action at the Alma, Inkerman and the Siege of Sebastopol; during the second battle he was shot twice, but escaped serious injury. In 1857 war was announced with China and Frederick was made AAG of the force. One officer noted his 'peculiarly conciliatory nature, which smoothed over many difficulties'. Shipwrecked on the way east, 'Old Ben', as everyone affectionately called him, displayed 'a calmness, firmness and self-posses-sion' that saved lives. Stephenson spent almost four years connected with the China War, seeing all the main actions, and did not leave Hong Kong until March 1861.

During the next decade he served with his regiment in Canada before returning to England for various home commands. He was made a major-general in 1868 and a lieutenant-general eleven years later. Following the Egyptian War he was pressed by the Duke of Cambridge to accept com-mand of the British army of occupation in Egypt. Finally he consented and left England in May 1883. When a relief expedition for **Gordon** was mooted Stephenson was strongly in favour of an overland dash from Suakin-Berber instead of the Nile route favoured by Wolseley – 280 miles as against 1,650 miles from Cairo to Berber. He described Wolseley's audacious plan as 'impracticable', the Suakin route offering 'a firm land base ... with facili-ties for the supply of meat, and the care of the sick, and one protected by the Fleet.' Later experts, such as Colonel Sandes, the historian of the Royal Engineers, supported Stephenson's judgement and said that Wolseley's plan 'doomed' **Gordon**. While considering Wolseley's expedition to be 'a very unnecessary fuss', Stephenson, ever the gentleman, supported his opponent even after he was supplanted by him as commander in Egypt. Wolseley, who could be very acid towards those who opposed him, always had respect for Stephenson, writing that he was 'in many ways the best man in Cairo ... His manners are perfect, and he is in every relation of life a high-minded

English Gentleman … in every sense so honest, straightforward and anxious to do right that I hate the idea of superseding him.'

Following **Gordon**'s death and the British retreat, it was Stephenson who took personal command at Ginniss on 30 December 1885 when the dervishes tried to invade Egypt. His two brigades of infantry, combining British and Egyptian troops fighting side-by-side, stopped the enemy in their tracks with a loss of just nine killed and thirty-six wounded. The Mahdists were then pursued 50 miles over the frontier. Stephenson returned to England two years later. He served as Constable of the Tower prior to his death on 10 March 1911. Writing in *The Times*, the Egyptian pro-consul Lord Cromer said his chief qualities were 'tact, firmness, patience and judgment'.

STEWART, FIELD-MARSHAL SIR D. – SOUND MAN

DONALD MARTIN STEWART spent his entire career in the Indian Army, a fine soldier and C-in-C, India, who is all but forgotten today. He was born on 1 March 1824 at Dyke, Scotland, from a long lineage of Highlanders. After a Hibernian education he entered the HEIC army as a cadet in 1840 and on 15 February 1841 landed at Calcutta to join the 9th BNI. Sixteen years of dull peacetime soldiering followed, relieved only by service in the 1854 Mohmand expedition and skirmishes with the Afridis in 1855, until 11 May 1857 when the 9th, like so many other Bengal regiments, mutinied at Alighur. After plundering the treasury and releasing gaoled prisoners, they marched off to Delhi leaving their officers unharmed. Captain Stewart reached Agra, 55 miles away, and offered his services to the lieutenant-governor of the North-West Provinces. All communication with Delhi had ceased and so Stewart volunteered to carry despatches. The 125-mile ride was full of risks and he encountered his fair share of perils; at one point, after his horse died, he was reduced to plodding on by donkey, but somehow he evaded rebels and reached the British on Delhi ridge. His reward was the appointment of DAAG of the Delhi Field Force. He served in the same role at the siege and capture of Lucknow by Campbell and the 1858 Rohilkhand campaign. In December 1857 he was made AAG of the Indian Army and seven months later promoted to lieutenant-colonel.

Following the transfer of the HEIC army to the Crown, Stewart stayed on in his department and won praise as he helped create the new Indian Army. He led the Bengal troops in the Abyssinian expedition with **Roberts** as his AQMG. As the years rolled by their mutual respect and friendship grew.

Donald meanwhile, whose hair was receding even as a young officer, turned grey and then a snowy white until his walrus moustache, eyebrows and hair made him look like everyone's favourite old uncle. When the Second Afghan War broke out, 'Old Stewart', as many contemporaries called him, was recalled from leave in England to command the Kandahar Field Force. In his history of the war, Brian Robson called Stewart at this juncture 'one of the most respected figures in the Indian Army. He was known as a calm, level-headed officer, a good organiser, not afraid to take decisions and of absolute integrity.' He had never held a field command and, ironically, was best known to the public for being chief commissioner of the Andaman penal colony in 1872 when the Viceroy, Lord Mayo, was stabbed to death by a convict.

During the 1878–79 invasion Stewart's column saw little fighting, but he displayed administrative skill and political acumen. Things changed during the second half of the war, when he was forced to leave Kandahar and go to Roberts' assistance at Kabul. On 19 April 1880 his 7,000-strong army ran into 12–15,000 fanatical *ghazis* at Ahmed Khel and had one of the most dramatic battles of the war: 'the enemy as thick as bees in a hive,' noted one private soldier, 'I stood almost petrified ...' Things got so critical that Stewart and his staff drew their swords in self-defence. Excellent British discipline and firepower saved the day with Afghan losses of around 3,000 (the British lost 130 killed and wounded). Robson gave little praise to Stewart and wrote that 'it would be difficult to think of a more tactically inept affair'.

At Kandahar, where he out-ranked a grumpy Roberts, Stewart was not to the taste of one staff officer who described him as 'very masterful and decided, but inclined to be cynical', admitting 'men have confidence in him, he does not go amongst them, nor court their liking'. There was a short spat between Stewart and Roberts when the latter accused his friend of spreading gossip back in Britain about the executions of Afghans at Kabul. Stewart was unrepentant and replied honestly: 'Never wrote to any one except **Norman**, to whom I expressed disapproval of your punishing persons who merely fought against you ... I probably gave my opinion very freely ... but he was not authorised to make public use of what I may have written.' After the war Stewart served as C-in-C, India, 1881–85 and gave up the appointment early to help Roberts step into his shoes. 'Bobs' later praised him as the most knowledgeable man in the Indian Army.

In May 1894 Stewart was made a field-marshal and a year later followed Pat Grant as Governor of the Royal Hospital. He died at Algiers on 26 May 1900, his body returned to London where it lies in Brompton Cemetery. In hindsight, he was not a great field commander but, as one contemporary wrote, he was 'shrewd, just and level-headed'. Another admired his 'supreme contempt for humbug … He told the plain truth and magnified nothing.'

STEWART, MAJOR-GENERAL G. – INDIAN CAVALRYMAN

A CLASSIC INDIAN Army cavalryman, George Stewart was born on 20 July 1839 and served as a subaltern in the volunteer cavalry with **Havelock**'s army from its formation right the way through to **Clyde**'s final operations at Lucknow. He then joined the 1st Sikh Cavalry for the central India campaign, being mentioned in despatches after the taking of Mhow; at Kookiekabund he was wounded and had a horse shot from under him.

Stewart's family were relatively poor, he could not afford to purchase promotions, and remained a lieutenant for many years. He served in the Second China War with the 1st Sikhs and got another mention in despatches for 'forward gallantry' in the action of Sinho, where he was wounded again. Transferring to the 11th Bengal Cavalry he joined General **Garvock** for the later stages of the Umbeyla campaign. A decade later, after serving in Manipur, he transferred to the Guides cavalry and fought under **Keyes** in the Jowaki Afridi expedition.

It is said that Stewart introduced polo to the Guides, a game he had played in Manipur. When the Second Afghan War broke out this handsome man with wavy dark hair and slim moustache was given command of the Guides cavalry. He led the corps at the taking of Ali Musjid in the Khyber, the engagements around Kabul in December 1879, where the Guides made several charges, and in the Battle of Charasiab. His reward was a brevet lieutenant-colonelcy. Stewart left the Guides in December 1884 to take over command of the 6th Punjab Infantry. He retired with the rank of major-general in 1887, but in 1904 his association with the Guides was revived when he was made their honorary colonel, a position he filled until his death on 12 January 1928.

STISTED, LIEUTENANT-GENERAL SIR H. – BRAVE OLD TIMER

FOR EVERY PROGRESSIVE general whose career is sketched in these pages there was an old-school officer who thought reform was poppycock. One of these was Henry William Stisted, a soldier who was once described by his subordinate, Garnet **Wolseley**, as a 'drivelling' idiot.

He was born in 1817, the son of a colonel in the 3rd Hussars, educated at Sandhurst and made an ensign in the 2nd Foot in 1835. Henry was soon off to India and was wounded attacking the gateway at the storming of Ghazni in 1839. He recovered and served at the taking of Khelat and the occupation of Kabul. Eleven years later he transferred to the 78th Foot as a lieutenant-colonel by purchase. During the Persian War he commanded a brigade at the night battle of Khoosh-ab before leading his own regiment at Mohammerah. By now a seasoned warrior, Stisted led the advanced guard of **Havelock**'s little army at the entry to Lucknow and, after the death of the fiery Brigadier Neill, was appointed to command the 1st Brigade. In May 1858 he commanded a brigade under **Clyde** at the tough Battle of Bareilly. Transferring again, this time to the 93rd Foot, he served in the later stages of the 1863 Umbeyla campaign.

In 1867 Stisted was sent to Canada and became the first Lieutenant-Governor of Ontario. A portrait of him at this time shows an old warrior with wavy white hair and mutton-chop whiskers. Garnet Wolseley disliked serving under him when he replaced his mentor, John **Michel**. He complained: 'I cannot help thinking that our Army System is rotten when it permits of such men ever rising to command anything … It is hard that England's soldiers, and perhaps even England's honour, should be at the mercy of such incapables.'

Stisted died in December 1875, a brave if old-fashioned soldier. He was survived by his wife, Maria, a sister of the explorer Richard Burton. He is buried in West Norwood Cemetery, London.

SYMONS, MAJOR-GENERAL SIR W. – OPTIMISTIC FAILURE

OPTIMISM IS A quality that generals need to use sparingly: too little and they can seem defeatist, too much and it can be their undoing. One who was fatally over-optimistic was William Penn Symons.

He was born at Hatt, Cornwall, on 17 July 1843, educated privately and commissioned an ensign in the 24th Foot in 1863, joining the 2nd Battalion in Mauritius. Promoted captain in 1878, Symons served with the 24th in the Ninth Xhosa War 1877–78 and the Zulu War of 1879. He was with **Chelmsford**'s returning column to Isandlwana and wrote: 'All was still as death.' Many of his long-serving friends had died on the battlefield.

In 1885 Major Symons went to Burma with his battalion and did good service fighting *dacoit*s in the Chindwin district until 1889. He was commended by Sir George **White** and given command of one of the two columns of the Chin-Lushai expedition that year. His reward was a CB. An excellent shot, Symons was promoted to lieutenant-colonel and made AAG for musketry in India. The winter 1894–95 saw him commanding a brigade (with local brigadier rank) during the Waziristan expedition. In 1897 he commanded the 2nd Brigade of the Tochi Field Force before being sent to Tirah to lead the 1st Division under **Lockhart**. A young Winston Churchill wrote that Symons 'commanded with prudent skill. His brigades had no misfortune, his rearguards came safely into camp ... Everyone talked of Symons, of his energy, of his jokes, of his enthusiasm. It was Symons who built a racecourse on the stony plain ... who won the principal event himself, to the delight of the private soldiers, with whom he was intensely popular'. Rewarded with a knighthood, Symons was sent to Natal in 1899 and by October was a major-general with local lieutenant-general rank. He looked every inch a soldier, with slick dark hair, a wavy moustache and a cheery smile. One officer serving under him said Symons was 'one of the most charming people I have ever met'. His motto was, 'To do my duty and to do it in the spirit of a high-minded gentleman.' The Natal governor noted that Symons had 'lots of energy and was as keen as mustard' to get at the Boers. Yet Sir William was no fool; he told HM Govt that he needed at least 5,600 troops to hold Natal and that his current force was 'insufficient', the situation was 'critical' and the Boer needed to be respected for 'his love of independence, for his powers of mobility, and for his marksmanship'. This good-natured man made the mistake of moving his line too far north, so keen was he to meet the enemy. 'I wish every commando in the Transvaal was there in a bunch,' he told one of White's staff, 'so that I could make one sweep of the lot of them.' Sir George White was appointed to supersede Symons, who was by now entrenched 70 miles north of Ladysmith at Dundee. On 20 October 1899 the Boers attacked at dawn. Symons was about to eat his breakfast and resented their 'impudence'. Replying with his artillery, allowing his cavalry to act on their own initiative, he then sent his infantry in close order formation to dislodge the enemy from Talana Hill. It was old textbook fighting that was about to be shot to ribbons in the war by Afrikaner tactics. Pinned down at the foot of the hill by the Boers' long-range rifles, casualties mounting, Sir William decided to impress his troops by leading from the front. His general's red pennant fluttering in the breeze, he stepped through a gap in the wall at the bottom of the hill and was shot in the stomach. Remounting his horse in terrible pain, he refused to be put on a stretcher until out of sight of his troops. 'Have they the hill?' he asked.

The British did indeed win the battle, but it was decided to retreat from Dundee and Symons became a prisoner-of-war. He died three days later and his last words were 'Tell everyone I died facing the enemy.' There is a memorial cairn to him on the Talana battlefield and a fine stone obelisk in Victoria Park, Saltash.

TANNER, LIEUTENANT-GENERAL SIR O. – DESERT CAMPAIGNER

ORIEL VIVEASH TANNER was a Bombay Army officer who seemed to spend his career fighting in desert country against Indians, Afghans, Egyptians and Baluchis. For much of this time he wore the green tunic and red pantaloons of the 29th Bombay Native Infantry (2nd Baluchis).

He was born in Australia, but managed to see early active service against rebels during the 1857–58 mutiny in the southern Mahratta country. Over two decades of peacetime soldiering followed, but during the Second Afghan War, and by now a lieutenant-colonel, Tanner was stationed at Khelat-i-Ghilzai in southern Afghanistan with just 250 men of his regiment and two companies of the 66th (Berkshire) Regiment. He held it until **Roberts** arrived and earlier, on 2 May 1880, during a punitive operation against some Afghan villages, managed to defeat an Afghan force of similar size, killing fourteen of the enemy, including their leader, with a loss of just one Baluchi wounded. He went on to serve under Roberts and was mentioned in despatches.

Made a colonel, Tanner was one of the last soldiers to leave Afghanistan in 1881, responsible for seeing the final troops across the Indus. The following year he served as commander of the Indian Army infantry brigade sent to support **Wolseley**'s invasion of Egypt. In this role he led his foot-slogging regiments along the canal bank and into attack at Tel-el-Kebir.

Raised to a brigadier, knighted, and sent to command at Quetta, Baluchistan, Tanner was the ideal man to lead an expedition into the hitherto little known Zhob Valley in 1884. He had with him 4,220 infantry, 561 cavalry and ten heavy guns along with a photo unit from the Royal Engineers. On 23 October news came in that a tribal army of between 500 and 1,000 men had assembled in the nearby hills. Possibly taking a tip from Wolseley's celebrated 'night march' prior to his Egyptian victory, Tanner moved his force before daybreak and, after offering the enemy a chance to surrender, hit them with well-aimed artillery fire and some quick hill-climbing which took the Zhobis by surprise. With about seventy enemy dead, including their leaders, the tribesmen soon sued for peace. Rebel forts were blown up and Tanner's army departed.

Two years later Tanner, who stares out from photographs as a florid man with receding hair and a white moustache, incurred the C-in-C's displeasure when Roberts visited Quetta; he wrote to the Viceroy that he was neither efficient or very active (one must remember that 'Bobs' saw Quetta as a southern gateway to Afghanistan and the Russian threat was by 1886 his abiding obsession). Tanner was removed, but he continued to serve a while longer before his retirement. He died at his London home in 1909.

TAYLOR, GENERAL SIR A. – HEROIC INDIAN ARMY ENGINEER

'TAYLOR TOOK DELHI, and if I live through this, the world shall know it,, said Brigadier John Nicholson as he lay dying in 1857. His remark referred to the diligent engineer who worked unceasingly to breach the city walls. Alex Taylor served in one more war, but Victorian soldiers always associated him with this deed.

He was born on 27 January 1826 into a family of engineers. His mother died when he was 7 and Alex was brought up by a talented but cold and irritable father. The lad was educated in Switzerland and Addiscombe before joining the Bengal Army as a sapper in 1845. Barely 19, Alex found himself in charge of the fort at Ferozepore near the battlefield of Ferozeshah during the First Sikh War. Later, while building a bridge near Sobraon, he was stricken with smallpox. In the Second Sikh War he served under Robert **Napier** at the Siege of Multan and was wounded in his left arm while leading one of the attacking parties on 2 January 1849. He was fit enough to serve at the final battle at Gujerat where, seeing an error in the Sikh movements, he galloped up to the headquarters staff and made a report – then took the liberty of suggesting a plan. The commanding engineer, General **Cheape**, retorted: 'Taylor, your modesty will be your ruin.' Much amused, Lord **Gough** added, 'It seems to me, Cheape, you had better *act* on his advice.'

Over the next eight years, under Napier's supervision, Taylor constructed the Grand Trunk Road between Lahore and Peshawar. By 1857, as James Lunt wrote, he was noted as 'a man of courage, energy and resource, a fine football player, a champion at jumping and, for some reason known in the Brigade as "Musha". Although only thirty-one, he was senior in years to the Engineer Brigade, which consisted almost entirely of young and untried subalterns.' It was the chief commissioner of the Punjab, John Lawrence, who asked Taylor to go to Delhi after the rising. He did the 500-mile journey from Attock in just five days at the height of the summer. Taylor was for a short time senior engineer with the Delhi Field Force and urged a dying General Barnard to try a *coup de main*, but this was cancelled. Richard Baird Smith, a brilliant but also ailing man, now became senior engineer and relentlessly urged the new commander, Archdale **Wilson**, a man also in poor health, to agree to an assault. It was left to Taylor to supervise the sappers and create and co-ordinate a plan, while Baird Smith convinced Wilson of its worth. After the city was re-taken Taylor went to Lucknow and served under Napier again. In the assault on the Begum's Palace on 15 March 1858 he was shot and badly wounded in the leg.

Six years later, fully recovered, Taylor saw action again as commanding engineer in the Umbeyla campaign. Building roads, stockades, abattis and breastworks kept him and his small team of sappers busy under intense enemy fire. He was wounded slightly in the arm during one attack and a few days later another bullet zipped through his sleeve without injury. In the final drama, when a group of officers, surrounded by thousands of fanatics, visited the tribal stronghold of Malka, Taylor went too.

A few years later he was struck by partial blindness, but recovered sufficiently to return to India as deputy inspector-general of military works, and president of the Defence of India Committee. In 1879 he returned to Britain and was made president of the Royal Indian Engineering College. He lived on until 10 February 1912. While the Siege of Delhi is forgotten by most folk, thousands of travellers every day still use the road Taylor constructed, his lasting legacy.

TAYLOR, GENERAL R. – FRONTIER PALADIN

ONE OF THE young men chosen to bring justice and administration along the North-West Frontier of India, Reynell George Taylor was born at Brighton on 25 January 1822, son of a colonel in the 10th Hussars. He was educated privately and at Sandhurst before arriving in India aged 18 as a cornet in the 2nd (which soon became the 11th) Bengal Light Cavalry.

Within three years he had fought in his first battle at Punniar in the brief Gwalior War. On 18 December 1845 he was in the thick of things at Mudki against the Sikhs:

I remembered stopping the cut of the first man I met and giving him a return blow across the face. Another fellow rode at me with a lance, and I turned it off with my sword when close to my breast; and I believe it was while making a return cut at him that another man who had come up on my bridle-hand, administered a severe 'smeller' in the face … which cutting through my shako peak, hit me half-way down the forehead, and, passing down, split my nose like a pea and deluged my left eye with blood. Another man with whom I met rode close up to my sword-hand, and with his teeth set, and standing up in his stirrups, gave a downright cut at my head, which I stopped … In the melee I received a severe cut on the shoulder … and cut a great piece out of the deltoid muscle as well. I had another wound on my left wrist.

It seems astonishing but using a fine needle a surgeon was able to mend Taylor's wounds leaving just the faintest trace of a scar.

Chosen by Henry Lawrence to be entrusted with administering the Punjab and Kashmir, Taylor started to carve out a reputation as a just and hard-working official as well as a Christian soldier. When a second Sikh War erupted he served for a time at Multan and then defended the fort at remote Lukkee. Resuming his duties in 1849, he was appointed deputy commissioner at Bannu in Waziristan. One of Taylor's assistants called him 'a saint on earth', but added that 'he worked slowly and over-consciously,' allowing himself no recreation except a daily ride at sundown.

During the Mutiny this able political officer watched over one of the Punjab districts. In 1860 he went with his old friend, Neville **Chamberlain**, on an expedition against the Mahsuds acting as political officer. Scouting ahead of the main column one day, Taylor and his small escort were attacked by tribesmen. In a letter he wrote: 'I saved one man's life with my revolver by shooting another who was pressing him. I put two barrels into him before he fell … tried two more on another man … so I had to take to my sword again.' Chamberlain and Taylor frequently worried their subordinates on this campaign by riding ahead and exposing themselves to danger.

A year later came the disastrous Umbeyla expedition in which Taylor was chief political officer. By now he was worn down by years of over-work and made the mistake of not giving the tribes notice of the expedition's intentions. It was not until the army was in full view at the foot of the Black Mountain that he sent word. Taylor's scouts also reported that the track had few obstacles and was wide enough for the army. They were wrong on both counts. Fatally, as it turned out, Taylor told his superiors that he thought it unlikely the influential ruler of Swat would support the *Wahhabi* fanatics who lived on the mountain. This also proved to be wrong. After weeks of intensely savage fighting in which one-sixth of the original British force was killed or wounded, Taylor managed, in the words of Charles Allen, 'to salvage something from the political disaster for which he was largely responsible'. He got an agreement from the tribes that they would destroy the fanatics' base at Malka and expel them provided the British withdrew their army. On 19 December a grim Taylor led the small group of officers (including **Adye**, **Roberts** and Alex **Taylor**), who watched Malka set ablaze. Roberts praised Reynell Taylor's coolness in the face of thousands of angry tribesmen.

Taylor served as a commissioner in the Punjab for a further fifteen years before retiring in 1877. He died at his home in South Devon on 28 February 1886 and is buried in East Ogwell churchyard. There is a memorial to him in Lahore Cathedral. One of his old friends, Dighton **Probyn**, wrote: 'Poor, dear Reynell! Where was his equal in honesty, generosity, bravery, or in any good and Christian qualities for a man … I don't suppose an evil thought ever crossed his mind.'

THACKWELL, LIEUTENANT-GENERAL SIR J. – SMART CAVALRY COMMANDER

A TALL, SLIM man with a long face, a mass of dark hair and a smart black moustache, Joseph Thackwell looked every inch a cavalryman down to his spurs. He is best remembered as a cavalry general in the first Afghan and both Anglo-Sikh wars. The son of a country squire, Joseph was born on 1 February 1781. Sixteen years later he joined the Worcestershire Regiment of Provisional Cavalry and in 1800 transferred to a cornetcy in the elite 15th Light Dragoons. He fought with them at Corunna, pursued the French over the Pyrenees and rode on, eventually, to Waterloo, where Captain Thackwell led the 15th in a celebrated charge late in the battle; he was shot through the bridle hand and instantly placed the reins in his teeth, but within seconds a bullet shattered his left arm and he fell to the ground. The arm was amputated and Thackwell promoted to major and, within a year, to lieutenant-colonel.

Always fit (it was said that Thackwell never rode less than 40–60 miles every day), he had a quiet time in the 1820s and got married. A decade later he was sent to deal with industrial unrest in the Midlands and was stoned by irate mill workers on one occasion. Bored by inactivity, he paid £4,000 for an exchange into the 3rd Light Dragoons destined for Indian service and set sail in 1837. Within a year he found himself commanding the cavalry with the Army of the Indus. Losses on the march to Kabul appalled him. 'How the army is to subsist, Heaven only knows,' he wrote. 'It has completely ruined this fine cavalry, and will reduce us to a state of starvation.'

Returning to India late in 1839, Thackwell was soon on active service again in Gwalior, where he once again commanded the cavalry division of four brigades (thirty-two squadrons) divided between the armies of generals **Gough** and Grey. Serving at Maharajpore, Thackwell's troopers in the battle lost fifty-nine killed and wounded and he was criticised for not pursuing the enemy, but he blamed the AG, Harry **Smith**, for refusing to 'allow the cavalry to turn the ravines, or cross the ford to fall on the enemy's rear, therefore as my superior officer, I was bound to obey'.

During the First Anglo-Sikh War, serving under Gough, a man who valued infantry and the bayonet above all else, Thackwell had little chance to shine, but at Sobraon he led his old regiment single-file through a narrow gap in the Sikh defences to attack their right wing. Smith later praised him for 'the most gallant "go" of you and the 3rd Dragoons I ever witnessed'. The biggest mistake of his career came during the Second Sikh War, when he delayed crossing the Chenab in pursuit of the Sikhs after Ramnagar. This failure at Sadullapur was, in the words of historian George Bruce, 'a serious tactical error'. It cost the lives of twenty-one men as well as fifty-one wounded and caused an angry Gough to exclaim that he had 'placed the ball at Thackwell's foot and Thackwell had declined to kick it'. Shortly after this came the confused Battle of Chillianwallah, in which some of the cavalry acted shamefully, though Sir Joseph was on a different part of the field and beyond blame. In the final battle at Gujerat the cavalry at last had a major role; Thackwell showed skill in the handling of his soldiers and the timing of the mounted attack, most effectively in the famous charge of **Malcolm**'s Sind Horse.

After the war Sir Joseph bought the colonelcy of the 16th Lancers and took cavalry command at Meerut. In May 1853 he returned to England and was for a few months Inspecting General of Cavalry, but ill health caused him to retire to estates purchased in Ireland. He died on 8 April 1858.

TOMBS, MAJOR-GENERAL SIR H. – BEAU IDEAL VC GUNNER

PERHAPS NO SOLDIER in the Victorian army so perfectly illustrated the ideal of a dashing, handsome warrior quite like Harry Tombs VC. He was, in the words of Colonel Julian Jocelyn, one of the finest soldiers the Army has ever produced. He was not only brave in himself, he was the cause of the bravery that was in other men. Time after time he distinguished himself by conspicuous and always useful courage. One of seven sons born to an old Indian campaigner who had led the 3rd Bengal Cavalry at the Siege of Bhurtpore, Henry (called 'Harry' by his friends) was born in Calcutta on 10 November 1825. Aged 14, he arrived at Sandhurst but moved on to Addiscombe, being gazetted a second lieutenant to the Bengal Artillery in 1841. One month after his eighteenth birthday Tombs served in his first battle at Punniar in the Gwalior War and was immediately mentioned in despatches for having 'done good service by firing with effect on the enemy', whilst commanding two guns. In the first war against the Sikhs he served as an aide to Harry Smith in two of the battles, during the second campaign acted as DAQMG of artillery. By war's end he was 23 years old and had served in at least eight major actions with several mentions in despatches.

Promoted to major while young, Harry in 1856 took over command of the 2nd Troop, 1st Brigade BHA. Already a distinguished unit, under Tombs it was to see even greater glory in the heady days of 1857–59. Marching to the relief of Delhi under Archdale **Wilson**'s command, Tombs showed his mettle at Ghazi-ud-din-Nagar, 10 miles from the city. A witness, Hervey **Greathed**, wrote: 'I cannot cease talking of the splendid behaviour of Tombs' troop: the gun-carriages are pitted with grape and shot marks, and Tombs continues the same gentle, modest fellow. He has lost, killed and wounded, thirteen men out of fifty, but the action of the troop never ceased for a moment.' During the Siege of Delhi there was no rest for Tombs and his men: on 17 June, when he was instrumental in a fierce fight around the Idgah mosque, he lost five horses killed under him. On that day he yelled above the din for the men of the 60th Rifles to keep the rebels locked down in the building, then had a train of gunpowder laid up to the doors and blew thirty-nine of them to smithereens. The C-in-C described Tombs' action as 'glorious'. In the famous fight on 9 July, in which he twice saved the life of his junior officer, Lieutenant **Hills** (described elsewhere in this book), an action that resulted in a VC for both of them, Tombs with characteristic modesty omitted to say much about himself in his report. His commanding officer tore up the paper and told Wilson the true version.

Twice wounded in the Mutiny, Harry became a brigadier in 1863 with command at Gwalior. A man of firm beliefs, he was the most senior officer to defend the actions of those white enlisted men who mutinied at the demand they relinquish their East India Company service in favour of the new Crown Army. At headquarters he was criticised for not entertaining 'a very proper feeling' towards his position in the new Royal Artillery. The C-in-C, India, Sir Hugh Rose, realised that he had to tread carefully with one of the army's heroes and reprimanded him 'with the utmost caution'.

This spat was settled by 1865 when Rose gave Tombs command of the right column of the Bhutan Field Force. After a successful little campaign in which his troops captured the enemy stronghold of Dewangiri, Tombs was knighted, promoted to major-general and got married. He held various district commands until 1874, when he suddenly fell very sick with what seems to have been cancer. Operated on in Marseilles, he returned to England to die and is buried at Carisbrooke on the Isle of Wight.

No man is perfect. Tombs had a fierce temper at times and could take a strong dislike to some men; he told Sergeant Nathaniel Bancroft, a trooper who later wrote one of the best accounts of life in the Indian Army, that they would 'never be friends' and duly found an excuse to court-martial the man and reduce him to the ranks. Generally, Tombs was noted for his bright and cheerful manner, charm and good looks, but Lord **Roberts** recalled that 'He was something of a martinet and was more feared than liked by his men.' They realised nevertheless that as a cool, bold leader he was 'unsurpassed'. James Hills rated Tombs a better commander than Stewart or Roberts, 'and that is saying a great deal'.

Sir Henry and his wife seem to have had uncommon bad luck. He was just fifty when he died; Lady Tombs re-married in 1877 to Herbert Stewart, a leading member of the Wolseley Ring, but he was killed in action eight years later in the Sudan. Their son, Geoffrey, died on the Western Front.

THORNTON, DEPUTY-SURGEON-GENERAL SIR J. – SEVEN CAMPAIGNS

IT IS SOMETIMES forgotten that medical men who accompanied the troops on campaign were themselves often in the thick of the fighting. The most famous of these in the Victorian period is probably James Reynolds, who won the VC at Rorke's Drift. I cannot even begin to do justice to these heroes in this book, yet James Howard Thornton's career, spanning seven campaigns, must stand testament to so many other warriors.

He was born on 7 January 1834, the son of a major in the 78th Highlanders. He was educated at Ramsgate and King's College, London, where he took his medical degrees, winning a post in the HEIC medical establishment by competition, and arrived in India during June 1856. Within a few weeks he set off up-country to join the 37th BNI at Benares. When the regiments stationed at Benares rose in revolt in 1857 a lucky Thornton avoided death and moved on to Chinsura to assist HM 5th Fusiliers, who were setting off towards Lucknow. The regiment was diverted to aid Major Vincent Eyre (an old hero of the First Afghan War), who was planning to relieve a small siege at Arrah. Thornton, along with Eyre and 200 men, had a ten-hour battle against an army of rebels thirty times their number. Their success was due to Eyre's brilliant command, some courage and the lucky fact that the mutineers had no artillery (the British had two 9-pounders and one 24-pounder howitzer). Thornton went on to serve in Campbell's two attempts to relieve Lucknow – wandering into the enemy's part of the city on one occasion and having a narrow escape. During the Oudh campaign in 1858 he was attached to 1st Bengal Europeans.

Soon he was off on campaign again to China. He served with the 15th PNI and witnessed the actions at Sinho and the Taku Forts; he entered Peking with the troops and declared the destruction of the Summer Palace to be a 'useless act of vandalism'.

Returning to India after six months' leave in 1861 he was appointed to the 28th BNI at Sylhet on the eastern frontier. Within months came the little-known Khasia and Jaintia expedition 1862–63. Fought in swampy, disease-ridden, hilly jungle, rain teeming down for much of the time, this twenty-two month campaign (with a seven-month breather), was caused by high taxes and some excessive policing policies. Thornton recorded British losses as 'very heavy', one regiment alone losing four white officers wounded and 200 other ranks killed or wounded; on one occasion, while serving with the 44th BNI, he was almost captured but escaped under a hail of rocks and arrows, one heavy stone giving him a nasty head injury. Fully recovered by 1864, Thornton was off to the front again serving as a senior medical officer with Harry **Tombs'** column in the Bhutan War, a campaign of modest fighting, but excessive sickness among the troops.

Almost two decades of peacetime medical work followed before Thornton was sent to Egypt in 1882 charged with the Indian Contingent's base hospital at Suez. Three years later he returned to the Nile desert as PMO of the Indian brigade sent to reinforce **Graham** at Suakin. Thornton had his hands full attending to the sick and dealing with night attacks by dervishes who frequently eluded sentries and stabbed sleeping patients. On the day of the Battle of Tofrek, gunfire just 6 miles distant alarmed Thornton in camp; he set off to see if he could help and pluckily collected twenty-four wounded men.

In 1886, on his return to India, Thornton was promoted deputy-surgeon-general and PMO of the Punjab Frontier Force. With the 'Piffers' he did not have long to wait before the next frontier war: this came in 1888 with the Black Mountain expedition, a campaign he called 'arduous', with marches in excess of 9,000ft, but thankfully carried out in good weather, and losses of just 100 men in killed and wounded.

Retiring in 1891, James Thornton was knighted three years later. He retired to Hove and died there on 6 January 1919, one day before his eighty-fifth birthday.

TRAILL-BURROUGHS, MAJOR-GENERAL SIR F. – COURAGEOUS LITTLE DESPOT

IN AN AGE when height was no bar to an officer's career, Frederick Traill-Burroughs was undoubtedly the most pint-sized general in the army. His courage, though, was in no proportion to his height and he remains one of the heroes of the Indian Rebellion. On his retirement to his Scottish estates he found himself in a new war – against his own belligerent crofters – a dispute labelled by its historian as 'the worst of the nineteenth-century Orkney lairds.'

A diminutive man, known in the 93rd Highlanders as 'Wee Frenchie', Frederick was born in 1831, educated on the continent (hence the nick-name), and joined his regiment in 1848. After six years' home service the young officer sailed with the 93rd to the Crimea. Never absent on sick leave for a single day of the war, the hardy little man fought at the Alma and commanded a company at Balaklava, where the regiment served as 'the thin red line tipped with steel'.

Not long after returning home the regiment was off again: they landed at Calcutta in September 1857 to be reunited with Sir Colin Campbell, who had led the Highland Brigade at Balaklava. Now he and the 93rd were destined for Lucknow. Frederick slogged up-country, fighting in several actions along the way and in the bloody attack on the Sikanderbagh during the first entry into Lucknow a controversy arose regarding Burroughs' claim that he was the first man through the breach. The regiment maintained that he was and a recommendation was sent to Campbell that he be given a Victoria Cross. Inundated for similar requests after a fight that had seen 1,840 rebels slaughtered, Campbell permitted the 93rd to one VC for each officer, non-commissioned officer and private soldier, the choice by private ballot. To his intense disappointment, Burroughs lost to a more popular officer. During Campbell's second relief of the city, brave as always, Burroughs pursued some rebels onto the roof of a building, unaware that it was about to be blown up. The explosion buried him in the debris and almost cost him a leg. During his recovery, waited upon by his servants, he noted drily: 'They ought to be glad I cannot kick now.'

Before leaving India he commanded the 93rd in the latter stages of the Umbeyla expedition. In 1870, after thirteen years in India, the regiment returned to Scotland. Four years later Burroughs retired after a quarter century with the 93rd. By then he had the grudging respect of the rankers who called the bald little man 'a monkey'. Beneath his pride and haughty manner, Burroughs could show kindness: the private soldier who labelled him an ape during the Mutiny died at Lucknow, but Burroughs sent the fellow's widowed mother a small pension out of his own pocket for the rest of her life.

Burroughs' later years are outside the scope of this book and are well documented by his biographer; suffice it to say that as an Orkney laird he evicted crofters on Rousay who wished to speak to a visiting Royal Commission in the 1880s. Matters escalated to the point where a gunboat had to be sent to keep the peace. After his death in London on 9 April 1905, old army friends mourned a gallant officer, while in the Orkneys this 'bad landlord', as he is still recalled, 'remained a curiously alien figure. He might own Rousay, but he never belonged to it'.

TREVOR, MAJOR-GENERAL W. – VICTORIA CROSS HERO OF BHUTAN

EXPERT SWORDSMAN, DEADLY shot with a revolver, William Spottiswoode Trevor's life was devoted to the Indian Army. At 10 years of age he and his mother were taken hostage in Afghanistan by Akbar Khan after William's father, Captain Robert Trevor, was dragged from his horse and hacked to pieces during the murderous assault on the British envoy, Macnaghten.

During his nine months of captivity young William learned Hindustani and Persian and was forced to amuse his gaolers by fighting Afghan boys for the prize of a leg of mutton.

Released by Pollock's army, William joined two of his brothers in going to Addiscombe and returned to India in February 1852 as an engineer. Quickly sent to Burma, he was praised for his conduct at the storming of Rangoon, where he was the first on the ladder of an escalading party until felled by a bullet that shattered his lower arm. Before war's end in 1854 Trevor had recovered sufficiently to fight alongside Garnet **Wolseley** at Donabew and, like his comrade, was wounded. He remained in Burma, returning to strength and building roads, until October 1857. His only Mutiny service was with the Darjeeling Field Force in pursuit of rebels, but he was present at an action with them near Cherabunder on the Bhutan frontier.

Kept busy constructing mountain roads in the region, Captain Trevor was attached to **Tombs**' column of the Bhutan Field Force in February 1865. At Dewangiri the enemy stronghold, reached 'by an exceedingly steep ascent with heavy jungle on both sides', consisted of three stockades. One of these, a blockhouse of wood and stone, commanded the plateau and Brigadier Tombs ordered that it be taken. After an artillery barrage the bugles were sounded and Trevor and his fellow engineer Lieutenant Dundas were the first men to scale a 14ft high wall, and then squeeze through a narrow entrance between the top of the wall and the roof of the build-ing into the blockhouse defended by 200 Bhutanese. The fight lasted thirty minutes and over 100 of the enemy were killed. 'How Trevor and Dundas escaped death was a marvel', wrote one contemporary historian. Trevor was wounded several times, however, including by a spear thrust from below through the bamboo floor of the gallery.

On 2 June 1866 the gallant Trevor found himself promoted to major and he and Dundas both got VCs. It was his last campaign, although he held several more appointments, including Chief Engineer in Burma. He retired in 1887, settled in London and died there twenty years later. His only child, Florence, was the much-loved second wife of Henry **Brackenbury**.

TULLOCH, MAJOR-GENERAL SIR A. – EXTRAORDINARY SPY

EARLY IN 1882 a balding Englishman with a strange accent was on a duck-shooting expedition near the Egyptian Army fortifications at Tel-el-Kebir. Locals were puzzled as the stranger missed birds within easy range and tried to pot others by starlight. The lunatic was in fact a Scot named Alexander Bruce Tulloch, and he was a War Office spy. He had a long association with army intelligence in the days when it depended on a quick brain, guile and a notebook or sharp memory. He also saw his fair share of campaigning.

The son of a Highland gentleman, Alex was educated in England before going to Sandhurst in 1852. Three years later he joined the Royal Scots and was soon en route for the Crimea, where his regiment formed part of the 2nd Brigade, Highland Division. Next the Royal Scots went to Central India, where young Tulloch was stationed at Hyderabad, a city returning to an uneasy peace in 1858. Action awaited the young officer in China two years later; at Tongku he was allowed to carry the Queen's Colour of his regiment and uncased it, enjoying the sight of it floating in the breeze, until a Chinese gun crew took aim at him, the 'round-shot so close that the earth thrown up just brushed the colour-party'. In the looting of the Summer Palace at Peking a large collection of jade was acquired by Tulloch, but he gave it all up to the prize agents so that the proceeds could be shared with the rest of the soldiers.

Over the next two decades Tulloch rose to become a major and travelled widely – Singapore, St Helena, Nova Scotia, Gibraltar. In 1875 he introduced himself to the Intelligence Department, giving them papers on the Spanish, French and Belgian armies. Most importantly, he wrote up an outline of how Cairo could be attacked via the newly acquired Suez Canal. In late 1881, as war clouds gathered over Egypt, Tulloch managed to gain the ear of **Wolseley** and obtained permission for a spying mission. His report, circulated secretly to top brass, was the major intelligence document which helped Wolseley in his planning for invasion. Intelligence historian William Beaver has written that the Egyptian general, Arabi Pasha, 'complained that the English major knew more about the coastal fortresses than he did'. Tulloch was sent early to Egypt and had a grandstand view of the bombardment of Alexandria sitting in the rigging of *HMS Invincible*; at the Second Battle of Kassassin he was nearly killed by a shell while standing next to General **Graham**; at Tel-el-Kebir he rode into the enemy lines with the headquarters staff. By this stage of the war Tulloch had been ousted as intelligence chief by Wolseley in favour of his protégé, Redvers **Buller**, much to Tulloch's fury. This humiliation rankled him so much because Tulloch had an immense ego (Wolseley complained privately that he felt Tulloch exaggerated facts and figures). Interviewed after the war by a Royal Commission, he made much of his secret role and in 1903 published a boastful autobiography. Reviewing this book, *The Times* acidly commented that 'Future generals ... will not find their work any easier if their predecessors are not habitually reticent ... as to every detail of their employment.'

In 1884, just as he was preparing to join General **Warren** in Bechuanaland, news came that the colonel of the Welsh Regiment had died of snake bite in Natal. Tulloch agreed instead to this new promotion. In 1889 he became a major-general and served for some time in Australia before retirement in 1895. He was knighted in 1902 and died on 25 May 1920.

TYTLER, MAJOR-GENERAL J. – WISE VC COMMANDER

ONE OF THE better field commanders of the Second Afghan War was John Adam Tytler VC. Under fire on several occasions, he displayed a cool nerve in tricky situations. He was also for much of his career the proud colonel of the hardy 4th Gurkhas. His premature death in 1880 robbed the army of a soldier destined for even higher office.

The third son of an HEIC surgeon, John was born on 29 October 1825, sent from India to England for his education at just 5 years old, returning thirteen years later as a cadet with the 66th BNI. His first active service came in 1851 during Campbell's frontier expeditions. The North-West Frontier remained his place of service, but in February 1858 his regiment came under attack at Chupara. The men wavered in the face of a heavy fire of grape, so Lieutenant Tytler 'dashed on ahead, and alone attacked the rebel gunners; for a few seconds he was personally engaged in a hand-to-hand fight, and before his men reached him had been dangerously wounded in three places'. Such courage won him his Victoria Cross. Promoted to captain in 1863, Tytler led the 4th Gurkhas bravely at Umbeyla and was mentioned in despatches. Four years later he commanded them again under **Wilde** in the Hazara expedition. Promoted to colonel in 1870, Tytler was soon on campaign again in the north-eastern jungles against the Lushais.

Not many men can claim to have started a war or led an invasion, but Tytler did both when, at 17.20 p.m. on 20 January 1878, he led the 2nd Brigade of the Peshawar Valley Field Force out of Jamrud, 'thus inaugurating the Second Afghan War'. Much of the first phase of this campaign involved punishing unfriendly tribes; a first easy expedition against the Shinwarris led to a second foray where Tytler had 'a serious fight on his hands' when 3,000 warriors descended on his 650 troops and two mountain guns. In a remarkable display of cool, wise leadership, Tytler succeeded in destroying his village-objective, then executed a retreat as the enemy came

repeatedly within 80yd of his rear and flanks. He lost just two killed and
twelve wounded, the Shinwarris suffering over 150 dead.

Ill health led Tytler to relinquish his command, but when the second
phase of the war broke out he was sent to punish the Zaimukhts in
Afghanistan, a tribe living near the Kurram River who continuously harassed convoys. Tytler took with him 3,200 soldiers and six mountain guns.
He managed to reach the 'impregnable' village of Zawo, at the end of
an 8-mile ravine that was only 10ft wide in places, before moving east to
punish the Orakzais on the frontier. Ordered to make some 'demonstra-
tion' to take pressure off Roberts, who was in difficulty at Kabul, Tytler
knew that a retreat could lead to an even greater tribal uprising, with multiple chances for catastrophe. He managed to release two regiments to join
troops in the Kurram Valley, but held onto the rest of his force and forced
the Orakzais to sue for peace.

Twelve months of hard campaigning had exhausted Tytler; old wounds
plagued him and he caught a virulent dose of pneumonia. Too weak to
make a recovery, he died at Thal on the frontier early in February 1880,
another victim to one of the harshest environments where British soldiers
have fought and died.

VAUGHAN, GENERAL SIR J. – WISE FRONTIER CAMPAIGNER

J. LUTHER VAUGHAN, along with his friend Alfred **Wilde** was one of the
best infantry colonels in the Punjab Frontier Force in the mid-nineteenth
century. On occasions he led expeditions and, much later, he took part in
Roberts' famous march from Kabul to Kandahar in the role of a newspaper reporter.

He was born on 6 March 1820, was educated at Rugby and accepted a
cadetship in the Bengal Army in 1840. In the spring of the following year he
joined the 21st BNI and within three years was adjutant, quartermaster and
interpreter of his regiment. By then he had fought his first battle and been
mentioned in despatches as aide to General **Littler** at Maharajpore.

A bright soldier, Vaughan wrote a memo to high command suggesting
how an electric battery might be used to detonate mines in front of advancing troops. This fanciful notion was shelved immediately, but it brought the
young officer to the attention of John Lawrence, burly Chief Commissioner
of the Punjab, who in 1850 made him second-in-command of the 2nd
PNI, part of the newly created Punjab Irregular Force. Within two years

Vaughan was promoted to commandant of the 5th Punjabis, a hardy mix of Sikhs, Dogras and mountain Pathans.

In 1855 he set off for home leave after fourteen years' continuous service in India, but was encouraged by a comrade to join him in an attempt to serve with a Turkish Contingent being assembled in Constantinople for service against the Russians. Within weeks, following a spot of reconnaissance near Sebastopol and a written report to the War Office, Vaughan found himself with the local rank of major acting as AQMG with the Turks. Sidelined to garrison duties at Kertch for a year, he fulminated that his troops, all regular veterans, were wasted, and so eventually after peace was declared he returned to India.

On the outbreak of the Mutiny it was imperative that order be maintained in the Punjab. Vaughan was ordered to seize the bridge over the Indus at Attock from the possibly disloyal 55th BNI who, a short time later, did indeed mutiny. Their colonel committed suicide and left a letter blaming Vaughan for driving his *sepoys* to disgrace. The mutineers fled towards the frontier and took refuge on the Black Mountain with hardened fanatics. Vaughan was sent in pursuit and at Narinji, an almost inaccessible hill village, had a stiff fight on his hands before finally expunging this nest of hornets on 3 August 1857. He and his regiment were then left to police the Punjab until late in the rebellion, when they lost track of Nana Sahib, the most wanted rebel, deep within the jungles of Nepal.

After these years of relative inactivity, the 5th PNI under Vaughan were at the forefront of the fighting at Umbeyla in 1863; General **Chamberlain** gave him command of the left side of the British defences and on 26 October he had to co-ordinate a major attack by thousands of tribesmen on his lines. This tough and bloody campaign dragged on until the British finally advanced out of the pass and pursued their enemy on 15 December. Vaughan was given overall command of the base camp, which was slyly attacked by the tribesmen. In this fight he was ably assisted by two other 'Piffer' colonels – **Brownlow** and **Keyes**.

Vaughan was back two years later for a third campaign against the Black Mountain tribes, commanding one of two brigades sent to exact punishment. Tribal resistance after the troops forced a way to the two highest peaks was, he noted, 'almost nil'. He was rewarded by promotion to brigadier and given command at Gwalior, but 'I missed the friends I had left on the frontier.' He went on to command the Allahabad Division. With no immediate employment after his term of duty ceased, a disheartened Vaughan returned to England. He had always enjoyed writing and when the Second

Afghan War broke out he offered his services to *The Times* as a reporter. He was with Sam **Browne**'s column in the early stages and much later joined Roberts at Kabul. His *Times* despatches, especially after the march to Kandahar, were instrumental in developing the cult of 'Bobs Bahadur'.

Vaughan also sailed to South Africa for the Transvaal War in 1881, but peace was declared before he reached the front. He went home to write numerous articles and even authored a Pushtu grammar that went through several editions. He was knighted in 1887, was subsequently awarded a GCB and died on 2 January 1911 aged 90. The happiest moment of his old age came in 1903 when he was informed, to his great pride, that the 5th PNI would henceforth be known as the 58th (Vaughan's Rifles) Frontier Force Regiment.

WARREN, GENERAL SIR C. – THE SPECTRE OF SPION KOP

THE NATURE OF warfare causes generals to become associated forever with their greatest victories – or disasters. Thus Lord **Clyde** remains linked with Lucknow, Robert **Napier** with Magdala, Lord **Chelmsford** with Isandlwana – and Charles Warren with Spion Kop. His superior, Redvers **Buller**, called him 'a duffer' and most historians have agreed: Farwell thought him 'perhaps the worst' general in the South African War and easily the most 'preposterous', a view echoed by Griffith, who described him as 'very eccentric' and 'incompetent'. Indeed, when historians usually debate Spion Kop, it is accepted that Warren acted badly and the question usually revolves around how the blame for this British disaster should be apportioned between Warren, as the general in charge, and Buller, his chief, who sat back and watched the calamity unfold, yet did little except send conflicting 'advice'.

In this sketch we will, for once, ignore Buller's despatches after the battle which laid the blame at Warren's door, and Sir Redvers' attempt next day to make Coke a scapegoat. Without excusing Warren's action, we will examine his mindset as revealed in his private account not published until forty years after the event.

He was born in Bangor on 7 February 1840 and commissioned a second lieutenant in the Royal Engineers in 1857. Just over three years later he was sent to Gibraltar to conduct a survey that lasted four years (his 8m model of the Rock and all its buildings is in the Gibraltar Museum). Captain Warren was next recruited by the Palestine Exploration Fund and his digs on Temple Mount revealed a network of tunnels and cisterns.

Six years later, at the request of the Colonial Office, this expert surveyor went out to the diamond-laden boundary between Griqualand West and the Orange Free State. During the Ninth Xhosa War he was told to form a mounted unit, which he called the Diamond Fields Horse, and aid the colonists in the Transkei. During the next five months the corps saw plenty of action: he was wounded when a tree fell on him in a stiff fight on 21 March 1878, while on 4 April he commanded his men against 1,200 warriors 'confident of surrounding and assegaiing us ... by throwing out horns to either flank ...' Warren kept his cool and directed fire towards the chiefs, who were on horseback. 'This was the signal for the entire demoralization of the army,' he wrote. 'We now, some on horses and some on foot, dashed into the midst of them, and a hand-to-hand fight commenced ...' Back in Griqualand West, a native rebellion broke out and Warren stormed a fortified mountain at Paardekloof and routed the enemy, while in a final battle on 24 June, with a loss of just seven wounded, he attacked 'rebels' on the Witsand Heights, the enemy fighting 'desperately to the last. Numbers were shot ...' Within days Warren was in action again in what became known as the First Bechuana War, fighting the Batlapin tribe on the northern frontier of Griqualand West who were murdering settlers. On 24 July he led troops against the enemy's well-entrenched position on the steep Takoon Mountain. The tribesmen fought with incredible courage, losing 200 killed and many wounded (to Warren's five dead). In October, after more disputes, he returned for a short one-month second campaign and the occupation of south Bechuanaland. During these fights one old soldier who had served under Harry **Smith** wrote how amazed he was to see 7-pounders dragged to the top of mountains, adding, 'I believe myself that Colonel Warren could get men to do anything.'

In 1880 and for the next four years Warren was chief instructor at the School of Military Engineering. This work was interrupted in 1882 when he was sent to the Sinai to discover what had happened to the expedition of Professor Palmer, a noted orientalist recruited by the War Office to get the Bedouin on the British side during the Egyptian War. Warren found the remains of Palmer's party and brought their killers to justice. In 1884 he led a third expedition into Bechuanaland that ended peacefully. He next decided to stand for parliament on a Liberal ticket, but lost, and went out to Suakin as commander. Within a few weeks, following the resignation of the London police commissioner, Warren was offered the job, probably due to his skill in the Palmer enquiry. He accepted but had a stormy time, blamed by the press for mishandling riots in Trafalgar Square on 'Bloody Sunday', while he fudged the Jack the Ripper murders investigation and person-ally destroyed material that could have served as evidence. In 1889 he was shunted off to Singapore and, despite promotion to lieutenant-general in 1894, was placed on the reserve list.

The choice of Warren in 1899 to lead the 5th Division in South Africa does not seem to me to be the 'enigma' it was to Byron Farwell; eight years younger than **Roberts**, a year younger than Buller and only five years older than **Lyttelton**, Warren was in fact just twenty days older than **Kelly-Kenny**. His surveying and instructional skills implied an intelligent man, his command in numerous mountain encounters proved he had led men in battle in other South African wars, and he ought to have had a keen eye for the terrain (though badly armed native tribesmen were hardly in the same league as well-mounted Boers with mausers).

Warren's delay in getting to Spion Kop, key to the relief of Ladysmith, was, in the words of the official history, 'painfully slow'. He was, by nature, the kind of man who disliked doing things in a hurry, and maintained in his personal account that 'I wanted three days for what I called "blood-ing" the troops' before sending his men into a major battle. He also barely used his cavalry, leaving their commander 'completely puzzled'. Warren later excused this mistake – since reconnaissance might have prevented the mishap – by saying that he feared the 1,800 mounted men in the mountain passes (as opposed to the open veldt), would be 'short work' for Boer heavy guns (a somewhat lame excuse).

Buller's later evidence, 'obscure, contradictory and sometimes non-sensical', muddies the waters of what really happened on 23–24 January 1900. Sir Charles's troops took the hill, but then found themselves in an 'acre of massacre'. Several historians agree that Buller had charged Warren 'with an impossible task'. As conflicting reports arrived from different commanders, Warren's grasp of things fell apart. 'From start to finish I never had a chance', he later told an aide. As the hours passed and the body count grew on the hill, Sir Charles moved not an inch towards Spion Kop. 'Why did he not go there himself?' asks Pakenham. In his private account Warren said that he had asked Buller for permis-sion to lead the assault, but was commanded 'to carry on my duties by getting directions from down below'. Buller also ordered him 'to remain at one spot getting my reports from the Generals I sent out'. Even so, Warren's biographer (his grandson), can find no excuse for his failure to tell **Coke**, fighting on the hill, that he had been super-seded by Thorneycroft. When an exhausted Thorneycroft ordered a retreat it appalled both Coke and Warren. Ironically it also shocked the Boers, who were 'utterly exhausted' and later admitted they were near defeat. In his summing-up of the debacle Lord Roberts did not excuse Warren of errors, but principally blamed Buller for not taking charge and Thorneycroft for a 'wholly inexcusable' withdrawal.

A few months later Sir Charles was recalled, but he lived on for over a quarter of a century. In old age he got involved with the Boy Scout movement, dying of pneumonia on 21 January 1927. He is buried at Westbeare, Kent. His generalship was certainly vacillating and torpid when he was not up against natives; he also had too high an opinion of his own abilities, but it seems a shame he is remembered only for Spion Kop and not for his successes. That battle, as one senior officer wrote three days later, was down to Buller: 'He *should* have been there and in chief command.'

WATSON, GENERAL SIR J. – UP IN THE SADDLE

JOHN WATSON WAS a VC-winning cavalryman of strong views who championed riding high in the stirrups as opposed to bumping the saddle. Dighton **Probyn** said he rode 'like a huntsman and not like a soldier'. Watson argued it was more comfortable for his men and their horses. 'Nonsense, nonsense,' replied the Duke of Cambridge, C-in-C of the British Army. 'We must have discipline, sir, discipline.' Nevertheless, as one of Watson's sons remarked, his gallant father 'lived long enough to see his views adopted'. Blonde, blue-eyed, of medium height but strong, he 'cared less for appearances than for practical efficiency'. A superb swordsman, Probyn used to say that 'Old John' jogged along on horseback 'like an old farmer'.

Watson was born in Essex on 6 September 1829, entered the Bombay Army in 1848 and within weeks was at the Siege of Multan, where he carried the colours of his regiment, the Bombay Fusiliers, up to the breach. After a couple of exchanges he joined the newly created 1st Punjab Cavalry and was soon its adjutant. In 1857 he served in the Bozdar expedition before arriving at Delhi alongside his best friend, Probyn of the 2nd PC. Watson spent his time in the thick of things, carving out a reputation as a brilliant and brave cavalry officer. He next joined Greathed's column marching towards Lucknow; at Cawnpore, in a fight with a young rebel *sowar*, he got a nick on one finger and Frederick **Roberts**, another friend, joked that he was almost killed by a mere boy. Watson quickly retorted to the pint-sized Roberts, 'Well, boy or not, he was bigger than you.'

The VC was awarded to Watson for incredible bravery before Lucknow on 14 November 1857. In an encounter with a senior rebel cavalry officer he had a narrow shave when a pistol fired at less than 3ft failed to explode. Running the *resaldar* through with the curved blade he always used, Watson was attacked by the man's comrades and received 'a blow on his head from a tulwar, another on the left arm, which severed his chain gauntlet glove, a tulwar cut on his right arm … a bullet also passed through his coat and he received a blow on his leg that lamed him for some days afterwards'.

Just as Probyn was tasked with raising a cavalry regiment, so Watson did the same; it was first called the 4th Sikh Cavalry, but became more famous as the 13th Bengal Lancers, Watson's Horse.

In 1863 Captain Watson fought at Umbeyla. Promotions followed and in 1878 he led the cavalry brigade sent to Cyprus when it was feared there might be a regional conflict. Returning to India, he commanded the Kurram Valley Field Force during the latter part of the Second Afghan War. After the campaign he moved into the diplomatic sphere and was Agent at Baroda 1881–86. He was made a lieutenant-general one year later and full general in 1891. Watson had three sons who all rose to prominence in the Indian Army. He died in his ninetieth year on 23 January 1919.

WAUCHOPE, MAJOR-GENERAL A. – TRYING TO CHEAT DEATH

HOW MANY TIMES can a man cheat death? Andrew Gilbert Wauchope was wounded in so many of his battles that it seemed only a matter of time before an unlucky shot ended his career. This is exactly what happened on 11 December 1899 at Magersfontein, South Africa.

Andrew, the son of a Scottish landowner, was born on 5 July 1846. Aged 13 he was sent, like Evelyn **Wood**, to be a naval cadet, in his case training on *HMS Britannia*. Disliking life at sea, the young man purchased the commission of a second lieutenant in the Black Watch just prior to his 18th birthday. Eight years later he saw his first fighting while serving with a Hausa regiment in Ashanti. He was twice wounded in that war and mentioned in despatches. His chief, **Wolseley**, remembered the young Scotsman and in 1878 got him the job of a regional governorship of Cyprus for two years. In typical Wolseley style, he both admonished and praised the young officer in his journal: 'What a quaint, illiterate, and uneducated fellow it is, and yet what a good, honest, hard-working chap it is.' Captain Wauchope served on the staff during the 1881 Transvaal War and then joined Wolseley for a third time in Egypt. During hand-to-hand fighting in the trenches at Tel-el-Kebir he got a bullet through his helmet and another in his scabbard. Later, surveying the carnage, he remarked philosophically: 'What brutes we men are.'

That same year, 1882, Wauchope married, but his wife died tragically giving birth to twin boys. Fighting in the Sudan in 1884 he was severely wounded at El Teb on 29 February and was noted again for his bravery. Promoted to major in March, then quickly given a brevet lieutenant-colonelcy, he was wounded once more at Kirbekan in February 1885. The 1890s saw him recover and re-marry; his Scottish estates yielded huge reserves of coal and made him an extremely wealthy man. A lifelong Tory, Wauchope stood for Parliament, challenging Gladstone at Midlothian (and losing heavily against the 'Old Thunderer'). In 1894 he was given command of the 2nd Battalion, The Black Watch. His steady climb up the ladder was rewarded in 1898 with command of the 1st British Brigade in the final reconquest of the Sudan. His fellow brigadier, **Lyttelton**, thought Wauchope 'the direct opposite of **Gatacre**, equally brave, but very quiet and reserved. It was amusing to see him listening to Gatacre's harangues, looking pensively at him, with a far-away glance as if he saw something through and beyond him.' Highlanders liked serving under this tall, slim man who displayed a quiet intelligence.

In 1899, as the troopships set sail for the Cape, Wauchope was given the 3rd (Highland) Brigade. He led his men well at Belmont and Modder River as Lord **Methuen**'s army marched to relieve Kimberley. Finally, on the night of 10 December, he was ordered to lead the Highlanders in a night march. Wauchope made it plain that he disliked the idea. Under an inky sky lit by dramatic flashes of lightning and rolls of thunder, the officer guiding the brigade told Wauchope, 'This is as far as it is safe to go, Sir, in a mass.' The general replied: 'I'm afraid my men will lose direction. I think we will go a little further.' Daylight was fast coming on and a few minutes later, as he led his men towards hidden Boer trenches, 'a river of flame', like 'a million electric lights', flashed death from the muzzles of hundreds of rifles. After an initial paralysis, Wauchope had time to mutter to his ADC, 'This *is* fighting, A.G.' before he was shot dead and the aide badly wounded.

Wauchope was not blameless in the debacle which ended his life: some of his officers felt that he had advanced 'much too near not to be extended', and thought to deploy only after 200yd. Yet he clearly had reservations about the night attack and, as soon as the Boer fusillade started, kept his cool and quickly began issuing orders for the brigade to deploy to the right and try and outflank the enemy. Various glorious last words have been attributed to him, but all are probably false. He lies buried beneath a simple Gaelic cross of stone on the battlefield.

WHITE, FIELD-MARSHAL SIR G. – UPS AND DOWNS

A TALL, ATHLETIC man of impeccable manners, George White was 45 years old and already balding before he saw his first real action. Then, under the patronage of **Roberts**, his meteor shot into the firmament over the next two decades. This fast-track Indian career was halted at Ladysmith, his star quickly losing its brightness when he foolishly allowed himself and a large army to get trapped by the Boers, a mistake that ultimately cost the lives of hundreds of men on both sides.

An Ulsterman, George was born on 6 July 1835, entered Sandhurst at 15 and joined the 27th Inniskillings as an ensign in 1853. The regiment sailed for India after a few weeks and was there during the Mutiny, but frustratingly for White, it saw no active service. In 1863 he transferred into the 92nd Highlanders, a move that returned him to India. Three more terms of Indian service and a marriage saw White rising to major, before 14 March 1879 when he finally set out on his first campaign with the 92nd bound for Afghanistan as part of Roberts' army. 'Bobs' looked 'very worn and old', wrote White, while he himself felt 'as strong as an ibex'. The historian Brian Robson praised White's 'great coolness' in leading one wing of the attack in the action at Charasiab and then holding onto a hill against large numbers of regular Afghan troops. It is said that he grabbed a rifle and 'potted' the leading Afghan on the way up. He was just as brave at Kandahar, leading a bayonet charge, and was the first officer to capture a gun. For these and other acts of heroism he was awarded the Victoria Cross. At war's end he was promoted to lieutenant-colonel and given a CB.

White's fast track now began in earnest: in 1881 he was made Military Secretary to the Viceroy, then for three months in 1885 sent to the Egyptian-Sudan frontier as AG to **Dormer**. Next, under 'Bobs'' benevolent eyes, White was given a brigade in the Third Burmese War; he was responsible for cataloguing the loot of King Thebaw's palace and wrote, with his usual realism (a quality which sometimes bordered on pessimism in White's case), that 'our position here is ill-considered and much too extended', the people 'very loyal to the House of Alompra' and British rule 'must be hedged in by British bayonets for a long time to come'. White stayed on in Burma as successor to **Prendergast** since, Roberts claimed, 'he is the best man in India for the position.' A year later the elder soldier thought his protégé had done 'wonderfully well' and White, who left Burma in 1888 as a major-general, knew that 'I owe it all to my worthy chief, Sir Fred.' In 1890 White commanded in the relatively bloodless second Zhob Valley expedition. Under Roberts' patronage the plum role of C-in-C, India, fell into his lap in 1893 and he fulfilled this role during the heyday of imperial expansion, including the Chitral and Tirah campaigns. Not everyone liked him: Paul **Methuen** in this period called White 'a cold, unsympathetic man'.

Before he left Burma, Sir George made a point of praising Colonel **Symons**, commandant of the mounted infantry, whose services were 'of equal value to the Chief Commissioner and myself'. Against the wishes of **Lockhart**, a division in Tirah was given to Symons by White, who said he was 'the most competent man' in the entire British and Indian armies. This odd pair – Symons the optimist and White the realist – were now about to bring about a chain of military blunders. In South Africa the gung-ho Symons, who seemed to think the Boers could be dealt with like *dacoit*s and tribesmen, over-extended the British forward line in Natal and got himself killed. White, GOC in Natal, to the chagrin of his superior, Sir Redvers **Buller**, had been given strict instructions that he must not get besieged in Ladysmith, a forward base dominated by surrounding hills which was Natal's major supply and training camp. Yet that is what he did, bottling up most of the colony's British troops. White hoped to perform a 'knock-down blow' on the Boers, but on 'Mournful Monday', 28 October 1899, with Ladysmith almost surrounded, he lost 106 men killed, 347 wounded and 1,284 captured, compared to sixteen Boers killed and seventy-five wounded. In one of the most brutally honest letters ever penned by a Victorian general, White wrote to his wife: 'It was my plan, and I am responsible, and I have said so to the Secretary of State, and I must bear the consequences ... I played a bold game, too bold a game, and I have lost ... I think after this venture the men will lose confidence in me, and that I ought to be superseded ... I don't think I can go on soldiering ... It is far into the night, but I don't expect to sleep.' In daylight White decided not to retreat because he argued that the loss of the town and its munitions would give the Boers a significant victory and could lead to the fall of the rest of the colony. The British press rallied to his defence. So did the Queen, who telegraphed her support. In the corridors of Whitehall things were different: politicians said he was 'too old and doddery' for command; Lord **Wolseley**, C-in-C of the British Army, urged the war minister to sack him. In Natal a furious Redvers Buller called White 'weak and vacillating' and blamed the decision to create a siege on Ian

Hamilton, 'a dangerous advisor'. Modern historians have been no more kind: Pakenham describes White as lacking the 'moral strength' to make a fighting retreat. It could also be argued that his pride would not allow this, or it may have been his realistic assessment that many men would die in the attempt. Whatever White's reasons, the results were disastrous.

Before he could be got rid of, he had to be rescued. The Ladysmith garrison settled down to a tough 118-day siege. As the days wore on, their general grew increasingly depressed and removed from day-to-day events. Luckily for him – and the garrison – he had some clever and stalwart officers under his command, including Hamilton and **Hunter**. Meanwhile, Buller and the troops slogged towards the town fighting and dying along the way at Spion Kop, Vaal Krantz, Hart's Hill, Colenso and a score of minor actions. The Ladysmith siege was finally lifted on 28 February 1900. White, 'a stooped, patient, almost pathetic figure', who had seemingly aged ten years during the siege, told a cheering mob, 'Thank God we kept the flag flying!' His ill health provided a suitable excuse to repatriate him to England where the jingoistic press raved about his courage. The top brass considered him a failure. Only Roberts, his old mentor, stayed loyal. 'The officials have condemned White,' he wrote to Kitchener, 'but any trouble he got into was their doing not his – He had to deal with things as he found them and though he made mistakes, he showed considerable pluck and resolution and it was the latter quality Buller so signally lacked.'

Raised to a field-marshal, made Governor of Gibraltar and then of the Chelsea Hospital, Sir George was well aware he was being put out to pasture. His health never really recovered from the siege and in his last years he suffered memory loss. He died on 24 June 1912 a much respected man.

WHITLOCK, LIEUTENANT-GENERAL SIR G. – CAUTION PAYS A DIVIDEND

ROBERT CORNISH WHITLOCK had a reputation for being slow and over-cautious. In his case, it turned out for the best, since his gradual march on Kirwi and Banda in 1858 led to one of the biggest hauls of booty ever seized by a British army.

He was born in 1798 and joined the 8th Madras Native Infantry in June 1818. Eleven months later, he served at the storming of Copaul Droog in the Second Mahratta War. In 1823 young Lieutenant Whitlock transferred to the 36th MNI and was with them in the First Burmese War, although they played no special part. In 1834, while officially a captain, he commanded the 36th at the taking of a well-defended stockade in the little known Coorg campaign fought near Mysore against a cruel and virulently anti-British rajah. In 1853 Whitlock was selected to raise the 3rd Madras European Regiment and became its first commanding officer.

When the 1857 rising broke out, Whitlock was serving as a brigadier at Kurnool in the Madras Presidency. In theory the Bengal rebellion was a long way away, but Colin Campbell proposed to the Governor-General that two armies be created from the Bombay and Madras presidencies to take the field against rebels in Central India. Sir Hugh Rose took command of the Bombay troops and Whitlock, as a major-general, replaced Pat **Grant** in charge of the Madras force. The historian P.J.O. Taylor has called Whitlock 'a poor commander, slow, overcautious not to say timid'. One officer serving with Rose, admittedly biased, wrote disparagingly that Whitlock 'would never ride save on a mule which could not be persuaded to go forward, and that he was likened to a bad revolver, always going round but never going off.' He was slow in comparison to Rose's dexterous handling of situations, soldiers, deficient supplies and the blistering summer heat. Yet Rose, while trying to hurry along Whitlock, also told Campbell that he 'is … very good-natured and we get on famously together'.

The Nerbudda Field Force marched over 1,300 miles in trying conditions. Whitlock's biggest mistake as he marched northwards was a refusal to dismantle rebel forts near his track, meaning that the country was not properly pacified. The result was that the mutineers simply formed up again behind his column. The fame of his little army rests not on its military successes, like Rose's soldiers, but on the loot it acquired at Kirwi and Banda. Jealous rivals whispered that Whitlock's claim was a 'shameless lie', or that he at least exaggerated his claim that stores of rebel guns and powder had been found at Kirwi just so the fabulous treasure of its boy-ruler could be seized. The booty from Kirwi and Banda totalled £700,000 in gold, silver and jewels, a fabulous sum (multiply today by over 100 times). Everyone wanted a share, including the C-in-C, India, and other generals who fought in other parts of Central India, and all claimed some assistance in gaining this prize. A legal battle raged in the High Court for nine years until the prize money (less legal fees and a chunk for the government), went to the C-in-C, India, headquarters staff and Whitlock and his troops. Lord Clyde got a handsome £60,000, but Whitlock had no time to enjoy his £12,000 share before he died in his native Devon on 30 January 1868.

WILDE, LIEUTENANT-GENERAL SIR A. – PALADIN OF THE 'PIFFERS'

BIG, BURLY AND bearded, Alfred Wilde was one of the most famous infantry officers on the North-West Frontier. The son of a wealthy London solicitor and nephew of a Lord Chancellor, he was born on 1 November 1819, educated at Winchester and joined the 15th Madras Native Infantry in 1839, quickly transferring to the 19th MNI. He served with them in disturbances on the Malabar coast in 1843 and seven years later, then acting as the 19th's adjutant, interpreter and quartermaster, was invited to be adjutant of the recently formed 3rd PNI. A year later he transferred as second-in-command of the 4th PNI. Wilde played a prominent role in a night attack on Waziris during the occupation of the Bahadur Khel Valley in November 1851. He was given command of the 4th on 21 February 1853 and led them in operations the next year. Promoted to captain in 1856, Alfred led his men again in the Bozdar expedition.

Joining the regiment shortly before the Bozdar campaign was Assistant-Surgeon James Fairweather, who left vivid impressions of Wilde in his memoirs. It appears that Alfred's nickname was 'Jonathan' (after the eighteenth-century thief-taker). Fairweather described him as 'a big powerful looking man and although under forty his baldness made him look quite that age'. During the Siege of Delhi in 1857 he was wounded and also contracted cholera. According to Fairweather, in the evenings, regardless of the roar of cannon and musketry, Wilde liked the regimental band to play as he sat smoking his pipe. He was promoted major, wounded again, this time more seriously in the groin, on 21 March 1858 in the Lucknow assault. He returned to England, was given a CB having been mentioned several times in despatches, but returned to India in time to lead the 4th PNI in the 1860 Mahsud Waziri expedition.

In 1862 Wilde was made Commandant of the Guides Regiment and a year later led them in the Umbeyla campaign. He actually concocted the original plan for this expedition, based on the quick 'in-and-out' theory of Sydney **Cotton**'s 1858 expedition. This time the tribesmen would be attacked from the north, 'forcing them to fight with their backs to the plains'. Wilde's ideas for a speedy operation and a carefully chosen fighting force fell apart when the Lieutenant-Governor of the Punjab, Sir Robert Montgomery, radically increased the size of the army against the advice of the C-in-C, India, Sir Hugh Rose. The campaign, as we have shown several times in this book, was tough and Wilde was in plenty of fights.

When **Garvock** finally led the advance on Malka and Mandi, strongholds of the fanatics, Wilde headed the 2nd Brigade.

On 8 February 1865 Wilde was promoted to brigadier with command of the Punjab Irregular Force, known as 'the Piffers'. In 1868 it was thought necessary to send another expedition to the Black Mountain and this time Wilde was in overall command. In barely a week that October he led troops to the highest, strongly defended peak, and routed the tribesmen. The campaign was later criticised because the bulk of the fanatics kept one step ahead of the British and the campaign ended quickly. However Wilde cannot be blamed for following his orders since the Indian government was clearly nervous of having another costly and humiliating war on its hands so soon after Umbeyla.

Alfred was made a KCB in 1869 and promoted to major-general. He left India in 1871 but six years later, on his promotion to lieutenant-general, became a member of the Council of India. He died not long after on 7 February 1878.

WILLSHIRE, GENERAL SIR T. – 'TIGER TOM'

RECOGNISED AS AN efficient soldier, Thomas Willshire rose to prominence in the long war against Napoleon, then fought the Xhosa in South Africa and finally the Afghans. He seems to have been an interesting person – a great lover of animals with a pack of eight dogs that used to follow his heels, a cat at Poona who rode with him on his horse, and in Africa a pet monkey called 'Jacko', who sometimes did the same thing – yet the man who could not kill an animal used the lash freely on his soldiers to maintain discipline and was fearless in battle.

He was born in Nova Scotia while his father was quartermaster there with the 38th Foot. Astonishingly, his father procured a commission for the boy as a child. Aged 9, young Thomas joined the 38th as a lieutenant, and was a captain at 15! In 1807 he fought in the disastrous expedition to Buenos Aires and by his twenty-first birthday he had been bloodied in the Peninsular War at Vimerio and Corunna. He arrived back in England with no clothes, emaciated, and wrapped in an old tiger skin. The 38th next served in the useless Walcheren expedition, then sailed for Spain, where Willshire fought nobly at Vittoria, Salamanca and other battles as the French were pursued over the Pyrenees. He returned to England in 1815 as a lieutenant-colonel.

The 38th were sent to the Cape of Good Hope in 1828 and Willshire was soon made Commandant of British Kaffraria on the Xhosa frontier.

The conflict that broke out in 1819, the fifth fought against the Xhosa, was called by one statesman 'the Willshire war' due to the way he dominated its proceedings and on the whole led a skilful campaign against the chiefs Hintsa and Nxele. The tribes almost surprised Willshire at Grahamstown on 22 April, when a large Xhosa army attacked with some ferocity. He stayed cool, telling his soldiers not to fire until the enemy were just thirty-five paces away; over 1,000 natives were wounded or killed, to Willshire's loss of just eight men. He then plunged into the Fish River bush country, harassing the Xhosa at every turn. One trick he introduced was a new weapon which terrified the natives – the Congreve rocket. Eventually Nxele was handed over and sent to Robben Island (known today as Nelson Mandela's prison).

In 1822 the 38th moved to India and Willshire transferred to the 46th Foot. He was described at this time as 'handsome, with large black whiskers, tall and active'. Two years later he fought at Kittoor, where a Mahratta ruling family objected to British intervention after the death of its rajah. Willshire led a storming party at bayonet point and got £1,200 in prize money.

When the Army of the Indus was formed in 1838, one of the three Bombay Brigades was led by Willshire. He was one of the few generals to get any praise; Surgeon Kennedy, who wrote an account, thought he acted wisely, and James Outram, who was at times political agent and Willshire's aide, commended his 'gallant' behaviour at the storming of Khelat. Here Willshire led from the front, yelling to his troops, 'Loosen cartridges', as he rode to check that the gate was blown in before pointing with his sword to announce the storming party were to advance. He then rode into the city with the body of his troops and when the Baluchi chieftain, Mehrab Khan, was killed in the fighting the cheering soldiers presented Willshire with his sword.

Knighted in 1840, Sir Thomas left India in ill health but later commanded at Chatham. In his fifties he retired, married and raised a large family. 'Tiger Tom' retired eventually to Windsor and died there on 31 May 1862.

WILSON, LIEUTENANT-GENERAL SIR A. – CONQUEROR OF DELHI

THERE ARE VICTORIAN generals, such as **Buller**, **Chelmsford**, **Methuen** and **Warren**, whose failures have been reassessed in recent years. A smaller body, such as **Graham** and **Wood**, have had their victories challenged. Within the latter group also falls Archdale Wilson, the man charged with recovering Delhi during the 1857 Indian Rising. He was accused of over-caution and almost cowardice in his own lifetime, libelled by the biographer of Lord Lawrence – an attack re-fuelled by the biographer of his chief siege engineer, whose assertions seem to have influenced later Victorian writers, such as Lord **Roberts**. Given time, these distortions have led more recent writers to label him 'a manic-depressive' (Collier) whose 'nerve finally failed him' (Dalrymple). Luckily for anyone studying Wilson at Delhi, we have a very different perspective on the man from soldiers like **Hills-Johnnes** and **Norman**, who were also at the siege, along with administrators of the calibre of Sir George Campbell.

Wilson, the son of a Norfolk gentleman-rector, was educated at Norwich and Addiscombe and joined the Bengal Artillery in 1819. His first fight was the siege and storming of Bhurtpore in 1825–26, for which he was mentioned in despatches. During the Second Sikh War Lt-Colonel Wilson commanded the artillery at the capture of Kalawalla and Dulla, minor affairs which led to his command of artillery at 'John Company's' great arsenal at Dum Dum.

When the Mutiny erupted in May 1857 Wilson was commanding the artillery at its source – the cantonment of Meerut near Delhi. 'A tall man with very large contemplative eyes, a high forehead, grizzled (grey) hair, no whiskers but a moustache and goatee beard' is how one contemporary described him. Noting he was a keen whist player (and amateur gardener), the historian Christopher Hibbert called Wilson 'kindly, quiet, though short-tempered', an officer who after almost forty years in India wanted nothing more than a small cottage in his beloved Norfolk with his 'dear old woman', something he described as 'heaven'. Wilson was later criticised for not heeding warnings that the Meerut *sepoys* might mutiny or march on Delhi. Caution was always Wilson's by-word and if he failed to realise the dangers, then so did most other officers. He refused to set out in haste after the mutineers until his little army was properly organised and his belief that the rebels would not go to Delhi, but return to their homes was right in many cases.

In the weeks that followed, through all the fights, arguments, plans and battles, it must be remembered that Wilson was exhausted from a recent bout of smallpox, suffering much of the time from fever and confined to his sick bed. During the first three weeks after the outbreak of the mutiny he slept in his boots and on the march to Delhi 'suffered agonies from the heat and dust'. Despite his ill health, he met the rebels at Ghazi-ud-din-Nagar on 30 May, driving them from their guns, and fought 'brilliant and successful actions both on that and the next day when he was again attacked' (Vetch – DNB).

Combining with Sir Henry Barnard's troops, Wilson was with the force that routed the rebels at Badli-ki-Serai and helped reinforce the British huddled on the ridge above Delhi. After Barnard's death his successor, Thomas Reed, resigned on account of ill health. Wilson was still feverish, but did not shirk the huge responsibility of agreed chief command. He was quickly promoted to the rank of major-general on special service.

One of Wilson's first acts was to reinforce discipline and try to create a semblance of authority in his rag-tag army. He pressurised John Lawrence in the Punjab and Earl Canning in Calcutta to send reinforcements. His refusal to rush headlong into an attack annoyed many of the young bloods, but Wilson stuck by his cautious methods. Attack was necessary when and where it served success; on 25 August he authorised Brigadier Nicholson, one of his sternest critics, to take 2,200 men and twelve heavy guns and prevent the rebels from attacking his rear, an order the fiery Ulsterman carried out with gusto. During the early part of the siege Wilson wrote, 'My force is too weak to go out and attack them properly. Our artillery men are worked night and day, and are all getting knocked up.' Younger officers clamouring for immediate action were 'know-nothings' who foolishly thought 'a force under 2,000 bayonets (Europeans) can easily hop over the walls of Delhi covered with heavy guns and massacre with ease the 30,000 or 40,000 men defending it as easily as toasting cheese.'

Just about all historians seem to overlook Wilson's contribution to the storming of the city: as an artilleryman he took a keen interest in the sighting of the guns. Unfortunately, delays in planning infuriated his chief engineer, Richard Baird Smith, who raged about Wilson's obstinacy and ignorance, admitting he had no respect for him whatsoever. Wilson, perhaps over-cautious but possibly wise, fretted about Smith's 'impracticable' plans and bemoaned the fact, as he told his wife, that most of the engineers were 'very zealous', but being young men had 'little or no experience' of siege warfare. Slurs against Wilson started with Baird Smith and Nicholson. These were taken up by John Lawrence, who had no idea of the problems Wilson was facing at Delhi. A later critic was Lord Roberts, who seems to have been influenced by the writings of Lawrence's biographer, Bosworth Smith, and H.M. Vibart, the biographer of Baird Smith. As an example of this, I note that on p. 150 (vol ii) of Lawrence's biography, Bosworth Smith uses a letter written by Wilson to imply he was contemplating retreat but *omits* the vital words, 'I have determined to hold the position we now have to the last.' Sir George Campbell, an administrator who served as a political officer at Delhi and on the march to Lucknow, later wrote of Wilson, 'I do believe that to him individually the success was in a very great measure due. He was not a showy or a very brilliant man, but he was a good, cool, solid man.'

The chief criticism levelled at Wilson has been that after the initial assault on Delhi he then suggested a retreat. In fact he wrote a letter to Neville Chamberlain saying that unless Hindo Rao's house, a major Picquet, was captured, 'we shall not be strong enough to take the city.' It is said that on hearing this news, John Nicholson rose up in bed and shouted: 'Thank God, I have strength yet to shoot him if necessary.' Yet Wilson's note of caution, so typical of his character, is not the same as advocating a withdrawal. Henry Norman, who as AG stood by Wilson's side daily, was offended by Vibart's and Roberts' slurs in the 1890s and replied that he 'never heard him breathe a word about retiring'. Nor did Hills-Johnes VC ever hear 'a whisper of any intentions on his part to withdraw', thus disputing Roberts' comments. The best summing up I have read is by another Mutiny officer, General Sir Frederick Maunsell, who wrote of Wilson 'that he may have dropped expressions of the anxiety all felt is probable enough, but a General is judged by his acts and success, not by what he does not do!'

After Delhi's successful capture, a benevolent government turned a blind eye to any criticisms, adopting Maunsell's attitude; Wilson, who went on to command the artillery at the second relief of Lucknow, was made a KCB and on 8 January 1858, while still fighting, created a baronet of Delhi. Ill-health had taken its toll by that summer. He returned to England and the post of colonel-commandant of horse artillery. Awards followed and a promotion to lieutenant-general in 1868 before Wilson returned to Norfolk, where he died on 9 May 1874.

WOLSELEY, FIELD-MARSHAL LORD G. & WOLSELEY, LIEUTENANT-GENERAL SIR G. – MODERN MAJOR-GENERALS

IN THE 1870S he was known as 'England's only general' (so that his great rival, Roberts, a decade later had to be 'England's only *other* general'). When George Grossmith satirised him brilliantly on stage in *The Pirates of Penzance* as 'the very model of a modern major-general' everyone in the audience knew who he was singing about and were in on the joke. He fought in steamy Burmese and West African jungles, from the rocky Lulu Mountains of Africa to the banks of the sweltering Nile, and marched armies through the pine clad forests of Canada to the gates of Peking. In the years 1870–85 he proved himself the master of the 'small war', then dominated British military thought and reform of the army for a further fifteen years. He was arguably the greatest Victorian soldier, adored by those officers close to him, hated by reactionaries and pushy rivals alike, all subject to his privately vented scorn and withering wit. He was Garnet Joseph Wolseley.

He rose from Anglo-Irish Protestant obscurity to greatness. His father was not a general with connections (like Abraham **Roberts**) who could help his son. Garnet's father, a relatively poor major, died when he was 7. Throughout his life the boy, as eldest child, would feel financially responsible for his three sisters and three brothers. He was born on 4 June 1833 near Dublin and all his attempts to obtain a commission without purchase fell on deaf ears until Garnet was just past his 19th birthday, when a begging letter from his mother to Horse Guards saw him enter the service. He was only 5ft 7in tall, with a weak chin, 'handsome, clean-cut, slight but well-knit'.

Wolseley arrived in India early in 1853 as an ensign in the 80th Foot. Sent to the Burmese War, he recorded the first man he saw killed in action as an 'unpleasant sensation', but found leading men into battle was 'supremely delightful … The blood seems to boil, the brain to be on fire.' In an attack on a stockade under General **Cheape** he was severely wounded in the thigh, 'the blood squirting in jets through the fingers of my pipe-clayed gloves'. Promotion and a mention in despatches saw Garnet transfer to the 90th Light Infantry and leave for the Crimea in 1854. Promoted captain, he volunteered to serve in the firing line as an assistant engineer, was wounded in the right thigh and shortly afterwards severely mauled by a shell which killed the two men standing next to him. Sent to a monastery to convalesce, he accepted the post of DAQMG and was one of the last officers to leave the Crimea. The following year Garnet sailed for China with his regiment, but events in India changed everything; he fought in Campbell's advance on Lucknow, almost winning a VC leading a storming party into the city, 'the first of Sir Colin's army to reach the beleaguered garrison'.

The Indian Mutiny was the first campaign of Garnet's younger brother, George, who had joined the 84th Foot. Two years younger, far less mature, always impecunious, George was, in Garnet's opinion, 'one of the damnedest young fools I have ever known let loose upon the army, and I never expect anything brilliant or noble from him'.

After the final relief of Lucknow in March 1858 young Garnet was promoted to major and selected to be QMG to Sir Hope **Grant**'s Oudh Division. His regimental days were over and a glittering series of staff appointments now beckoned. 'I am now a great swell', he wrote home proudly. Hope Grant and Wolseley respected one another (he later dedicated his autobiography to the older man) and he followed his chief as AQMG to China in 1860. In January 1862 he was sent to Canada in the same department. While there he found time to wed and woo a shapely English girl, Louisa Erskine. She was to be, forever after, his psychological soul-mate and the only person in whom he truly confided. He also authored a *Soldier's Pocket-Book* – a compendium on everything from tactics to making Irish stew. This work also ruffled feathers at Horse Guards, since it allowed Wolseley to promote several army reforms. Luck, so important to a soldier's career, continued and in 1870 he led a logistically brilliant and bloodless expedition across the Canadian north-west to squash a revolt by half-breeds along the Red River. The press lauded this victory and in 1871 he arrived at the War Office as AAG. Now began a thirty-year struggle to reform an institution mired in the thinking of half a century earlier, thanks to the reactionary Duke of Cambridge as C-in-C.

Two years later he was sent to West Africa to deal with an invasion of British territory by the Ashanti tribe. Utilising the talents of a select group of 'special service' officers, along with a hand-picked staff, some of them veterans of Red River, Wolseley's 'garnet ring' took firm shape – **Buller, Brackenbury, Colley, Greaves, Maurice, McNeill, Russell, Wood** and others. Wolseley claimed that he chose members 'on merit alone' but, as Ian Beckett has noted, 'Wolseley, in particular, became something of a prisoner of the initial success of his ring.' He soon noticed failings in some of his acolytes, as the officers began arguing among themselves, threatening to tear the circle apart. Problems aside, it was a remarkable collection of minds and talents, unlike anything seen before or since in the British Army.

One thing Wolseley did very well was plan in advance, 'in contrast to Roberts who was an indifferent organizer'. Thus his march on Coomassie, the Ashanti capital, along with pitched battles in dense jungle in 1874, the defeat of the wily Pedi chieftain, Sekhukhune, on his rocky Lulu Mountain stronghold in 1879 and an infantry attack at dawn after a night march through the desert to Tel-el-Kebir in 1882 were all meticulously planned. Between spats at the War Office, where Cambridge tried to apply the brakes, Wolseley supported reforming politicians such as Edward Cardwell. 'Our only General' was sent, as if he were a military saviour, to settle affairs in Natal (1875) and Cyprus (1878), restore honour in Zululand (1879) and crush Egyptian nationalists (1882). Wolseley's last active campaign in 1884–85 was his boldest: playing for high stakes he attempted to save his friend, Charles **Gordon**, besieged in Khartoum, using a combination of land and river forces. This scheme involved French-Canadian boatmen, colonial volunteers from Australia, Life Guardsmen riding camels and regular British infantry. Despite a late start and the weirdness of it all, the plan narrowly failed. Recriminations soon followed.

One of Wolseley's failings, alongside an ego that grew over the years, was a failure to cultivate and court popularity with politicians. He had 'neither the personality nor the inclination to create legends', wrote Joseph Lehmann, one of his biographers. The surviving campaign journals of Wolseley have now all been published. These, along with his letters to Louisa, reveal a waspish and sarcastic man, full of bitterness, ego, dislike of politicians and royals. They were never intended for publication and anyone study-ing them soon realises that Wolseley's campaign frustrations, set down often with sharp invective, made the journals his emotional safety valve. Face to face, his subordinates only ever met a cheery or cool man, always seemingly in control. Thus an officer criticised in Wolseley's private writings one day could just as easily be praised on the next.

In his autobiography Ian **Hamilton**, a close friend of Roberts, called Wolseley 'the most impersonal commander I ever met', a description that has stuck to him. Yet Wolseley's writings – notably the waspish journals, and his autobiography – reveal a very witty man, and witty men are rarely dull company. Louisa loved soirees with literary and artistic celebrities such as the writer Henry James. Elizabeth Butler, the celebrated war artist, recalled Wolseley had the same hearty laugh as a man from her childhood – Charles Dickens. Thus Hamilton's invective must be set against William Butler, who called his chief 'The best and most brilliant brain I have ever met … on whom command sat so easily and fitting that neither he nor the men he commanded had ever to think about it …' More than a decade after Wolseley's death a junior ring member, the son of General **Adye**, dedicated his own autobiography simply to 'the finest soldier I have ever known'.

In 1895, after much huffing and puffing, Cambridge stepped down and Wolseley became C-in-C, although he almost lost the job to Buller. Queen Victoria never warmed to him. Her soldier son, Arthur, Duke of Connaught, who was given command of the Guards Brigade at Tel-el-Kebir, disagreed. On one occasion Her Majesty complained to Disraeli and the great man reminded her that 'Men of action, when eminently successful in early life, are generally boastful and full of themselves.'

Short-term memory loss, a sense of ennui and growing fatigue began affecting Wolseley in the 1890s when he needed to be at the height of his powers. In a famously hot debate in parliament on the conduct of the South African War the C-in-C was brutally criticised, notably by the War Minister,

Lord Lansdowne, who threw him to the wolves. A former Viceroy of India and confidante of Roberts, Lansdowne accused Wolseley of not preparing Britain better for the war and of allowing White to get trapped in Ladysmith. A gloating Roberts told **Kitchener** that his rival allowed Ladysmith to be held against his own judgement and ... did nothing to 'have it protected. The whole truth is that neither he nor any one at the War Office had the slightest idea of the fighting power of the Boers. They all thought it would be a simple affair if we went to war'. This criticism is not entirely valid since Wolseley had told Cambridge before the war started that a fight with the Boers 'will be the most serious war England has *ever* had', allowing for the army's size and logistical difficulties. In parliament he admitted that the war had not been 'fully anticipated', but resented suggestions that Ladysmith was his responsibility. It had always been the British way to allow field commanders a great deal of latitude. Having spent much time in Natal the field-marshal was well aware of the dangers of being bottled in that place and advised White to make his stand on the Biggarsberg heights. It was all to no avail; Wolseley retired amid recriminations in the press, never forgiving 'that little reptile', Lansdowne, and the 'charlatan' Roberts, whose generalship in South Africa left him cold.

Brother George died in 1907, killed head-on in a bizarre accident crossing a railway line. He had followed Garnet to Egypt (arriving just in time for Tel-el-Kebir) and up the Nile, also seeing fighting in the Second Afghan War and the pacification of Burma. In debt for most of his career to Garnet and others, George was unhappy in India. One of the few times Wolseley and Roberts agreed on something was when 'Bobs' refused to give George Wolseley a brigade. He was finally made a major-general in 1892 and commanded as a lieutenant-general in the Punjab 1897–98 and held the Madras command 1898–1904.

Garnet Wolseley died at his winter home near Mentone on 26 March 1913, ironically on the eve of a vastly different kind of war. His body was brought back to London, where it lies close to that of Roberts in St Paul's Cathedral. He had championed numerous reforms (machine-guns among them) and his determination to drag the British Army away from its fusty Napoleonic days makes him the 'father' of the modern British Army, especially the organisation into army corps ready for mobilisation for service at home or abroad. One expert writing in the 1930s declared:

> Nothing is more certain than it was Lord Wolseley, and Lord Wolseley alone, who conceived the idea of an Expeditionary Force ... when we recall the incomparable little British Expeditionary Force of 1914 let us do justice to a

great soldier, a great public servant and a great man and, while we speak of it affectionately as the Old Contemptibles, let us think of it as Wolseley's Army.

One suspects he would have been pleased with that epitaph.

WOOD, FIELD-MARSHAL SIR E. – 'GOOD OLD EVELYN'

WHEN A SECOND war with the Boers broke out in 1899 there was a certain gentle irony in the fact that the second most senior post in the British Army was occupied by the man who had negotiated the settlement of the earlier Transvaal conflict. Almost as popular as 'Bobs', friend to scores of ambitious officers – from subalterns to generals – courageous, intelligent (some said cunning), eccentric, vain and deaf (when it suited him), Evelyn Wood was a unique individual. In recent years his career has been intelligently and sympathetically re-examined by historian Stephen Manning, while his generalship in the Zulu War has been sharply criticised by, among others, Huw Jones.

Evelyn was born on 9 February 1838, the son of an aristocratic Essex vicar who later became Lord Mayor of London. His siblings included two sisters who became famous: the popular novelist 'Anna Steele' and Katherine, better known as Kitty O'Shea, lover of the Irish patriot Charles Stewart Parnell. Sent to Marlborough but unhappy, the boy convinced his adoring mother to let him join the Navy at 14; he served as a midshipman in the Crimean War and was wounded in an assault on the Redan, Lord Raglan loaning his coach to take the youth back to *HMS Queen*. Wanting to see more action after recovery, Wood used the influence of Raglan to obtain a commission without purchase into the army's 13th Light Dragoons. Back in the Crimea he got typhoid and pneumonia, a situation made worse by a sadistic nurse at Scutari Hospital, until his mother arrived to rescue her boy and restore him to health back home.

It was 1858 and the Indian Mutiny was winding down, yet Wood typically managed within weeks of arrival to see fighting in Central India under **Michel**, win a VC after charging a party of rebels – and also mash his nose and ears after falling off a giraffe's back when he tried to ride the animal for a bet!

In the 1860s Evelyn almost left the army to become a lawyer, but things changed in 1873 when he was accepted by **Wolseley** as a special service officer in his West Africa expedition. At the Battle of Amoaful, true to form, Wood got hit in the stomach by a nail gun. Impressed by his resourcefulness and pluck, Wolseley said he was 'the only one' of his team to whom he would entrust command if he was incapacitated in some way.

Turning down the chance to be commandant of Sandhurst in preference to active service against the Xhosa in 1877, Wood soon won the praise of General Thesiger, who liked his 'marked abilities and tact'. When the Zulu War started he was given command of the no. 3 (left flank) column operating in the northern part of the territory. A fellow officer described his bearded and balding superior as 'a most bloodthirsty man' and 'the most ambitious man I ever met … he is a hard master to serve – everything must go straight, and success is everything'. On 28 March Colonel Wood launched an attack on the Zulu position on Hlobane Mountain intended to distract attention from **Chelmsford**'s advance to relieve Eshowe. This expedition was, in the words of Greaves and Knight, 'poorly planned and badly executed'. Following the grisly death of one of his staff officers (and close friends), Wood was so badly shaken that he left his troops in splintered groups to fend for themselves. Next day at Kambula, his composure seemingly restored, he fought bravely and directed the defence under a heavy fire. This decisive victory allowed Wood (and **Buller**) to blame the debacle at Hlobane on their cavalry commander, John Russell, along with a conveniently dead scapegoat, Commandant Weatherley of the Border Horse.

Returning home the glib Wood met his Queen, who thought him 'wonderfully lively' and witty. Always naive politically, he misread the situation in the Transvaal and the character of the Boers. In 1881, back in South Africa, Wood wanted to fight on after his friend **Pomeroy-Colley**'s death, but found himself negotiating a peace settlement that gave the Transvaal its independence. This led to strong words between Wood and critics who included the Queen and Wolseley. In 1882 a humiliated Wood was punished by Wolseley with a minor role in Egypt. His ego badly bruised, the following year he accepted the role of Sirdar of a newly reformed Egyptian Army. Wolseley later wrote that Wood's work in improving the Egyptian soldiers was 'for purposes of self-glorification', and that the man's vanity and self-seeking would have been 'positively disgusting' if Evelyn was not, at times, so laughable. During the 1884–85 Sudan War he worked as Director of the Lines of Communication.

For the rest of his life, Wood grew into a walrus-moustachioed, white haired, venerated old warrior working partly at the War Office, partly as a military fixture. Any officer wanting advancement and needing a helping hand, such as pushy Lieutenant W.S.L. Churchill, tended to lean on Wood. His eccentricities and love of riding continued; an aide complained he needed to carry around 'a chemist's shop' to treat all of Evelyn's maladies. Wolseley, who made him Adjutant-General in 1897, wrote: 'What a good fellow he is when his vanity is not over-excited.' After his death in 1919 *The Times* recalled him with truth as 'a magnificent if not a very great man, who lived a magnificent life'.

WOODGATE, MAJOR-GENERAL E. – IN JUNGLE AND ON VELDT

EDWARD ROBERT PREVOST Woodgate was a good-looking, fair-haired member of **Wolseley**'s outer circle and a close friend of Evelyn **Wood**. Today he is best remembered for being mortally wounded on Spion Kop in 1900. Less than two years earlier he had successfully commanded operations in Sierra Leone during the hard-fought 'Hut Tax War' against the Temne and Mendi tribes.

He was born in 1845, was educated at Radley and joined the 4th 'King's Own' in 1865. The regiment was at the centre of things during the Abyssinian expedition and Woodgate took part in the Battle of Aroghi and storming of Magdala. In 1873 he was selected as a special service officer in Wolseley's expedition against the Ashantis. Here he served under Wood, fighting with the advanced guard. Wood found him an energetic subaltern: despite a fever he agreed to lead a covering party for road cutters early one morning. 'Yes sir, I'll start at once.' 'Have some breakfast,' urged Wood. 'Oh no,' replied Woodgate, 'I've got some biscuit, and there's plenty of water about the track.' A battle developed and Wood was hit by a slug. He found his pockets had been stuffed by Woodgate with War Office notebooks, the younger man remarking chirpily, 'Well, as you are sure to be in front I should like to save your chest.' Years later, Sir Evelyn repaid this act by helping to defray Woodgate's costs on preparing for the Staff College.

Passing out of Camberley in 1877, Captain Woodgate accompanied Wood again to South Africa in 1878 and served as his principal staff officer. During the tense Battle of Kambula he led the attack on the cattle *kraal*, waving his sword aloft at the head of two companies of the 90th, 'marching as leisurely and unconcernedly as if he were pacing a piece of ground for cricket wickets'. In this brutal fight forty-four men of the 90th were killed or wounded but the *kraal* was re-captured from the Zulus.

During the 1880s Woodgate served on staff in the West Indies and in 1893 was given command of his regiment's 1st battalion. Five years later, perhaps with his Ashanti war service in Wolseley and Wood's minds, their old comrade was sent to raise a new regiment in Sierra Leone. Given overall command of troops in the country, Woodgate had to face a tough situation when the Temne tribe, under its remarkable war chief, Bai Bureh, rose in revolt against a hut tax. Bureh showed himself to be a superb guerrilla leader and the situation worsened after the Mendi tribe also joined the uprising. The result was, in the words of one scholar, 'By far one of the most difficult campaigns the British fought during the occupation of their West African possessions.' Fighting ended in November 1898, Bai Bureh refusing to quit in the swamps (he was eventually freed on legal grounds as he had never sworn allegiance to the Queen). Woodgate accompanied some of his columns and was, for example, in the fighting on 10 May near Foaio when five stockades had to be rushed. Each day brought more ambushes and deaths until the town of Kwasu was relieved and a small battle fought by Woodgate's 145 regular troops and 650 friendlies, using rockets and 7-pounders at the stockaded town of Senahu, this just one of scores of fights.

Hardly surprisingly, Woodgate's health suffered from this second West African campaign and he returned home to England to be made a KCMG. When war broke out with the Boers he was offered the Lancashire Brigade, which included his old regiment, part of **Warren**'s division. Sent to capture the peak of Spion Kop at the head of 1,700 men, Woodgate ousted 200 Boers from the summit. Unfortunately, Warren had given him no clear instructions about what to do next. There was thick fog and at dawn the Boers returned in greater numbers, supported by artillery. Woodgate had made no stone sangars or dug trenches and his men were mown down in the appalling fire. The historian Kenneth Griffith castigated this 'murderous blunder', but praised the way the general moved 'amongst his poor men with consummate bravery'. He signalled **Buller**: 'Am exposed to terrible cross-fire, especially near first dressing station. Can barely hold our own. Water badly needed. Help us.' About 8.30 a.m. he was mortally wounded by a shell splinter just above his right eye. One officer and four Tommies from the 2nd Lancashires carried him away; Private Quirk, a Wigan lad, had his arm blown off after three paces and was then hit in the lung, and the officer was also badly wounded on the way down the steep hill. At one point Woodgate had to be restrained from returning to the fray, and it has been suggested that this activity precipitated memory loss during his remaining days, with no recall of the battle.

He finally passed away on 23 March 1900, two months exactly after his injury, and lies buried at St John's churchyard, Mooi River, Natal. A small stone block augmented by a metal cross signifies where he fell on the battlefield.

YEATMAN-BIGGS, MAJOR-GENERAL A. – DARGAI AND TIRAH

THE ARDUOUS TIRAH campaign of 1897–98 hastened the end of the life of its commanding general, William **Lockhart**, and definitely ended that of the man who led his 2nd division, Arthur Godolphin Yeatman-Biggs.

Arthur was born in March 1843 and his Wiltshire landowning family hoped he would become a lawyer. He opted instead for a military career, joining the Royal Artillery in 1860 as the youngest officer in the service. In his first year this teenager was slightly wounded at the taking of the Taku Forts in China and stayed on after the war, at the suggestion of his friend, Charles **Gordon**. He remained until 1862 and served briefly against the Taiping rebels. One of several officers sent out to South Africa after Isandlwana, Yeatman (the Biggs came later) was QMG in the latter part of the Zulu War and staff officer of the eastern column in the attack on the BaPedi 'fighting kopje' at the climax of **Wolseley**'s campaign against Chief Sekhukhune. He was mentioned in despatches for his 'very energetic' work. Wolseley wrote in his journal that Yeatman was 'a first-rate officer whom I shall hold onto in future.' Three years later Yeatman served as brigade major, Royal Artillery, in Egypt, but missed the major battles, though he won a brevet of lieutenant-colonel.

In 1894 he was promoted to AAG in India and was sent to the front when the Great Frontier Rising occurred in 1897. Under his command was Brigadier Kempster, later to be criticised for his handling of troops, who wrote that his divisional commander was 'nice … He does not bother one & trusts you! He is one you feel you *will* work for.' One of the most difficult times for Yeatman-Biggs came after the fall of the small fort at Saragirhi, defended to the last by twenty-one brave Sikhs. He had to judge whether his base at Hangu might also suffer a mass attack by tribesmen, or whether he could press on to relieve Fort Gulistan (which duly took place). Then came the famous storming of the heights of Dargai, during which wounded Piper Findlater won a VC for playing the pipes. Two of Yeatman-Biggs' brigadiers, Westmacott and Kempster, were later censured by General Lockhart for a bloody and preventable action (if Westmacott had retained control of the heights from an earlier seizure) that saw 197 casualties. Campaigning into the winter in the rain and cold of Tirah killed many a soldier and Yeatman-Biggs was just one more of the war's many deaths. He passed away on 4 January 1898. His grave is in Taikal Cemetery, Peshawar, where the stone says he 'died of exhaustion when his duty was ended'. The real cause of his death, like that of so many others, was enteric dysentery.

ACRONYMS

The following abbreviations are used throughout the book:

AAG = Assistant-Adjutant-General
ADC = Aide-de-Camp
AG = Adjutant-General
AQMG = Assistant-Quartermaster-General
BNI = Bengal Native Infantry
C-in-C = Commander-in-Chief
CO = Commanding Officer
DAG = Deputy-Adjutant-General
DAAG = Deputy-Assistant-Adjutant-General
DAQMG = Deputy-Assistant-Quartermaster-General
DQMG = Deputy-Quartermaster-General
GCB = Knight Grand Cross of the Order of the Bath
GCIE = Knight Grand Commander of the Order of the Indian Empire
HEIC = Honourable East India Company
KCB = Knight Commander of the Order of the Bath
KCMG = Knight Grand Cross of the Order of St Michael and St George
NI = Native Infantry
PNI = Punjab Native Infantry
QMG = Quartermaster-General

APPENDIX A

THE GENERALS AND THEIR CAMPAIGNS

1837

ACCESSION OF QUEEN VICTORIA

1838

FIRST AFGHAN WAR (TO 1842)
Airey – Chamberlain (C.) – Chamberlain (N.) – Drysdale – Durand
– England – Fraser-Tytler – Havelock – Keane – Lawrence – Lugard –
Lumsden (H.) – Malcolm – McCaskill – Outram – Pollock – Roberts (A.)
– Sale – Stisted – Thackwell – Trevor – Willshire

1840

FIRST CHINA WAR
Clyde – Gough (Lord) – Grant (H.)

1842

SAUGOR RISING
Olpherts

1843

GWALIOR WAR
Airey – Chamberlain (N.) – Bourchier – Drysdale – Durand – Gough (Lord) – Grant (P.) – Havelock – Littler – Maude – Olpherts – Taylor (R.) – Thackwell – Tombs – Vaughan

SIND WAR
Malcolm – Napier (C.) – Olpherts – Outram – Phayre

1844

SOUTHERN MAHRATTA CAMPAIGN (TO 1845)
Outram

1845

FIRST SIKH WAR (TO 1846)
Drysdale – Edwardes – Franks – Fraser-Tytler – Garvock – Gilbert – Gough (Lord) – Grant (H.) – Grant (P.) – Haines – Havelock – Lawrence – Littler – Lugard – McCaskill – Napier (R.) – Sale – Sandhurst – Taylor (A.) – Taylor (R.) – Thackwell – Tombs

FIRST NEW ZEALAND WAR
Middleton

1846

SEVENTH XHOSA WAR (TO 1847)
Bisset – Clifford – Garvock – Horsford – Smith – Somerset

1848

CAPE AFRIKANER RISING
Clifford – Garvock – Smith

SECOND SIKH WAR (TO 1849

Browne (S.) – Brownlow – Chamberlain (C.) – Chamberlain (N.) – Cheape
– Clyde – Coke (J.) – Daly – Dillon – Durand – Edwardes – Franks – Fraser-
Tytler – Gilbert – Gough (C.) – Gough (Lord) – Grant (H.) – Grant (P.)
– Greathed – Haines – Lawrence – Lugard – Lumsden (H.) – Malcolm
– Napier (R.) – Norman – Sandhurst – Smith – Taylor (A.) – Taylor (R.) –
Thackwell – Tombs – Watson – Wilson

1849

UTMAN KHEL AFRIDI EXPEDITION
Lumsden (H.)

1850

MOHMAND EXPEDITION
Clyde

AFRIDI EXPEDITION
Clyde – Coke (J.) – Dillon – Keyes – Lawrence – Lumsden (H.) – Napier
(C.) – Norman – Sandhurst

EIGHTH XHOSA WAR (TO 1853)
Bisset – Cathcart – Garvock – Michel – Primrose – Smith – Somerset

1851

MIRANZAI TURRI-BAGWASH EXPEDITION
Coke (J.) – Daly

WAZIRI EXPEDITION (TO 1852)
Browne – Coke – Wilde

MOHMAND EXPEDITION (TO 1852)
Clyde – Coke – Lumsden (H.) – Tytler

1852

BORI AFRIDI EXPEDITION
Edwardes – Norman

RANIZAI UTMAN KHEL EXPEDITION
Clyde – Coke (J.) – Lumsden (H.) – Norman

HAZARA EXPEDITION (TO 1853)
Brownlow – Napier

SECOND BURMESE WAR (TO 1854)
Appleyard – Cheape – Trevor – Wolseley (FM)

1853

KOHAT PASS AFRIDI EXPEDITION
Coke (J.) – Napier – Olpherts – Roberts (A.)

SHIRANNI EXPEDITION
Keyes

KASRANI EXPEDITION
Keyes

1854

MOHMAND EXPEDITION
Brownlow – Chamberlain (C.) – Cotton – Stewart (D.)

CRIMEAN WAR (TO 1856)
Adye – Airey – Alison – Appleyard – Baker – Black – Bright – Brown
– Cathcart – Chelmsford – Clifford – Clyde – Crealock (H.) – Dillon –
Dormer – Drury-Lowe – Earle – East – Elles – England – Glyn – Gordon
– Graham – Haines – Home – Horsford – Maude – O'Connor – Olpherts
– Rogers (VC) – Rowlands – Staveley – Stephenson – Traill-Burroughs –
Tulloch – Vaughan – Wolseley (FM) – Wood

1855

ORAKZAI EXPEDITION
Chamberlain (N.)

SANTHAL REBELLION (TO 1856)
Middleton – Norman

1856

TURI EXPEDITION
Chamberlain (N.)

PERSIAN WAR (TO 1857)
Havelock – Havelock-Allan – Lugard – Macpherson – Malcolm – Outram – Phayre – Prendergast – Stisted

1857

BOZDAR EXPEDITION
Browne (S.) – Brownlow – Chamberlain (N.) – Coke (J.) – McQueen – Probyn – Watson – Wilde

BLACK MOUNTAIN NARINJI EXPEDITION
Browne (S.) – Vaughan – Wilde

INDIAN REBELLION (TO 1859)
Adye – Alison – Battye – Bourchier – Brackenbury – Browne (S.) – Brownlow – Chamberlain (N.) – Clyde – Coke (J.) – Cotton – Crealock (J.) – Delafosse – Dillon – Dormer – Drysdale – Drury-Lowe – Durand – East – Edwardes – Elles – Franks – Fraser-Tytler – Glyn – Grant (H.) – Grant (P.) – Greathed – Harrison – Havelock – Havelock-Allan – Hills-Johnes – Home – Horsford – Lawrence – Low – Lugard – Lumsden (P.) – Macgregor – Macintyre – Macpherson – McNeill – McQueen – Michel – Middleton – Napier (R.) – Norman – O'Connor – Olpherts – Outram – Palliser – Palmer – Prendergast – Primrose – Probyn – Roberts (F.) – Russell – Sandhurst – Sartorius – Stewart (D.) – Stewart (G.) – Stisted – Tanner

– Taylor (A.) – Tombs – Thornton – Traill-Burroughs – Trevor – Tytler – Vaughan – Watson – Whitlock – Wilde – Wilson – Wolseley (FM) – Wolseley (G.) – Wood

1858

BLACK MOUNTAIN SITANA EXPEDITION
Cotton – Edwardes – Greaves

SECOND CHINA WAR (TO 1860)
Brownlow – Buller – Clifford – Crealock (H.) – Dillon – Dormer – Gordon – Graham – Grant (H.) – Greathed – Harrison – Home – Kelly-Kenny – Lumsden (P.) – Macgregor – Michel – Napier (R.) – Pomeroy-Colley – Probyn – Rogers (VC) – Staveley – Stephenson – Stewart (G.) – Thornton – Tulloch – Wolseley (FM) – Yeatman-Biggs

1860

MAHSUD EXPEDITION
Browne (J.) – Chamberlain (N.) – Keyes – McQueen – Taylor (R.) – Wilde

KABUL KHEL WAZIRI EXPEDITION
Chamberlain (N.) –Lumsden (H.) – McQueen – Wilde

1861

FIRST SIKKIM EXPEDITION
Delafosse

1862

KHASIA AND JAINTIA EXPEDITION
Collett – Thornton

1863

UMBEYLA EXPEDITION

Adye – Browne (J.) – Brownlow – Chamberlain (N.) – Channer – Collett – Delafosse – Elles – Garvock – Gaselee – Keyes – Low – Probyn – Roberts (F.) – Stewart (G.) – Stisted – Taylor (A.) – Taylor (R.) – Traill-Burroughs – Tytler - Vaughan – Watson – Wilde

MOHMAND EXPEDITION (TO 1864)

Battye

SECOND NEW ZEALAND TARANAKI WAR (TO 1872)

Baker – Clarke – Greaves – Havelock-Allan – Home – McNeill

1864

BHUTAN WAR (TO 1865)

Bourchier -Fraser-Tytler – Gough (C.) – Lockhart – Lumsden (P.) – Macgregor – Sartorius – Tombs – Thornton – Trevor

1866

FENIAN CANADIAN RAID

Coke (J.T.) – Lyttelton

1868

ABYSSINIAN WAR

Collett – Dillon – Gaselee – Gerard – Gough (H.) – Hills-Johnes – Kelly-Kenny – Lockhart – Macgregor – Malcolm – Napier (R.) – Palliser – Palmer – Phayre – Prendergast – Roberts (F.) – Staveley – Stewart (D.) – Woodgate

BLACK MOUNTAIN EXPEDITION

Bright – Brownlow – Elles – Lockhart – Macpherson – Meiklejohn – Rogers (R.) – Tytler – Wilde

1869

BEZOTI EXPEDITION
Gaselee

ORAKZAI EXPEDITION
Keyes

KABUL KHEL WAZIRI EXPEDITION
Keyes

1870

FIRST RIEL CANADIAN RED RIVER EXPEDITION
Buller – Butler – McCalmont – McNeill – Wolseley (FM)

1871

LUSHAI EXPEDITION (TO 1872
Battye – Bourchier – Brownlow – Channer – East – Hills-Johnes – Macintyre – Macpherson – Roberts (FM) – Tytler

1872

DAWAR WAZIRI EXPEDITION
Keyes

1873

SIXTH ASHANTI WAR (TO 1874)
Alison – Baker – Barton – Brackenbury – Buller – Butler – Greaves – Hart-Synnot – Home – Maurice – McCalmont – McNeill – Methuen – O'Connor – Pomeroy-Colley – Russell – Sartorius – Wauchope – Wolseley (FM) – Wood – Woodgate

1874

DAFLA EXPEDITION (TO 1875)
Palmer

1875

PERAK EXPEDITION (TO 1876)
Channer

1876

AFRIDI EXPEDITION
Rogers (R.)

1877

NINTH XHOSA WAR (TO 1878)
Black – Buller – Carrington – Chelmsford – Crealock (J.) – Glyn – Grenfell – Molyneux – Parr – Symons – Warren – Wood – Woodgate

JOWAKI AFRIDI EXPEDITION (to 1878)
Blood – Channer – Gaselee – Keyes – McQueen – Meiklejohn – Rogers (R.) – Stewart (G.)

1878

GRIQUALAND REBELLION
Warren

FIRST PEDI EXPEDITION
Clarke – Clery – Rowlands – Wood – Woodgate

FIRST BECHUANA EXPEDITION
Warren

SECOND BECHUANA EXPEDITION (TO 1879)
Warren

SECOND AFGHAN WAR (TO 1880)
Appleyard – Baker – Baden-Powell – Battye – Blood – Bright – Browne (J.) – Browne (S.) – Carrington – Channer – Collett – Egerton – Gaselee – Gerard – Gough (C.) – Gough (H.) – Greaves – Haines – Hamilton – Hart – Hills-Johnes – Lockhart – Low – Lumsden (P.) – Macdonald – Macgregor – Macintyre – Macpherson – Maude – McCalmont – McQueen – Meiklejohn - Nicholson – Palliser – Palmer – Phayre – Pole-Carew – Pomeroy-Colley – Primrose – Roberts (F.) – Rogers (R.) – Stewart (D.) – Stewart (G.) – Tanner – Tytler -Vaughan – Watson – White – Wolseley (G.)

1879

ZULU WAR
Barton – Black – Blood – Brackenbury – Buller – Butler – Chelmsford – Clarke – Clery – Clifford – Crealock (H.) – Crealock (J.) – Drury-Lowe – East – Glyn – Grenfell – Harrison – Hart-Synnot – Hutton – Maurice – McCalmont – Molyneux – Parr – Pomeroy-Colley – Rogers (VC) – Rowlands – Rundle – Russell – Symons – Wolseley (FM) – Wood – Woodgate

SECOND PEDI EXPEDITION
Brackenbury – Carrington – Clarke – Harrison – Maurice – McCalmont – Russell – Wolseley (FM) – Yeatman-Biggs

BASUTO WAR (TO 1881)
Carrington – Clarke

1881

TRANSVAAL WAR
Hamilton – Hart-Synnot – Hutton – Macdonald – Pomeroy-Colley – Rundle – Wauchope – Wood

MAHSUD EXPEDITION
McQueen

1882

EGYPTIAN WAR
Adye – Alison – Barton – Blood – Buller – Butler – Clery – Dormer – Drury-Lowe – Earle – Gerard – Graham – Grenfell – Harrison – Hart – Hart-Synnot – Havelock-Allan – Hutton – Kitchener – Lyttelton – Macpherson – Maurice – McCalmont – McNeill – Meiklejohn – Methuen – Molyneux – Nicholson – Parr – Pole-Carew – Rogers (R.) – Rundle – Russell – Thornton – Tulloch – Wauchope – Wolseley (F.M.) – Wood – Yeatmann-Biggs

1884

FIRST ZHOB VALLEY EXPEDITION
Gaselee – Tanner

GORDON RELIEF EXPEDITION (TO 1885)
Barton – Brackenbury – Buller – Butler – Clery – Colville – Earle – French – Gordon – Graham – Greaves – Grenfell – Hamilton – Harrison – Hutton – Kitchener – Maurice – McCalmont – McNeill – Palmer – Parr – Rundle – Stephenson – Thornton – Warren – Wauchope – White – Wolseley (FM) – Wolseley (G.) – Wood

THIRD BECHUANA EXPEDITION (TO 1885)
Carrington – Methuen – Molyneux – Warren

1885

THIRD BURMESE WAR
East – Prendergast – White

SECOND RIEL CANADIAN REBELLION
Middleton

1886

PACIFICATION OF BURMA (TO 1891)
Baker – Collett – Hamilton – Lockhart – Low – Nicholson – Palmer – Pole-Carew – Roberts (F.) – Symons – White – Wolseley (G.)

SUDAN FRONTIER OPERATIONS (TO 1895)
Coke (J.T.) – Grenfell - Hunter – Kitchener – Macdonald – Rundle

1888

BLACK MOUNTAIN EXPEDITION
Channer – Egerton – Gatacre – McQueen – Thornton

1890

SECOND ZHOB VALLEY EXPEDITION
White

1891

MANIPUR EXPEDITION
Collett

MIRANZAI EXPEDITIONS I & II
Egerton – Lockhart

BLACK MOUNTAIN EXPEDITION
Elles – Gaselee – Lockhart

1892

ISAZAI EXPEDITION
Gaselee – Lockhart

1893

BUNYORO WAR (TO 1895)
Colville

1894

MAHSUD-WAZIRI EXPEDITION
Egerton – Gaselee – Lockhart – Meiklejohn – Symons

1895

CHITRAL RELIEF EXPEDITION
Blood – Channer – Gatacre – Hamilton – Low

SEVENTH ASHANTI WAR (TO 1896)
Baden-Powell

1896

MATABELE-MASHONA RISING
Baden-Powell – Carrington

RECONQUEST OF SUDAN (TO 1898)
Egerton – Gatacre – Hunter – Kitchener – Lyttelton – Macdonald – Rundle
– Wauchope

1897

INDIAN FRONTIER RISING (TO 1898)
Blood – Egerton – Gaselee – Hamilton – Hart – Havelock-Allan – Lockhart
– Meiklejohn – Methuen – Nicholson – Palmer – Symons – Yeatman-Biggs

1898

SIERRA LEONE HUT TAX WAR
Woodgate

1899

SOUTH AFRICAN WAR (TO 1902)
Baden-Powell – Barton – Blood – Buller – Carrington – Clery – Coke (J.T.)
– Colville – French – Gatacre – Hamilton – Hart-Synnot – Hills-Johnes
– Hunter – Hutton – Kelly-Kenny – Kitchener – Lyttelton – Macdonald
– Methuen – Nicholson – Pole-Carew – Roberts (F.) – Rundle – Symons –
Warren – Wauchope – White – Wolseley (F.M.) – Woodgate

1900

THIRD CHINA WAR
Gaselee

1901

DEATH OF QUEEN VICTORIA

APPENDIX B

THE MISSING GENERALS

A handful of famous generals were excluded from my book after a great deal of soul-searching. The reasons were varied. Perhaps the two who most deserve a place as fighting men are Lords Raglan and Strathnairn. Fitzroy Somerset, later Lord Raglan, fought in two theatres of war, the Napoleonic War in Europe and the Crimean War as C-in-C. Biographies of him are limited; the two best are Christopher Hibbert's classic *The Destruction of Lord Raglan* and, quite recently, John Sweetman's *Raglan*. Strathnairn, better known as Sir Hugh Rose, had served in a minor capacity in the Crimea as a liaison officer. Small, seemingly iron-framed, he arrived unknown at Calcutta in 1857 and then fought a brilliant, arduous, often over-looked campaign against rebels in Central India. Some of his Mutiny correspondence has been published, but he badly needs a full-scale modern re-evaluation.

Two Victorian brigadiers I regret omitting are John Jacob and John Nicholson of the Bombay and Bengal armies respectively. The best work on Jacob is by historian H.T. Lambrick (see bibliography). Nicholson, a controversial figure, cries out for a full modern interpretation, most works on him being hagiographies, though William Dalrymple does re-evaluate him in *The Last Mughal*. The same author also presents a fine pen portrait, in *The Return of a King*, of one other figure I had to omit, William Nott, a major character in the First Afghan War, although his only active earlier service had been an expedition to Sumatra (there is also a huge and very rare biography by Joachim Stocqueler).

One famous escapee from Isandlwana, Herbert Smith-Dorrien, became a major-general within weeks of Queen Victoria's death. His autobiography, *Memories of Forty-Eight Years' Service*, is hugely readable. So too are the two autobiographies of James Willcocks, *From Kabul to Kumasi*, and *The Romance of Soldiering and Sport*, both vivid accounts of the ten campaigns he had served in by 1901, including command of the relief column sent to the besieged fort of Kumasi in the hard-fought third Ashanti War. Astonishingly, he returned from West Africa to be promoted brevet of lieutenant-colonel after all this active service, and did not reach the rank of major-general until 1906. He is perhaps best remembered for what were jokingly called 'Willcocks's Weekend Wars' fought on the North-West Frontier in the Edwardian period.

SELECT BIBLIOGRAPHY

Unpublished Original Sources:
Author's Collection: *Papers of Lt-General Sir R. Rogers*
Killie Campbell Africana Library, Durban, South Africa: *Papers of Lt-General Sir G. Wolseley and Lt-Colonel H. Wood*
Gwent County Archives: *Papers of Major-General Sir A. Tulloch*Herefordshire Records Office: *Letters of Captain J. Airey*
National Army Museum: *Papers of Lt. H. De la Poer Gough, Colonel F. Kempster, Captain E. Maconchy & Field-Marshal Lord Wolseley; Canon Lummis Victoria Cross Archive.*
Tottenham Archive*: Papers of Major-General Sir W. Meiklejohn*

Printed Books
Autobiography & Biography:
Adye, Col. J., *Sitana* (London, 1867).
— Gen. Sir J., *Recollections of a Military Life* (London, 1895).
— Maj-Gen. Sir J., *Soldiers and Others I Have Known* (London, 1925).
Anglesey, Marquess of, ed., *Sergeant Pearman's Memoirs* (London, 1968).
Annand, A., ed., *Cavalry Surgeon* (London, 1971).
Anon. *Memoir of Major-General Sir Henry Tombs V.C., K.C.B., R.A.* (Woolwich, 1913).
— *General The Right Hon. Sir Edward Lugard G.C.B., P.C. 1810–1898* (Privately Printed. npp. nd., c. 1930).
Anson, H., ed., *With H.M. 9th Lancers during The Indian Mutiny* (London, 1896).
Appleyard, Maj-Gen. F., *A Resume of Thirty-Four Years' Army Service* (Privately Printed. npp. nd., c. 1904).
Arthur, Sir G., *The Letters of Lord and Lady Wolseley 1870–1911* (London, 1923).
Baird, J., ed. *Private Letters of the Marquess of Dalhousie* (Edinburgh, 1911).
Ball-Acton, G., *Colonel Ball-Acton* (Privately Printed. npp. nd., c. 1906).
Battye, F., *The Fighting Ten* (London, 1984).Beachey, R., *The Warrior Mullah* (London, 1990).
Beckett, I., ed., *Wolseley and Ashanti* (Brimscombe Port, 2009).
Bence-Jones, M., *The Viceroys of India* (London, 1982).
Bisset, Maj-Gen., *Sport and War* (London, 1875).
Blomfield, D., ed., *Lahore to Lucknow* (London, 1992).
Blood, Gen. Sir B., *Four Score Years and Ten* (London, 1933).
Brackenbury, Gen. Sir H., *Some Memories of My Spare Time* (Edinburgh, 1909).
Brice, C., *The Military Career of General Sir Henry Brackenbury 1856–1904* (PhD Thesis. DeMontfort University, 2009).
— *The Thinking Man's Soldier* (Solihull, 2012).
Brock, Rev. W., *A Biographical Sketch of Sir Henry Havelock* (London, 1858).

Brown, Rev. F., *From Tientsin to Peking* (London, 1902).

Brownlow, F.M. Sir C., *Stray Notes on Military Training and Khaki Warfare* 2nd Edition, Privately Published (London, nd. c. 1914).

Bruce, W., *Life of General Sir Charles Napier G.C.B* (London, 1885).

Buckland, C.E., *Dictionary of Indian Biography* (London nd. c. 1910).

Butler, Col. Sir W., *Sir Charles Napier* (London, 1894).

—— Lt.-Gen. Sir W., *The Life of Sir George Pomeroy-Colley* (London, 1899).

—— *Sir William Butler* (London, 1911).

Callwell, Maj-Gen. Sir C., *Stray Recollections* (London, 1923).

—— *The Memoirs of Major-General Sir Hugh McCalmont K.C.B., C.V.O.* (London, 1924).

Campbell, Sir G., *Memoirs of My Indian Career* (London, 1893).

Cavendish, A., ed. *Cyprus 1878* (Nicosia, 1991).

Cathcart, Sir G., *Correspondence* (London, 1856).

Churchill, W., *London to Ladysmith* (London, 1900).

Churchill, R., *Winston S. Churchill* (London, 1967).

Cobban, J., *Field-Marshal Lord Roberts V.C., K.P., G.C.B., G.C.S.I.* (London, 1900).

Collister, P., *'Hellfire Jack' VC* (London, 1989).

Colville, Col. Sir H., *The Land of the Nile Springs* (London, 1895).

Cooper, Pte. H., *What the Fusiliers Did* (Lahore, 1880).

Corvi, S. & Beckett I., ed., *Victoria's Generals* (Barnsley, 2009).

Creagh, Gen. Sir O. & Humphris E. ed., *The Victoria Cross 1856–1920* (Facsimile Reprint. Polstead nd. c. 1990).

—— *Autobiography* (London nd. c. 1926).

Daly, Maj. H., *Memoirs of General Sir Henry Dermot Daly G.C.B., C.I.E.* (London, 1905).

—— M., *The Sirdar* (Philadelphia, 1997).

Dictionary of National Biography – various editions.

Doolittle, D., *A Soldier's Hero* (Narragansett, 1991).

Douglas, Sir G., *The Life of Major-General Wauchope* (London, 1904).

Durand, H., *The Life of Major-General Sir Henry Marion Durand* (London, 1883).

—— Sir M., *The Life of Field-Marshal Sir George White V.C.* (London, 1915).

Edwardes, Maj. H., *A Year on the Punjab Frontier in 1848–49* (London, 1851).

Edwardes, Lady, *Memorials of the Life and Letters of Major-General Sir Herbert B. Edwardes* (London, 1886).

Edwards-Stuart, Lt.-Col. I., *A John Company General* (Bognor Regis, 1993).

Elsmie, G., *Field-Marshal Sir Donald Stewart G.C.B., G.C.I.E., C.I.E.* (London, 1903).

Exelby, J., The Secret Service Major and the Invasion of Egypt. *History Today*. Vol 56, Issue 11. 2006.

Farwell, B., *Eminent Victorian Soldiers* (London, 1986).

Forrest, G., *Sepoy Generals* (Edinburgh, 1901).

—— *Life of Field-Marshal Sir Neville Chamberlain G.C.B., G.C.S.I.* (Edinburgh, 1909).

—— *The Life of Lord Roberts* (London, 1914).

Fortescue-Brickdale, Sir C., ed., *Major-General Sir Henry Hallam Parr* (London, 1917).

French, Maj. The Hon G., *Lord Chelmsford and the Zulu War* (London, 1939).

Gatacre, B., *General Gatacre* (London, 1910).

Gerard, Lt.-Gen. Sir M., *Leaves from the Diaries of a Soldier and Sportsman during Twenty-Five Years' Service in India, Afghanistan, Egypt and other Countries 1865–1885* (London, 1903).

Gleichen, Maj-Gen. Lord E., *A Guardsman's Memories* (Edinburgh, 1932).

Goldsmid, Maj-Gen. Sir F., *James Outram* (London, 1881).

Gon, P., *'Send Carrington'* (Craighall, 1984).

Gough, Maj-Gen. Sir H., *Old Memories* (Edinburgh, 1897).

Greathed, H., *Letters Written During the Siege of Delhi* (London, 1858).

Greaves, Gen. Sir G., *Memoirs* (London, 1924).

Groser, H., *Field-Marshal Lord Roberts V.C., K.P., G.C.B., G.C.S.I.* (London, 1900).

Hamilton, Gen. Sir I., *Listening for the Drums* (London, 1944).

—— I., *The Happy Warrior* (London, 1966).

Hamilton-Browne, Col. G., *A Lost Legionary in South Africa* (London, nd. c. 1913).

Hannah, W., *Bobs* (London, 1973).

Harrington, A., *Sir Harry Smith – Bungling Hero* (Cape Town, 1980).

Harrison, Gen. Sir R., *Recollections of a Life in the British Army* (London, 1908).

Hart-Synnot, B., ed., *Letters of Major-General Fitzroy Hart-Synnot* (London, 1912).

Hibbert, C., *The Destruction of Lord Raglan* (London, 1962).

Hoe, S., *Women at the Siege* (Oxford, 1988).

Home, Surg-Gen. Sir A., *Service Memories* (London, 1912).

Hunter, A., *Kitchener's Sword-Arm* (Staplehurst, 1996).

Innes, Gen. J., *The Life and Times of General Sir James Browne R.E., K.C.B., K.C.S.I.* (London, 1905).

Ireland, W., *History of the Siege of Delhi* (Edinburgh, 1861).

James, D., *Lord Roberts* (London, 1954).

Jardine, D., *The Mad Mullah of Somaliland* (London, 1923).

Jeal, T., *Baden-Powell* (London, 1989).

Knight, I., & Greaves, A., *The Who's Who of the Anglo-Zulu War 1879* (Barnsley, 2007).

Knollys, Col. H., *Life of General Sir Hope Grant* (Edinburgh, 1894).

Kochanski, H., *Sir Garnet Wolseley* (London, 1999).

Laband, J., ed., *Lord Chelmsford's Zululand Campaign 1878–1879* (Far Thrupp, 1994).

Lakeman, Sir S., *What I Saw in Kaffir-Land* (Edinburgh, 1880).

Lambrick, H., *John Jacob of Jabobabad* (London, 1960).

Laurie, CO W., *Sketches of Some Distinguished Anglo-Indians* (London, 1886).

Lawrence, Lt.-Gen. Sir G., *Reminiscences of Forty-Three Years in India* (London, 1874).

Lawrence, R., *Charles Napier* (London, 1952).

Lee-Warner, Sir W., *Memoirs of Field-Marshal Sir Henry Wylie Norman* (London, 1908).

Lehman, J., *All Sir Garnet* (London, 1964).

—— *Remember you are an Englishman* (London, 1977).

Lewin, Lt-Col. T., *A Fly on the Wheel* (London, 1912).

Low, C., *The Life and Correspondence of Field-Marshal Sir George Pollock* (London, 1873).

—— *Soldiers of the Victorian Age* (London, 1880).

—— *Major-General Sir Frederick S. Roberts* (London, 1883).

—— *General Lord Wolseley* (London, 1883).

Lumsden, Gen. Sir P. & Elsmie, G., *Lumsden of the Guides* (London, 1899).

Lutyens, M., *The Lyttons in India* (London, 1979).

Lyttelton, Gen. Sir N., *Eighty Years* (London, nd. c. 1927).

Macgregor, Lady, *The Life and Opinions of Major-General Sir Charles Metcalfe Macgregor* (Edinburgh, 1888).

Mackenzie, Maj-Gen. C., *Storms & Sunshine of a Soldier's Life* (London, 1886).

Maclagan, M., *'Clemency' Canning* (London, 1962).

Macrory, P., ed., *Lady Sale* (London, 1969).

Magnus, P., *Kitchener* (London, 1958).

Manning, S., *Evelyn Wood VC* (Barnsley, 2007).

Maude, F. & Sherer, J., *Memories of the Mutiny* (London, 1894).

Maurice, Maj-Gen. Sir F. & Arthur, Sir G., *The Life of Lord Wolseley* (London, 1924).

McCourt, E., *Remember Butler* (London, 1967).

McKay, Sgt. J., *Reminiscences of the Last Kafir War* (Cape Town, 1970).

Miller, S., *Lord Methuen and the British Army* (London, 1999).

Molyneux, Maj-Gen. W., *Campaigning in South Africa and Egypt* (London, 1896).

Montgomery, J., *Toll for the Brave* (London, 1963).

Napier, Lt-Col. The Hon. H., *Lord Napier of Magdala G.C.B., G.C.S.I.* (London, 1927).

Nevill, Col. H., ed., The Mutiny Day by Day Being Extracts from the Letters of General Sir Archdale Wilson to his Wife. *Journal of the United Services Institution of India, Calcutta*, 1920–22.

Outram, Capt. J., *Rough Notes of the Campaign in Sinde and Afghanistan in 1838–39* (Bombay, 1840).

Parry, E., *Suakin, 1885* (London, 1885).

—— *Reynell Taylor* (London, 1888).

Payne, D. & E., *Henry Charles Harford* (London, 2008).

Phillips, L., *With Rimington* (London, 1901).

Pollock, J., *Kitchener* (London, 1998).

Powell, G., *Buller – A Scapegoat* (London, 1994).

Preston, A., ed., *In Relief of Gordon* (London, 1967).

—— *Sir Garnet Wolseley's South African Diaries (Natal) 1875* (Cape Town, 1971).

—— *Sir Garnet Wolseley's South African Journal 1879–80* (Cape Town, 1973).

Rait, R., *The Life and Campaigns of Hugh First Viscount Gough Field-Marshal* (London, 1903).

—— *The Life of Field-Marshal Sir Frederick Paul Haines* (London, 1911).

Raugh, H., *The Victorians at War 1815–1914* (Santa Barbara, 2004).

Rivett-Carnac, D., *Hawk's Eye* (Cape Town, 1966).

Roberts, F.M. Lord, *Forty-One Years in India* (London, 1897).

—— F., *Letters Written During the Indian Mutiny* (London, 1924).

Robinson, Comm. C., ed., *Celebrities of the Army* (London, 1900).

Robson, B., ed., *Roberts in India* (Far Thrupp, 1993).

—— *Sir Hugh Rose and the Central India Campaign 1858* (Far Thrupp, 2000).

Royle, T., *Death before Dishonour* (New York, 1982).

Russell, W., *My Diary in India in the Year 1858–59* (London. 1860).

Ryan, M., *William Francis Butler* (Dublin. 2003).

Saks, D., Tragic Failure – The Last Campaign of Maj-Gen. George Pomeroy Colley, 1881. *Journal of South African Military History*, Vol. 13, No. 6, 2006.

Sampson, V. & Hamilton, I., *Anti-Commando* (London, 1931).

Scott, D., ed., *Douglas Haig*. Barnsley 2006.

Shadwell, Lt-Gen., *The Life of Colin Campbell, Lord Clyde* (Edinburgh, 1881).

Singh, B., ed., *The Letters of the First Viscount Hardinge of Lahore to Lady Hardinge and Sir Walter and Lady James 1844–1847* (London, 1986).

Smith, G., ed., *The Autobiography of Lieutenant-General Sir Harry Smith* (London, 1902).

Smith, M., *General Sir William Stephen Alexander Lockhart*. Privately Published (Hunstanton, 2011).

Smith-Dorrien, Gen. Sir H., *Memories of Forty-Eight Years' Service* (London, 1925).

Stanley, G., *Louis Riel* (Toronto, 1963).

Stapleton, T., *Maqoma* (Cape Town, 1994).

Steevens, G., *With Kitchener to Khartum* (London, 1898).

Stephenson, Sir F., *At Home and on the Battlefield* (London, 1915).

Stewart, Col. C., *Through Persia in Disguise* (London, 1911).

Stocqueler, J., *Memoirs and Correspondence of Major-General Sir William Nott G.C.B.* (London, 1854).

Taylor, A., *General Sir Alex Taylor G.C.B., R.E.* (London, 1913).

Temple, A., *Our Living Generals* (London, 1898).

Thackeray, Col. Sir E., *Biographical Notices of Officers of the Royal (Bengal) Engineers* (London, 1900).

Thomson, W., *The Little General and the Rousay Crofters* (Edinburgh, 2000).

Thornton, Dep-Surg-Gen. J., *Memories of Seven Campaigns* (London, 1895).
Trotter, Capt. L., *The Bayard of India* (Edinburgh, 1903).
Trousdale, W., ed., *War in Afghanistan, 1879–80* (Detroit, 1985).
Tulloch, Maj-Gen. Sir A., *Recollections of Forty Years' Service*. (Edinburgh, 1903).
Vaughan, Gen. Sir J., *My Service in the Indian Army – and After* (London, 1904).
Vetch, Col. R., *Life, Letters and Diaries of Lieut-General Sir Gerald Graham V.C., G.C.B., R.E.*
    (Edinburgh, 1901).
Vibart, Col. H., *The Life of General Sir Harry N. D. Prendergast R.E., V.C., G.C.B.* (London, 1914).
Waller, J., *Gordon of Khartoum* (New York, 1988).
Wallis, C., *The Advance of our West African Empire* (London, 1903.
Wessels, A., ed., *Lord Roberts and the War in South Africa 1899–1902* (Far Thrupp, 2000).
Wilkinson, Maj-Gen. O & Maj-Gen. J., *The Memoirs of the Gemini Generals* (London, 1896).
Williams, C., *The Life of Lieutenant-General Sir Henry Evelyn Wood* (London, 1892).
Williams, W., *The Life of General Sir Charles Warren* (London, 1941).
—— *Commandant of the Transvaal* (Wrexham, 2001).
Wolseley, Lt-Col. G., *Narrative of the War with China in 1860* (London, 1862).
—— Field-Marshal Visc., *The Story of a Soldier's Life* (London, 1903).
Wood, F.M. Sir E., *From Midshipman to Field-Marshal* (London, 1906).
Wright, W., *Through the Indian Mutiny* (Brimscombe Port, 2011).
Wylly, Col. H., *The Military Memoirs of Lieut.-General Sir Joseph Thackwell* (London, 1908).

General:
Allen, C., *Soldier Sahibs* (London, 2000).
—— *God's Terrorists* (London, 2006).
Anglesey, Marquess of, *A History of the British Cavalry 1816–1913* (London, 1973–86).
Anon., *The British Army* (London, 1899).
—— *The Second Afghan War 1878–80* (London, 1908).
—— *Historical Records of the 20th (Duke of Cambridge's Own) Infantry* (Devonport, nd. c. 1909).
—— *Frontier & Overseas Expeditions from India* (Calcutta and Simla, 1907–11).
—— *History of the Guides 1846–1922* (Aldershot, 1938).
Asher, M., *Khartoum* (London, 2005).
Atkinson, C., *The South Wales Borderers 24th Foot 1689–1937* (Cambridge, 1937).
Aung, M., *Lord Randolph Churchill and the Dancing Peacock* (New Delhi, 1999).
Atwood, R., *The March to Kandahar* (Barnsley, 2008).
Barthorp, M., *The Frontier Ablaze* (London, 1996).
Bates, D., *The Abyssinian Difficulty* (Oxford, 1979).
Beattie, H., *Imperial Frontier* (Richmond, 2002).
Beaver, W., *Under Every Leaf* (London, 2012).
Beckett, I., *The Victorians at War* (London, 2003).
Bennett, I., *A Rain of Lead* (London, 2001).
Blackburn, T., ed., *The Defeat of Amarapura* (New Delhi, 2009).
Bruce, G., *Six Battles for India* (London, 1969).
Cantlie, Lt-Gen. Sir N., *A History of the Army Medical Department* (London, 1974).
Cardew, Lt. F., *A Sketch of the Services of the Bengal Native Army* (Calcutta, 1903).
—— Maj. F., *Hodson's Horse 1857–1922* (Edinburgh, 1928).
Castle, I. & Knight, I., *Fearful Hard Times* (London, 1994).
Chakravorty, B., *British Relations with the Hill Tribes of Assam* (Calcutta, 1980).
Claridge, W., *A History of the Gold Coast and Ashanti* (London, 1915).
Clarke, S., ed., *Invasion of Zululand 1879* (Johannesburg, 1979).
—— *Zululand at War 1879* (Johannesburg, 1984).

Clements, W., *The Glamour and Tragedy of the Zulu War* (London, 1936).

Collier, R., *The Sound of Fury* (London, 1963).

Cory, G., *The Rise of South Africa* (London, 1910–30).

Cowan, J., *The New Zealand Wars* (Wellington, 1922–23).

Crowder, M., ed., *West African Resistance* (London, 1971).

Dalrymple, W., *Return of a King* (London, 2013).

David, S., *The Indian Mutiny* (London, 2002).

—— *Zulu* (London, 2004).

—— *The Bengal Army and the Outbreak of the Indian Mutiny* (New Delhi, 2009).

Delavoye, Capt. A., *Records of the 90th Regiment* (London, 1880).

Dutton, R., *Forgotten Heroes* (Prenton, 2010).

Elliott, Maj-Gen. J., *The Frontier 1839–1947* (London, 1968).

Everett, Maj-Gen. Sir H., *The History of the Somerset Light Infantry (Prince Albert's) 1685–1914* (London, 1934).

Farwell, B., *Queen Victoria's Little Wars* (London, 1972).

Featherstone, D., *At Them with the Bayonet* (London, 1968).

Forrest, G., *A History of the Indian Mutiny* (Edinburgh, 1904–12).

Gardyne, Lt-Col. C., *The Life of a Regiment* (London, 1929).

Gilmour, D., *The Ruling Caste* (London, 2008).

Gough, Gen. Sir C. & Innes, A., *The Sikhs and the Sikh Wars* (London, 1897).

Griffith, K., *Thank God we Kept the Flag Flying* (London, 1974).

Hanna, Col. H., *The Second Afghan War 1878–79–80* (London, 1899–1910).

Hare, Maj-Gen. Sir S., *The Annals of the King's Royal Rifle Corps Vol IV* (London, 1929).

Harris, J., *Much Sounding of Bugles* (London, 1975).

Hasrat, B., ed., *The Punjab Papers* (Hoshiarpur, 1970).

Heath, I., *Armies of the Nineteenth Century: Asia* (St Peter Port, 1999).

Heathcote, T., *The Afghan Wars 1839–1919* (Staplehurst, 2003).

—— *Mutiny and Insurgency in India 1857–58* (Barnsley, 2007).

Hibbert, C., *The Dragon Wakes* (London, 1970).

—— *The Great Mutiny* (London, 1978).

Holmes, T., *A History of the Indian Mutiny: Fifth Revised Edition* (London, 1904).

Hughues, Maj-Gen. B., *The Bengal Horse Artillery 1800–1861* (London, 1971).

Huttenback, R., *British Relations with Sind 1799–1843* (Oxford, 2007).

Innes, Lt-Gen. M., *Lucknow and Oude in the Mutiny* (London, 1895).

James, L., *Raj* (London, 1997).

Jocelyn, Col. J., *The History of the Royal and Indian Artillery in the Mutiny of 1857* (London, 1915).

Jones, H., *The Boiling Cauldron* (Bisley, 2006).

Kaye, Sir J. & Malleson, Col., *History of the Indian Mutiny of 1857–8* (London, 1898–99).

Keppel-Jones, A., *Rhodes and Rhodesia* (Kingston, 1983).

Khera, P., *British Policy towards Sindh* (Delhi, 1963).

Knight, I., *Zulu Rising* (London, 2010).

Laband, J., *The Transvaal Rebellion* (London, 2005).

Laurie, Col. W., *Our Burmese Wars and Relations with Burma* (London, 1885).

Leasor, J., *The Red Fort* (London, 1956).

Lehmann, J., *The First Boer War* (London, 1972).

Lock, R., *Blood on the Painted Mountain* (London, 1995).

—— & Quantrill, P., *Zulu Vanquished* (London, 2005).

Macdonald, A., *Why Gordon Perished* (London, 1896).

Macrory, P., *Signal Catastrophe* (London, 1966).

Mann, M., *China, 1860* (Salisbury, 1989).

Mason, P., *A Matter of Honour* (London, 1974).

Maunsell, Gen. F., *The Siege of Delhi* (London, 1912).

Maurice, Maj-Gen. Sir F. & Grant, Capt. M., *History of the War in South Africa 1899–1902* (London, 1906–11).

Maxwell, L., *My God – Maiwand* (London, 1979).

Milton, J., *The Edges of War* (Cape Town, 1983).

Morton, D., *The Last War Drum* (Toronto, 1972).

Mostert, N., *Frontiers* (London, 1992).

Myatt, F., *The March to Magdala* (London, 1970).

Nevill, Capt. H., *Campaigns on the North-West Frontier* (London, 1912).

Norris, J., *The First Afghan War 1838–1842* (Cambridge, 1967).

O'Connor, R., *The Spirit Soldiers* (New York, 1973).

Paget, Lt-Col. W. & Mason, Lt. A., *A Record of the Expeditions against the North-West Frontier Tribes* (London, 1884).

Pakenham, E., *The Boer War* (London, 1979).

Parritt, Col. B., *Red with Blue Stripes* (Tunbridge Wells, 1974).

Pemberton, W., *Battles of the Crimean War* (London, 1962).

—— *Battles of the Boer War* (London, 1964).

Preston, D., *The Boxer Rebellion* (New York, 2000).

Pulford, C., *Two Kingdoms of Uganda* (Woodford Halse, 2011).

Reid, Surg-Lieut-Col. A., *Chin-Lushai Land* (Calcutta, 1893).

Sandes, Lt-Col. E., *The Royal Engineers in Egypt and the Sudan* (Chatham, 1937).

Settle, J., *Anecdotes of Soldiers in Peace and War* (London, 1905).

Sheppard, Maj. E., *The Ninth Queen's Royal Lancers 1715–1936* (Aldershot, 1939).

Sidhu, A., *The First Anglo-Sikh War* (Chalford, 2010).

Smith, K., *The Wedding Feast War*. Privately Published (Barnsley, 2010).

Smithers, A., *The Kaffir Wars, 1779–1877* (London, 1973).

Spiers, E., ed., *Sudan* (London, 1998).

—— *The Scottish Soldier and Empire 1854–1902* (Edinburgh, 2006).

Spilsbury, J., *The Indian Mutiny* (London, 2007).

Stanley, P., *White Mutiny* (London, 1998).

Stewart, J., *Crimson Snow* (Chalford, 2008).

Srivastava, K., *The Revolt of 1857 in Central India – Malwa* (Bombay, 1966).

Symons, J., *England's Pride* (London, 1966).

Taylor, P., ed., *A Companion to the 'Indian Mutiny' of 1857*. (Delhi, 1996).

Vibart, Maj. H., *The Military History of the Madras Engineers & Pioneers* (London, 1881).

Waller, J., *Beyond the Khyber Pass* (New York, 1990).

Walters, Capt. H., *The Operations of the Malakand Field Force and the Buner Field Force 1897–98* (Simla, 1900).

Ward, A., *Our Bones are Scattered* (New York, 1996).

Watson, Maj-Gen. W., *King George's own Central India Horse* (Edinburgh, 1932).

Watson, B., *The Great Indian Mutiny* (New York, 1991).

Woodthorpe, Lt. R., *The Lushai Expedition 1871–1872* (London, 1873).

Wright, W., *A Tidy Little War* (Brimscombe Port, 2009).

—— *Omdurman 1898* (Brimscombe Port, 2012).

Yorke, E., *Playing the Great Game* (London, 2012).

INDEX